Pro Objective-C

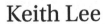

Keith Lee

Pro Objective-C

ISBN-13 (pbk): 978-1-4302-5050-0

ISBN-13 (electronic): 978-1-4302-5051-7

President and Publisher: Paul Manning
Lead Editor: Michelle Lowman
Development Editor: Douglas Pundick
Technical Reviewer: Felipe Laso Marsetti
Editorial Board: Steve Anglin, Mark Beckner, Ewan Buckingham, Gary Cornell, Louise Corrigan, Jonathan Gennick, Jonathan Hassell, Robert Hutchinson, Michelle Lowman, James Markham, Matthew Moodie, Jeff Olson, Jeffrey Pepper, Douglas Pundick, Ben Renow-Clarke, Dominic Shakeshaft, Gwenan Spearing, Matt Wade, Steve Weiss, Tom Welsh
Coordinating Editor: Mark Powers
Copy Editor: Kimberly Burton-Weisman
Compositor: SPi Global
Indexer: SPi Global
Artist: SPi Global
Cover Designer: Anna Ishchenko

Distributed to the book trade worldwide by Springer Science+Business Media New York, 233 Spring Street, 6th Floor, New York, NY 10013. Phone 1-800-SPRINGER, fax (201) 348-4505, e-mail orders-ny@springer-sbm.com, or visit www.springeronline.com. Apress Media, LLC is a California LLC and the sole member (owner) is Springer Science + Business Media Finance Inc (SSBM Finance Inc). SSBM Finance Inc is a Delaware corporation.

For information on translations, please e-mail rights@apress.com, or visit www.apress.com.

Apress and friends of ED books may be purchased in bulk for academic, corporate, or promotional use. eBook versions and licenses are also available for most titles. For more information, reference our Special Bulk Sales–eBook Licensing web page at www.apress.com/bulk-sales.

Any source code or other supplementary materials referenced by the author in this text is available to readers at www.apress.com/9781430250500. For detailed information about how to locate your book's source code, go to www.apress.com/source-code/.

To my wife Dinavia, for all of your love, support, and inspiration.

To the curly-haired kid, you are wise beyond your years.

—Keith

Contents at a Glance

Contents

About the Author

Keith Lee is a technologist with a longstanding passion for both Apple products and software development in general. He has over 20 years of experience designing and implementing software systems for devices and the desktop, along with server-side development. His primary interests these days are software development on the OS X and iOS platforms, and new programming languages. Keith is also a noted composer who has written works for diverse ensembles that have been performed in both the United States and abroad. He lives with his wife and daughter in California and can be reached via e-mail at ProObjectiveC@icloud.com.

About the Technical Reviewer

Felipe Laso Marsetti is an iOS programmer working at Lextech Global Services. He loves everything related to Apple, video games, cooking, and playing the violin, piano, or guitar. In his spare time, Felipe loves to read and learn new programming languages and technologies.

Felipe likes to write on his blog at http://iFe.li, create iOS tutorials and articles as a member of Ray Wenderlich's blog at www.raywenderlich.com, and work as a technical reviewer for Objective-C and iOS–related books. You can find him on Twitter as @Airjordan12345, on Facebook under his name, or on App.net as @iFeli.

Acknowledgments

This book would not exist without the encouragement and understanding of my wife Dinavia. You supported this work and the long hours it required, providing whatever I needed to see this through to the end. I am always and forever grateful.

Writing a book is a lot of work! I have been very fortunate in this endeavor to work with a great team at Apress. Douglas Pundick, development editor, and Mark Powers, coordinating editor, have been instrumental in keeping the book on track. Felipe Laso Marsetti was especially helpful with his detailed technical review of the book's chapters and the code. Kimberly Burton-Weisman did an excellent job performing the copyediting in a timely, efficient manner. In fact, the entire Apress editorial board was instrumental in making this process run smoothly and seamlessly. Thank you is not enough!

Finally, I would like to thank Apple, in particular Steve Jobs and Steve Wozniak, for this amazing technology that we are so fortunate to be able to use. Many years ago, I bought my first computer, a Mac SE 30, as a college student. From that point on, I have always been impressed by the quality of the systems, hardware, software, and the engineering that goes into each Apple product. Thanks to the vision and the perseverance of these pioneers, I have been able to write this book.

Introduction

The Objective-C programming language continues to grow in popularity and usage. This is due to the power and ease-of-use of the language itself, along with the numerous features that continue to be added to the platform. Many programmers have developed a basic knowledge of the language and now want to further their expertise. *Pro Objective-C* will take you to the next level.

What This Book Is

Pro Objective-C provides an in-depth, comprehensive guide to the language, its runtime, and key APIs. It explains the key concepts of Objective-C in a clear, easy-to-understand manner, along with detailed coverage of its more complex features. Its key topics include:

- Objective-C fundamentals and key language elements

- The Objective-C runtime system

- Foundation Framework APIs

- Objective-C advanced language features

The book also includes numerous practical examples—code excerpts and complete applications—that demonstrate how to apply in code what you're learning.

Each topic is covered clearly, concisely, and is packed with the details you need to develop Objective-C code effectively. The most important features are given in-depth treatment, and each chapter contains numerous examples that clearly demonstrate the use of Objective-C.

Who This Book Is For

This book is geared toward intermediate to advanced developers who already have some Objective-C experience. It's also great for developers who have not used Objective-C but have some C programming experience and also understand object-oriented programming.

What You Need

Before you begin writing Objective-C code for the Apple OS X and iOS platforms, you'll need an Intel-based Mac computer (MacBook, iMac, Mac Pro, etc.) running OS X Mountain Lion (OS X 10.6.8) or later. You will also need Xcode, Apple's toolset for iOS and Mac software development. Chapter 1 provides instructions for obtaining and installing Xcode.

What's in This Book

Here's a brief overview of the chapters of this book.

Chapter 1

This chapter introduces the Objective-C programming language and development environment. You will also download and install Xcode and write your first Objective-C program.

Chapter 2

Chapter 2 is all about classes, the major building block for object-oriented programming. It covers the key elements and unique features Objective-C provides for developing classes.

Chapter 3

In Chapter 2 you learned how to create classes; in this chapter you learn how to use them. Specifically, you learn about the concepts and details around Objective-C object creation, initialization, and messaging.

Chapter 4

Proper memory management is key to developing programs that perform both correctly and efficiently. In this chapter you'll learn how computer memory is allocated and released for Objective-C programs, the Objective-C memory model, and how to write programs that perform memory management properly.

Chapter 5

Objective-C includes a preprocessor that is used to translate source files prior to compilation. In this chapter you will learn how the preprocessor works and how the preprocessor language is used in Objective-C source files.

Chapter 6

As you learned earlier in this book, ARC is the recommended approach for Objective-C memory management. In this Expert Section chapter you will learn some of the finer details surrounding ARC memory management, as well as how to use ARC with toll-free bridged objects.

Chapter 7

Chapter 7 begins our study of the Objective-C runtime system by providing an in-depth exploration of the dynamic features of the Objective-C language. This includes runtime type determination, method resolution, object introspection, dynamic code loading, and other features.

Chapter 8

In Chapter 8 you will learn about the architecture and design of the Objective-C runtime system, and how its dynamic features are implemented. The chapter also shows how your code interacts with the runtime, both at compile time and during program execution.

Chapter 9

In this Expert Section chapter you will enhance your knowledge of the runtime system by developing several example programs that exercise some of its key features and APIs.

Chapter 10

In Chapter 10, you will learn about Foundation Framework classes that provide common, general-purpose functionality required by most Objective-C programs. The classes examined include root classes, strings, value objects, collections, XML data processing, and predicates.

Chapter 11

In Chapter 11, you will explore Foundation Framework classes that provide system services. These classes implement a variety of operating system services for networking, file management, interprocess communication, system information retrieval, text processing, threading, and concurrency.

Chapter 12

Chapter 12 covers several Foundation Framework classes that provide specialized system services, which implement functionality to support event-driven programming, object persistence, and distributed programming.

Chapter 13

In this chapter you'll learn about the Foundation Framework's general-purpose functions, data types, and constants, a set of APIs that provide a variety of essential functionality for Objective-C software development.

Chapter 14

Chapter 14 is an Expert Section dedicated to error handling. You will learn about the causes of runtime errors, the programming options for error handling, and the Foundation Framework APIs for handling errors and exception conditions.

Chapter 15

In Chapter 15 you will learn how to program with blocks, a powerful extension to the Objective-C language. It explores block syntax and semantics, block memory management, how to develop blocks in your own code, and how to use blocks in existing APIs.

Chapter 16

Objective-C literals are a recent addition to the language. In this chapter you will learn their syntax, associated semantics, and general guidelines for usage.

Chapter 17

The Objective-C platform provides a variety of language extensions, APIs, and operating system services that are designed to enable you to safely and efficiently implement concurrent programming. In Chapter 17 you will explore this technology in depth.

Chapter 18

In Chapter 18 you will learn the fundamentals of key-value programming (key-value coding, key-value observing). The chapter includes relevant implementation details, and also shows how to use key-value programming in your code.

Appendix A

Appendix A provides a concise summary of the basic elements of the Objective-C language. Its scope is the Objective-C language extensions to ANSI C.

Appendix B

Appendix B presents an in-depth exploration of Xcode, including its basic concepts, major functional elements, and how to use its key features.

Appendix C

Appendix C provides a detailed overview of LLDB, the Xcode debugger. You will learn the architecture and design of LLDB, briefly review how it's integrated with Xcode, and learn how to efficiently debug programs in Xcode with LLDB.

Chapter 1

Getting Started

For those of you new to Objective-C, welcome on board! In this chapter, you'll receive an introduction to the language and then dive right in by writing some code. You'll start with an overview of the Apple Objective-C development environment and discuss some of the reasons why Objective-C is such a popular language for application development. Next, you begin using Xcode, Apple's integrated development environment (IDE), and see how it makes Objective-C programming both enjoyable and efficient.

Introduction

Objective-C is the primary programming language for developing applications on Apple's OS X and iOS (iPod, iPhone, iPad) platforms. In recent years, these platforms have become some of the most popular application development environments. A key reason for this success is due, in fact, to features of the Objective-C language.

Apple released version 2.0 of Objective-C in 2007. It added many new features to the language, including declared and synthesized properties, dot notation, fast enumeration, exception support, runtime performance improvements, and 64-bit machine support.

The Objective-C language has continued to evolve and acquire features that make Objective-C programming more powerful and expressive. Some of the more significant recent additions to the language include automatic reference counting for Objective-C objects, improved support for data hiding, improved type safety for enumerations, as well as new language constructs for block objects, literals, and other features.

Apple Objective-C Platform

Apple's Objective-C development environment consists of several parts:

- Objective-C programming language
- Objective-C runtime environment
- Software libraries
- Software development tools

Object-oriented software development using Objective-C is the main subject of this book. As such, Part 1 of this book covers the programming language and the way it supports object-oriented programming.

Objective-C programs execute within the Objective-C runtime environment; it enables the dynamic programming capabilities of the language. Part 2 of this book explores the Objective-C runtime environment in depth and demonstrates how to use its application programming interfaces (APIs).

The software libraries include a set of frameworks, libraries, and services that provide general-purpose functionality to simplify application development. This software provides, out-of-the-box, much of the functionality needed to develop applications on the OS X and iOS platforms. Part 3 of this book covers the Foundation Framework, the base APIs that are used for any type of Objective-C program.

Part 4 focuses on advanced features of Objective-C that are of particular interest to programmers as they develop more sophisticated applications.

The software development tools enable source code editing and compilation, user interface development, version control, project management, testing and debugging, and other features. They also simplify application development and enable developers to be more efficient when developing, managing, and maintaining Objective-C software. Throughout this book, instructions are provided for using these tools to develop programs. Appendix B offers additional tips and recommendations.

Why Objective-C?

So, what are the benefits of Objective-C compared to the many other programming languages available today? After all, quite a few languages support object-oriented programming. Is its being the primary programming language for developing applications on Apple's OS X and iOS platforms the biggest reason for its popularity? Well, Objective-C is a great programming language on its own merits, with a variety of features that make it incredibly powerful, versatile, and easy to use for application development:

- *Object-oriented programming*: The Objective-C programming language provides complete support for object-oriented programming (OOP), including capabilities such as object messaging, encapsulation, inheritance, polymorphism, and open recursion.

- *Object messaging*: Object messaging enables objects to collaborate by passing messages between themselves. In effect, Objective-C code (e.g., a class/object method or a function) sends a message to a receiving object *(the receiver)* and the receiver uses the message to invoke its corresponding method, returning a result if required. If the receiver does not have a corresponding method, it can handle the message in other ways, such as forwarding it to another object, broadcasting it to other objects, introspecting it and applying custom logic, and so forth.

- *Dynamic runtime*: Compared to many other languages that support OOP, Objective-C is very dynamic. It shifts much of the responsibility for type, message, and method resolution to the runtime, rather than compile or link time. These capabilities can be used to facilitate developing and updating programs both in real time, without the need to recompile and redeploy software, and over time, with minimal or no impact to the existing software.

- *Memory management*: Objective-C provides a memory management capability, Automatic Reference Counting (ARC), which both simplifies application development and improves application performance. ARC is a compile-time technology that incorporates many of the benefits of traditional automatic memory management mechanisms (i.e., garbage collectors). However, compared to these traditional technologies, ARC provides better performance (memory management code is interleaved with your program code at compile time), however, and it doesn't introduce memory management-induced pauses into program execution.

- *Introspection and Reflection*: The Objective-C language includes features that enable a program to query an object at runtime, provide information (its type, properties, and the methods it supports), and modify its structure and behavior. This enables a program to be modified during its lifetime of execution.

- *C language support*: Objective-C is primarily an object-oriented extension to the C language. It constitutes a superset of C. This means that the raw power of C is available and that C libraries can be accessed directly.

- *Apple technologies*: Apple provides a wealth of software libraries and tools for Objective-C application development. The development kits have frameworks and libraries that include the infrastructure, enabling you to focus on developing your application-specific logic. Xcode, Apple's integrated development environment, provides all the tools you'll need to develop great applications using Objective-C.

These are just some of the reasons why Objective-C continues to grow in popularity among developers—and I'm sure you'll discover more as you continue through this book. OK, enough talk. Now let's use Xcode to take Objective-C out for a test drive and find out what it's really capable of!

Developing a Simple Objective-C Program

The best way to become proficient in a programming language is to learn by doing, so now you are going to start writing some code! But first, let's download and install Xcode.

Xcode is a complete IDE for Objective-C software development on the Mac. It is fully integrated with both iOS and OS X, and it includes all the tools necessary for writing and compiling source code, developing sophisticated user interfaces, software testing and debugging, release build and version management, project management, and a host of other features. Xcode is a free download for all members of the Apple iOS and Mac Developer Programs. If you are not a member of either program, it is also available as a free download from the Mac App Store. The examples in this book were developed using Xcode 4.5, the current release. This version of the IDE will run on any Intel Mac computer that has OS X Lion or later installed.

Creating the Project

Once you have downloaded and installed Xcode, launch the program. The Xcode welcome window shown in Figure 1-1 will display.

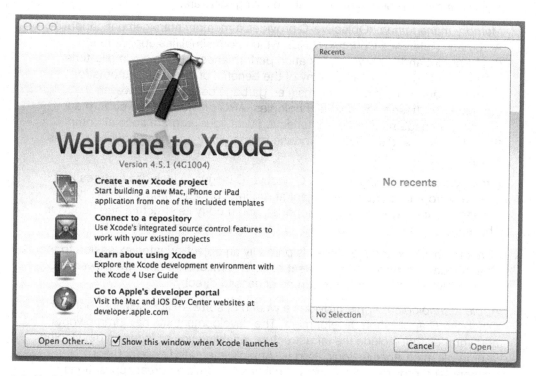

Figure 1-1. Xcode welcome window

> **Note** If you have an iOS device (e.g., iPhone/iPod/iPad) connected to your computer, you may see a message asking whether or not you want to use that device for development. Because you will not be developing a mobile app here, you should click the *Ignore* button.)

This screen presents you with a variety of options: you can visit Apple's developer portal, learn more about Xcode, and so forth. Because you want to create a new application, select the **Create a new Xcode project** option by selecting **New ➤ Project ...** from the Xcode File menu. The Xcode workspace window will be displayed, followed by the New Project Assistant pane on top of that, as shown in Figure 1-2.

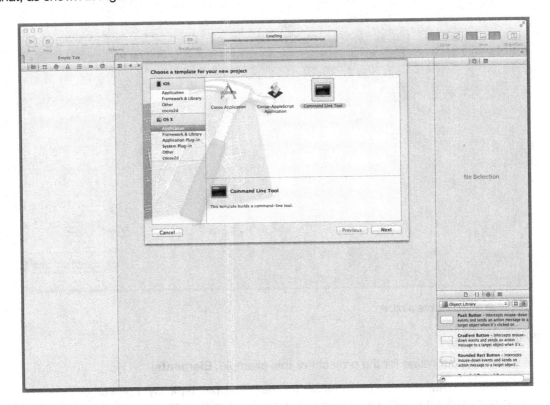

Figure 1-2. Xcode New Project Assistant

The left side of the New Project Assistant is divided into iOS and OS X sections. You are going to start by creating a command-line application, so select **Application** under the OS X section. In the upper-right pane, you'll see several icons that represent each of the project templates that are provided as starting points for creating OS X applications. Select **Command Line Tool** and click **Next**. The project options window will be displayed (as shown in Figure 1-3) for you to input project-specific information.

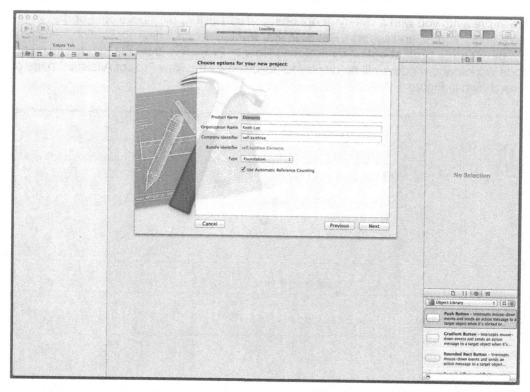

Figure 1-3. Xcode project options window

Specify the following:

- The *Product Name* for the project (for this example, **Elements**).

- The *Organization Name* (an identifier for the developer, typically a person or organization; this name will be included in the copyright comments at the top of your source files).

- A *Company Identifier* (this is a name used to provide an identifier for your application; typically you input something like your domain name in reverse order, but any name will suffice).

- The *Type* of application (Xcode supports various application types, including C, C++, etc.; here you select **Foundation** for an Objective-C project that uses the Foundation Framework).

- And finally, select the check box to specify that the project will use *Automatic Reference Counting* for memory management.

After this information has been provided, click **Next** to display the window for entering the name and location of your project (see Figure 1-4).

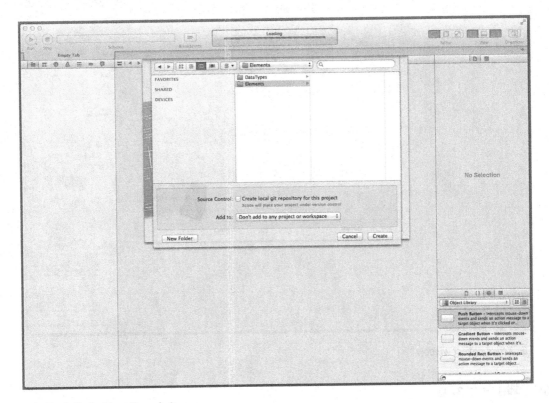

Figure 1-4. Xcode Project Location window

Specify the location in your file system where you want the project to be created (if necessary, select **New Folder** and enter the name and location for the folder); also be sure to uncheck the **Source Control** check box. Next, click the **Create** button. The project (workspace) window, as shown in Figure 1-5, is opened.

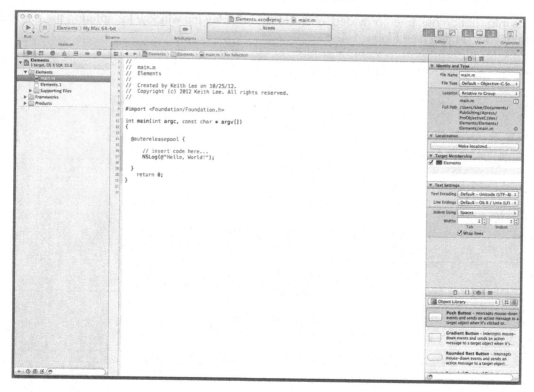

Figure 1-5. Xcode project window

Xcode Workspace

The project window consists of a toolbar and three main areas, as illustrated in Figure 1-6.

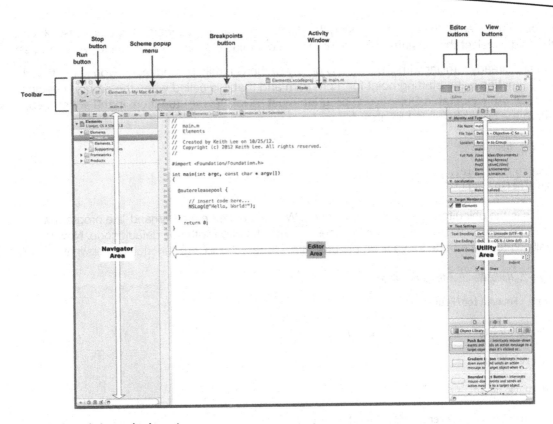

Figure 1-6. Project window main elements

The toolbar includes controls to start and stop running your project (the **Run** and **Stop** buttons); a pop-up menu to select the **Scheme** you want to run (a scheme defines information used to build and execute one or more targets); a **Breakpoints** button for toggling breakpoints on/off while debugging your program; the **Activity View** in the middle of the toolbar; a set of **Editor** buttons; a set of **View** buttons; and an **Organizer** button.

The three areas below the toolbar comprise the navigator area, editor area, and the utility area. The *navigator area* is used to view and access different resources (files, etc.) within a project. The *editor area* is where you write most of your program. The *utility area* is used to view and access Help and other inspectors, and to use ready-made resources in your project.

This has been a (very) high-level overview of the elements that comprise the Xcode workspace, so don't worry about understanding all of it right now. You will gain plenty of experience using Xcode and its associated tools as you develop code throughout this book.

Completing Your Test Drive

You have now created an Xcode project named Elements. If you look at the navigator area of the project window, at the top you'll see a selector bar comprised of seven buttons and below that the main navigator area. Click the leftmost button (a folder icon) to see the Project Navigator view. The project navigator shows the contents (files, resources, etc.) of a project or Xcode workspace.

Now open the Elements folder by clicking the disclosure triangle alongside the Elements folder icon. In the folder, select the file named **main.m**; this file contains the main() function for your program.

If you are already familiar with Objective-C or any of the C family of languages, you know that the main() function is the starting point for a program and that it is called when the program begins execution. An executable Objective-C program must have a main() function. In the editor area, observe the code shown in Listing 1-1.

Listing 1-1. Hello, World!

```
// insert code here...
NSLog(@"Hello, World!");
```

Yes, this is the ubiquitous Hello, World! greeting. When you create a command-line program with Xcode, it creates a main.m file, which includes a main() function with this default code. Now let's actually write a little code for your simple program. Update the main() function as shown in Listing 1-2.

Listing 1-2. Hello, World! with Current Date

```
#import <Foundation/Foundation.h>

int main(int argc, const char * argv[])
{
  @autoreleasepool
  {
    NSLog(@"Hello, World!");

    // Display the current date, formatted nicely
    NSDate *dateTime = [NSDate date];
    NSDateFormatter *dateFormat = [[NSDateFormatter alloc]init];
    [dateFormat setDateFormat:@"EEE MMM d, yyyy"];
    NSString *dateString = [dateFormat stringFromDate:dateTime];
    NSLog(@"Today's date is %@", dateString);
  }
  return 0;
}
```

In addition to Hello, World!, the program also displays the current day and date. You can compile and run this program now by clicking the **Run** button on the toolbar (or by selecting **Run** from the Xcode Product menu). The output pane (located below the editor area) displays the Hello, World! message and the date (see Figure 1-7).

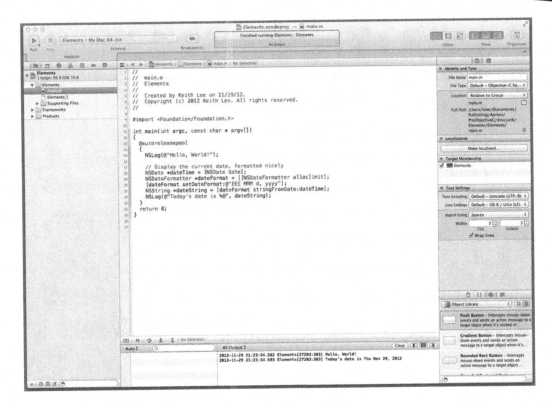

Figure 1-7. Hello, World! example

Perfect. You have learned how to create an Xcode project and how to compile and run a simple Objective-C program. Feel free to continue exploring the Xcode project window to become more familiar with its contents.

Roundup

This chapter introduced Objective-C. You downloaded and installed Xcode, and used it to write an Objective-C program. The Objective-C language, combined with the tools and software provided by Apple, make this a great platform for software development. With this introduction completed, you're now prepared to begin learning the language in depth. When you're ready, turn the page and let's start developing some classes!

Chapter 2

Using Classes

Classes are the building block for object-oriented programming (OOP). In fact, programs created using OOP consist primarily of a network of interacting *class instances* (i.e., objects). The Objective-C language provides full support for OOP, including language features that enable design-time specification of classes and the runtime creation of class instances, along with multiple mechanisms to support object interaction.

This chapter focuses on Objective-C's key elements and unique features for developing classes. It covers key areas such as Objective-C class structure, class design and implementation, and some additional language features that support class development and OOP. The chapter also includes plenty of examples (along with a program that you will develop) to reinforce your understanding of the concepts. Sounds like fun, right? OK, so let's get started!

Developing Your First Class

Object-oriented programming is a style of computer programming that emphasizes the creation and use of software objects to write programs. A *software object* provides a representation of the characteristics or attributes of the thing/concept being modeled (its *state*) along with a definition of the things it can do (its *methods*). With Objective-C, you create the specification or blueprint for an object with a class *interface* and a corresponding *implementation*. In the interface, you specify the structure of the class (i.e., its properties and methods). In the implementation, you specify the variables that store the classes' internal state, and implement its logic by defining its properties and methods. The Objective-C language also provides several additional features for developing classes, specifically *protocols* and *categories*, which you'll learn about later in this chapter. For now, let's start with the basics by adding a class to the Elements project.

Adding a Class to the Project

From Xcode, select the **Elements** folder in the navigator area and then create a new file by selecting **New ➤ File...** from the Xcode File menu. The New File template will be displayed. Next, select

Cocoa under OS X; this reveals templates for Objective-C class elements. Select the **Objective-C class icon** to create an Objective-C class with implementation and header files, and then click the **Next** button (as shown in Figure 2-1).

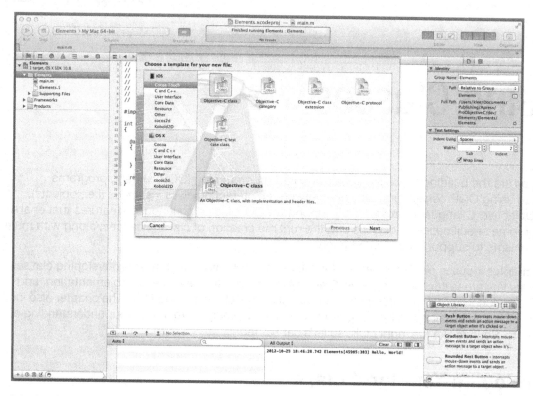

Figure 2-1. *Creating an Objective-C class*

A window for choosing the options for your class, specifically its name and the name of its subclass, is displayed. As shown in Figure 2-2, enter **Atom** for the class name, select **NSObject** (or type the name of the subclass in the list) from the subclass drop-down list, and then click **Next**.

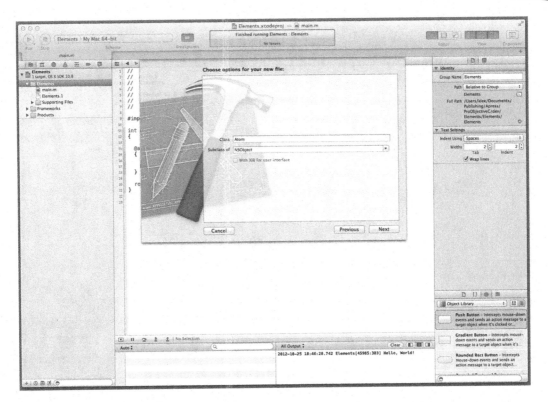

Figure 2-2. *Specifying Atom class options*

Next, you'll be prompted to specify the project target for the class and where in your file system to save the class files. Leave the location as the Elements folder and the project target as the Elements project, and then click the **Create** button (see Figure 2-3).

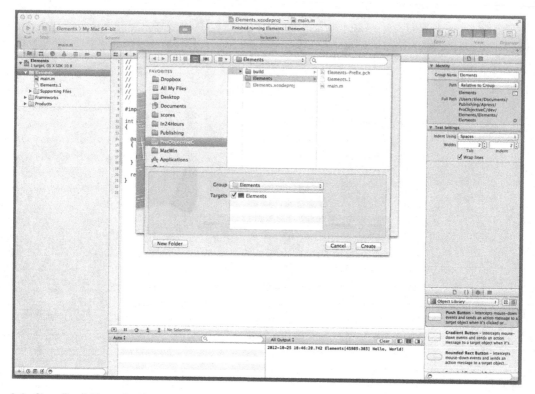

Figure 2-3. Class files folder and project target

You have created a class using Xcode! In the Xcode project navigator pane, you will see that the Atom class is split into two files (`Atom.h` and `Atom.m`) that have been added to the project under the Elements folder. Next, you'll develop the Atom class in these files.

Coding the Atom Class Interface

The interface for the `Atom` class is specified in the `Atom.h` header file, and the implementation in the `Atom.m` file. The names of these files reflect the Objective-C convention whereby header files are suffixed with `.h` and implementation files are suffixed with `.m`. Let's examine the `Atom.h` interface file created by Xcode. In the project navigator pane, select **Atom.h** and view the Atom interface in the editor pane (see Listing 2-1).

Listing 2-1. Atom Class Base Interface

```
#import <Foundation/Foundation.h>

@interface Atom : NSObject
@end
```

The #import <Foundation/Foundation.h> line is an Objective-C *preprocessor* directive to include the header file for the Foundation Framework in this (the Atom) header file. The preprocessor is used to transform Objective-C code prior to compilation (you'll learn more about the preprocessor in Chapter 5 of this book). The Foundation Framework provides a base layer of APIs that can be used for any type of Objective-C program (Part 3 of this book explores the Foundation Framework APIs in depth). The remainder of the header file declares the interface for the Atom class.

A class interface declaration begins with the @interface directive and the name of the class; it ends with the @end directive. The formal syntax for declaring a class interface is shown in Listing 2-2.

Listing 2-2. Class Interface Syntax

```
@interface ClassName : SuperclassName
// Property and method declarations
@end
```

So, you can see from Listing 2-1 that the Atom class has a superclass named NSObject. A superclass establishes a common interface and implementation, which specialized subclasses can inherit, modify, and supplement. Hence, the Atom class *inherits* the functionality of the NSObject class. NSObject is the root (i.e., base) class of most Foundation Framework class hierarchies and it provides a basic interface to the Objective-C runtime. Thus, the vast majority of the classes you implement here will descend from the NSObject class hierarchy. Now let's declare the custom properties and methods for the Atom class (i.e., those that aren't inherited from NSObject). In the editor pane, update the Atom.h file as shown in Listing 2-3 (the code updates are shown in **bold**).

Listing 2-3. Atom Interface

```
@interface Atom : NSObject
@property (readonly) NSUInteger protons;
@property (readonly) NSUInteger neutrons;
@property (readonly) NSUInteger electrons;
@property (readonly) NSString *chemicalElement;

- (NSUInteger) massNumber;
@end
```

This code adds several properties and an *instance* method to the class declaration. The property chemicalElement is of type NSString * (i.e., a pointer to a text string) and has a readonly attribute, meaning that you can retrieve its value but cannot set it. The properties protons, neutrons, and electrons are each of type NSUInteger (i.e., non-negative integer values) and are read-only. The instance method, named massNumber, returns a non-negative integer value. You'll learn the specifics on declaring class properties and methods later in this chapter. In the meantime, let's complete this example by coding the class implementation.

Coding the Atom Class Implementation

The implementation for the Atom class is provided in the Atom.m file. In the project navigator pane, select the **Atom.m** file and view the base Atom implementation in the editor pane, as shown in Listing 2-4.

Listing 2-4. Atom Class Base Implementation

```
#import "Atom.h"

@implementation Atom
@end
```

The import directive includes the contents of the Atom.h header file (i.e., its preprocessor directives, interface declarations, and other included header files). Now let's define the custom properties and methods for the Atom class that were declared in the Atom interface. In the editor pane, update the Atom.m file as shown in Listing 2-5 (the code updates are displayed in **bold**).

Listing 2-5. Atom Class Implementation

```
@implementation Atom

- (id) init
{
  if ((self = [super init]))
  {
    _chemicalElement = @"None";
  }

  return self;
}

- (NSUInteger) massNumber
{
  return 0;
}

@end
```

All methods declared in a class interface must be defined in its class implementation. Hence, the Atom implementation in Listing 2-5 defines two methods: init() and atomicMass(). The massNumber() method is declared in the Atom interface, so the actual program logic for the method is defined here; it just returns the value 0 for the atomic mass number. The init() method is also defined here, but why? After all, this method isn't declared in the Atom interface. Well, the init() method is declared in NSObject, which is a subclass (i.e., parent) of the Atom class. The NSObject init() method is used to initialize a new object immediately after memory has been allocated for it; hence if you have any custom initialization functionality to perform (set instance variables to known values, etc.), it should be performed here. In this implementation, the init() method initializes the instance variable backed by the chemicalElement property to the text string None.

Once you finish making the updates to the Atom class implementation, you should test your class. First, go back to the main() method and edit it as shown in Listing 2-6.

Listing 2-6. Atom Project main() Method

```
#import <Foundation/Foundation.h>
#import "Atom.h"
```

```
int main(int argc, const char * argv[])
{
  @autoreleasepool
  {
    Atom *atom = [[Atom alloc] init];
    NSLog(@"Atom chemical element name: %@", atom.chemicalElement);
  }

  return 0;
}
```

In the `main()` method, create an `Atom` object and then use the Foundation Framework `NSLog` function to display the object's chemical element name to the output pane. Save all the files of the project by selecting **Save** from the Xcode File menu, and then compile and run the program by clicking the **Run** button in the toolbar. (You can also simply compile and run the program, and it will automatically save any changes to its files). The output pane (see Figure 2-4) displays the message "Atom chemical element name: None".

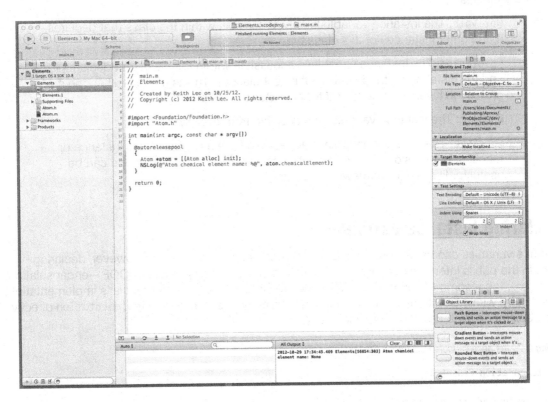

Figure 2-4. Testing the Atom class

Great. You have just implemented and tested your first Objective-C class. With this introduction, you are now ready to "look under the hood" to learn about classes in depth—so let's begin!

Instance Variables

Instance variables, sometimes referred to as *ivars*, are variables declared for a class that exist and hold their value throughout the life of a corresponding class instance (i.e., object). The memory used for instance variables is allocated when an object is first created, and freed when the object is deallocated. Instance variables have an implicit scope and namespace corresponding to the object. Objective-C provides features to control direct access to instance variables, as well as a convenient mechanism for getting/setting their values.

Instance Variable Access

Access to an object's instance variables is a function of its scope. Within an object, its instance variables can be accessed directly from any of its instance methods. Direct access to an object's instance variables from an external class instance is a function of the variable's scope. Objective-C provides several compiler directives used to explicitly specify the scope of (i.e., control access to) instance variables:

- @private: The instance variable is only accessible within the class that declares it and other instances of this class type.

- @protected: The instance variable is accessible within the class that declares it and the instance methods of any of its subclasses. This is the default scope if a protection level is not specified for an instance variable.

- @public: The instance variable is accessible from everywhere.

- @package: The instance variable is accessible from any other class instance or function, but outside the package, it is treated as private. This scope can be useful for libraries or framework classes.

Declaring Instance Variables

Instance variables can be declared in a class interface or implementation; however, declaring them in the public interface of a class would violate one of the key tenets of OOP—encapsulation. Therefore, the recommended practice is to declare instance variables in the class implementation; specifically, within a statement block placed immediately after the class @implementation directive. The declaration syntax is shown in Listing 2-7.

Listing 2-7. Instance Variable Declaration Syntax

```
@implementation ClassName
{
  // Instance variable declarations
}
...
@end
```

If the access control compiler directives are used, the syntax for declaring each instance variable within the statement block is updated as shown in Listing 2-8.

Listing 2-8. Instance Variable Declaration with Access Control Directives

```
{
  protection_directive ivar_declaration_list
  protection_directive ivar_declaration_list
  ...
}
```

An example class that declares instance variables with access control compiler directives is shown in Listing 2-9.

Listing 2-9. Example Class with Instance Variable Declarations

```
@implementation MyTestClass
{
  @protected
    int myInt1;
    int myInt2;
  @private
    float myFloat;
  @package
    double myDouble;
}
...
@end
```

This class declares two protected variables named myInt1 and myInt2; a private variable named myFloat; and a package-protected variable named myDouble.

Accessing Instance Variables

Instance variables are directly bound to and exist within the context of the corresponding object. As a consequence, an object's instance methods can directly access its instance variables. For example, if the class MyTestClass shown in Listing 2-9 defines an instance method myTestMethod, the method can directly access the instance variable myInt1 (see Listing 2-10).

Listing 2-10. Instance Variable Access Declarations

```
-(void) myTestMethod
{
  myInt1 = 1;
  ...
}
```

Although instance variables provide convenient, direct access to an object's state, they expose the internals of a class—and this violates the OOP principle of encapsulation. Therefore, instance variables should only be declared when necessary, and the declaration should be in the class implementation, not the public interface. The preferred approach for publicly exposing the internal state of an object is through *declared properties.* Let's look at those next.

Properties

In many programming languages, methods that access an object's internal state—often referred to as *getter/setter* methods—must be manually coded. Objective-C provides declared properties to both automate and simplify this task. A property differs from an instance variable in that it doesn't directly access an object's internal state, but rather provides a convenient mechanism (i.e., getter/ setter methods) for accessing this data, and thus may include other logic. Objective-C *declared properties* enable the compiler to generate these methods automatically according to your provided specification. This reduces the amount of code you have to write and maintain, and increases program consistency and reliability.

Property Declaration

A property is declared using the @property keyword followed by an optional set of attributes (enclosed within parentheses), the property type, and its name.

```
@property (attributes) type propertyName;
```

For example, the Atom class you developed earlier (see Listing 2-3) declares the properties chemicalElement, protons, neutrons, and electrons. Properties can be declared in a *class interface*, a *category interface*, or a *protocol*. The declaration sets the signature for the getter/setter methods associated with a property, but does not generate the actual method definitions.

Property Attributes

Property declaration attributes are used to specify the storage semantics and other behaviors associated with a property. The most commonly-used property attributes are described in Table 2-1.

Table 2-1. Property Attributes

Category	Attribute	Description
Atomicity	nonatomic	Accessors are not atomic and, consequently, could provide different results when accessed concurrently by multiple threads. If not specified, accessors are atomic; that is, their values are always fully set/retrieved.
Setter Semantics	assign	The setter method performs a simple assignment of the property value without using copy or retain. This is the default setting.
	retain	On assignment, the input value will be sent a retain message and the previous value will be sent a release message.
	copy	A copy of the new message will be set on assignment and the previous value will be sent a release message.
	strong	This attribute (used when ARC memory management is applied on a property) is equivalent to the retain attribute.

(*continued*)

Table 2-1. (continued)

Category	Attribute	Description
	weak	This attribute (used when ARC memory management is applied on a property) is similar to the assign attribute except that if the affect property is released, its value is set to nil.
Read/Write	readwrite	The property can be read or written to. Both getter and setter methods must be implemented. This is the default setting.
	read-only	The property can be read but not written to. The getter method must be implemented.
Method names	getter=getterName	Renames the getter to the specified getterName.
	setter=setterName	Renames the setter to the specified setterName.

Property Definition

A property definition is performed in the implementation section of a class. In most cases, a property is backed by an instance variable; hence, the property definition includes defining getter and setter methods for the property, declaring an instance variable, and using that variable in the getter/setter methods. Objective-C provides several methods for defining a property: explicit definition, synthesis via keyword, and autosynthesis.

Explicit Definition

For this method of defining a property, its methods are explicitly defined in the corresponding class implementation. As an example, the setter method for a property named myIntProperty can be defined as shown in Listing 2-11.

Listing 2-11. Property Setter Method Definition

```
-(void) setMyIntProperty:(int) value
{
  _myIntProperty = value;
{
```

The name of the variable corresponding to the property is prefaced with an underscore. This name reflects the Objective-C standard naming convention for property instance variables, whereby the name of the variable is that of the property name, prefaced with an underscore.

Synthesis via Keyword

Through use of the @synthesize keyword, the compiler can autogenerate property definitions. A property is synthesized in the corresponding class implementation section. The syntax for synthesizing a property via keyword is

```
@synthesize propertyName [= instanceVariableName];
```

If the optional `instanceVariableName` assignment is not provided, the compiler will automatically generate the instance variable name following the standard naming convention for property-backed instance variables. If an `instanceVariableName` value is provided, the compiler will create the instance variable with the name provided. For a property named `myIntProperty`, the getter and setter methods will be autogenerated with the statement

```
@synthesize myIntProperty;
```

The compiler will create a corresponding instance variable named `_myIntProperty`.

Autosynthesis

The recommended Apple Objective-C compiler, Clang/LLVM (versions 4.2 and above) provides support for autosynthesis of declared properties. This means that the compiler will automatically synthesize declared properties that are neither: 1) synthesized by keyword (e.g., using `@synthesis`); 2) generated dynamically (via the `@dynamic` property directive); nor 3) having user-provided getter and setter methods. Thus, there is no need to include code to synthesize a declared property when using this feature. A declared property is automatically synthesized by the compiler, along with the corresponding instance variable. The `Atom` class implemented earlier (see Listing 2-3) uses autosynthesis of its declared properties.

Dynamic Generation

Accessor methods for a property can be delegated or dynamically created at runtime. The `@dynamic` property directive can be used to prevent compiler autogeneration of accessor methods in these cases. The compiler will not generate a warning if it cannot find implementations of accessor methods associated with the properties whose names follow the `@dynamic` property. Instead, the developer is responsible for creating these methods by either writing the accessor method implementations directly, using some other means to derive them (such as dynamic code loading or dynamic method resolution), or leveraging a software library (e.g., the Apple Core Data framework) that dynamically generates these methods.

Property-Backed Instance Variables

Most properties are backed by an instance variable, hence the mechanism by which properties hide the internal state of an object. Unless specified otherwise, the instance variable should have the same name as the property, but with an underscore prefix. In the `Atom` class implementation shown in Listing 2-5, the `init` method accesses the instance variable for the `chemicalElement` property, which is named `_chemicalElement`.

Property Access

Objective-C provides two mechanisms for accessing properties: accessor methods and dot notation. Accessor methods synthesized by the compiler follow standard naming conventions:

- The method used to access the value (the *getter* method) has the same name as the property.

- The method used to set the value (the *setter* method) starts with the word "set" prepended to the property name, with the first letter of the property name capitalized.

Using these conventions, the getter method for a property named `color` would be called `color`, and its setter method would be called `setColor`. So, for an object named `myObject`, the getter and setter accessor methods would be invoked as follows:

```
[myObject color];
[myObject setColor:value];
```

Objective-C provides a concise alternative to accessor methods: *dot notation*. The dot notation syntax for getting and setting a property of an object named `myObject` would be

```
myObject.propertyName;
myObject.propertyName = propertyValue;
```

The first statement invokes the getter accessor method to retrieve the value of the property and the second invokes the setter accessor method to set the property to the value of `propertyValue`.

In general, properties should be accessed using the two mechanisms mentioned. However, if the object associated with a property is not (or may not be) fully constructed, these mechanisms should not be used, and the property-backed instance variable should be used instead. This means that within a class `init` method or `dealloc` method, the instance variable should be accessed directly, as shown with the `Atom` class `_chemicalElement` instance variable in Listing 2-5.

Methods

Methods define the behavior exhibited by classes and class instances (objects) at runtime. They are directly associated with either an Objective-C class (class method) or object (instance method). Instance methods have direct access to an object's instance variables. Methods can be declared in a class interface, a protocol, and/or a category. Methods thus declared are defined in a corresponding class implementation.

Syntax

A method declaration consists of a method type, a return type, and one or more method segments that provide name, parameter, and parameter type information (see Figure 2-5).

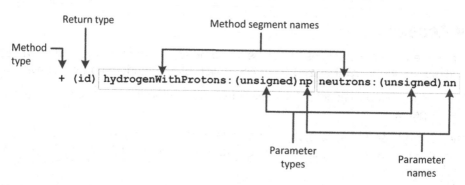

Figure 2-5. Method declaration syntax

The *method type* identifier specifies whether the method is a class or an instance method. A class method is declared with a + (plus) sign and indicates that the method has *class scope*, meaning that it operates at the class level and does not have access to the instance variables of the class (unless they are passed as parameters to the method). An instance method is declared with a − (minus) sign and indicates that the method has *object scope*. It operates at the instance level and has direct access to the instance variables of the object and its parent objects (subject to the access controls on the instance variables).

The *return type* indicates the type of the returned variable from the method, if any. The return type is specified within parentheses, following the method type. If the method does not return anything, the return type is declared as void. Figure 2-5. declares a class method with two parameters whose names are np and nn, each of which takes a non-negative integer value, and returns a value of type id, a special Objective-C type that I will discuss in the next chapter.

The method definition syntax is identical to that of the declaration syntax, but instead of a terminating semicolon, it is followed by the implementation logic enclosed within curly braces. The Atom class declares an instance method named massNumber; the implementation of this method is shown in Listing 2-5.

Invoking Methods

In Objective-C, an object (the *sender*) interacts with another object (the *receiver*) by sending it a message, thus causing the receiver to invoke a specific method. The syntax for invoking a method on an object is

```
[receiver methodSegmentName:parameterValue ...];
```

Braces surround the message. If the method has multiple segments, its name and parameter values are listed consecutively, each separated by a space. An example method invocation with multiple name/parameter value pairs is

```
[Atom withProtons:6 neutrons:6 electrons:6];
```

This method invocation has three segments and thus takes three input parameters: an integer number of protons, neutrons, and electrons.

Protocol

You have learned about the basic elements and structure of Objective-C classes, but the language provides several additional features for developing classes. In this section, you'll learn about one of these: protocols.

A *protocol* declares methods and properties that can be implemented by any class. A class interface is directly associated with a specific class and, hence, a class hierarchy. On the other hand, a protocol is not associated with any particular class, thus it can be used to capture similarities among classes that are not hierarchically related. Protocols provide Objective-C with the capability to support the concept of multiple inheritance of specification (i.e., of method declarations). A protocol can also be used to define the messages that an object can send (by specifying properties that conform to a protocol).

Syntax

A protocol declaration begins with the @protocol directive followed by the name of the protocol. It ends with the @end directive. Protocols can have both *required* and *optional* methods; optional methods do not require that an implementation of the protocol implement these methods. The directives @required and @optional (followed by the method name(s)) are used to mark a method appropriately. If neither keyword is specified, the default behavior is required. The syntax of a protocol declaration is shown in Listing 2-12.

Listing 2-12. Protocol Declaration Syntax

```
@protocol ProtocolName
// Property declarations
@required
// Method declarations
@optional
// Method declarations
@end
```

One protocol can incorporate other protocols by specifying the name of each declared protocol within braces; this is referred to as *adopting* a protocol. Commas are used to separate multiple protocols (see Listing 2-13).

Listing 2-13. Incorporating Other Protocols

```
@protocol ProtocolName<ProtocolName(s)>
// Method declarations
@end
```

An interface can adopt other protocols using similar syntax (see Listing 2-14).

Listing 2-14. Interface Adopting a Protocol

```
@interface ClassName : Parent <ProtocolName(s)>
// Method declarations
@end
```

To put this theory into action, you are going to add a protocol to the Atom project and have the Atom implementation conform to (i.e., implement) the required methods of this protocol. From the Xcode workspace window, select the **Elements** folder in the navigator area and then create a new file (by selecting **New ➤ File…** from the Xcode File menu) just as you did earlier. The New File template will be displayed. As before, select **Cocoa** under OS X, but instead of creating an Objective-C class, select the **Objective-C protocol icon** to create a protocol that conforms to the NSObject protocol. Next, click the **Next** button (see Figure 2-6).

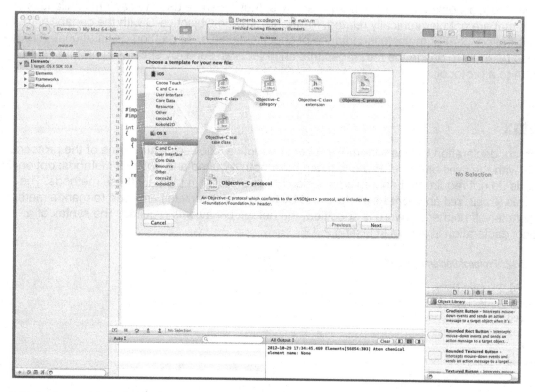

Figure 2-6. Create a protocol using Xcode

In the next window that specifies options for your new file, enter **Writer** for the protocol name and click the **Next** button. Next, you'll be prompted to specify where in your file system to save the class files and the project target for the class. Leave the location as the Elements folder, select **Elements** as the project target (if not already selected), and click the **Create** button. A header file named Writer.h has been added to the Xcode project navigator pane. Click this file to display the Writer protocol (see Listing 2-15).

Listing 2-15. Protocol Template File

```
#import <Foundation/Foundation.h>

@protocol Writer <NSObject>

@end
```

In the editor pane, update the `Writer.h` file as shown in Listing 2-16 (the code updates are shown in **bold**).

Listing 2-16. Protocol Method Declarations

```
#import <Foundation/Foundation.h>

@protocol Writer <NSObject>

- (void)write:(NSFileHandle *)file;

@end
```

This protocol declares a method named `write` that takes a reference to an `NSFileHandle` as its parameter and returns nothing. To make the Atom interface adopt this protocol, select the **Atom.h** file in the navigator pane and then make the updates shown in **bold** (see Listing 2-17).

Listing 2-17. Adopting a Protocol

```
#import <Foundation/Foundation.h>
#import "Writer.h"

@interface Atom : NSObject <Writer>

@property (readonly) NSUInteger protons;
@property (readonly) NSUInteger neutrons;
@property (readonly) NSUInteger electrons;
@property (readonly) NSString *chemicalElement;

- (NSUInteger) massNumber;

@end
```

The Atom interface has effectively been extended with methods from the Writer protocol. Select the **Atom.m** implementation file and add the code shown in Listing 2-18.

Listing 2-18. Atom Class Implementation

```
@implementation Atom
...

- (void)write:(NSFileHandle *)file
{
  NSData *data = [self.chemicalElement
                   dataUsingEncoding:NSUTF8StringEncoding];
  [file writeData:data];
  [file closeFile];
}
...
@end
```

The Atom class now conforms to the Writer protocol, and sending a write: message to an Atom object causes the chemical element name to be written out to a file. This is an example of how protocols can be used to provide common behaviors between classes in different hierarchies.

Category

A category enables the addition of new functionality to an existing class without subclassing it. The methods in a category become part of the class type (within the scope of the program) and are inherited by all its subclasses. This means that you can send a message to any instance of the class (or its subclasses) to invoke a method defined in the category. Typically, categories are used 1) to extend classes defined by others (even if you don't have access to the source code); 2) as an alternative to a subclass; or 3) to distribute the implementation of a new class into multiple source files (this can help simplify a large class being developed by multiple programmers).

A category interface declaration begins with the @interface keyword followed by the name of the existing class and the category name in parentheses followed by the protocols it adopts (if any). It ends with the @end keyword. Between these statements, the method declarations are provided. The syntax of a category declaration is shown in Listing 2-19.

Listing 2-19. Category Declaration Syntax

```
@interface ClassName (CategoryName)
// Method declarations
@end
```

Now let's extend the Atom class by adding a category. As before, from the Xcode workspace window, select the **Elements** folder in the navigator area and then create a new file (by selecting **New ➤ File...** from the Xcode File menu). Select **Cocoa** under OS X; this time, however, select the **Objective-C category icon** to create a category with implementation and header files, and then click the **Next** button.

In the next window that specifies options for your new file, enter **Nuclear** for the category name, select **Atom** in the Category on the drop-down list, and then click the **Next** button. Next, you'll be prompted to specify where in your file system to save the class files and the project target for the class. Leave the location as the Elements folder, select **Elements** as the project target (if not already selected), and click the **Create** button. In the Xcode project navigator pane, two new files have been added to the Elements folder: Atom+Nuclear.h and Atom+Nuclear.m. These files are the category interface and implementation files. In the Atom+Nuclear.h header file, update the category interface as shown in Listing 2-20.

Listing 2-20. Nuclear Category Interface

```
#import "Atom.h"

@interface Atom (Nuclear)

-(NSUInteger) atomicNumber;

@end
```

This category declares a method named atomicNumber that returns a non-negative integer number. Select the **Atom+Nuclear.m** source file and update the category implementation as shown in Listing 2-21.

Listing 2-21. Nuclear Category Implementation

```
#import "Atom.h"
#import "Atom+Nuclear.h"

@implementation Atom (Nuclear)

-(NSUInteger) atomicNumber
{
  return self.protons;
}

@end
```

This completes the implementation of the Nuclear category and thus adds the atomicNumber method to the Atom class and any classes that descend from it. Let's test the class now. In the main.m file, make the updates shown in Listing 2-22 to the main() method.

Listing 2-22. Code for Testing the Nuclear Category

```
#import <Foundation/Foundation.h>
#import "Atom.h"
#import "Atom+Nuclear.h"

int main(int argc, const char * argv[])
{
  @autoreleasepool
  {
    Atom *atom = [[Atom alloc] init];
    NSLog(@"Atomic number = %lu", [atom atomicNumber]);
  }

  return 0;
}
```

Save all the files of the project by selecting **Save** from the Xcode File menu, and then compile and run it by clicking the **Run** button in the toolbar. The output pane shown in Figure 2-7 displays the message "Atom number = 0".

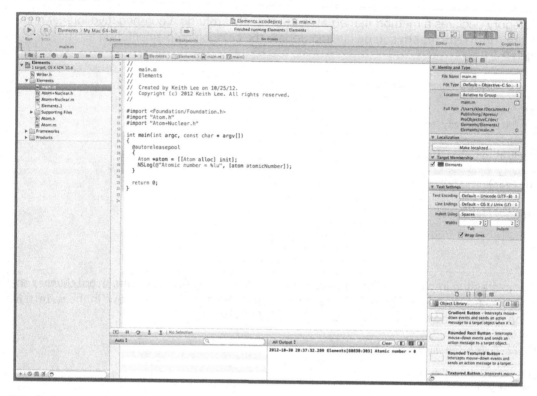

Figure 2-7. *Testing the Nuclear category*

And that's it. You have created a category for the Atom class that adds an instance method that returns the atomic number for an Atom object. Now let's look at extensions.

Extensions

An *extension* is considered an anonymous (i.e., unnamed) category. The methods declared in an extension *must* be implemented in the main @implementation block for the corresponding class (they cannot be implemented in a category). The syntax of a class extension is shown in Listing 2-23.

Listing 2-23. Extension Declaration Syntax

```
@interface ClassName ()
{
  // Instance variable declarations
}

// Property declarations
// Method declarations
@end
```

As shown in Listing 2-23, an extension differs from a category in that it can declare instance variables and properties. The compiler will verify that the methods (and properties) declared in an extension are implemented. A class extension is commonly placed in the same file as the class implementation file and it is used to group and declare additional required, private methods (e.g., not part of the publicly declared API) for use solely within a class.

Roundup

Whew. This has been quite an introduction to Objective-C and developing classes! You have covered a lot of ground in this chapter, so let's take a moment to recap what you've learned:

- An Objective-C class is comprised of an interface and an implementation.

  - The interface *declares* the class properties and methods.

  - The implementation *defines* the class instance variables, properties, and methods.

- An interface may employ *inheritance* to obtain the properties and methods of subclasses in a class hierarchy.

- By convention, a class interface is stored (on disk) in a header file (suffixed with .h) and its implementation is stored in a file suffixed with .m.

- A protocol declares methods and properties that can be implemented by any class. They are often used to provide common behaviors in classes that are not hierarchically related.

- A category enables the addition of new functionality to an existing class without subclassing it. Typically, categories are used 1) to extend classes defined by others (even if you don't have access to the source code); 2) as an alternative to a subclass; or 3) to distribute the implementation of a new class into multiple source files. An extension can be considered an anonymous category; however, its declarations must be implemented in the main implementation block of the class. Extensions can also declare instance variables and properties.

- Xcode provides templates for creating Objective-C classes, protocols, categories, and extensions, thereby making it easy to get started developing your own classes.

This has been a detailed primer on developing classes using Objective-C and Xcode, so this is a good time to take a break and review what you've gone over. In the next chapter, you'll pick up where you left off by exploring the details of object messaging using Objective-C.

Chapter 3

Objects and Messaging

Now that you have a good understanding of how to create classes using Objective-C, you may be wondering, "How do I use these classes?" That's the focus of this chapter; specifically object creation, initialization, and invoking methods on objects using Objective-C.

As you learned in Chapter 2, an Objective-C class is defined by its instance variables, properties, and methods. In addition, through OOP inheritance, a class also contains the state and behavior (i.e., methods and instance variables) of its parent class/classes. At runtime, an object-oriented program executes its logic by creating objects and invoking the desired operations on these objects using messaging—an OOP mechanism for invoking methods on objects and classes.

Creating Objects

A class instance (i.e., object) is created by allocating memory for it and initializing it appropriately. Objects of the same kind are said to be members of the same class. What this means is that they have the same methods and matching sets of instance variables. Thus, when you create objects of the same type, you are in effect creating a set of instance variables for the object—along with a set of pointers to the methods defined for the class.

Every class lives in its own namespace. The names assigned within a class definition don't conflict with names assigned anywhere outside it. This is true both of the instance variables in an object's data structure and of the object's methods. Hence, the meaning of a message must be understood relative to the particular object that receives the message. The same message sent to two different objects can invoke two distinct methods. This is a fundamental feature of OOP and simplifies a class interface, because the same names (corresponding to desired operations) can be reused in different classes.

The Foundation Framework provides functionality that simplifies object creation. Specifically, the NSObject class includes methods that are used to create class instances. The NSObject alloc class method returns a new instance of the specified class type; its syntax is

```
+ (id) alloc
```

An `id` is an Objective-C type used to hold a reference to any Objective-C object, regardless of its class. The `alloc` method can be invoked as

```
id varName = [ClassName alloc];
```

This creates an object of type `ClassName` and assigns it to a variable named varName of type id. You could also create the object as follows:

```
ClassName *varName = [ClassName alloc];
```

This would also create an object of type `ClassName` and assign it to a variable named varName; however, in this case, the variable is of type `ClassName *` (i.e., a pointer to a class of type `ClassName`). Explicitly defining the type for the variable provides static type checking, at the expense of flexibility. We'll discuss this more in Part 2 of the book, which explores the Objective-C runtime. In either case, the `alloc` method returns objects that are an instance of the receiving class's type, also known as a *related result type*. This means that the object returned from sending the `alloc` message will have the same type as that of the receiving class. Now in Chapter 2, you developed an `Atom` class. You can create an `Atom` object and assign it to a variable named atom using the `alloc` method.

```
Atom *atom = [Atom alloc];
```

As the receiving class of the `alloc` message is `Atom`, the created object will be of type `Atom`. Memory is allocated for the object and its instance variables are set to default values (zero).

OK, so this is great: Objective-C (and the Foundation Framework) provides everything you need to create objects. But what about initialization? Well, Objective-C also provides mechanisms to initialize newly created objects. You'll look at these next.

Object Initialization

The `alloc` method allocates storage for an object and sets its instance variables to zero, but it doesn't initialize the object's instance variables to appropriate values nor does it prepare any other necessary objects or resources needed by the object. Therefore, your classes should implement a method to complete the initialization process. NSObject implements an `init` method that provides the foundation for object initialization, and at a minimum, your classes should override this method to provide any custom initialization behavior required for them. The syntax for the NSObject `init` method is

```
- (id) init
```

Notice that `init` is an instance method, and like the `alloc` method, it returns objects of type id that are related result types. Remember the `init` method you developed in Chapter 2 for the `Atom` class? It's shown in Listing 3-1.

Listing 3-1. Atom Class init Method

```
- (id) init
{
  if ((self = [super init]))
```

```
{
  // Initialization code here.
  _chemicalElement = @"None";
}

return self;
}
```

Let's examine this code in detail to get a better understanding for the responsibilities of the init method. This line combines several operations in a single line of code:

```
if ((self = [super init]))
```

The expression within brackets [super init] performs initialization of the calling object using the init method of its parent class. Since this is the first statement in an init method, it guarantees a series of initializations for an object all the way up its inheritance chain to the root object of the hierarchy (see Figure 3-1).

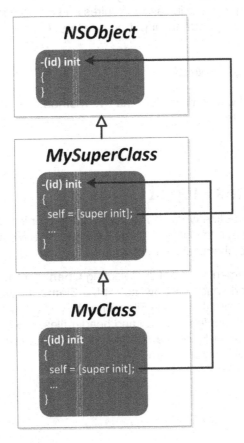

Figure 3-1. *Object initializations via init methods*

The result returned from the `init` method invocation is assigned to the special Objective-C `self` parameter. Each method has an implicit `self` parameter (it's not in the method declaration), which is a pointer to the object that received the message. So, the assignment statement

```
self = [super init]
```

invokes the superclass's `init` method and assigns the result to the calling object, thereby guaranteeing (see Figure 3-1) that any initialization required throughout the object's class hierarchy is performed.

Looking back at Listing 3-1, you see that the result of this assignment is surrounded (in parentheses) by a conditional `if` statement (Appendix A provides a complete overview of Objective-C conditional statements). This has the effect of performing conditional logic. In effect, if the superclass initialization succeeds (i.e., the expression `[super init]` returns a valid object), the custom initialization for the object is performed; otherwise, the `init` method returns `nil`.

By convention, the name of an initializer always begins with `init`. An initializer with no input parameters is simply named `init`. If the initializer requires one or more input parameters, the name is lengthened accordingly to incorporate the input parameters. A sample declaration of an initializer with one input parameter is

```
-(id)initWithNeutrons:(NSUInteger) neutrons
```

As object allocation is coupled with initialization, the two methods are usually performed together in a single line of code; for example,

```
Atom *atom = [[Atom alloc] init];
```

Extending the Elements Project

Now you're going to put into practice what you've learned about object allocation and initialization by extending the Elements project. In Chapter 2, you created an `Atom` class. Let's subclass this to create different types of atomic chemical elements!

Start Xcode and reopen the Elements project by selecting **Open ...** from the Xcode File menu. In the navigator area of the Xcode workspace window, select the **Elements** project, and then create a new file by selecting **New ➤ File ...** from the Xcode File menu. As you did when creating the `Atom` class, create an Objective-C class with implementation and header files. Next, in the window where you choose options for your class, enter **Hydrogen** for the class name, select **Atom** from the subclass drop-down list, and then click **Next** (see Figure 3-2).

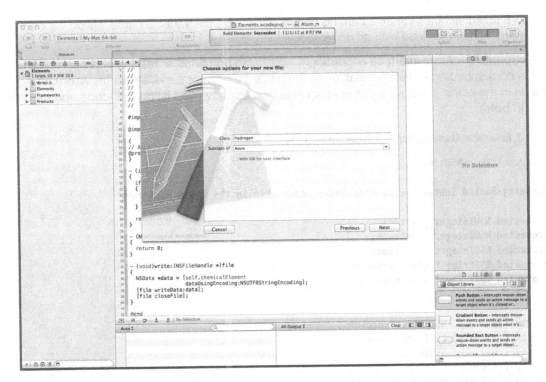

Figure 3-2. Specifying the Hydrogen class options

At the next prompt, leave the location as the Elements folder and the project target as the Elements project, and then click the **Create** button to create the Hydrogen class.

In the Xcode navigator pane, you see that two new files (Hydrogen.h and Hydrogen.m) have been created. Shortly, you are going to create an init method for the class and also a factory method that will both allocate and initialize new Hydrogen objects; but before doing that, you need to refactor the Atom class.

Refactoring the Atom Class

Refactoring means to restructure existing code without changing its external behavior. It's something that you'll do often while developing software to improve its design, facilitate the addition of new features, and so forth. In this case, you are going to refactor the Atom class so that its subclasses can access and update its instance variables during object initialization.

As shown in Chapter 2's Listing 2-3, the Atom class interface declares a single property named chemicalElement, which is defined using autosynthesis. When the compiler automatically synthesizes a property, it creates a backing instance variable whose scope is declared as *private*. A private instance variable cannot be directly accessed by its subclasses, so you need to refactor the class to enable instance variable access from its subclasses. You'll declare the variable in the instance variable declaration block with protected scope. In order to connect the property method generated using autosynthesis to the instance variable, you'll name it according to the standard property-backed instance variable naming conventions (e.g., the variable name will be the same as the property name, prefaced with an underscore).

So let's update the Atom interface accordingly. You'll also add another read-only property (and the corresponding instance variable). In the project navigator pane, select the **Atom.h** file, and then in the editor pane, update the Atom interface as shown in Listing 3-2 (code updates are shown in **bold**).

Listing 3-2. Refactored Atom Interface with Protected Variables

```
@interface Atom : NSObject

// Property-backed instance variables, only accessible in the class hierarchy
{
    @protected NSUInteger _protons;
    @protected NSUInteger _neutrons;
    @protected NSUInteger _electrons;
    @protected NSString *_chemicalElement;
    @protected NSString *_atomicSymbol;
}

@property (readonly) NSUInteger protons;
@property (readonly) NSUInteger neutrons;
@property (readonly) NSUInteger electrons;
@property (readonly) NSString *chemicalElement;
@property (readonly) NSString *atomicSymbol;

- (NSUInteger) massNumber;

@end
```

In Listing 3-2, you now declare the property-backed instance variables with `protected` scope, thereby enabling them to be directly accessed (and updated) by subclasses. You also added a new property that retrieves the atomic symbol for an `Atom` object.

Next, let's update the Atom implementation to reflect these changes. Select the **Atom.m** file and then update the Atom implementation of the `massNumber` instance method, as shown in Listing 3-3.

Listing 3-3. Atom Implementation massNumber Method

```
- (NSUInteger) massNumber
{
    return self.protons + self.neutrons;
}
```

As you can see, the mass number of an atom is computed as the sum of the number of protons and neutrons it has. OK, that's all the refactoring you'll do on the `Atom` class for now. Let's update the Hydrogen class next.

Creating the Hydrogen Initializer Method

Now you'll create a new init method for the Hydrogen class. It will initialize a Hydrogen object with the input number of neutrons, and set the chemical element name and atomic symbol appropriately. Select the **Hydrogen.h** file. In the editor pane, update the interface as shown in Listing 3-4.

Listing 3-4. Hydrogen Interface

```
#import "Atom.h"

@interface Hydrogen : Atom

- (id) initWithNeutrons:(NSUInteger)neutrons;

@end
```

This interface declares a Hydrogen init method with an input parameter that specifies the number of neutrons for the atom. Next, select the implementation file (**Hydrogen.m**) and update the implementation as shown in Listing 3-5.

Listing 3-5. Hydrogen Implementation

```
#import "Hydrogen.h"

@implementation Hydrogen

- (id) initWithNeutrons:(NSUInteger)neutrons
{
  if ((self = [super init]))
  {
    _chemicalElement = @"Hydrogen";
    _atomicSymbol = @"H";
    _protons = 1;
    _neutrons = neutrons;
  }

  return self;
}

@end
```

The initWithNeutrons: method first invokes the init method for the superclass Atom and then sets its initial values appropriately. For a Hydrogen object, this means setting the chemical element name (Hydrogen), its atomic symbol (H), the number of protons (by definition, hydrogen has one proton), and the number of neutrons provided as an input parameter.

Creating a Hydrogen Factory Method

Class *factory* methods are convenience methods used to perform class creation and initialization. They are class methods that are typically named following the convention

```
+ (id) className...
```

className is the name of the class and begins in lowercase. Now you're going to implement a factory create method for the Hydrogen class. In the Hydrogen interface file, add the method shown in Listing 3-6.

Listing 3-6. Hydrogen Interface with Factory Create Method

```
#import "Atom.h"

@interface Hydrogen : Atom

- (id) initWithNeutrons:(NSUInteger)neutrons;
+ (id) hydrogenWithNeutrons:(NSUInteger)neutrons;

@end
```

A class instance method named hydrogenWithNeutrons: was added to the interface. Notice that the name of the factory create method name is similar to that of the init method, but it is prefixed by the name of the class. This method creates a new Hydrogen object and initializes it using the input parameter. Open the Hydrogen implementation file and add the method definition, as shown in Listing 3-7.

Listing 3-7. Hydrogen Implementation with Factory Create Method

```
+ (id) hydrogenWithNeutrons:(NSUInteger)neutrons
{
  return [[[self class] alloc] initWithNeutrons:neutrons];
}
```

Observe that the method allocates memory for a Hydrogen object, calls the initWithNeutrons: method on this new instance, and then returns the newly created and initialized object. Also notice the use of the expression [self class] to retrieve the current class instance. Using this expression (as opposed to specifying the class directly), if the class is subclassed and the factory method is invoked by a subclass, the instance returned is the same type as the subclass. Now let's test the new class. Select the **main.m** file and update the main() function as shown in Listing 3-8.

Listing 3-8. Testing the Hydrogen Class

```
int main(int argc, const char * argv[])
{
  @autoreleasepool
  {
    Atom *atom = [Hydrogen hydrogenWithNeutrons:0];
    [atom logInfo];
```

```
    id atom1 = [[Hydrogen alloc] initWithNeutrons:1];
    [atom1 logInfo];

    Hydrogen *atom2 = [Hydrogen hydrogenWithNeutrons:2];
    [atom2 logInfo];
  }

  return 0;
}
```

The main() function uses both the Hydrogen init method and the class factory method to create and initialize Hydrogen objects, and then display information about the objects in the Xcode output window. Now save all the project files, and then compile and run the program (by clicking the **Run** button in the toolbar or by selecting **Run** from the Xcode Product menu). The output pane should display the results shown in Figure 3-3.

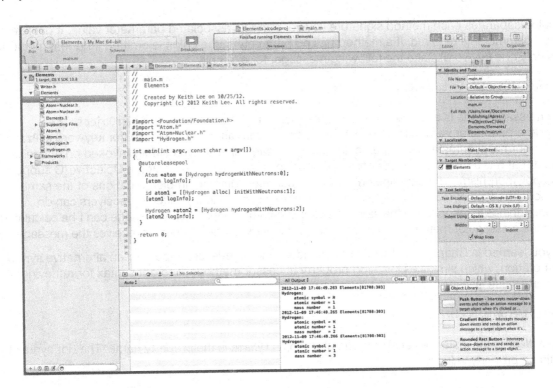

Figure 3-3. Testing the Hydrogen class

Great! You created a Hydrogen class with custom initialization and factory methods, and tested it to verify that it works as expected. Now that you are comfortable with object creation and initialization using Objective-C, let's focus on object messaging.

Message Dispatch

Messaging is a fundamental concept in OOP. It is the mechanism used to invoke a method on an object. The receiving object (i.e., receiver) of a message determines at runtime which of its instance methods to invoke. Instance methods have access to an object's instance variables along with its instance methods. The Objective-C syntax for sending a message to (i.e., invoking a method on) an object is

```
[receiver messageNameParams]
```

`receiver` is the object the message is sent to. The `messageNameParams` information identifies the method's actual name and parameter values (if any); and brackets enclose the message. The syntax for the `messageNameParams` is

```
keyword1:value1 keyword2:value2 ... keywordN:valueN
```

A colon separates each method signature keyword and its associated parameter value. It declares that a parameter is required. If a method has no parameters, the colon is omitted (and that method has only one keyword). Take the following message, for example:

```
[orderObject addItem:burgerObject forPrice:3.50];
```

The message name is `addItem:forPrice:`; the receiver of the message is `orderObject`. The message parameter values are `burgerObject` (for keyword `addItem`) and `3.50` (for keyword `atPrice`). Under normal circumstances, a particular message can only be successfully invoked on a receiving object that has a method with the corresponding message name. In addition, Objective-C supports type polymorphism, whereby different receivers can have different implementations of the same method. The type of receiver is determined at runtime; consequently, different receivers can do different things in response to the same message. In sum, the result of a message can't be calculated from the message or method name alone; it also depends on the object that receives the message.

As you learned in Chapter 2, Objective-C provides language-level support for an alternative syntax—dot notation, which simplifies invoking property accessor methods. The dot syntax for retrieving a property value is

```
objectName.propertyName
```

`objectName` is the instance variable name and `propertyName` is the property name. The dot syntax for setting a property value is

```
objectName.propertyName = Value
```

Dot syntax is merely an alternative syntax and not a mechanism for directly accessing a property-backed instance variable. The compiler transforms these statements into the corresponding property accessor methods.

Objective-C also provides language-level support for *class methods*. These are methods defined at the class level and invoked directly on a class. The syntax for invoking a class method is

```
[className messageNameParams]
```

Class methods work the same way as instance methods, except that they are invoked on a class, not an object. As a result, class methods do not have access to the instance variables and methods defined for the class. They are commonly used to create new instances of a class (i.e., as factory methods), or for accessing shared information associated with a class.

By separating the message (the requested behavior) from the receiver (the owner of a method that can respond to the request), object messaging directly supports the OOP paradigm of encapsulation.

Objective-C augments its support for object messaging with language-level features that enable you to determine at runtime the method to be invoked, and even change the method implementation. You'll explore these features in Part 2 of this book; but for now, let's learn how to handle scenarios where an object receives a message it cannot process.

Message Forwarding

Objective-C object messaging finds and executes a method on an object based on the message it receives. The object type can either be specified in the code and statically bound at compile time (*static typing*) or be unspecified with its type resolved at runtime (*dynamic typing*). In either case, at runtime, the receiving object interprets the message to determine which method to invoke. This runtime resolution of method calls makes it easy to change and/or extend programs dynamically, but also carries with it a certain risk: it permits a program to send a message to an object that may not have a corresponding method attached to it. Under the default scenario, if this happens, a runtime exception is thrown. However, Objective-C provides another option: through a mechanism called *message forwarding*, it is possible to configure an object to perform user-defined processing when it receives a message not mapped to its set of methods. Message forwarding enables an object to perform a variety of logic on any unrecognized message it receives, perhaps parceling it out to a different receiver who can respond to the message, sending any unrecognized messages to the same destination, or simply silently "swallowing" the message (i.e., performing no processing nor causing a runtime error to be thrown).

Forwarding Options

Objective-C provides two types of message forwarding options that you can use.

- *Fast forwarding*: Classes that descend from NSObject can implement fast forwarding by overriding the NSObject forwardingTargetForSelector: method to forward the method to another object. This technique makes it appear like the implementations of your object and the forwarding object are combined. This simulates the behavior of multiple inheritance of class implementations. It works well if you have a target class that defines all the possible messages that your object can consume.

- *Normal (full) forwarding*: Classes that descend from NSObject can implement normal forwarding by overriding the NSObject forwardInvocation: method. This technique enables your object to use the full contents of the message (target, method name, parameters).

Fast forwarding works well if you have a target class that defines all the possible messages that your object can consume. Full fowarding should be used if you don't have such a target class or you would like to perform other processing on message receipt (for example, just logging and swallowing the message).

Adding Fast Forwarding to the Hydrogen Class

To give you an idea of how message forwarding can be used, you're going to add this capability to the Hydrogen class you just implemented. You'll extend the class to provide fast forwarding, and then you'll create a helper target class that handles the forwarded message by implementing the corresponding method.

Message Forwarding Helper Class

First, you'll create the helper class. In Xcode, create a new Objective-C class. Name it **HydrogenHelper** and make the Elements project its target. In the Xcode navigator pane, observe that two new files (HydrogenHelper.h and HydrogenHelper.m) have been created. Select the **HydrogenHelper.h** file, and then in the editor pane, update the interface as shown in Listing 3-9.

Listing 3-9. HydrogenHelper Interface

```
#import <Foundation/Foundation.h>

@interface HydrogenHelper : NSObject

- (NSString *) factoid;

@end
```

This interface declares a single instance method, factoid, which returns a pointer to an NSString (NSString *). Next, select the implementation file (**HydrogenHelper.m**) and define the factoid method as shown in Listing 3-10.

Listing 3-10. HydrogenHelper Implementation

```
#import "HydrogenHelper.h"

@implementation HydrogenHelper

- (NSString *) factoid
{
  return @"The lightest element and most abundant chemical substance.";
}
```

As you can see from Listing 3-10, the HydrogenHelper factoid method returns a simple fact about the Hydrogen element. Now you are going to update the Hydrogen class to support fast forwarding. In the Hydrogen implementation (Hydrogen.m), add the following code to overwrite the default implementation of the forwardingTargetForSelector: method, as shown in Listing 3-11 (updates are shown in **bold**).

Listing 3-11. Hydrogen Class Message Fast Forwarding Updates

```
@implementation Hydrogen
{
@private HydrogenHelper *helper;
}
...
- (id) initWithNeutrons:(NSUInteger)neutrons
{
  if ((self = [super init]))
  {
    // Initialization code here.
    _chemicalElement = @"Hydrogen";
    _atomicSymbol = @"H";
    _protons = 1;
    _neutrons = neutrons;

    // Create helper for message forwarding
    helper = [[HydrogenHelper alloc] init];
  }

  return self;
}

- (id) forwardingTargetForSelector:(SEL)aSelector
{
  if ([helper respondsToSelector:aSelector])
  {
    return helper;
  }
  return nil;
}
...
@end
```

First, the Hydrogen class adds a HydrogenHelper* instance variable. Next, in the init method, the HydrogenHelper object is created and initialized. This is the target object that will be used for message forwarding. Finally, the forwardingTargetForSelector: method is implemented. The method first checks to see if the message is one that the target (HydrogenHelper) object can process. If it can, it returns that object; otherwise, it returns nil. Recall that the HydrogenHelper class has a single instance method, factoid. Thus if a Hydrogen object receives a message for an instance method named factoid, it will be redirected to send that message to its HydrogenHelper object (see Figure 3-4).

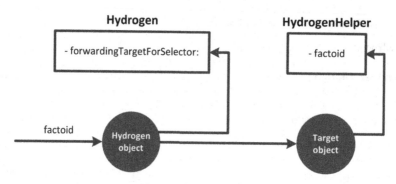

Figure 3-4. *Fast forwarding the factoid method for the Hydrogen class*

Great! You have implemented fast forwarding for the Hydrogen class. Now let's test the class using fast forwarding. Select the **main.m** file and update the main() function, as shown in Listing 3-12.

Listing 3-12. Testing Fast Forwarding of the Hydrogen Class

```
int main(int argc, const char * argv[])
{
  @autoreleasepool
  {
    Atom *atom = [Hydrogen hydrogenWithNeutrons:0];
    [atom logInfo];

    id atom1 = [[Hydrogen alloc] initWithNeutrons:1];
    [atom1 logInfo];

    // Use message forwarding to get a fact about Hydrogen
    Hydrogen *atom2 = [Hydrogen hydrogenWithNeutrons:2];
    NSString *fact = [atom2 factoid];
    [atom2 logInfo:fact];
  }

  return 0;
}
```

On the left side of the editor pane, you'll probably see an exclamation point in a red circle located on the line NSString *fact = [atom2 factoid]. If you click this exclamation point, you will see an error message (see Figure 3-5).

Figure 3-5. Hydrogen class object messaging error

This error, "No visible @interface for 'Hydrogen' declares the selector 'factoid'," occurs because the Hydrogen class does not have a `factoid` instance method declared in its interface. The compiler needs to know the full method signature of every message that a program can possibly send—even those that are forwarded. The solution is to declare the unknown method, either in a class interface or in a category. In Xcode, create a new Objective-C category, enter **Helper** for the name, and select **Atom** in the category drop-down list. Make the Elements project its target and the Elements folder the location where the files will be saved. In the Xcode project navigator pane, two new files have been added to the Elements folder: `Atom+Helper.h` and `Atom+Helper.m`. These files are the category interface and implementation files. Because you don't need the implementation, delete the **Atom+Helper.m** file by selecting it in the navigator pane and then selecting **Delete** from the Xcode Edit menu. Next, in the `Atom+Helper.h` header file, update the category interface as shown in Listing 3-13.

Listing 3-13. Atom Helper Category Interface

```
#import "Atom.h"

@interface Atom (Helper)

- (NSString *) factoid;

@end
```

In Listing 3-13, the factoid method has been added to the category interface. Since the Hydrogen class is a subclass of the Atom class, the compiler will now see the factoid method, thereby resolving the error. The main.m file should include the Atom helper category interface in its list of imports (see Listing 3-14).

Listing 3-14. Imports for main() function

```
#import <Foundation/Foundation.h>
#import "Atom.h"
#import "Atom+Nuclear.h"
#import "Atom+Helper.h"
#import "Hydrogen.h"

int main(int argc, const char * argv[])
{
    ...
}
```

If you compile and run the project, the output should be as shown in Figure 3-6.

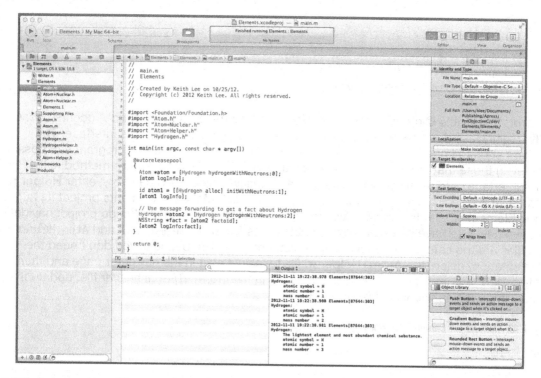

Figure 3-6. Hydrogen class with message forwarding test

Roundup

This chapter examined the concepts and details around Objective-C object creation, initialization, and messaging. The following are the key takeaways:

- The `NSObject alloc` method is used to allocate memory for an object, initializing its instance variables to zero. The method returns objects that are an instance of the receiving class's type, also known as a "related result type."

- `NSObject` provides an `init` method that serves the foundation for object initialization. Your classes should override this method to provide any custom initialization behavior required for them. Typically, instance allocation and initialization are performed with a single line of code: `[[ClassName alloc] init]`.

- Initializer methods should be implemented such that they perform a series of initializations for an object all the way up its inheritance chain to the root object of the hierarchy.

- Objective-C messaging supports OOP type polymorphism, whereby different receivers can have different implementations of the same method. In addition, the type of the receiver is determined at runtime. Consequently, different receivers can do different things in response to the same message.

- Objective-C message forwarding enables an object to perform user-defined processing when it receives a message not mapped to its set of methods. Message forwarding can be used to provide many of the features typically associated with OOP multiple inheritance.

- Objective-C provides two types of message forwarding: fast forwarding and normal (full) forwarding. Both are implemented by overriding the appropriate `NSObject` instance method, along with implementing any required supporting classes.

In the last two chapters, you learned the ins and outs of developing classes using Objective-C: class design and implementation, object creation and initialization, and object interaction. In fact, why not take a moment to look back over what you have covered so far. This is a great time to go over your example programs and tinker with them to get a better feel for the language. Coming soon (in the next chapter, to be precise), you'll explore another key topic of Objective-C programming: memory management.

Chapter 4

Memory Management

So far, you've learned how to develop classes and create and initialize objects. Now is a great time to study the details of Objective-C memory management. Proper memory management is key to developing programs that perform both correctly and efficiently. In this chapter, you'll look into how computer memory is allocated and released for Objective-C programs, the Objective-C memory model, and how to write programs that perform memory management properly.

The overall quality of a program is often directly related to its management of system resources. A computer's operating system allocates a finite amount of main memory for program execution, and if a program attempts to use more memory than the amount allocated by the O/S, it will not operate correctly. Hence, a program should use only as much memory as needed, neither allocating memory that it does not use nor trying to use memory that is no longer available. The Objective-C language and runtime provide mechanisms to support application memory management in alignment with these goals.

Program Memory Usage

In order to better understand the role of memory management, you need to understand how a program is stored and used in computer memory. An executable Objective-C program is composed of (executable) code, initialized and unitialized program data, linking information, relocation information, local data, and dynamic data. The program data includes statically-declared variables and program literals (e.g., constant values in the code that are set during program compilation).

The executable code and program data, along with the linking and relocation information, are statically allocated in memory and persist for the lifetime of the program.

Local (i.e., automatic) data consists of data whose scope is delimited by the statement block within which it is declared and is not retained after the block has been executed. Syntactically, an Objective-C *compound statement block* is a collection of statements delimited by braces (as shown in Listing 4-1).

Listing 4-1. Example Statement Block

```
{
  int myInt = 1;
  float myFloat = 5.0f;
  NSLog(@"Float = %f, integer =  %d", myFloat, myInt);
}
```

The example in Listing 4-1 includes two local variables, `myInt` and `myFloat`, which exist within this statement block and are not retained after the block has been executed. Automatic data resides in the program *stack*, a block of memory whose size is usually set prior to program/thread execution. The stack is used to store local variables and context data for method/function invocation. This context data consists of method input parameters, return values, and the return address where the program should continue execution after the method completes. The operating system automatically manages this memory; it is allocated on the stack for and subsequently deallocated at the end of the scope where it was declared.

At runtime, an Objective-C program creates objects (via the `NSObject alloc` method, as discussed in Chapter 3) stored in dynamically allocated memory referred to as the program *heap*. Dynamic object creation implies the need for memory management, because objects created on the heap never go out of scope.

A diagram depicting the allocation and usage of memory during program execution is shown in Figure 4-1.

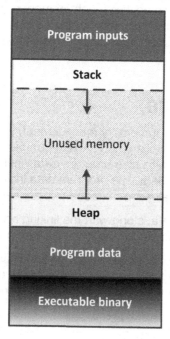

Figure 4-1. Objective-C program memory usage

The memory allocated for the program code is set at compilation time and, hence, accounted for in the overall amount of system memory used. The memory allocated on the program stack (usually) has a maximum size determined at program startup, and is automatically managed by the O/S. On the other hand, Objective-C objects are dynamically created during program execution and are not automatically reclaimed by the O/S. Thus, Objective-C programs require memory management to ensure proper utilization of system memory. Typical results of no or incorrect program memory management include the following:

- *Memory leaks*: These are caused when a program does not free unused objects. If a program allocates memory that it doesn't use, memory resources are wasted; if it continually allocates memory without releasing it, the program will eventually run out of memory.

- *Dangling pointers*: These are caused when a program frees objects still being used. This condition results in a dangling pointer; if the program attempts to access these objects later, a program error will result.

Objective-C Memory Model

Objective-C memory management is implemented using reference counting, a technique whereby unique references to an object are used to determine whether or not an object is still in use. If an object's reference count drops to zero, it is considered no longer in use and its memory will be deallocated by the runtime system.

The Apple Objective-C development environment (for both the OS X and iOS platforms) provides two mechanisms that can be used for memory management: Manual Retain-Release and Automatic Reference Counting. In the next few paragraphs, you'll learn how these work and you'll develop a few programs to become familiar with their usage.

Implementing Manual Retain-Release

Manual Retain-Release (MRR) is a memory-management mechanism based on the concept of object ownership: as long as there are one or more owners of an object, it will not be deallocated by the Objective-C runtime. You write your code to explicitly manage the life cycle of objects, obtaining an ownership interest in objects that you create/need to use, and releasing that ownership interest when you no longer need the object(s). To see how this is applied, first you need to understand how objects are accessed and used, and the difference between object access and ownership.

Object Reference and Object Ownership

An Objective-C object is accessed by *indirection* through a variable that points to the memory address of the Objective-C object. This variable, also called a *pointer*, is declared by prefixing its name with an asterisk. The following statement

```
Hydrogen *atom;
```

declares a pointer variable named atom that points to an object of type Hydrogen. Note that pointers and indirection can be used for any Objective-C data type, including primitives and C data types; however, object pointers are used specifically for interacting with Objective-C objects.

An *object pointer* enables access to an Objective-C object, but does not by itself manage ownership. Look at the following code:

```
Hydrogen *atom = [Hydrogen init];
...
Hydrogen *href = atom;
```

The pointer href is declared and assigned to a Hydrogen object named atom, but href does not (by assignment) claim an ownership interest in this object. Hence, if atom is deallocated, href will no longer point to a valid object. Thus, to manage the life cycle (i.e., the existence) of an object using MRR, your code must observe a set of memory management rules. You'll look at these next.

Basic Memory Management Rules

To use MRR correctly, your code needs to balance ownership claims on an object with those releasing ownership claims on the object. In order to support this requirement, you should write your code observing the MRR basic memory-management rules, as follows:

- *Claim ownership interest in any object that you create.* You create an Objective-C object with a method whose name begins with alloc, new, copy, or mutableCopy. You also dynamically create an Objective-C block object by sending the copy message to the block.

- *Take ownership interest in an object (that you don't already own) using the* retain *method.* NSObject implements a retain method that is used to take ownership interest in an object. Under normal circumstances, an object is guaranteed to remain valid both within the method it is received (as a parameter), and as a return value. The retain method is used to take ownership of an object that you want to use over a long period of time, typically to store it as a property value, or to prevent it from being deallocated as a side effect of some other operation.

- *You must relinquish ownership of objects you own when no longer needed.* NSObject implements the release and autorelease methods that are used to relinquish ownership interest in an object. The autorelease method relinquishes ownership interest of an object at the end of the current autorelease block. The release method immediately relinquishes ownership interest in an object. Both methods send the dealloc method on an object if its retain count equals zero.

- *You must not relinquish ownership of objects you do not own.* This could cause such objects to be released prematurely. If a program attempts to access an object that has already been deallocated, it will cause an error.

Listing 4-2 shows an example that illustrates application of the MRR basic memory-management rules.

Listing 4-2. MRR Example Usage

```
Hydrogen *atom = [Hydrogen init];
...
Hydrogen *href = [atom retain];
...
[atom release];
...
[href release];
```

A Hydrogen object is created and assigned to a variable named atom. Since the object is created with an alloc message, atom has an ownership interest in this object. Later in the code, a variable named href takes an ownership interest in this object, thereby increasing the retain count (i.e., the number of ownership interests) in the object. Later, a release message is sent to the atom variable. As href still has an ownership interest in the object, it is not deallocated. Once href sends a release message to the object, its retain count drops to zero and it can be deallocated by the runtime.

Deallocating Memory

When an object's retain count drops to zero, the runtime frees the memory it uses via the NSObject dealloc method. This method also provides a framework for your subclasses to relinquish ownership of any objects it owns. Each of your classes (which nominally descend from NSObject) should override the dealloc method, invoking the release method on each object it has an ownership interest in, and then call the dealloc method of its superclass. This approach enables each of your classes to properly relinquish ownership of any objects it owns throughout its class hierarchy, as shown in Figure 4-2.

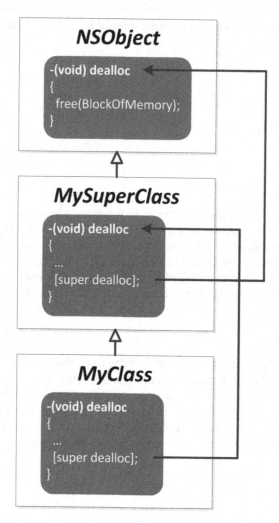

Figure 4-2. A dealloc method implementation

Delayed Release via Autorelease

NSObject provides an autorelease method that is used to invoke the release method on an object at the end of an autorelease pool block. *Autorelease pool blocks* provide a mechanism that enables you to relinquish ownership of an object at some time in the future, thereby eliminating the need to explicitly invoke the release method on the object and also avoiding the possibility of it being deallocated immediately. Autorelease pool blocks are defined using the @autorelease directive, as shown in Listing 4-3.

Listing 4-3. Autorelease Pool Block Syntax

```
@autorelease
{
  // Code that creates autoreleased objects
  ...
}
```

Autoreleased objects should always be coded within an autorelease pool block, otherwise they will not receive release messages and would therefore leak memory. The Apple UI frameworks used to create iOS and Mac OS X apps (specifically AppKit and UI Kit) provide autorelease blocks automatically; hence, you would normally only code an autorelease block if

- You are writing a program that is not based on a UI framework, such as a command-line tool.

- Your implementation logic includes a loop that creates many temporary objects. In order to reduce the maximum memory footprint of an application, you may use an autorelease pool block inside a loop to dispose of those objects before the next iteration.

- Your application spawns one or more secondary threads. You must create your own autorelease pool block as soon as a thread begins executing; otherwise, your application will leak memory.

In the example shown in Listing 4-4, the autorelease block surrounds all the code within the main() function, and an object is dynamically allocated with the autorelease message.

Listing 4-4. Command-Line Program with Autorelease Block

```
int main(int argc, const char * argv[])
{
  @autorelease
  {
    Hydrogen *atom = [[[Hydrogen alloc] init] autorelease];
    ...
  }
  return 0;
}
```

Note that the autorelease message is sent immediately after the object has been created and initialized, usually in a single, combined statement. This design ensures that any objects created with autorelease will be released at the end of the autorelease block, prior to program end.

Using MRR

Now that you've gone over Objective-C memory management and MRR, it's time to apply what you've learned by developing an example program! This example will demonstrate the application of the MRR basic memory-management rules, along with usage of the corresponding APIs. Briefly, the program consists of three classes: an OrderEntry class used to record product orders, and the dependent classes OrderItem and Address. The OrderItem class encapsulates the state and behaviors specific to an order entry item, and the Address class consists of the state and behavior associated with an order entry shipping address. Each OrderEntry object has a corresponding OrderItem object and Address object (as shown in Figure 4-3).

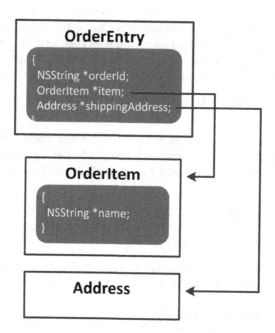

Figure 4-3. Order entry classes

You will develop these classes using MRR memory management, and then test them to demonstrate proper use of this memory-management technique. In Xcode, create a new project by selecting **New ➤ Project ...** from the Xcode File menu. In the New Project Assistant pane, create a command-line application (choose **Command Line Tool** from the Mac OS X Application selection) and click **Next**. In the Project Options window, specify MRR Orders for the Product Name, set the Type to Foundation, select MRR memory management by unchecking the **Use Automatic Reference Counting** check box (as shown in Figure 4-4), and then click **Next**.

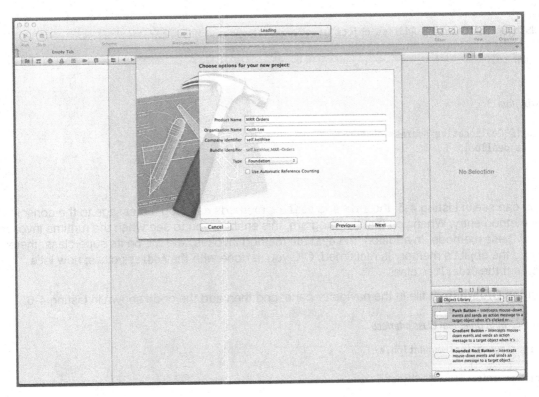

Figure 4-4. Creating an MRR order entry project

Specify the location in your file system where you want the project to be created (if necessary, select **New Folder** and enter the name and location for the folder), uncheck the **Source Control** check box, and then click the **Create** button.

Now let's add the OrderEntry, OrderItem, and Address classes. As you've done in previous chapters, add each class to the project by selecting **New ➤ File ...** from the Xcode File menu, selecting the Objective-C class template, naming the class appropriately (each is a subclass of NSObject), then selecting the MRR Orders folder for the files location and the MRR Orders project as the target.

Your project now has files for three classes along with the main.m file. Next, let's implement the Address class. You are not going to add any instance variables, properties, or methods to the class, so you won't be editing the Address interface. However, you will edit the Address implementation by overriding the default init and dealloc methods provided by its superclass (NSObject). Select the **Address.m** file in the navigator pane, and then add the code shown in Listing 4-5.

Listing 4-5. MRR Address Class Implementation

```objc
#import "Address.h"

@implementation Address
- (id) init
{
  if ((self = [super init]))
```

```
  {
    NSLog(@"Initializing Address object");
  }
  return self;
}

- (void)dealloc
{
  NSLog(@"Deallocating Address object");
  [super dealloc];
}
@end
```

As you can see in Listing 4-5, the init and dealloc methods each log a message to the console to show method entry. When you test the program, this enables you to see when the runtime invokes each of these methods. In addition, the dealloc method invokes dealloc on its superclass, thereby ensuring the object's memory is reclaimed. OK, you're done with the Address class; now let's implement the OrderItem class.

Select the **OrderItem.h** file in the navigator pane, and then add the code shown in Listing 4-6.

Listing 4-6. MRR OrderItem Class Interface

```
#import <Foundation/Foundation.h>

@interface OrderItem : NSObject
{
@public NSString *name;
}

- (id) initWithName:(NSString *)itemName;
@end
```

The OrderItem class adds a public instance variable named *name* of type (NSString *), and a custom initializer (initWithName:) that takes an input parameter also of type (NSString *). Next, select the **OrderItem.m** file and implement the OrderItem class, as shown in Listing 4-7.

Listing 4-7. MRR OrderItem Class Implementation

```
#import "OrderItem.h"

@implementation OrderItem
- (id) initWithName:(NSString *)itemName
{
  if ((self = [super init]))
  {
    NSLog(@"Initializing OrderItem object");
    name = itemName;
    [name retain];
  }
  return self;
}
```

```
- (void)dealloc
{
  NSLog(@"Deallocating OrderItem object");
  [name release];
  [super dealloc];
}
@end
```

The custom initializer assigns the instance variable to the input parameter. Since the OrderItem object did not create the input parameter, it doesn't have an ownership interest in it. However, as you don't want this object to be deallocated as a side effect of some other operation (and also require it to be valid throughout the object's lifetime), you send a retain message to the name variable, thereby taking an ownership interest in the object. In the dealloc method, you send a release message to the name object, then invoke dealloc on its superclass to relinquish the OrderItem object's memory.

Now let's implement the OrderEntry class. Select the **OrderEntry.h** file and code the interface (as shown in Listing 4-8).

Listing 4-8. MRR OrderEntry Class Interface

```
#import <Foundation/Foundation.h>
#import "OrderItem.h"
#import "Address.h"

@interface OrderEntry : NSObject
{
@public OrderItem *item;
NSString *orderId;
Address *shippingAddress;
}

- (id) initWithId:(NSString *)oid;
@end
```

Listing 4-8 shows that an OrderEntry object has three instance variables and a custom initializer (initWithId:). Next, select the **OrderEntry.m** file and implement the OrderEntry class, as shown in Listing 4-9.

Listing 4-9. MRR OrderEntry Class Implementation

```
#import "OrderEntry.h"

@implementation OrderEntry
- (id) initWithId:(NSString *)oid
{
  if ((self = [super init]))
  {
    NSLog(@"Initializing OrderEntry object");
    orderId = oid;
    [orderId retain];
```

```
    item = [[OrderItem alloc] initWithName:@"Doodle"];
    shippingAddress = [[Address alloc] init];
  }

  return self;
}

- (void)dealloc
{
  NSLog(@"Deallocating OrderEntry object");
  [item release];
  [orderId release];
  [shippingAddress release];
  [super dealloc];
}
@end
```

The custom initializer assigns the input parameter to the orderId instance variable, and then creates and initializes OrderItem and Address objects. As the OrderEntry object has an ownership interest in the OrderItem and Address objects, and also the orderId instance, it is responsible for releasing them prior to it being deallocated. This is accomplished in the dealloc method, which then invokes dealloc on its superclass to relinquish the OrderEntry object's memory.

So you've implemented the order entry classes, now test the classes to validate the implementation and also verify that you used MRR correctly. Select the **main.m** file in the navigator pane, and then update the main() function as shown in Listing 4-10.

Listing 4-10. MRR main() Function Implementation

```
#import <Foundation/Foundation.h>
#import "OrderEntry.h"

int main(int argc, const char * argv[])
{
  @autoreleasepool
  {
    // Create an OrderEntry object for manual release
    NSString *orderId = [[NSString alloc] initWithString:@"A1"];
    OrderEntry *entry = [[OrderEntry alloc] initWithId:orderId];

    // Release orderId (retained by OrderEntry, so object not deallocated!)
    [orderId release];
    NSLog(@"New order, ID = %@, item: %@", entry->orderId, entry->item->name);

    // Must manually release OrderEntry!
    [entry release];

    // Create an autorelease OrderEntry object, released at the end of
    // the autorelease pool block
```

```
    OrderEntry *autoEntry = [[[OrderEntry alloc] initWithId:@"A2"] autorelease];
    NSLog(@"New order, ID = %@, item: %@", autoEntry->orderId, autoEntry->item->name);
  }
  return 0;
}
```

The main() function demonstrates MRR memory management by creating OrderEntry objects and releasing them, along with the objects it has an ownership interest in, according to the memory-management rules. The first OrderEntry object is manually released, while the second is created with autorelease, and thus is released at the end of its surrounding autorelease pool block.

Now save, compile, and run the MRR Orders program and observe the messages in the output pane (as shown in Figure 4-5).

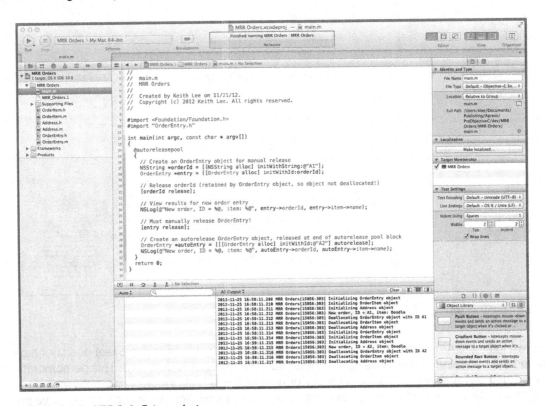

Figure 4-5. Testing the MRR OrderEntry project

The messages show the sequence of calls to initialize and deallocate the dynamically created objects. It looks like all the object create/retain and release messages are correctly balanced, and the tests you ran displayed the appropriate output, so you're all done, right? Well, not quite. After all, how do you know for sure that the program doesn't have a memory leak—it could display the correct output but still have an undetected problem. So, how do you verify that the program isn't leaking memory or has some other undetected problem? Xcode has a suite of tools that can be used to analyze your program and detect potential problems. In Appendix B, you'll learn how to use the Xcode Instruments tool to do just that, but here you'll use Xcode's Build and Analyze tool to perform an initial check of the application.

Select **Analyze** from the Xcode Product menu. The tool performs an analysis of the program, detecting, among other things, any potential memory leaks or dangling pointers. If an error(s) is detected, it identifies the error. Now observe the Activity View in the middle of the toolbar; it should display "Analyze Succeeded," meaning that no memory-management errors were detected. In the `main()` function, comment-out the [orderId release] statement, and then run the Build and Analyze tool again. It should display the message shown in Figure 4-6.

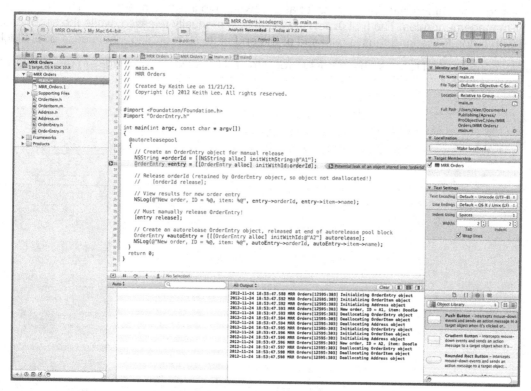

Figure 4-6. *Analyzing MRR for the OrderEntry project*

As shown in Figure 4-6, when a dynamically allocated object (`orderId` in this case) does not have a balanced set of retain/release messages, a potential memory leak is detected. This demonstrates that the Build and Analyze tool is great for performing an initial first-check on program memory management. Now, go ahead and remove the comment markers from your program—you've proven that it manages memory correctly using MRR. Great job!

Using Automatic Reference Counting

With MRR memory management, you are directly responsible for managing the life cycle of your program's objects. This enables fine-grain control of memory usage, at the cost of placing a significant burden on the programmer. Even with the simple example you just implemented, it requires a lot of diligence (and testing with the proper tools) to make sure that you are balancing your retains and releases properly and in a timely manner. In general, manual reference counting is an error-prone task, which, if not done correctly, can cause a program to leak memory and/or crash. In fact, this type of infrastructure is best relegated to a tool, thereby freeing programmers to focus on the actual business logic your programs are designed to implement. Enter Automatic Reference Counting (ARC), a memory-management enhancement that automates this task, thereby eliminating the responsibility for the programmer. ARC employs the same reference counting model as MRR, but utilizes the compiler to manage the object life cycle. Specifically, at program compilation, the compiler analyzes the source code, determines the life cycle requirements for dynamically created objects, and then automatically inserts retain and release messages where necessary in the compiled code. ARC provides other benefits as well: application performance is (potentially) improved and errors associated with memory management (e.g., releasing an object that is still in use, retaining an object no longer in use) are eliminated. In addition, as opposed to garbage collection technology, ARC is deterministic (the statements are inserted at compile time) and doesn't introduce pauses into program execution for garbage collection.

ARC provides automatic memory management for Objective-C objects and block objects. It is the recommended approach for memory management in new Objective-C projects. ARC can be used across a project or on a per-file basis if there is a need for manual reference counting in some cases. Note that ARC does not automatically handle reference cycles, where objects have circular references. Objective-C provides language features for declaring weak references on objects as necessary to manually break these cycles. You'll look at these later in this chapter.

Rules and Conventions for Using ARC

As mentioned, ARC greatly simplifies memory management with respect to the MRR method. As a result, there are different sets of rules for object memory management under ARC. These rules are as follows:

- You cannot send retain, retainCount, release, autorelease, or dealloc messages. ARC forbids programmatic control of an object life cycle and automatically inserts these messages where required during compilation. This includes @selector(retain), @selector(release), and related methods. You may implement a dealloc method if you need to manage resources other than instance variables. ARC automatically creates a dealloc method in your classes (if not provided) to release the objects it owns, and invokes [super dealloc] in your implementation(s) of the dealloc method.

- You can't cast directly between id and (void *) types. ARC only manages Objective-C objects and blocks, thus the compiler needs to know the types of the objects it is processing. Because a *pointer to void* (void *) is a generic pointer type that can be converted to any other pointer type (even those that are not Objective-C pointer types), this restriction is necessary. This scenario is common when casting between Foundation Framework objects and Core Foundation types (Core Foundation is an Apple software library that provides C-language APIs). A set of APIs is provided for ownership transfer of variables between ARC and non-ARC environments.

- Autorelease pool blocks should be used to perform ARC-managed autorelease of objects.

- You cannot call the Foundation Framework functions NSAllocateObject and NSDeallocateObject. These functions provide the capability to allocate and deallocate memory for an object in a specific memory zone. Because zone-based memory is no longer supported, these functions cannot be used.

- You cannot use object pointers in C structures (structs). ARC does not perform memory management for dynamically allocated C structures, thus the compiler cannot determine where to insert the necessary retain and release messages.

- You cannot use memory zones (NSZone). As mentioned, zone-based memory is no longer supported.

- To properly cooperate with non-ARC code, you cannot create a method or a declared property (unless you explicitly choose a different getter) that begins with "copy".

- By default, ARC is not exception-safe: it does not end the lifetime of __strong variables whose scope is abnormally terminated by an exception, and it does not perform releases of objects that would occur at the end of a full-expression if that full-expression throws an exception. The compiler option -fobjc-arc-exceptions can be used to enable exception handling for ARC code. ARC does end the lifetimes of weak references when an exception terminates their scope, unless exceptions are disabled in the compiler.

ARC Lifetime Qualifiers

There are a set of ARC-specific qualifiers that declare the object lifetime for both regular variables and properties. The following are those for regular variables:

- __strong: Any object created using alloc/init is retained for the lifetime of its current scope. This is the default setting for regular variables. The "current scope" usually means the braces in which the variable is declared (a method, for loop, if block, etc.)

- __weak: The object can be destroyed at anytime. This is only useful if the object is somehow strongly referenced somewhere else. When destroyed, a variable with __weak is set to nil.

- __unsafe_unretained: This is just like __weak but the pointer is not set to nil when the object is deallocated. Instead, the pointer is left dangling (i.e., it no longer points to anything useful).

- __autoreleasing: Not to be confused with calling autorelease on an object before returning it from a method, this is used for passing objects by reference.

When using ARC lifetime qualifiers to declare variables for Objective-C objects, the correct syntax is

```
ClassName *qualifier varName;
```

ClassName is name/type of the class (OrderEntry, etc.), qualifier is the ARC lifetime qualifier (as previously listed), and varName is the name of the variable. If no qualifier is specified, the default is __strong. The ARC-specific lifetime qualifiers for properties are as follows:

- ■ strong: The strong attribute is equivalent to the retain attribute (the complete list of property attributes is provided in Appendix A).

- ■ weak: The weak attribute is similar to the assign attribute, except that if the affected property instance is deallocated, its instance variable is set to nil.

Under ARC, strong is the default ownership attribute for object-type properties.

Using ARC

Now you are going to develop an example program that uses ARC. You'll take the program you built earlier that uses MRR memory management (OrderEntry) and create a new version that uses ARC memory management. This will enable you to get some hands-on experience programming with ARC and also see how it simplifies application memory management. As you may recall, the OrderEntry program you developed earlier consists of three classes: an OrderEntry class used to record product orders, and the dependent classes OrderItem and Address.

In Xcode, create a new project by selecting **New ➤ Project ...** from the Xcode File menu. In the New Project Assistant pane, create a command-line application (choose **Command Line Tool** from the Mac OS X Application selection) and click **Next**. In the Project Options window, specify **ARC Orders** for the Product Name and select ARC memory management by checking the **Use Automatic Reference Counting** check box, and then click **Next**.

Specify the location in your file system where you want the project to be created (if necessary, select **New Folder** and enter the name and location for the folder), uncheck the **Source Control** check box, and then click the **Create** button.

Now let's add the OrderEntry, OrderItem, and Address classes. As you've done before, add each class to the project by selecting **New ➤ File ...** from the Xcode File menu, selecting the Objective-C class template, naming the class appropriately (each is a subclass of NSObject), and then selecting the ARC Orders folder for the files location and the ARC Orders project as the target.

Your project now has files for three classes along with the main.m file. Next, implement the Address class. Proceeding as you did with the MRR Orders project, you'll edit the Address class implementation by overriding the default init and dealloc methods provided by its superclass (NSObject). Select the **Address.m** file in the navigator pane, and then add the code, as shown in Listing 4-11.

Listing 4-11. ARC Address Class Implementation

```
#import "Address.h"

@implementation Address
- (id) init
{
  if ((self = [super init]))
```

```
{
    NSLog(@"Initializing Address object");
}
    return self;
}

- (void)dealloc
{
    NSLog(@"Deallocating Address object");
}
@end
```

Listing 4-11 shows the init method is the same as that provided for MRR Address class. The dealloc method is different; it does not invoke dealloc on its superclass because this is automatically performed by ARC. Now let's implement the ARC OrderItem class.

The ARC OrderItem interface is the same as that provided for the MRR OrderItem class. Select the **OrderItem.h** file and copy the interface shown in Listing 4-6. Next, select the **ARC OrderItem.m** file and implement the OrderItem class, as shown in Listing 4-12.

Listing 4-12. ARC OrderItem Class Implementation

```
#import "OrderItem.h"

@implementation OrderItem
- (id) initWithName:(NSString *)itemName
{
    if ((self = [super init]))
    {
        NSLog(@"Initializing OrderItem object");
        name = itemName;
    }
    return self;
}

- (void)dealloc
{
    NSLog(@"Deallocating OrderItem object);
}
@end
```

The custom initializer is very similar to that provided for the MRR OrderItem class. It differs in that it doesn't invoke the retain method on the name instance variable, as you cannot send retain, release, or autorelease messages with ARC. The dealloc method is also different from that provided for the MRR OrderItem class; it merely logs a message to the output console. ARC automatically sends a release message to all the objects that the OrderItem class has an ownership interest in, and also invokes dealloc on its superclass.

Now you'll implement the ARC OrderEntry class. The interface is identical to that of the MRR OrderEntry class. Select the **ARC OrderEntry interface** (OrderEntry.h) and copy the interface shown in Listing 4-8.

Next, select the **OrderEntry.m** file and implement the OrderEntry class, as shown in Listing 4-13.

Listing 4-13. ARC OrderEntry Class Implementation

```
#import "OrderEntry.h"

@implementation OrderEntry
- (id) initWithId:(NSString *)oid
{
  if ((self = [super init]))
  {
    NSLog(@"Initializing OrderEntry object");
    orderId = oid;
    item = [[OrderItem alloc] initWithName:@"Doodle"];
    shippingAddress = [[Address alloc] init];
  }

  return self;
}

- (void)dealloc
{
  NSLog(@"Deallocating OrderEntry object with ID %@", orderId);
}
@end
```

The custom initializer is very similar to that provided for the MRR OrderEntry class. It differs in that it doesn't invoke the retain method on the orderId instance variable; as noted previously, you cannot send retain/release/autorelease messages with ARC. The dealloc method is also different from that provided for the MRR OrderEntry class; it merely logs a message to the output console. ARC automatically sends a release message to all the objects that the OrderItem class has an ownership interest in, and also invokes dealloc on its superclass.

Now let's implement the ARC Orders main() function. Select the **main.m** file in the navigator pane, and then update the main() function, as shown in Listing 4-14.

Listing 4-14. ARC main() Function Implementation

```
#import <Foundation/Foundation.h>
#import "OrderEntry.h"

int main(int argc, const char * argv[])
{

  @autoreleasepool
  {
    // Create an OrderEntry object for manual release
    NSString *a1 = @"A1";
    NSString *orderId = [[NSString alloc] initWithString:a1];
    OrderEntry *entry = [[OrderEntry alloc] initWithId:orderId];
```

```
    // Set ID to nil to verify that value was retained by ARC!
    a1 = nil;

    // View results for new order entry, should display valid ID!
    NSLog(@"New order, ID = %@, item: %@", entry->orderId, entry->item->name);

    // Now set OrderEntry object to nil, it can now be deallocated by ARC!
    entry = nil;

    // Create another OrderEntry object
    OrderEntry *autoEntry = [[OrderEntry alloc] initWithId:@"A2"];
    NSLog(@"New order, ID = %@, item: %@", autoEntry->orderId,
        autoEntry->item->name);
  }
  return 0;
}
```

The main() function demonstrates ARC memory management by creating OrderEntry objects. They are automatically released by ARC when the objects are no longer in use. The function also demonstrates that classes developed with ARC acquire ownership interest in dependent objects as necessary, thereby preventing objects from being changed or deallocated while they are still in use.

Now save, compile, and run the ARC Orders program, and observe the messages in the output pane (as shown in Figure 4-7).

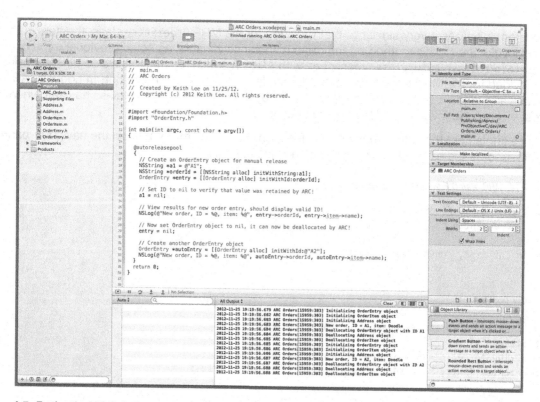

Figure 4-7. Testing the ARC OrderEntry project

The messages show the sequence of calls to initialize and deallocate the dynamically created objects. You can see that ARC memory management performed correctly, releasing all dynamically created objects when they were no longer in use. You can also perform an initial first-check of program memory management by selecting **Analyze** from the Xcode Product menu. Comparing the MRR Orders project and the ARC Orders project, notice how it significantly reduced the amount of code you had to write. As your projects grow in size and complexity, the advantages of ARC become even more pronounced. Because ARC can be selected on a file-by-file basis and ARC-compiled code can be used alongside existing code built using MRR, there's no reason not to use it on your projects. In fact, ARC is the Apple-recommended mechanism for memory management on new Objective-C projects.

Avoiding Circular References

The Objective-C reference counting model is implemented by taking ownership interest in an object (via a retain message), and then releasing ownership interest (via a release message) when that object is no longer needed. This process is automated with ARC, which automatically inserts retain/release/autorelease messages in the code where needed. However, in an object graph, a problem of circular references can arise if two objects in the graph have circular references. For example, in the preceding ARC Orders project, an OrderEntry object has an OrderItem instance variable, which is by default a strong reference. Now if an OrderItem object also had an OrderItem instance variable, this could create a circular reference between the two objects. If this were to occur, neither object could ever be deallocated, therefore causing a memory leak. In effect, the OrderEntry object could not be released until the OrderItem object is released, and the OrderItem object couldn't be released until the OrderEntry object is released. The solution to this problem is to use weak references. A weak reference is a *non-owning relationship*; that is, the object declared as a weak reference is not owned by the declaring object, hence eliminating the circular reference. The Apple Objective-C convention for object graphs is for the parent object to maintain a strong reference to each of its child objects, while the child objects maintain a weak reference (if necessary) to the parent object. Thus, in this example, the OrderEntry object would have a strong reference to its OrderItem object, while the OrderItem object would have a weak reference to its parent, OrderEntry object. A weak reference would be declared in the OrderItem class (as shown in Listing 4-15).

Listing 4-15. Declaring a Weak Reference

```
#import <Foundation/Foundation.h>

@interface OrderItem : NSObject

{
@public NSString *name;
OrderEntry *__weak entry;
}

- (id) initWithName:(NSString *)itemName;

@end
```

When destroyed, the entry variable is set to nil, thereby avoiding a circular reference.

Roundup

This chapter examined the details of Objective-C memory management, including the Objective-C memory model, how memory is allocated and released for Objective-C programs, and how to use the two methods provided for Objective-C memory management. The following are the key takeaways:

- At runtime, an Objective-C program creates objects (via the NSObject alloc method) stored in dynamically allocated memory referred to as the program heap. Dynamic object creation implies the need for memory management, because objects created on the heap never go out of scope. Typical results of incorrect or no memory management include memory leaks and dangling pointers.

- Objective-C memory management is implemented using reference counting, a technique whereby unique references to an object are used to determine whether or not an object is still in use. If an object's reference count drops to zero, it is considered no longer in use and its memory is deallocated by the runtime system.

- The Apple Objective-C development environment provides two mechanisms that can be used for memory management: Manual Retain-Release (MRR) and Automatic Reference Counting (ARC).

- With MRR, you write your code to explicitly manage the life cycle of objects, obtaining an ownership interest in objects that you create/need to use, and releasing that ownership interest when you no longer need the object(s).

- ARC employs the same reference counting model as MRR, but utilizes the compiler to manage the object life cycle. At program compilation, the compiler analyzes the source code, determines the life cycle requirements for dynamically created objects, and then automatically inserts retain and release messages where necessary in the compiled code.

- ARC is augmented with new object lifetime qualifiers that are used to explicitly declare the lifetime of object variables and properties, and also includes functionality (weak references) that can be used to prevent circular references in object graphs.

- ARC can be used across a project or on a per-file basis, thereby enabling code that uses ARC to still work with existing code that is not ARC-compliant. Apple also provides a conversion tool for migrating existing Objective-C code to ARC. ARC is the recommended tool for memory management on all new Objective-C projects.

Memory management is very important for Objective-C software development. It has a major impact on the application user experience and the overall system operation. A well-written Objective-C program uses only as much memory as it requires, and doesn't leak memory or try to access objects that are no longer in use. You now understand the Objective-C memory model and the methods provided for application memory management: MRR and ARC (the Apple-recommended approach). In the next chapter, you're going to tackle another key element of the Objective-C platform—the preprocessor. And guess what? This means that you'll be learning a new programming language as well! So why not take a break and give yourself a well-deserved rest. When you're ready, turn the page to begin the next chapter.

Chapter 5

The Preprocessor

The Objective-C programming language includes a preprocessor that is used to translate source files prior to compilation. Some of the translation is performed automatically, and a portion is performed based on the preprocessor language elements that you include in your source files. If you look at publicly available Objective-C source code, such as Apple's Objective-C source code for example, you'll most likely observe liberal use of the preprocessor language. So you may be wondering, what are the features of the preprocessor and how do you best use this language in your programs? Those are the subjects of this chapter, so let's get started!

Overview

The general process of source code compilation takes input source files and transforms them into output files that can be executed on a target computing platform. The Objective-C compiler divides this process into several phases, as shown in Figure 5-1.

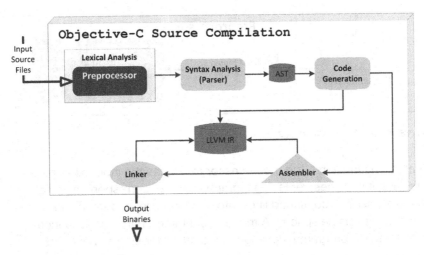

Figure 5-1. Compiling Objective-C source files

Together, these phases perform lexical analysis, syntax analysis, code generation and optimization, assembly, and linking operations to produce the output binaries. During the *lexical analysis* phase, the source code is broken down into tokens. Each *token* is a single element of the language; for example, a keyword, operator, identifier, or symbol name within the context of its grammar.

The *syntax analysis* (or parsing) phase checks the tokens for the correct syntax and verifies that they form a valid expression. This task concludes with the creation of a hierarchical parse tree or an abstract syntax tree (AST) from the tokens.

During *code generation and optimization*, the AST is used to generate code in the output language, which may be a machine language or an intermediate language representation (IR). The code is also optimized into a functionally equivalent but faster and smaller form.

The *assembly* phase takes the generated code and converts it into executable machine code for the target platform.

Finally, during the *linking* phase, one or more machine code outputs from the assembler are combined into a single executable program.

The preprocessor is used during the lexical analysis phase (as shown in Figure 5-1) prior to parsing. To understand its role in this phase, let's review the operation of the preprocessor in detail.

Operations

The preprocessor works by substituting the input character sequences for other character sequences according to a set of predefined rules. These operations, depicted in Figure 5-2, are performed in the following order:

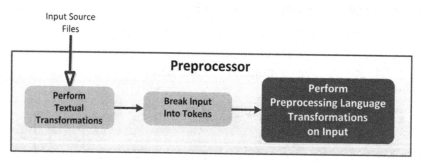

Figure 5-2. Preprocessing Objective-C source files

1. *Textual translation*: First, the preprocessor translates the input source file by breaking it into lines, replacing trigraphs by their corresponding single characters, merging continued lines into one long line, and replacing comments with single spaces. A trigraph is a three-character sequence defined by the C programming language to stand for single characters.

2. *Token conversion*: Next, the preprocessor converts the translated file into a sequence of tokens.

3. *Preprocessor language-based transformation*: Finally, if the token stream contains any preprocessing language elements, they are transformed based on these inputs.

The first two operations are performed automatically, and the last is a function of the *preprocessor language* elements added to the source files.

Preprocessor Language

That's right, the preprocessor language is a separate programming language that's distinct from Objective-C. The source-file transformations performed using the language are primarily source file inclusions, conditional compilation, and macro expansions. Preprocessor language elements operate on a source file prior to program compilation, and the preprocessor has no knowledge of the Objective-C language itself.

The preprocessor language defines directives to be executed and macros to be expanded. A preprocessor *directive* is a command that is executed by the preprocessor, not the compiler. A preprocessor *macro* is a named code fragment. Wherever the name is used in the source code, the code fragment is substituted for it. The preprocessor language also defines several operators and keywords.

> **Note** It's important to understand the capabilities and limitations of the preprocessor language because incorrect use can cause subtle compilation problems that are difficult to diagnose. You should keep this in mind as you look at the language in detail.

Directives

Preprocessor directives are indicated in Objective-C source files with a unique syntax that causes these lines to be treated by the preprocessor, not the compiler. A preprocessor directive has the following form:

```
#directiveName directiveArguments
```

A directive begins with a hash sign (#), immediately followed by the directive name, and then its corresponding arguments. The following line

```
#import "Elements.h"
```

is an example of a preprocessor directive; each directive is terminated by a newline. To extend a directive through more than one line, a backslash (\) is placed at the end of the line to be continued on another line. The following example

```
#define DegreesToRadians(x)  \
                ((x) * 3.14159 / 180.0)
```

is a preprocessor directive that extends across two lines, as indicated by the backslash at the end of the first line of the directive.

The following is the complete set of preprocessor directives and the functionality that they provide:

- Header file inclusion (#include, #import)
- Conditional compilation (#if, #elif, #else, #endif, #ifdef, #ifndef)
- Diagnostics (#error, #warning, #line)
- Pragmas (#pragma)

Header File Inclusion

The preprocessor has two directives (#include and #import) that enable header file inclusion; basically, they tell the preprocessor to take the text of a file and insert it into the current file. As such, they facilitate code reuse, because a source file can use external class interfaces and macros without having to copy them directly.

The syntax of the *include* directive has two forms:

```
#include "HeaderFileName"
```

or

```
#include <HeaderFileName>
```

HeaderFileName is the name of the header file to be inserted. The only difference between both expressions is the locations (i.e., directories) where the compiler looks for the file:

- *Header file name between double quotes* ("HeaderFileName"). The compiler first searches for the file in the same directory that includes the file containing the directive. If the file is not found there, the compiler searches for the file in the default directories, where it is configured to look for the system-standard header files.
- *Header file name between angle brackets* (<HeaderFileName>). The compiler searches for the file in the default directories, where it is configured to look for the standard header files.

By convention, standard header files are usually included using the angle brackets because they are normally located in the default directories, whereas other header files (such as those for your Objective-C classes) are included using double quotes.

The *import* directive (#import) also performs header file inclusion. Like the #include directive, the included header file is enclosed in either double quotes or angle brackets. This directive differs from #include in that it ensures a header file is only included once in a source file, thereby preventing recursive includes. For example, in the Elements program you implemented in Chapters 2 and 3, the main.m source file includes the Hydrogen.h and Atom+Nuclear.h header files. Now each of these files includes the Atom.h file, and hence you have a scenario that could result in duplicate includes of the Atom header file (in the main.m file). However, since main.m includes the Hydrogen and Atom+Nuclear header files using the #import directive (as shown in Listing 5-1), the Atom header file will only be included once (in the main.m source file).

Listing 5-1. Using the #import Directive to Prevent Recursive Includes

```
#import <Foundation/Foundation.h>
#import "Atom.h"
#import "Atom+Nuclear.h"
#import "Atom+Helper.h"
#import "Hydrogen.h"
```

Without the #import directive, it would be necessary to provide an include guard in a header file to prevent recursive inclusion. An *include guard* is a set of preprocessor statements that are used to prevent duplicate inclusion of a header file. It is typically constructed using the #ifndef conditional compilation expression and a #define directive. An example include guard for the Atom.h header file is shown in Listing 5-2.

Listing 5-2. Atom.h Header File Include Guard

```
#ifndef  ATOM_H
#define  ATOM_H
@interface Atom : NSObject
// Atom interface declarations
...
@end
#endif
```

The #import directive is typically used to include Objective-C header files, thus there is generally no need to implement include guards in your Objective-C source files. Now let's look at the conditional compilation directives.

Conditional Compilation

The *conditional compilation* directives (#if, #elif, #else, #endif, #ifdef, #ifndef) enable you to include or exclude part of the source text if a certain condition is met.

The #if directive enables you to test the value of an expression and include/exclude a portion of the source text based on the result. The syntax for using this directive is shown in Listing 5-3.

Listing 5-3. Syntax for the #if Preprocessor Directive

```
#if ArithmeticExpression
// conditional text (preprocessor or Objective-C source code)
...
#endif
```

An #if directive is used to test an arithmetic expression. As shown in Listing 5-3, it is paired with an #endif directive, which together enclose conditional text. The arithmetic expression is of integer type and may contain the following elements:

- Integer and character constants.

- Arithmetic operators, bitwise operations, shifts, comparisons, and logical operations (as defined in Appendix A).

- Preprocessor macros. The macros are expanded before computation of the expression.

- Uses of the *defined* operator, which is used to check whether a macro is defined.

- Identifiers that are not macros, which are all assigned the value zero when being evaluated.

The preprocessor evaluates the expression according to these rules. If the result of the evaluation is nonzero, the conditional text (typically source code but possibly also other preprocessor directives) is included for compilation or further preprocessing; otherwise, it is skipped. Look at the following example:

```
#if INPUT_ARGS <= 0
#warning "No input arguments defined"
#endif
```

The preprocessor would process these lines as follows:

1. Expand the identifier INPUT_ARGS. If identifier is a macro, it is replaced with its corresponding value; if it is not a macro or the macro has no value, the identifier is replaced with the value zero.

2. Calculate the value of the expression. If the value is nonzero (i.e., the value of the INPUT_ARGS identifier is less than or equal to zero), the text between the #if directive statement and the #endif directive is included (i.e., not filtered by the preprocessor). In this case (due to the #warning message), it would ultimately cause the compiler to generate a warning message.

This type of directive is often used to perform conditional compilation of platform-specific code for a designated target environment. For example, if you have Objective-C code that has customizations for several different compilers, these could be encapsulated using #if directives and the appropriate compiler-specific identifiers.

The #elif directive stands for "else if"; it augments the #if directive by enabling you to check for two or more possible conditions. It is placed between the #if and #endif directives; the conditional text following the #elif directive is processed only if the original #if directive (and any preceding #elif directive(s)) failed. The syntax for the #elif directive is shown in Listing 5-4.

Listing 5-4. Syntax for the #elif Preprocessor Directive

```
#if ArithmeticExpression1
// Conditional text 1

...
#elif ArithmeticExpression2
// Conditional text 2

...
#elif ArithmeticExpressionN
// Conditional text N

...
#endif
```

The preprocessor would process the text of Listing 5-4 as follows: if ArithmeticExpression1 succeeds then Conditional text 1 is processed; else if ArithmeticExpression2 succeeds then Conditional text 2 is processed; else if ArithmeticExpressionN succeeds then Conditional text N is processed. If multiple conditional expressions within the group of #if-#elif would succeed, only the first will be processed.

The #else directive augments the #if and #elif directives by providing a mechanism for conditional text to be executed if none of the associated #if and #elif expressions succeed. It is placed between the #if, #elif (if any #elif directives provided), and #elif directives, as the last directive immediately preceding the #endif. The syntax for the #else directive is shown in Listing 5-5.

Listing 5-5. Syntax for the #else Preprocessor Directive

```
#if ArithmeticExpression1
// Conditional text 1

...
#elif ArithmeticExpression2
// Conditional text 2

...
#else
// Else conditional text

...
#endif
```

The preprocessor would process the Else conditional text of Listing 5-5 if none of the other conditional expressions succeed.

At most, one #else directive can be placed between the #if and its corresponding #endif directive, and it must be the last directive before the #endif. Finally, also note that the #if, #elif, #else, and #endif directives can be nested; in this case, the #endif matches the closest preceding #if directive.

The #ifdef directive enables conditional text to be processed only if the macro that is specified as its parameter has been defined, no matter what its value is. It is paired with an #endif directive, which is enclosed by the conditional text. The syntax for this directive is shown in Listing 5-6.

Listing 5-6. Syntax for the #ifdef Preprocessor Directive

```
#ifdef MacroName
// Conditional text
...
#endif
```

The #ifndef directive functions as the complement to the #ifdef directive; it enables conditional text to be processed only if the macro that is specified as its parameter has not been defined. The syntax for this directive is shown in Listing 5-7.

Listing 5-7. Syntax for the #ifndef Preprocessor Directive

```
#ifndef MacroName
// Conditional text
...
#endif
```

The behavior of the #ifdef and #ifndef directives can also be achieved by using the defined operator in an #if or #elif conditional expression.

The defined operator is used to test whether a name is defined as a macro. It is equivalent to the #ifdef directive. The syntax for using the defined operator in a conditional expression is

```
#if defined MacroName
```

or

```
#elif defined MacroName
```

The macro name can be surrounded with parentheses, if desired. One of the reasons for using the defined operator (in lieu of the #ifdef directive) is when you need to test more than one macro in a single expression, as in the following example:

```
#if defined (MacroName1) || defined (MacroName2)
// insert source text here
#endif
```

Diagnostics

The preprocessor includes several directives that provide diagnostics for problems that occur during program compilation. The #error directive causes the preprocessor to generate an error message and fail compilation. The syntax for this directive is

```
#error "ErrorMessage"
```

The error message is surrounded in double-quotes. This directive is commonly used if a conditional compilation check fails; for example, the following code fragment

```
#ifndef    INPUT_ARGS
#error "No input arguments provided"
#endif
```

causes compilation to fail and generates an error message ("No input arguments provided") if the macro INPUT_ARGS is not defined.

The #warning directive causes the preprocessor to generate a compile-time warning message, but allows compilation to continue. The syntax for this directive is

```
#warning "WarningMessage"
```

The warning message is surrounded in double-quotes. The following code fragment

```
#ifndef    OUTPUT_FILE
#warning "Output filename not provided"
#endif
```

generates a warning message ("Output filename not provided") if the macro OUTPUT_ARGS is not defined; compilation will continue.

The #line directive is used to supply a line number for compiler messages. If an error happens during the compiling process, the compiler shows an error message with references to the name of the file where the error happened and a corresponding line number, thereby making it easier to find the code that generated the error. The syntax for the #line directive is

```
#line LineNumber "FileName"
```

LineNumber is the new line number that will be assigned to the next code line. The line numbers of successive lines will be increased one by one from this point on. The "FileName" (surrounded in double-quotes) is an optional parameter that enables you to redefine the file name that will be displayed. Xcode and the Objective-C compiler use of the #line directive are illustrated in the following code fragment:

```
...
#line 10 "Elements.m"
int ?numProtons;
```

This code will generate an error that will be shown as error in file "Elements.m" at line 11.

The Xcode IDE displays the line numbers of source files and automatically displays errors and warnings while you enter code and at compilation; hence, you rarely have need to use this directive in your source files.

Pragma

The *pragma* directive (#pragma) is used to specify additional options to the compiler, beyond that conveyed by the Objective-C language itself. These options are specific for the platform and the compiler being used. The syntax for the #pragma directive is

```
#pragma PragmaOptions(s)
```

The pragma options are a series of characters that correspond to a specific compiler instruction (and arguments, if any), and cause an implementation-defined action. If the compiler does not support a specific argument for a #pragma directive, it is ignored and no error is generated.

The Apple Objective-C compiler supports numerous pragma options; the exact options available can be found in the reference documentation for the compiler.

Xcode includes support for several `#pragma mark` directives. You would use these directives in implementation source files to categorize methods when viewing them within the IDE. Let's look at an example to see how this works. The Xcode workspace window contains a *jump bar* at the top of the editor area; it is used to hierarchically view items in the workspace. If you click an item in the jump bar, it displays items at the same level within the hierarchy (as shown in Figure 5-3).

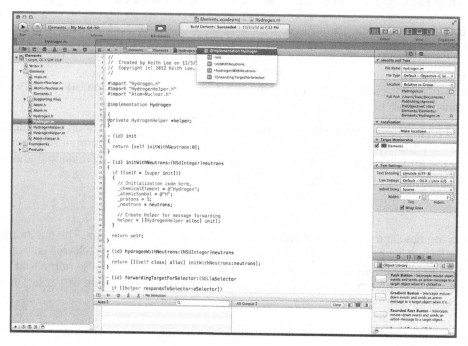

Figure 5-3. *Using the Xcode jump bar to display methods*

Figure 5-3 shows that clicking a class implementation in the Xcode jump bar brings up a pop-up window that displays a list of the Hydrogen class implementation's methods. Now this is where pragma mark directives enter the picture—they can be used to organize how these methods are displayed in the jump bar pop-up. You can create a divider visible in the jump bar pop-up using the directive

```
#pragma mark -
```

You create a label used to categorize one or more methods using the directive

```
#pragma mark MarkName
```

MarkName is the label for the methods that will be displayed in the pop-up.

The following example includes pragma mark directives for the Hydrogen class implementation created in Chapters 2 and 3. These updates (shown in **bold** in Listing 5-8) categorize the class custom initialization methods.

Listing 5-8. Example #pragma mark Directive Usage

```
#pragma mark -
#pragma mark Custom Initializers

- (id) initWithNeutrons:(NSUInteger)neutrons
{
  if ((self = [super init]))
  {
    // Initialization code here.
    _chemicalElement = @"Hydrogen";
    _atomicSymbol = @"H";
    _protons = 1;
    _neutrons = neutrons;

    // Create helper for message forwarding
    helper = [[HydrogenHelper alloc] init];
  }

  return self;
}


#pragma mark -
```

If you now click the Hydrogen implementation in the Xcode jump bar (as shown in Figure 5-4), the pop-up display lists the method initWithNeutrons:, prefaced with a label of Custom Initializers, and surrounded by dividers.

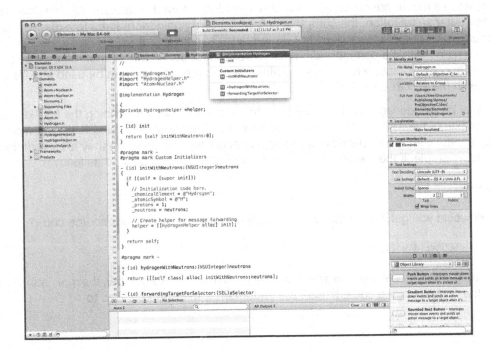

Figure 5-4. Using the #pragma mark directives

Particularly for large projects and classes that contain a large number of methods, #pragma mark directives provide a mechanism that facilitates the categorization and organization of class methods and make the jump bar more efficient to use.

Macros

A preprocessor *macro* is a named code fragment. Wherever the name is used in the source code, the code fragment is substituted for it. Preprocessor macros can be used to define constant values or to provide function-like substitutions complete with input parameter values. Macros are defined with the #define preprocessor directive, and removed with the #undef directive. The syntax for an object-like macro that defines a constant value is

```
#define MacroName [MacroValue]
```

The optional macro value is placed after the name; the macro value may be an arithmetic expression composed of constant values. The syntax for a function-like macro is

```
#define MacroName(MacroArguments) Code
```

The macro name includes one or more arguments (separated by commas) surrounded by parentheses, and the code fragment substituted for it. An example function-like macro that adds two values is

```
#define SQUARE(x)  ((x) * (x))
```

All arguments to a macro are completely macro-expanded before they are substituted into the macro body. After substitution, the complete text is scanned again for macros to expand, including the arguments. The preprocessor does not understand Objective-C; it simply replaces occurrences of the macro name with the corresponding macro value or code. Also note that macros are not affected by Objective-C scope rules. Once defined, a macro exists and can be used in a file until it is undefined with the #undef directive.

Now you may be wondering: why did I use all of those parentheses for defining the SQUARE macro? This reflects one of the issues with macros; because they merely perform simple substitution, you have to be careful with macro definitions to avoid unexpected results when they are expanded. Consider, for example, if the SQUARE macro listed earlier was instead defined as follows:

```
#define SQUARE(x)  x * x
```

What result would you get if you later wrote the following statement in your source code?

```
int product = SQUARE(4 + 2);
```

Guess what? It's not 36! Let's see exactly how the macro works. Remember, it simply substitutes the macro for the corresponding code; hence, the statement is macro-expanded to

```
int product = 4 + 2 * 4 + 2;
```

Due to Objective-C operator precedence and associativity rules (listed in Appendix A), in the preceding statement, the multiplication of 2 * 4 is performed before the addition; thus, this statement will return a value of 14—probably not what you expect! To avoid these types of issues (due to macro expansion), you can surround the macro arguments and the macro itself with parentheses, as shown in the initial definition for the ADD macro.

```
#define SQUARE(x)  ((x) * (x))
```

In fact, parentheses should be used for both function-like and object-like macros. On the other hand, multiline function-like macros that are being used to perform a computation rather than return a value should be surrounded by curly braces ({ }). For example, the following macro is surrounded with curly braces:

```
#define SWAP(a, b)  {a^=b; b^=a; a^=b;}
```

Function-like macro definitions accept two special operators (# and ##) in the replacement sequence. The *stringification* operator (represented by the # symbol) is used to replace a macro input parameter with the corresponding text string (surrounded by double-quotes). The *concatenation* operator (represented by the ## symbol) is used to concatenate two tokens, leaving no blank space between them.

Warning, Don't Overuse Macros!

Macros, particularly function-like macros, are a powerful feature, but can be very dangerous to use. Because preprocessor replacements happen before the source is parsed, it can be difficult to define macros that correctly expand in all cases. It is often problematic to pass arguments with *side effects* (i.e., changes the value of an argument(s)) to function-like macros. This can result in one or more of these arguments being evaluated multiple times (i.e., duplication of side effects), and therefore making unexpected changes to their values, which are difficult to diagnose.

Finally, code that relies heavily on complicated macros may be difficult to maintain because their syntax is, on many occasions, different from that used in Objective-C.

Roundup

This has been fun. You just learned a programming language in one chapter! Well, perhaps it hasn't been that extreme, but now you have a good understanding of how the Objective-C preprocessor works and how the preprocessor language is used in Objective-C source files. Particularly, if you want to understand many publicly available software libraries and frameworks, or would like to examine Apple's Objective-C source code, detailed knowledge of the preprocessor language is invaluable. To summarize, the following are the key takeaways from this chapter:

- The preprocessor is used during the lexical analysis phase of compilation, which occurs prior to parsing. It works by substituting the input character sequences (of source files) for other character sequences, according to a set of predefined rules. These operations perform textual translation, token conversion, and preprocessor-based language transformation.

- The preprocessor language is a separate programming language that's distinct from Objective-C. The source file transformations performed using the language are primarily source file inclusions, conditional compilation, and macro expansions.

- The preprocessor language defines *directives* to be executed and *macros* to be expanded. A preprocessor directive is a command that is executed by the preprocessor, not the compiler. A preprocessor macro is a named code fragment. Wherever the name is used in the source code, the code fragment is substituted for it.

- Preprocessor directives perform header file inclusion, conditional processing, diagnostics, and platform-specific operations (pragmas).

- A preprocessor macro is a named code fragment. Wherever the name is used in a source file, the code fragment is substituted for it. Preprocessor macros define constant values and/or provide function-like substitutions complete with input parameter values.

- Macros, particularly function-like macros, are a powerful feature, but can be very dangerous. Improper use can cause misnesting, operator precedence problems, duplication of side effects, and other problems. In addition, code that relies heavily on complicated macros may be difficult to maintain because their syntax is often different from that used in Objective-C. In general, you should minimize your use of macros in your Objective-C source code.

Chapter 6

Expert Section Using ARC

Believe it or not, you're approaching the end of Part 1 in this book. So far, so good! Part 1 concludes with this Expert Section chapter. *Expert Section* chapters are designed to provide additional details and more in-depth coverage of a subject presented earlier in the book. In this chapter, you'll learn some of the finer details surrounding ARC memory management. You'll review some key points about ARC memory management and object ownership, and also learn how to use ARC with toll-free bridged objects.

ARC and Object Ownership

Recall from Chapter 4 that Objective-C code creates objects stored in dynamically allocated memory (the heap). Objects created on the heap never go out of scope, thus application memory management is required to ensure that these objects are removed from memory when no longer in use, and that a program doesn't erroneously free objects still being used. Objective-C implements memory management using a reference counting model, whereby unique references to an object are used to determine whether or not an object is still in use. ARC automates this task by inserting code (at compile time) to properly balance `retain` and `release` messages on objects, per the reference counting model. ARC prohibits programmatic control of object life cycle. Specifically, you can't send `retain` or `release` messages to control ownership interest in objects. Hence, it is very important to understand the rules pertaining to object ownership under ARC.

Claiming Ownership Interest in Objects

Your Objective-C code takes an ownership interest in any object that it creates using any method that has a name beginning with `alloc`, `new`, `copy`, or `mutableCopy`. The `main()` function shown in Listing 6-1 creates an `Atom` object using the `alloc` method, and thus claims an ownership interest in this object.

Listing 6-1. Creating an Atom Object

```
int main(int argc, const char * argv[])
{
  @autoreleasepool
  {
    Atom *atom = [[Atom alloc] init];
    [atom logInfo];
  }

  return 0;
}
```

Your code can also take an ownership interest in a `block` object if it creates one using a copy message.

> **Note**   A *block* is an implementation of a closure, a function that permits access to variables outside of their typical scope. Blocks can be dynamically allocated on the heap and are also managed by ARC, as with standard Objective-C objects. Programming with blocks will be covered in depth in Part 4 of this book.

Releasing Ownership Interest in Objects

As mentioned previously, ARC prohibits programmatic use of the `release`, `autorelease`, `dealloc`, or related messages on an object. Your code gives up ownership interest in an object when it performs any of the following: 1) variable reassignment, 2) `nil` assignment, or 3) its owner is deallocated.

Variable Reassignment

If a variable that points to a dynamically created object is changed to point to another object, the object loses an owner. At compile time, ARC inserts code to send a `release` message to this object. At this point, if there are no more owners of the object, it will be deallocated. Listing 6-2 illustrates an example of variable reassignment.

Listing 6-2. Object Ownership—Variable Reassignment

```
Atom *myAtom = [[Atom alloc] initWithName:@"Atom 1"];
// Other code
...
myAtom = [[Atom alloc] initWithName:@"Atom 2"];
```

In Listing 6-2, an Atom object (let's call it Atom 1) is created and assigned to the myAtom variable; later in the code, this variable is assigned to another Atom object (let's call it Atom 2). Because the myAtom variable has been reassigned to Atom 2, Atom 1 loses an owner and will be deallocated if there are no other owners of this object.

nil Assignment

If the value of a variable that currently points to a dynamically created object is set to nil, the object loses an owner. Listing 6-3 illustrates an example of nil assignment.

Listing 6-3. Object Ownership—nil Reassignment

```
Atom *myAtom = [[Atom alloc] init];
// Other code
...
myAtom = nil;
```

In Listing 6-3, an Atom object is created and assigned to the myAtom variable; later in the code, this variable is set to nil. Because the myAtom variable has been set to nil, the Atom object loses an owner. Again, ARC inserts code to send a release message to this object after the statement that sets the myAtom variable to nil.

Owner Deallocation

Owner deallocation. Now that doesn't sound very pleasant, does it? Actually this phrase refers to object ownership and how ARC transparently manages the object life cycle of both object graphs and collections. Object-oriented programs consist of webs of interrelated objects. These objects are linked together through OOP inheritance and/or composition, collectively referred to as an *object graph*. In an object graph, objects contain references to other (child) objects through the principle of composition. If a (parent) object creates another (child) object, it has claimed an ownership interest in it. In Chapter 4, you created a program with an object graph consisting of an OrderEntry class and two dependent (child) classes; its object graph is depicted in Figure 6-1.

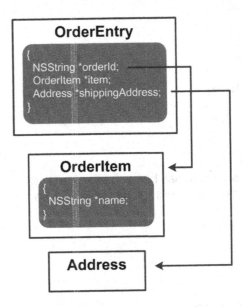

Figure 6-1. OrderEntry object graph

When an OrderEntry object is created and initialized, its init method also creates instances of its two child classes; thus, the OrderEntry object claims an ownership interest in each of these objects. Later, when an OrderEntry object is deallocated, ARC automatically sends a release message to each of its child objects. Specifically, at compile time, ARC creates code that inserts a dealloc method for the OrderEntry object (if one doesn't already exist), inserts a release message for each child object it owns, and then sends a dealloc message to the superclass of the OrderEntry object. Hence, ARC automatically manages the life cycle of object graphs.

The Apple Foundation Framework includes a variety of collection classes, so named because they are used to hold instances of other objects. When an object is stored in an instance of a collection class, the collection class claims an ownership interest in the object. Conversely, when a collection class instance is deallocated, ARC automatically sends a release message to each of the objects in the collection.

Creating Multiple Order Entries

To illustrate the use of ARC memory management and owner deallocation, you are going to extend the Order Entry project created in Chapter 4 by adding the capability to collect and store multiple order entries. You'll use a collection class to store the entries, and then demonstrate how ARC performs memory management with collection classes and the objects stored therein.

In Xcode, open the ARC Orders project (if not already opened) by selecting **Open Recent ➤ ARC Orders.xcodeproj** from the Xcode File menu. The source code for the project consists of seven files that implement the OrderEntry, OrderItem, and Address classes, and the main function. Let's start by making some updates to the OrderItem class. Select the **OrderItem.h** file in the navigator pane and then update the OrderItem interface, as shown in Listing 6-4.

Listing 6-4. ARC OrderItem Class Interface

```
#import <Foundation/Foundation.h>

@interface OrderItem : NSObject

@property (readonly) NSString *name;

- (id) initWithName:(NSString *)itemName;

@end
```

In Listing 6-4, the instance variable name has been changed to a read-only property. Next, select the **OrderItem.m** file and update the OrderItem implementation, as shown in Listing 6-5.

Listing 6-5. ARC OrderItem Class Implementation

```
#import "OrderItem.h"

@implementation OrderItem

- (id) initWithName:(NSString *)itemName
{
  if ((self = [super init]))
```

```
{
    _name = itemName;
    NSLog(@"Initializing OrderItem object %@", _name);
  }
  return self;
}

- (void)dealloc
{
  NSLog(@"Deallocating OrderItem object %@", self.name);
}

@end
```

This code is very similar to the original implementation; the custom initializer method (initWithName:) has been modified to initialize the property-backed instance variable. The log messages have also been slightly updated to display the OrderItem object name. Recall from Chapter 3, that for an autosynthesized property, the standard naming convention for its instance variable is the property name prefaced with an underscore. Now let's update the OrderEntry class. Select the **OrderEntry.h** file in the navigator pane and then update the OrderEntry interface, as shown in Listing 6-6.

Listing 6-6. ARC OrderEntry Class Interface

```
#import <Foundation/Foundation.h>
#import "OrderItem.h"
#import "Address.h"

@interface OrderEntry : NSObject

{
  Address *shippingAddress;
}

@property (readonly) NSString *orderId;
@property (readonly) OrderItem *item;

- (id) initWithId:(NSString *)oid name:(NSString *)order;

@end
```

The OrderEntry interface now has a single instance variable, two read-only properties, and an updated custom initializer (initWithId:name:). The properties are read-only and they replace two of the instance variables in the original interface from Chapter 4. Next, you'll update the class implementation. Select the **OrderEntry.m** file in the navigator pane and update the implementation, as shown in Listing 6-7.

Listing 6-7. ARC OrderEntry Class Implementation

```
#import "OrderEntry.h"

@implementation OrderEntry

- (id) initWithId:(NSString *)oid name:(NSString *)order;
{
  if ((self = [super init]))
  {
    NSLog(@"Initializing OrderEntry object");
    _orderId = oid;
    _item = [[OrderItem alloc] initWithName:order];
    shippingAddress = [[Address alloc] init];
  }

  return self;
}

- (void)dealloc
{
  NSLog(@"Deallocating OrderEntry object with ID %@",
        self.orderId);
}

@end
```

The custom initializer method (initWithId:name:) has been modified to initialize the two property-backed instance variables. The log message has also been slightly updated to display the OrderEntry ID using the property getter method.

Now that you've updated the classes, let's update the main function to create some order entries and store them in a collection class. Select the **main.m** file in the navigator pane and then update the main function, as shown in Listing 6-8.

Listing 6-8. ARC Orders main() Function Implementation

```
#import <Foundation/Foundation.h>
#import "OrderEntry.h"

int main(int argc, const char * argv[])
{

  @autoreleasepool
  {
    // Create an OrderEntry object
    OrderEntry *entry1 = [[OrderEntry alloc] initWithId:@"A-1"
                                             name:@"2 Hot dogs"];
    NSLog(@"Order 1, ID = %@, item: %@", entry1.orderId, entry1.item.name);
```

```
    // Create another OrderEntry object
    OrderEntry *entry2 = [[OrderEntry alloc] initWithId:@"A-2"
                                            name:@"1 Cheeseburger"];
    NSLog(@"Order 2, ID = %@, item: %@", entry2.orderId, entry2.item.name);

    // Add the order entries to a collection
    NSArray *entries = [[NSArray alloc] initWithObjects:entry1, entry2, nil];
    NSLog(@"Number of order entries = %li", [entries count]);

    // Set OrderEntry object to nil, ARC sends a release message to the object!
    NSLog(@"Setting entry2 variable to nil");
    entry2 = nil;

    // Set collection to nil, ARC sends a release message to all objects
    NSLog(@"Setting entries collection variable to nil");
    entries = nil;

    // Set OrderEntry object to nil, ARC sends a release message to the object!
    NSLog(@"Setting entry1 variable to nil");
    entry1 = nil;

    // Exit autoreleasepool block
    NSLog(@"Leaving autoreleasepool block");
  }
  return 0;
}
```

The updates to the main() function are extensive, so you'll go over them line by line. First, the code creates two OrderEntry objects, each time logging a message to the console displaying the ID and name for the entry. Next, the code creates and initializes an NSArray object with the two order entries. An NSArray is a Foundation Framework class for managing order collections of objects (you'll learn about NSArray and other Foundation Framework collection classes in Part 3 of this book). As you learned earlier, when an object is stored in an instance of a collection class, the collection class claims an ownership interest in the object. Thus, the NSArray object claims an ownership interest in each order entry. Next, the variable currently pointing to one of the OrderEntry objects (entry2) is set to nil, thereby releasing an ownership interest in the object. Because the NSArray object still "owns" the entry2 object, it is not deallocated. Next, the variable pointing to the NSArray object is set to nil, thereby releasing ownership interest in the entry2 object and in all objects for which it claims an ownership interest. Finally, the variable pointing to the other OrderEntry object (entry1) is set to nil, thereby releasing an ownership interest in that object. A message is also logged to the console immediately before leaving the autorelease pool block.

Now save, compile, and run the updated ARC Orders program and observe the messages in the output pane (see Figure 6-2).

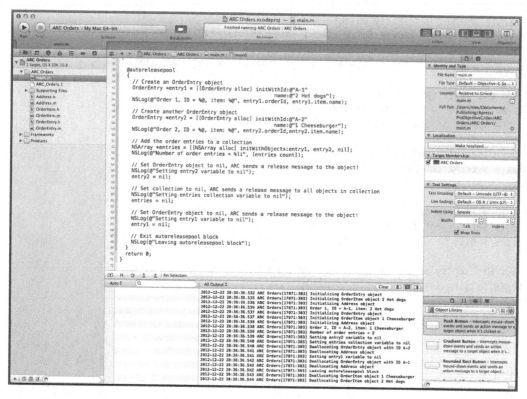

Figure 6-2. Testing the updated ARC Order Entry project

The messages in the output pane (depicted in more detail in Figure 6-3) show the sequence of calls to initialize and deallocate the dynamically created objects.

```
All Output ▼                                                    Clear  ▯ ▮ ▯
2012-12-22 20:36:36.532 ARC Orders[17071:303] Initializing OrderEntry object
2012-12-22 20:36:36.535 ARC Orders[17071:303] Initializing OrderItem object 2 Hot dogs
2012-12-22 20:36:36.536 ARC Orders[17071:303] Initializing Address object
2012-12-22 20:36:36.536 ARC Orders[17071:303] Order 1, ID = A-1, item: 2 Hot dogs
2012-12-22 20:36:36.537 ARC Orders[17071:303] Initializing OrderEntry object
2012-12-22 20:36:36.537 ARC Orders[17071:303] Initializing OrderItem object 1 Cheeseburger
2012-12-22 20:36:36.538 ARC Orders[17071:303] Initializing Address object
2012-12-22 20:36:36.538 ARC Orders[17071:303] Order 2, ID = A-2, item: 1 Cheeseburger
2012-12-22 20:36:36.539 ARC Orders[17071:303] Number of order entries = 2
2012-12-22 20:36:36.539 ARC Orders[17071:303] Setting entry2 variable to nil
2012-12-22 20:36:36.540 ARC Orders[17071:303] Setting entries collection variable to nil
2012-12-22 20:36:36.540 ARC Orders[17071:303] Deallocating OrderEntry object with ID A-2
2012-12-22 20:36:36.541 ARC Orders[17071:303] Deallocating Address object
2012-12-22 20:36:36.541 ARC Orders[17071:303] Setting entry1 variable to nil
2012-12-22 20:36:36.542 ARC Orders[17071:303] Deallocating OrderEntry object with ID A-1
2012-12-22 20:36:36.542 ARC Orders[17071:303] Deallocating Address object
2012-12-22 20:36:36.542 ARC Orders[17071:303] Leaving autoreleasepool block
2012-12-22 20:36:36.543 ARC Orders[17071:303] Deallocating OrderItem object 1 Cheeseburger
2012-12-22 20:36:36.544 ARC Orders[17071:303] Deallocating OrderItem object 2 Hot dogs
```

Figure 6-3. ARC object deallocation

In Figure 6-3, a series of messages show the initialization of two OrderEntry object graphs, including their corresponding dependent objects (OrderItem and Address). A message indicating the number of order entries stored in the NSArray collection class is then displayed. Next, the entry2 variable (corresponding to an OrderEntry object) is set to nil; however, because the NSArray instance still has an ownership interest in this OrderEntry object, it is not deallocated. The entries variable (corresponding to the NSArray instance) is then set to nil. This causes the NSArray instance to be deallocated and a release message to be sent to each of the objects in this collection. At this point, the OrderEntry object corresponding to the entry2 variable has no more owners, so it is deallocated, along with its dependent objects. Next, the entry1 variable is set to nil, causing a release message to be sent to its corresponding OrderEntry object. Because this object now has no owners, it is also deallocated along with its dependent objects. The output pane now displays a message indicating that the code is leaving the autorelease pool block. Following this message, the corresponding OrderItem object for each of the OrderEntry objects is deallocated.

ARC memory management has properly managed the life cycle of this object graph and the collection class. However, if you look closely at the output from the output pane, you may have noticed that the OrderItem objects were deallocated at the end of the autorelease pool (as shown by the log messages in Figure 6-3). So why weren't they deallocated when the corresponding OrderEntry parent objects were deallocated? The answer lies in how ARC manages the life cycle of property accessors—specifically in this case, property get methods. Your code needs to claim an ownership interest in any object it obtains (i.e., hasn't created programmatically via a method beginning with alloc, new, copy, or mutableCopy) and may use over a long period of time. Because ARC prohibits you from programmatically sending retain messages to objects, it must be capable of detecting these scenarios and inserting the necessary code to manage object life cycle appropriately. Specifically, if an object is retrieved via a property get method, ARC detects this and automatically inserts code to send retain and autorelease messages to this object, thereby preventing it from being deallocated prematurely. Recall from Listing 6-6 that the OrderEntry interface declares a (read-only) property named item of type OrderItem. In Listing 6-8, the following statement retrieves the OrderItem object item via the property get method (entry1.item):

```
NSLog(@"Order 1, ID = %@, item: %@", entry1.orderId, entry1.item.name);
```

At compile time, ARC will automatically insert code that sends retain and autorelease messages to this OrderItem object. Later in the code, the OrderItem object (entry2.item) is retrieved with the following statement:

```
NSLog(@"Order 2, ID = %@, item: %@", entry2.orderId, entry2.item.name);
```

In sum, when an object is retrieved via a property getter, ARC sends retain and autorelease messages to the object to prevent it from being deallocated. This explains why the OrderItem objects were deallocated at the end of the autorelease pool block, and not when the parent (OrderEntry) objects were deallocated.

Let's comment-out the preceding two log statements and then save, compile, and rerun the program. Because the OrderItem objects are no longer retrieved via a property get method, you should observe that the OrderItem objects are now deallocated when the corresponding OrderEntry objects are deallocated, not at the end of the autorelease pool block (see Figure 6-4).

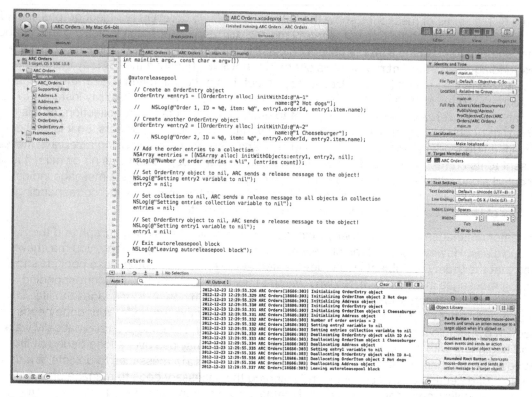

Figure 6-4. Running the updated ARC Order Entry project

This example demonstrates the details of how code compiled using ARC can programmatically release ownership interest in objects and how ARC manages object life cycle for both object graphs and collections. Understanding these details will become invaluable as you develop larger and more complex Objective-C applications.

Using ARC with Apple Frameworks and Services

Apple includes numerous software libraries (i.e., frameworks and services) that provide the interfaces needed to write software for the OS X and iOS platforms. Some of the most commonly used libraries for application development are depicted in Figure 6-5.

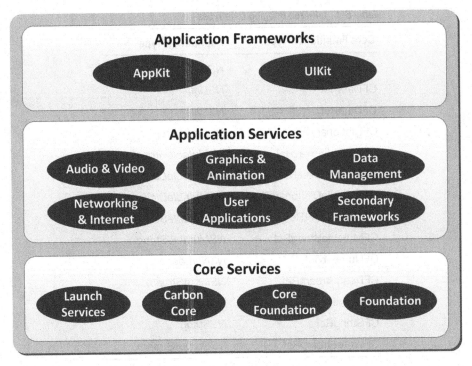

Figure 6-5. Apple Application frameworks and services

The application programming interfaces (APIs) for some of these libraries are written in Objective-C, and thus may be used directly in your Objective-C programs. The APIs for the majority of these libraries are written in ANSI C, and hence may also be used directly in your Objective-C programs.

You may recall from Chapter 4 that ARC provides automatic memory management for Objective-C objects and block objects. The Apple software libraries with C-based APIs do not integrate with ARC. Thus, you are responsible for programmatically performing memory management when dynamically allocating memory with these C-based APIs. In fact, when using ARC, it is prohibited to perform standard casts between pointers of Objective-C objects and pointers of other types (e.g., one that is a part of an Apple C–based API). Apple provides several mechanisms (toll-free bridging and ARC bridged casts) to facilitate the use of C-based APIs in Objective-C programs. You will look at these next.

Objective-C Toll Free Bridging

Interoperability is provided for a number of data types in the C-based Core Foundation Framework and the Objective-C-based Foundation Framework. This capability, referred to as *toll-free bridging*, allows you to use the same data type as the parameter to a Core Foundation function call or as the receiver of an Objective-C message. You can cast one type to the other to suppress compiler warnings. Some of the more commonly used toll-free bridged data types are listed in Table 6-1; it includes the Core Foundation type and the corresponding Foundation Framework type.

Table 6-1. *Toll-Free Bridging Data Types*

Core Foundation Type	Foundation Type
CFArrayRef	NSArray
CFDataRef	NSData
CFDateRef	NSDate
CFDictionaryRef	NSDictionary
CFMutableArrayRef	NSMutableArray
CFMutableDataRef	NSMutableData
CFMutableDictionaryRef	NSMutableDictionary
CFMutableSetRef	NSMutableSet
CFMutableStringRef	NSMutableString
CFNumberRef	NSNumber
CFReadStreamRef	NSInputStream
CFSetRef	NSSet
CFStringRef	NSString
CFWriteStreamRef	NSOutputStream

With toll-free bridging, the compiler implicitly casts between Core Foundation and Foundation types. For example, a variable of type CFStringRef is used as an argument to an Objective-C method in Listing 6-9.

Listing 6-9. Toll-Free Bridging Implicit Cast

```
CFStringRef cstr = CFStringCreateWithCString(NULL, "Hello, World!",
                                             kCFStringEncodingASCII);
NSArray *data = [NSArray arrayWithObject:cstr];
```

The [NSArray arrayWithObject:] class method takes a parameter of type id (in other words, an Objective-C object pointer) as an argument, but is passed as CFStringRef. Because CFStringRef is a toll-free bridged data type, the cstr parameter is implicitly cast to an NSString object (see Table 6-1). To remove the compiler warning for the implicit cast, the parameter is cast, as shown in Listing 6-10.

Listing 6-10. Toll-Free Bridging Explicit Cast

```
CFStringRef cstr = CFStringCreateWithCString(NULL, "Hello, World!",
                                             kCFStringEncodingASCII);
NSArray *data = [NSArray arrayWithObject:(NSString *)cstr];
```

As mentioned in the previous section, the Objective-C compiler does not automatically manage the lifetimes of Core Foundation data types. Therefore, to use Core Foundation toll-free bridged types in ARC memory managed Objective-C programs, it is necessary to indicate the ownership semantics involved with these types. In fact, the code in Listing 6-10, as is, will not compile when using ARC!

For Objective-C programs that use ARC memory management, you must indicate whether the life cycle of a toll-free bridged type is to be managed by ARC or managed programmatically. You do this by using ARC bridged casts.

ARC Bridged Casts

ARC bridged casts enable the use of toll-free bridged types when using ARC. These casting operations are prefaced with the special annotations __bridge, __bridge_retained, and __bridge_transfer.

- The __bridge annotation casts an object from a Core Foundation data type to a Foundation object (or vice-versa) without transfer of ownership. In other words, if you dynamically create a Foundation Framework object, and then cast it to a Core Foundation type (via toll-free bridging), the __bridge annotation informs the compiler that the object's life cycle is still managed by ARC. Conversely, if you create a Core Foundation data type and then cast it to a Foundation Framework object, the __bridge annotation informs the compiler that the object's life cycle must still be managed programmatically (and is not managed by ARC). Note that this annotation removes the compiler error but doesn't transfer ownership; thus, care is required when using it to avoid memory leaks or dangling pointers.

- The __bridge_retained annotation is used to cast a Foundation Framework object to a Core Foundation data type and transfer ownership *from* the ARC system. You are then responsible for programmatically managing the lifetime of the bridged data type.

- The __bridge_transfer annotation is used to cast a Core Foundation data type to a Foundation object and also transfer ownership of the object *to* the ARC system. ARC will then programmatically manage the lifetime of the bridged object.

The syntax for using a bridged cast annotation in a cast operation is

```
(annotation castType)variableName
```

This differs from a regular cast operation in that the annotation is prepended to the cast type. The ARC bridged casts can be used not only for toll-free bridged types, but also anywhere your Objective-C code needs to use access memory not managed as Objective-C objects. Listing 6-11 updates the previous example with an ARC bridged cast.

Listing 6-11. Toll-Free Bridging with an ARC Bridged Cast

```
CFStringRef cstr = CFStringCreateWithCString(NULL, "Hello, World!",
                                    kCFStringEncodingASCII);
NSArray *data = [NSArray arrayWithObject:(__bridge_transfer NSString *)cstr];
```

Notice that the annotation precedes the type being cast to. This annotation transfers ownership of the bridged object to ARC, which will now manage the object's life cycle. OK, enough theory, now let's create some examples that demonstrate the use of ARC bridged casts!

Using ARC Bridged Casts

Now you'll develop an example program that applies what you've learned about toll-free bridging and ARC bridged casts. In Xcode, create a new project by selecting **New ➤ Project ...** from the Xcode File menu. In the New Project Assistant pane, create a command-line application (choose **Command Line Tool** from the Mac OS X Application selection) and click **Next**. In the Project Options window, specify **ARC Toll Free Bridging** for the Product Name, choose **Foundation** for the Project Type, choose ARC memory management by selecting the **Use Automatic Reference Counting** check box, and then click **Next**.

Specify the location in your file system where you want the project to be created (if necessary, select **New Folder** and enter the name and location for the folder), uncheck the **Source Control** check box, and then click the **Create** button.

First, you'll create a toll-free bridged Core Foundation data type. Select the **main.m** file in the navigator pane and create a CFStringRef, as shown in Listing 6-12.

Listing 6-12. A main() Function Toll-Free Bridged Data Type

```
#import <Foundation/Foundation.h>

int main(int argc, const char * argv[])
{
  @autoreleasepool
  {
    CFStringRef cstr = CFStringCreateWithCString(NULL, "Hello, World!",
                                        kCFStringEncodingASCII);
  }
  return 0;
}
```

A CFStringRef is a Core Foundation data type that represents a unicode string of characters. It is a toll-free bridged type and it can be cast to a Foundation Framework NSString object. To demonstrate the use of toll-free bridging, update the code, as shown in Listing 6-13.

Listing 6-13. Implicit Toll-Free Bridging

```
#import <Foundation/Foundation.h>

int main(int argc, const char * argv[])
{
  @autoreleasepool
  {
    CFStringRef cstr = CFStringCreateWithCString(NULL, "Hello, World!",
                                        kCFStringEncodingASCII);
    NSArray *data = [NSArray arrayWithObject:cstr];
    NSLog(@"Array size = %ld", [data count]);
    ...
}
```

The variable cstr, of type CFStringRef, is a parameter for the Objective-C NSArray object. From a toll-free bridging perspective, this is all fine, but because you are using ARC memory, the code will not compile. It displays an error indicating that a bridged cast is required (see Figure 6-6).

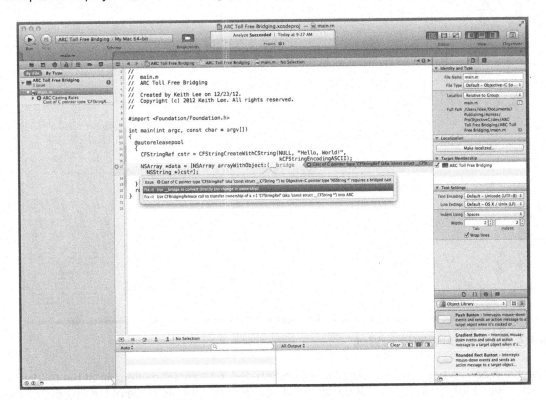

Figure 6-6. Toll-Free bridging compilation error

The Xcode pop-up message recommends that you update the code with a bridged cast using the __bridge annotation. If you make this update, the code now compiles and runs. There is a potential problem, however. Can you guess what it is? Well, if you analyze this program (by selecting **Analyze** from the Xcode Product menu), there is a potential memory leak of the object stored in the cstr variable (see Figure 6-7).

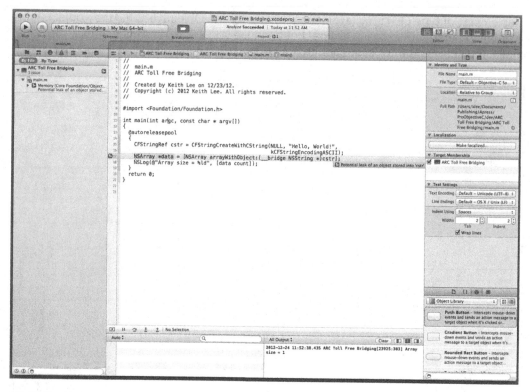

Figure 6-7. Bridged cast potential memory leak

This problem occurs because the __bridge annotation doesn't transfer ownership of the toll-free bridged object; thus, your code must programmatically manage the life cycle of the object pointed to by cstr. Because your code created the CFStringRef, it owns this dynamically created object and can send a release message to it, as in the following, for example:

```
CFRelease(cstr);
```

This will eliminate the potential memory leak. A better solution (which will avoid having to programmatically manage the life cycle of this object), however, is to use the __bridge_transfer annotation. This will transfer ownership of the object to ARC, which will then automatically manage the object's life cycle.

```
NSArray *data = [NSArray arrayWithObject:(__bridge_transfer NSString *)cstr];
```

If you analyze the program again after making this change, no memory leaks are detected. Cool. Now let's create another example. This one casts a Foundation Framework object to a Core Foundation data type. Add the code shown in Listing 6-14.

Listing 6-14. Implicit Toll-Free Bridging

```
// Now cast a Foundation framework object to a Core Foundation type
NSString *greeting = [[NSString alloc] initWithFormat:@"%@",
                     @"Hello, World!"];
CFStringRef cstr1 = (__bridge CFStringRef)(greeting);
printf("String length = %ld", CFStringGetLength(cstr1));
```

This code creates a Foundation Framework NSString instance and uses the __bridge annotation to cast it to a Core Foundation CFStringRef. This code compiles and runs, but has a potential dangling pointer because ARC immediately sends a release message to the NSString object (stored in the variable greeting) when the bridged cast is performed. To resolve this problem, change the cast annotation to __bridge_retained. This transfers ownership of the object from ARC, thereby preventing ARC from sending the release message to the object. You must now programmatically manage the life cycle of the object (now cast to a CFStringRef). Add a CFRelease function call after the printf statement.

```
CFRelease(cstr1);
```

If you analyze the program now, there are no potential memory leaks detected. When you compile and run the program, you'll see the output shown in Figure 6-8.

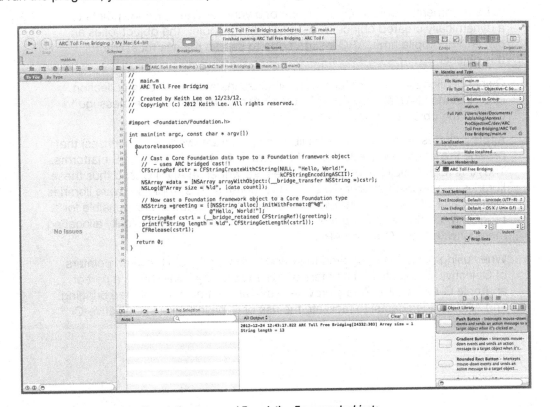

Figure 6-8. Bridged casts to Core Foundation types and Foundation Framework objects

Great! You now have a good handle on toll-free bridging and the use of ARC bridged casts. Feel free to experiment with other toll-free bridged types to get familiar with this technology under ARC.

Roundup

This Expert Section chapter explored some of the finer details surrounding ARC memory management. Because ARC is the Apple-recommended approach for memory management on all new Objective-C projects, it is critical to have a good understanding of how to use this technology. In this chapter, you focused on the details of ARC object ownership, block objects, and toll-free bridging. To recap, the following are the key takeaways:

- ARC prohibits programmatic use of the release, autorelease, dealloc, or related messages on an object. Your code gives up ownership interest in an object when it performs any of the following: 1) variable reassignment, 2) nil assignment, or 3) its owner is deallocated.

- Variable reassignment occurs when a variable that points to a dynamically created object is changed to point to another object. At this point, the object loses an owner; at compile time, ARC inserts code to send a release message to this object.

- nil assignment occurs when the value of a variable that currently points to a dynamically created object is set to nil. At this point, the object loses an owner. At compile time, ARC inserts code to send a release message to this object.

- Owner deallocation occurs for collection class instances. When a collection class instance is deallocated, ARC automatically sends a release message to each of the objects in the collection.

- Apple includes numerous software libraries (i.e., frameworks and services) that provide the interfaces needed to write software for the OS X and iOS platforms. The APIs for the majority of these libraries are written in ANSI C, and thus these libraries can be used in your Objective-C programs. The Apple software libraries with C-based APIs do not integrate with ARC; so your code is responsible for programmatically performing memory management when dynamically allocating memory with these C-based APIs.

- When using ARC, it is prohibited to perform standard casts between pointers of Objective-C objects and pointers of other types (e.g., one that is a part of an Apple C-based API). Apple provides several mechanisms (toll-free bridging and ARC bridged casts) to facilitate the use of C-based APIs in Objective-C programs.

- Toll-free bridging, provided for a number of data types in the Core Foundation and Foundation Frameworks, enables your code to use the same data type as the parameter to a Core Foundation function call or as the receiver of an Objective-C message. You can cast one type to the other to suppress compiler warnings. Under ARC memory management, you cannot directly cast toll-free bridged types; they must be prepended with special ARC bridged cast annotations.

- ARC bridged casts enable the use of toll-free bridged types when using ARC. These casting operations are prefaced with the special annotations `__bridge`, `__bridge_retained`, and `__bridge_transfer`.

Well, Part 1 has been quite a journey! You have learned many of the fundamentals of the Objective-C language. Take your time to review everything that you have learned in these six chapters, because having a sound foundation with this material is critical to becoming proficient in programming with Objective-C. Next up is Part Two, where you explore the Objective-C Runtime. When you're ready, turn the page and let's begin!

Chapter 7

Runtime System

Objective-C has a considerable number of *dynamic features*, which are functionality and behaviors that are executed at runtime, rather than when the code is compiled or linked. These features are implemented by the Objective-C runtime system, and are what provides much of the power and flexibility of the language. They can be used to facilitate developing and updating programs both in real time, without the need to recompile and redeploy software, and over time, with minimal or no impact to the existing software.

Understanding how the Objective-C runtime works will help you gain a much deeper understanding of the language and how your programs are run. In this chapter, you will explore the dynamic features of the language in detail and demonstrate how you can use them in your programs.

Dynamic Features

At runtime, the Objective-C language performs many common behaviors—such as type determination and method resolution—that other languages perform during program compilation or linking, if at all. It also provides APIs that enable you to perform additional runtime operations such as object introspection and the dynamic creation and loading of code. These features are made possible through the architecture and implementation of the Objective-C runtime. In the next few sections, you'll examine these features in more detail and learn how they are used in your programs.

Object Messaging

In OOP terminology, *message passing* is a style of communication used to send and receive messages between objects. Objective-C message passing (e.g., object messaging) is used to invoke methods on both classes and class instances (i.e., objects). The example in Figure 7-1 depicts the syntax for sending a message to an object/class.

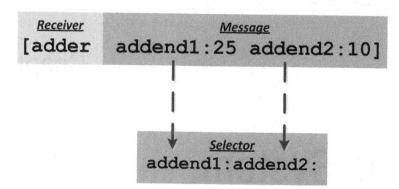

Figure 7-1. *Objective-C message passing*

In the message-passing expression shown in Figure 7-1, the *receiver* (adder) is the target of the message (i.e., the object or class), and the message itself (addend1:25 addend2:10) is composed of a *selector* along with any corresponding input parameters.

Object messaging is implemented as a dynamic feature—the actual type of the receiver of the message and the corresponding method to be invoked on the receiver is determined at runtime (see Figure 7-2).

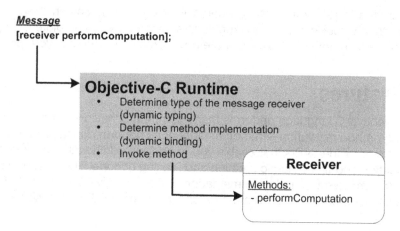

Figure 7-2. *Objective-C object messaging*

Figure 7-2 depicts how the Objective-C runtime implements the mapping of messages to method calls via dynamic typing and dynamic binding, both of which you'll look at shortly. Object messaging provides tremendous flexibility with its dynamic programming features. In addition to simplifying the programming interface, these capabilities also enable the development of modular applications that can be modified and/or updated during program execution.

Because Objective-C method calls are resolved at runtime, there is a certain amount of overhead associated with dynamic binding. The Objective-C runtime system caches method calls—saving the message-to-method association in memory—to reduce this overhead.

The other consequence of runtime resolution of method calls is that the receiver is not guaranteed to be able to respond to a message. If it cannot, it will raise a runtime exception. The Objective-C language provides several features (e.g., object introspection and message forwarding) that can be used to mitigate this scenario.

To summarize, the following are the key elements of Objective-C object messaging:

- *Message*: A name (the selector) and a set of parameters sent to an object/class.

- *Method*: An Objective-C class or instance method that has a specific declaration comprised of a name, input parameters, a return value, and the method signature (the data type(s) for the input parameters and return value).

- *Method binding*: The process of taking a message sent to a particular receiver and finding and executing the appropriate method. The Objective-C runtime performs dynamic binding of messages to method calls.

You're probably pretty comfortable with methods, receivers, and messages because you've discussed these terms throughout this book, but what about selectors and method signatures? Let's look at these in the coming paragraphs.

Selectors

In Objective-C object messaging, a *selector* is a text string that refers to a method and can be sent to an object or a class. The Objective-C runtime uses selectors to retrieve the correct method implementation for a target object/class. A selector is represented as a text string broken up into segments, with a colon placed at the end of each segment that is followed by a parameter:

```
nameSegment1:nameSegment2:nameSegment3:
```

This selector has three segments, each of which is followed by a colon, thereby indicating that the corresponding message has three input parameters. The number of parameters for a message corresponds to the number of segments in its selector. If a message has no parameters, the selector has one segment without a colon. Some examples of valid selectors are shown in Listing 7-1.

Listing 7-1. Example Valid Selectors

```
description
description:
setValue:
sumAddend1:addend2:
sumAddend1::
```

In Objective-C source code, a message selector directly maps to one or more class/instance method declaration. Listing 7-2 depicts a class interface that includes a single instance method declaration.

Listing 7-2. Calculator Class Interface

```
@interface Calculator : NSObject
- (int) sumAddend1:(NSInteger)a1 addend2:(NSInteger)a2;
@end
```

The selector for the Calculator class instance method shown in Listing 7-2 is sumAddend1:addend2:.
If a Calculator object is instantiated and assigned to a variable named myCalculator, this instance
method is invoked using the receiver object (myCalculator) followed by the selector with the desired
input parameters, as in the following, for example:

```
[myCalculator sumAddend1:25 addend2:10];
```

OK, so this is all well and good. These examples show the role of selectors in object messaging,
but you may still be wondering how all this stuff works. You probably guessed it: the Objective-C
runtime! When your source code is compiled, the compiler (a component of the runtime) creates
data structures and function calls that support the dynamic mapping of receiver class/objects and
message selectors to method implementations. When your code is executed, the runtime library
(another component of the runtime) uses this information to find and invoke the appropriate method.
Later in this chapter, you'll review the components of the Objective-C runtime in detail.

Empty Selector Segments

If you were really paying attention in the previous section, you may have noticed one of the examples
in Listing 7-1 has a selector that looks a little different from the others; it's the example **sumAddend1::**.
For this selector, the first name segment has a text string (sumAddend1) but the second one doesn't!
Actually, a method declaration with more than one argument can have empty argument names;
hence a selector with more than one segment can have *empty selector segments* (i.e., segments
without names). Listing 7-3 extends the Calculator class interface with an instance method that
includes an empty segment.

Listing 7-3. Instance Method with Empty Selector Segment

```
@interface Calculator : NSObject
- (int) sumAddend1:(NSInteger)a1 addend2:(NSInteger)a2;
- (int) sumAddend1:(NSInteger)a1 :(NSInteger)a2;
@end
```

This instance method can be invoked with the following expression:

```
[myCalculator sumAddend1:25 :10]
```

As with any message-passing expression, each selector name segment is followed by a parameter.
In a selector with one or more empty segments, the name segment is not provided but the
parameter is still required, hence the message sumAddend1:25 :10 in the preceding example. You
won't normally see many method declarations with empty argument names (thus, empty selector
segments), because a typo in an object message used to invoke such a method could easily lead to
errors that are hard to debug.

The SEL Type

Up to this point, you have defined a selector as a text string that is part of a message in a message-
passing expression; now, you'll examine the selector type. A *selector type* (SEL) is a special
Objective-C type that represents a unique identifier that replaces a selector value when the source

code is compiled. All methods with the same selector value have the same SEL identifier. The Objective-C runtime system ensures that each selector identifier is unique. A variable of type SEL can be created using the @selector keyword.

```
SEL myMethod = @selector(myMethod);
```

So why would you create SEL variables? Well, the Objective-C runtime system (via NSObject) includes many methods that utilize variables of type SEL as parameters to dynamic methods. In addition to obtaining information about objects and classes, NSObject includes several methods for invoking a method on an object using a selector parameter. The following example uses the NSObject instance method performSelector:withObject:withObject: to invoke a method specified by the selector variable.

```
[myCalculator performSelector:@selector(sumAddend1::) withObject:[NSNumber numberWithInteger:25]
                    withObject:[NSNumber numberWithInteger:10]];
```

The @selector directive creates a selector variable at compile time. You can also create a selector at runtime with the Foundation Framework NSSelectorFromString function. In this case, the previous example is updated as follows:

```
SEL selector = NSSelectorFromString(@"sumAddend1::");
[myCalculator performSelector:selector withObject:[NSNumber numberWithInteger:25]
                    withObject:[NSNumber numberWithInteger:10]];
```

Method Signatures

Now that you have examined message receivers, selectors, and the SEL type, let's look at method signatures and their role in object messaging. A *method signature* defines the data type(s) for the input parameters of a method along with its returned result (if any). Now you may be thinking: OK, so that's all well and good, but why is this important when sending a message to an object? To understand that, let's take a moment to discuss some of the internals of how the runtime system implements object messaging.

> **Note**   In the next chapter, you are going to examine the details of the runtime system and how its dynamic behaviors (such as object messaging) are implemented. In this chapter, you focus on the runtime system architecture and not its implementation details.

The compiler translates an object message of the form [receiver message] into a (ANSI) C function call whose declaration includes the method signature. Thus, in order to generate the correct code for object messaging, the compiler needs to know both the selector value and the method signature. Now the selector is easily extracted from the object message expression, but how does the compiler determine the method signature? After all, the message may include input parameters, but you don't know how these types map to the actual method to be invoked because the receiver (and corresponding method) isn't determined until runtime. Well, to determine the correct method signature, the compiler makes a guess based on the methods it can see from the declarations it has parsed so far. If it can't find one, or there's a mismatch between the declarations it sees and the method that will actually be executed at runtime, a method signature mismatch can occur, resulting in anything from compiler warnings to runtime errors.

To demonstrate a scenario that could cause a method signature mismatch, let's say that your program uses three classes whose interfaces are as shown in Listing 7-4.

Listing 7-4. Calculator Classes Methods

```
@interface Calculator1 : NSObject
- (int) sumAddend1:(NSInteger)a1 addend2:(NSInteger)a2;
@end

@interface Calculator2 : NSObject
- (float) sumAddend1:(float)a1 addend2:(float)a2;
@end

@interface Calculator3 : NSObject
- (NSInteger) sumAddend1:(NSInteger)a1 addend2:(NSInteger)a2;
@end
```

So what happens when your code sends the message [receiver sumAddend1:25 addend2:10] where the receiver is of type id? Depending upon the interface(s) your code imports and the runtime type of the receiver (using Listing 7-4 the receiver could be of type Calculator1, Calculator2, or Calculator3), a method signature mismatch may occur. This condition can cause a variety of errors, such as stack overflow, invalid method inputs, or an invalid returned result.

This example illustrates the danger of method signature mismatch. To avoid this scenario, it's best to try to ensure that methods with different signatures also have different names.

Using Object Messaging

Now you'll create an example program to illustrate the use of selectors and the SEL type. In Xcode, create a new project by selecting **New ➤ Project ...** from the Xcode File menu. In the **New Project Assistant** pane, create a command-line application (choose **Command Line Tool** from the OS X Application selection) and click **Next**. In the **Project Options** window, specify **Calculator** for the Product Name, choose **Foundation** for the Project Type, select ARC memory management by checking the **Use Automatic Reference Counting** check box, and then click **Next**.

Specify the location in your file system where you want the project to be created (if necessary, select **New Folder** and enter the name and location for the folder), uncheck the **Source Control** check box, and then click the **Create** button.

Next, you'll create a Calculator class. Add the class to the project. Select **New ➤ File ...** from the Xcode File menu, select the **Objective-C** class template, name the class **Calculator** (in the Subclass Of drop-down list, select **NSObject**), select the **Calculator** folder for the files location and the **Calculator** project as the target, and then click the **Create** button.

You're done creating the program files, now let's implement the code. Select the **Calculator.h** file in the navigator pane, and then add the code shown in Listing 7-5.

Listing 7-5. Calculator Class Interface

```
#import <Foundation/Foundation.h>

@interface Calculator : NSObject

- (NSNumber *) sumAddend1:(NSNumber *)adder1 addend2:(NSNumber *)adder2;
- (NSNumber *) sumAddend1:(NSNumber *)adder1 :(NSNumber *)adder2;

@end
```

The Calculator class adds two instance methods: sumAddend1:addend2: and sumAddend1::. Each method takes two input parameters of type NSNumber * and returns an NSNumber *. Also note that the second parameter for the second method takes an empty argument name. Now select the **Calculator.m** file and implement the Calculator class, as shown in Listing 7-6.

Listing 7-6. Calculator Class Implementation

```
#import "Calculator.h"

@implementation Calculator

- (NSNumber *) sumAddend1:(NSNumber *)adder1 addend2:(NSNumber *)adder2
{
  NSLog(@"Invoking method on %@ object with selector %@", [self className],
      NSStringFromSelector(_cmd));
  return [NSNumber numberWithInteger:([adder1 integerValue] +
                                      [adder2 integerValue])];
}

- (NSNumber *) sumAddend1:(NSNumber *)adder1 :(NSNumber *)adder2
{
  NSLog(@"Invoking method on %@ object with selector %@", [self className],
      NSStringFromSelector(_cmd));
  return [NSNumber numberWithInteger:([adder1 integerValue] +
                                      [adder2 integerValue])];
}

@end
```

Each method simply returns the sum of the two input parameters. The methods also log to the console the class name of the (receiver) object and a selector text string. This string is obtained using the Foundation function NSStringFromSelector.

```
NSStringFromSelector(_cmd)
```

The input parameter for this function is a variable of type SEL. So what's this _cmd parameter and where did it come from? Well, _cmd is an implicit parameter (available in the implementation of every Objective-C method but not declared in its interface) that holds the selector of the message being sent. Thus, the expression NSStringFromSelector(_cmd) returns a text string for the selector of the method being invoked.

You've implemented the `Calculator` class, now let's implement the `main()` function. Select the **main.m** file in the navigator pane and then update the `main()` function, as shown in Listing 7-7.

Listing 7-7. Calculator main() Function Implementation

```
#import <Foundation/Foundation.h>
#import "Calculator.h"

int main(int argc, const char * argv[])
{
  @autoreleasepool
  {
    Calculator *calc = [[Calculator alloc] init];
    NSNumber *addend1 = [NSNumber numberWithInteger:25];
    NSNumber *addend2 = [NSNumber numberWithInteger:10];
    NSNumber *addend3 = [NSNumber numberWithInteger:15];
    NSLog(@"Sum of %@ + %@ = %@", addend1, addend2,
        [calc sumAddend1:addend1 addend2:addend2]);
    NSLog(@"Sum of %@ + %@ = %@", addend1, addend3,
        [calc sumAddend1:addend1 :addend3]);
  }
  return 0;
}
```

The `main()` function creates a `Calculator` object and uses it to add two numbers, logging the result to the output pane. When you compile and run the program, the output should look like Figure 7-3.

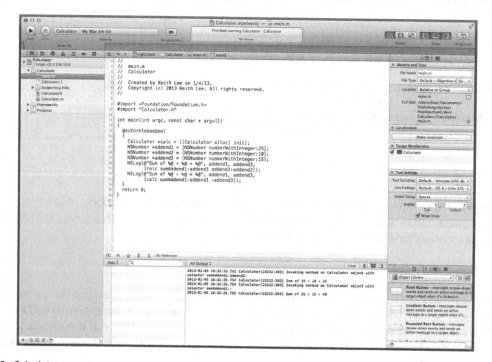

Figure 7-3. Calculator program

Now let's add code to invoke a dynamic method on an object. You'll use the `NSObject` instance method `performSelector:withObject:withObject:`, which requires a selector input parameter. Update the `main()` function as shown in Listing 7-8.

Listing 7-8. main() Function Using the performSelector: Method

```objc
#import <Foundation/Foundation.h>
#import "Calculator.h"

int main(int argc, const char * argv[])
{
  @autoreleasepool
  {
    Calculator *calc = [[Calculator alloc] init];
    NSNumber *addend1 = [NSNumber numberWithInteger:25];
    NSNumber *addend2 = [NSNumber numberWithInteger:10];
    NSNumber *addend3 = [NSNumber numberWithInteger:15];

    SEL selector1 = @selector(sumAddend1:addend2:);
    id sum1 = [calc performSelector:selector1 withObject:addend1
                withObject:addend2];
    NSLog(@"Sum of %@ + %@ = %@", addend1, addend2, sum1);

    SEL selector2 = NSSelectorFromString(@"sumAddend1::");
    id sum2 = [calc performSelector:selector2 withObject:addend1
                withObject:addend3];
    NSLog(@"Sum of %@ + %@ = %@", addend1, addend3, sum2);
  }
  return 0;
}
```

The code creates a selector for each instance method and then computes the sum of the two numbers using the NSObject `performSelector:withObject:withObject:` method. The first selector is created using the `@selector` directive, thus, at compile time. The second selector is created at runtime using the Foundation function `NSSelectorFromString`. The results of the method invocation are logged to the output pane. OK, this all looks good—but wait a minute, when you compile the program now, you see a couple of warnings in the `main()` function (see Figure 7-4).

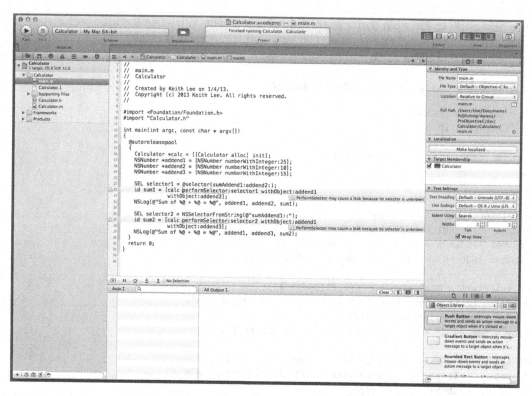

Figure 7-4. *Calculator program selector warning*

This warning, *PerformSelector may cause a leak because its selector is unknown*, is generated because the method will throw an exception if no method matching the selector is found, potentially causing a memory leak. You can remove this warning by adding pragma directives to the code (shown in bold in Listing 7-9).

Listing 7-9. Pragma Directives for performSelector: Warnings

```
#pragma clang diagnostic push
#pragma clang diagnostic ignored "-Warc-performSelector-leaks"
    SEL selector1 = @selector(sumAddend1:addend2:);
    id sum1 = [calc performSelector:selector1 withObject:addend1
            withObject:addend2];
    NSLog(@"Sum of %@ + %@ = %@", addend1, addend2, sum1);

    SEL selector2 = NSSelectorFromString(@"sumAddend1::");
    id sum2 = [calc performSelector:selector2 withObject:addend1
            withObject:addend3];
    NSLog(@"Sum of %@ + %@ = %@", addend1, addend3, sum2);
#pragma clang diagnostic pop
```

The pragma directive clang diagnostic ignored is used to disable specific compiler warnings. The syntax for this directive is

```
#pragma clang diagnostic ignored "DiagnosticName"
```

The name of the diagnostic is specified within double quotes. In this case, the diagnostic -Warc-performSelector-leaks disables compiler warnings for a potential memory leak when invoking the performSelector:withObject:withObject: method. The pragma clang diagnostic push and pragma clang diagnostic pop directives are used to save and restore the current compiler diagnostic settings. This ensures that the compiler will continue with its usual compiler options when compiling the rest of the source file. When you compile and run the program now, you should see expected output without the compiler warnings (see Figure 7-5).

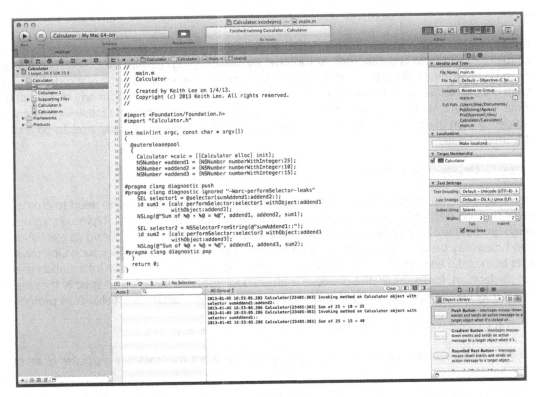

Figure 7-5. Calculator program using performSelector

Great job. Now that you've covered object messaging, selectors, and method signatures in detail, let's examine the other dynamic features of the runtime.

Dynamic Typing

Dynamic typing enables the runtime to determine the type of an object at runtime; thereby letting runtime factors dictate what kind of object is to be used in your code. This is particularly beneficial when it isn't known in advance the type of object that needs to be assigned to a variable, such as when passing arguments to methods. Objective-C supports both static and dynamic typing. When a variable is statically typed, its type is specified upon variable declaration. For example, the following statement declares that the variable myAtom is a pointer to an object of type Atom.

```
Atom *myAtom;
```

With static typing, the compiler can perform type checking at compile time and thus detect type errors prior to program execution. With dynamic typing, on the other hand, type checking is performed at runtime. Objective-C provides support for dynamic typing via the id data type. The id type is a unique Objective-C type that can hold a pointer to any type of Objective-C object, regardless of its class. The following statement declares that the variable myAtom is a pointer to an object of type id.

```
id *myAtom;
```

Hence, the variable myAtom may actually point to an object of type Atom, Hydrogen, and so forth—the actual type of the variable is determined at runtime. Dynamic typing permits associations between objects to be determined at runtime rather than forcing them to be encoded in a static design. This can make it much easier to write a single method that can handle an object from any class, rather than write a different method for each class in an application. For example, the following instance method declaration uses dynamic typing, thereby enabling the single input parameter to be an object from any class.

```
- (NSInteger) computeValue:(id)parameter;
```

Dynamic typing can be used to simplify your class interfaces because there is no need to create a different method declaration for each possible input parameter type. Dynamic typing also gives you much greater flexibility because the types used by a program can evolve during its execution and new types may be introduced without the need to recompile or redeploy. Because Objective-C supports both static and dynamic typing, you can provide different levels of type information to a method declaration; for example, the previous method declaration is modified to specify that the input parameter may be an object of any type that conforms to the NSDecimalNumberBehaviors protocol.

```
- (NSInteger) computeValue:(id<NSDecimalNumberBehaviors>)parameter;
```

Next, the method declaration is modified to specify that the input parameter is a pointer to an object of type NSNumber.

```
- (NSInteger) computeValue:(NSNumber *)parameter;
```

Finally, the method declaration is further refined to specify that the input parameter is a pointer to an object of type NSNumber that conforms to the NSDecimalNumberBehaviors protocol.

```
- (NSInteger) computeValue:(NSNumber<NSDecimalNumberBehaviors> *)parameter;
```

Objective-C also provides APIs for runtime object introspection (for example, asking a dynamically typed, anonymous object what its class is) to partially mitigate the loss of static type checks. Introspection enables the runtime to verify the type of an object and thus validate its suitability for a particular operation. You'll learn about object introspection later in this chapter.

Dynamic Binding

Dynamic binding is the process of mapping a message to a method at runtime, rather than at compile time. In effect, the message and the object receiving the message aren't set until the program is running and the message is sent. Since the same method could be implemented by potentially many (receiver) objects, the exact method invoked can vary dynamically. Dynamic binding thus enables OOP polymorphism. Dynamic binding allows new objects and code to be interfaced with or added to a system without affecting existing code, therefore decreasing coupling between objects. It also enables a reduction in program complexity by eliminating the need for conditional logic to handle multiple-choice scenarios (typically implemented with a switch statement). Dynamic binding implies the use of dynamic typing. In the following code fragment, the variable atom of type id is sent the message logInfo.

```
id atom = [[Hydrogen alloc] initWithNeutrons:1];
[atom logInfo];
```

When this code executes, the runtime determines the actual type of the variable atom (via dynamic typing), and then uses the message selector (logInfo) to map the message to a corresponding instance method implementation for the receiver object atom. In this case, the variable atom resolves to the type Hydrogen *, hence the runtime searches for a Hydrogen instance method logInfo. If none is found, it searches for a corresponding instance method in its superclass. The runtime continues searching the class hierarchy until it finds the instance method (see Figure 7-6).

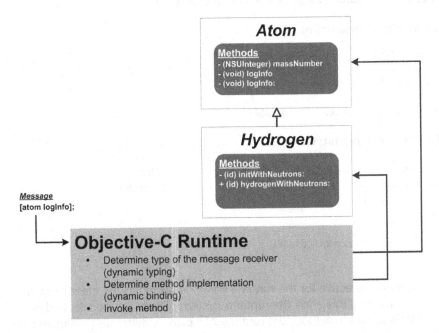

Figure 7-6. Objective-C dynamic binding

Dynamic binding is an inherent feature of Objective-C and it doesn't require any special APIs. Dynamic binding even allows the message that's sent (the message *selector*) to be a variable determined at runtime.

Dynamic Method Resolution

Dynamic method resolution enables you to provide the implementation of a method dynamically. Objective-C includes the @dynamic directive, which tells the compiler that the methods associated with a property will be provided dynamically. The Apple Core Data Framework makes use of the @dynamic directive to generate efficient attribute accessor methods and relationship accessor methods for managed object classes.

The NSObject class includes the methods resolveInstanceMethod: and resolveClassMethod: to dynamically provide an implementation for a given selector for an instance and class method, respectively. You override one or both of these methods to dynamically implement instance/class methods. In the next section, you'll learn how to use these methods by developing code to dynamically resolve a method implementation for a selector.

Providing a Method Implementation Dynamically

Now you're going to demonstrate dynamic method resolution by updating the Calculator program to dynamically provide the implementation of a method. Start Xcode (if not already started) and open the Calculator project by selecting **Open Recent ➤ Calculator.xcodeproj** from the Xcode File menu. First, you'll update the Calculator class implementation. Select the **Calculator.m** file in the navigator pane and then update the Calculator implementation by overriding the resolveInstanceMethod: class method, as shown in Listing 7-10.

Listing 7-10. Calculator Class Dynamic Method

```
#import <objc/runtime.h>
...
+ (BOOL) resolveInstanceMethod:(SEL)aSEL
{
  NSString *method = NSStringFromSelector(aSEL);

  if ([method hasPrefix:@"absoluteValue"])
  {
    class_addMethod([self class], aSEL, (IMP)absoluteValue, "@@:@");
    NSLog(@"Dynamically added instance method %@ to class %@", method,
          [self className]);
    return YES;
  }
  return [super resolveInstanceMethod:aSEL];
}
```

In Listing 7-10, an import directive for the runtime library is added to the class implementation (#import <objc/runtime.h>); this adds the runtime system APIs to your code. In the resolveInstanceMethod: class method, the runtime API class_addMethod() is used to dynamically add a function as an instance method to a class. This function takes as its input parameters the class the method will be added to, the selector for the new method, the address for the function, and an array of characters that describe the types of the arguments to the method. As you can see from

Listing 7-10, the function being added as an instance method is called absoluteValue; it takes an id as its input parameter and returns an id as its result. Now let's add the absoluteValue() function to the Calculator class implementation. Add the code shown in Listing 7-11.

Listing 7-11. Calculator Class Dynamic Method

```
id absoluteValue(id self, SEL _cmd, id value)
{
  NSInteger intVal = [value integerValue];
  if (intVal < 0)
  {
    return [NSNumber numberWithInteger:(intVal * -1)];
  }
  return value;
}
```

Notice that the function's input parameters include the implicit parameters self and _cmd; self is the receiving object and _cmd is the selector for the method.

Now let's update the main() function to test dynamic method resolution. Select the **main.m** file from the navigator pane and update the function, as shown in Listing 7-12.

Listing 7-12. Calculator Class main() Function with Dynamic Method

```
#import <Foundation/Foundation.h>
#import "Calculator.h"

int main(int argc, const char * argv[])
{
  @autoreleasepool
  {
    Calculator *calc = [[Calculator alloc] init];
    NSNumber *addend1 = [NSNumber numberWithInteger:-25];
    NSNumber *addend2 = [NSNumber numberWithInteger:10];
    NSNumber *addend3 = [NSNumber numberWithInteger:15];

#pragma clang diagnostic push
#pragma clang diagnostic ignored "-Warc-performSelector-leaks"
    SEL selector1 = @selector(sumAddend1:addend2:);
    id sum1 = [calc performSelector:selector1 withObject:addend1
              withObject:addend2];
    NSLog(@"Sum of %@ + %@ = %@", addend1, addend2, sum1);

    SEL selector2 = NSSelectorFromString(@"sumAddend1::");
    id sum2 = [calc performSelector:selector2 withObject:addend1
              withObject:addend3];
    NSLog(@"Sum of %@ + %@ = %@", addend1, addend3, sum2);

    SEL selector3 = NSSelectorFromString(@"absoluteValue:");
    NSLog(@"Invoking instance method %@ on object of class %@",
        NSStringFromSelector(selector3), [calc className]);
```

```
    id sum3 = [calc performSelector:selector3 withObject:sum2];
    NSLog(@"Absolute value of %@ = %@", sum2, sum3);
#pragma clang diagnostic pop
  }
  return 0;
}
```

The code dynamically creates a selector for the new method and then invokes an instance method using the selector. Dynamic resolution causes the method to be added to the runtime and invoked, returning its result. The result is then displayed in the output pane. Now save, compile, and run the updated Calculator program and observe the messages in the output pane (see Figure 7-7).

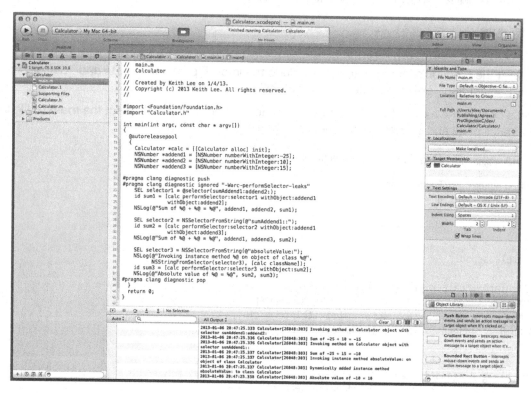

Figure 7-7. Objective-C dynamic method resolution

As you can observe in the output pane, the new method (`absoluteValue:`) is added to the `Calculator` class by the Objective-C runtime when the message using the selector `absoluteValue:` is dynamically invoked via the method `performSelector:withObject:`. As shown by this example, dynamic method resolution can be used to add methods to classes at runtime.

Dynamic Loading

Dynamic loading enables an Objective-C program to load both executable code and resources, as they are needed, instead of having to load all program components at application startup. The executable code (which is linked prior to loading) can contain new classes that become integrated into the runtime image of the program. This *lazy-loading* of program code and resources improves overall performance by placing lower memory demands on the system. This also enhances program extensibility because new software can be added dynamically without change to an existing program. Apple provides the bundle mechanism to support the dynamic loading of software on the iOS and OS X platforms.

A bundle is a software delivery mechanism. It consists of a directory with a standardized hierarchical structure that holds executable code and the resources used by that code. A bundle can contain executable code, images, sound files, or any other type of code or resource. It also contains a runtime configuration file called the information property list (Info.plist). Bundles define the basic structure for organizing the code and resources associated with your software; they come in several types:

- *Application bundle*: An application bundle manages the code and resources associated with a process (e.g., a program).

- *Framework bundle*: A framework bundle manages a dynamic shared library and its associated resources, such as header files. Applications can link against one or more frameworks, for example the Foundation Framework.

- *Loadable bundle*: A loadable bundle (also referred to as a plug-in) is a type of bundle that an application can use to load custom code dynamically.

The Foundation Framework NSBundle class can be used to manage bundles. An NSBundle object represents a location in the file system that groups code and resources that can be used in a program. Listing 7-13 uses an NSBundle object to dynamically load the path of an application's information property list named Info.plist.

Listing 7-13. Dynamically Loading a Property List File

```
NSBundle *bundle = [NSBundle mainBundle];
NSString *bundlePath = [bundle pathForResource:@"Info" ofType:@"plist"];
```

As mentioned, bundles can be used to dynamically load executable code. Listing 7-14 uses an NSBundle object to dynamically load a framework bundle and then create an instance of a class from the framework.

Listing 7-14. Dynamically Loading a Framework Object

```
NSBundle *testBundle = [NSBundle bundleWithPath:@"/Test.bundle"];
id tester = [[[bundle classNamed:@"Tester"] alloc] init];
```

Introspection

The Foundation Framework NSObject APIs include numerous methods for performing object introspection. These methods dynamically query the runtime for the following types of information:

- Information about methods
- Testing object inheritance, behavior, and conformance

Because Objective-C defers much of its behaviors to the runtime, rather than compile or link time, object introspection can be a critical capability to help you avoid runtime errors such as message-dispatch errors, erroneous assumptions of object equality, and other problems.

The following statement uses the NSObject isKindOfClass: method to test whether the receiver of a message is an instance of the Calculator class or an instance of any class that inherits from the Calculator class.

```
BOOL isCalculator = [myObject isKindOfClass: [Calculator class]];
```

The next statement checks whether an object responds to a selector; that is, whether it implements or inherits a method that can respond to a specified message.

```
BOOL responds = [myObject respondsToSelector:@selector(sumAddend1::)];
```

The next statement checks whether an object conforms to a given protocol.

```
BOOL conforms = [myObject conformsToProtocol:@protocol(MyProtocol)];
```

The following statement obtains the method signature for a selector.

```
NSMethodSignature *signature = [myObject methodSignatureForSelector:@selector(sumAddend1::)];
```

This is just a sample of the NSObject methods for performing object introspection. In Part 3 of this book, you'll look at the NSObject APIs in more detail.

Roundup

In this chapter, you examined in detail the features of the Objective-C runtime and reviewed the key components of the runtime system architecture. To recap, the following are the key takeaways:

- Objective-C message passing (e.g., object messaging) is used to invoke methods on both classes and objects. Object messaging is implemented as a dynamic feature—the actual type of the receiver of the message and the corresponding method to be invoked on the receiver is determined at runtime.

- A message-passing expression consists of a receiver (the target object/class of the message) and the message itself. The message is composed of a selector along with any corresponding input parameters.

- A selector is represented as a text string broken up into segments, with a colon placed at the end of each segment that is followed by a parameter. A selector with more than one segment can have empty selector segments (i.e., segments without names).

- A selector type (SEL) is a special Objective-C type that represents a unique identifier that replaces a selector value when the source code is compiled. A variable of type SEL can be created using the @selector keyword or with the Foundation Framework function NSSelectorFromString().

- A *method signature* defines the data type(s) for the input parameters of a method along with its returned result (if any). Method signature mismatch—where the compiler can't determine the appropriate method for an object message, or there's a mismatch between the declarations it sees and the method that will actually be executed at runtime—can result in anything from compiler warnings to runtime errors. To avoid this scenario, it's best to try to ensure that methods with different signatures also have different names.

- Dynamic typing enables the runtime to determine the type of an object at runtime, thereby letting runtime factors dictate what kind of object is to be used in your code. Objective-C provides support for dynamic typing via the id data type.

- Dynamic binding is the process of mapping a message to a method at runtime, rather than at compile time. Dynamic binding enables OOP polymorphism and allows new objects and code to be interfaced with or added to a system without affecting existing code, therefore decreasing coupling between objects.

- Dynamic method resolution enables you to provide the implementation of a method dynamically. Objective-C includes the @dynamic directive, which tells the compiler that the methods associated with a property will be provided dynamically. The NSObject class includes the methods resolveInstanceMethod: and resolveClassMethod: to dynamically provide an implementation for a given selector for an instance and class method, respectively.

- Dynamic loading enables an Objective-C program to load both executable code and resources, as they are needed, instead of having to load all program components at application startup. Apple provides the bundle mechanism to support the dynamic loading of software on the iOS and OS X platforms. The Foundation Framework NSBundle class can be used to manage bundles. An NSBundle object represents a location in the file system that groups code and resources that can be used in a program.

- The Foundation Framework NSObject APIs include numerous methods for performing object introspection. These APIs dynamically query the runtime for information about methods. They also perform tests for object inheritance, behavior, and conformance.

Now that you know the features of the runtime system and how they can be used in your programs, let's examine the runtime system's architecture and implementation. When you're ready, turn the page to begin!

Chapter 8

Runtime Architecture

The runtime system is a key element of the Objective-C platform. It's what implements the dynamic features and object-oriented capabilities of the language. Its structure enables you to develop Objective-C code without being exposed to the internals of the runtime, yet also provides a public API that enables you to write code to directly invoke runtime services.

In the last chapter, you reviewed the dynamic features of Objective-C; in this one, you'll explore the architecture and design of the runtime system and how it implements these features. You'll identify the runtime's major components, examine key implementation details, and then look at how your code interacts with the runtime, both at compile time and during program execution. By the end of this chapter, you'll have a thorough understanding of the function of the runtime system in the Objective-C language.

Runtime Components

The Objective-C runtime system has two main components: the compiler and the runtime library. Let's take out a magnifying glass to examine these in more detail and see how they are used to implement the runtime system.

Compiler

In Chapter 5, you briefly reviewed the general process of Objective-C source code compilation. As depicted in Figure 5-1, the compilation process takes input Objective-C source files and proceeds, in multiple phases (consisting of lexical analysis, syntax analysis, code generation and optimization, assembly, and linking operations), to produce the output binaries that form an executable program.

Just as the C standard library provides a standard API and implementation for the C programming language, the runtime library provides a standard API and implementation for the object-oriented features of Objective-C. This library is linked (during the linking phase) to all Objective-C programs. It's the job of the compiler to take your input source code and generate code that uses the runtime library to produce a valid, executable Objective-C program.

Both the object-oriented elements and dynamic features of the Objective-C language are implemented by the runtime system. Together, this consists of the following:

- Class elements (interface, implementation, protocols, categories, methods, properties, instance variables)
- Class instances (objects)
- Object messaging (including dynamic typing and binding)
- Dynamic method resolution
- Dynamic loading
- Object introspection

In summary, when the compiler parses Objective-C source code that uses these language elements and features, it generates code with the appropriate runtime library data structures and function calls to implement the language-specified behaviors. To clarify how this works, let's look at a few examples that demonstrate how the compiler generates code for Objective-C classes and objects, and how it performs object messaging.

Object Messaging Code Generation

When the compiler parses an object message (a *message send* expression), such as

```
[receiver message]
```

for example, it generates code that calls the runtime library function objc_msgSend(). This function takes as its input parameters the receiver and the selector of the message, along with any parameters passed in the message. Thus the compiler converts each messaging expression in the source code (i.e., of the form [receiver message]) to a call on the runtime library messaging function objc_msgSend(...), passing along any supplied parameters to the call. Each message is dynamically resolved, meaning that the message receiver type and the actual method implementation to be invoked are determined at runtime. For each class and object in the source code, the compiler builds the data structures required to perform object messaging.

Class and Object Code Generation

When the compiler parses Objective-C code containing class definitions and objects, it generates corresponding runtime data structures. An Objective-C class corresponds to a runtime library Class data type. According to the Apple Runtime Reference, the Class data type is a pointer to an opaque type with an identifier of objc_class.

```
typedef struct objc_class *Class;
```

An *opaque data type* is a C struct type that is incompletely defined in its interface. Opaque types provide a form of data hiding, in that their variables can only be accessed through functions designed specifically for them. Runtime library functions are used to access the variables of the Class (i.e., objc_class) data type.

Just as Objective-C classes have a runtime data type, Objective-C objects also have a corresponding runtime data type. When the compiler parses Objective-C code for objects, it generates code that creates a runtime object type. This data type, defined in Listing 8-1, is a C struct with an identifier of objc_object.

Listing 8-1. objc_object Data Type

```
struct objc_object
{
  Class isa;
  /* ...variable length data containing instance variable values...  */
};
```

When you create an object, memory is allocated for an objc_object type that consists of an isa pointer directly followed by the data for the instance variables of the object.

Note that, as with the Class data type, the objc_object type contains a variable named isa of type Class; in other words, a pointer to a variable of type objc_class. In fact, the runtime data type for all Objective-C objects and classes begin with an isa pointer. The runtime equivalent for the Objective-C id type is a C struct defined as a pointer to an objc_object, for example.

Listing 8-2. id Type Definition

```
typedef struct objc_object
{
  Class isa;
} *id;
```

In other words, an id is just a pointer to a C struct with the identifier objc_object. The runtime data structure for Objective-C block objects follows the same convention, thereby enabling them to also be properly managed by the runtime system.

Viewing Runtime Data Structures

Before you go any further with these concepts, let's create an example that will allow you to see how Objective-C objects and classes map to the runtime data structures discussed earlier. In Xcode, create a new project by selecting **New ➤ Project ...** from the Xcode File menu. In the **New Project Assistant** pane, create a command-line application (choose **Command Line Tool** from the Mac OS X Application selection) and click **Next**. In the **Project Options** window, specify **Runspector** for the Product Name, choose **Foundation** for the Project Type, select ARC memory management by checking the **Use Automatic Reference Counting** check box, and then click **Next**.

Specify the location in your file system where you want the project to be created (if necessary, select **New Folder** and enter the name and location for the folder), uncheck the **Source Control** check box, and then click the **Create** button.

Now let's implement the code. Select the **main.m** file in the navigator pane, and then add the code shown in Listing 8-3.

Listing 8-3. Runspector main.m File

```
#import <Foundation/Foundation.h>
#import <objc/runtime.h>


// Test class 1
@interface TestClass1 : NSObject { @public int myInt; }
@end
@implementation TestClass1
@end

int main(int argc, const char * argv[])
{
  @autoreleasepool
  {
    // Create a few instances of one class and display its data
    TestClass1 *tc1A = [[TestClass1 alloc] init];
    tc1A->myInt = 0xa5a5a5a5;
    TestClass1 *tc1B = [[TestClass1 alloc] init];
    tc1B->myInt = 0xc3c3c3c3;
    long tc1Size = class_getInstanceSize([TestClass1 class]);
    NSData *obj1Data = [NSData dataWithBytes:(__bridge const void *)(tc1A)
                                     length:tc1Size];
    NSData *obj2Data = [NSData dataWithBytes:(__bridge const void *)(tc1B)
                                     length:tc1Size];
    NSLog(@"TestClass1 object tc1 contains %@", obj1Data);
    NSLog(@"TestClass1 object tc2 contains %@", obj2Data);
    NSLog(@"TestClass1 memory address = %p", [TestClass1 class]);
  }
  return 0;
}
```

OK, let's review this code. At the beginning of the `main.m` file, observe the import statement

```
#import <objc/runtime.h>
```

This statement is required to include the runtime library APIs in the file. Immediately after the import statements, the code defines the class `TestClass1`. This simple class has no methods and a single public instance variable. In the `main()` function, two `TestClass1` objects are created and initialized, with the instance variable for each assigned a value. After the objects are created, the Foundation Framework `NSData` class is used to retrieve the data (in bytes) for each object. The Runtime Library function `class_getInstanceSize()` is used to retrieve the size (in bytes) of a class instance. Once the data is retrieved, it is displayed in the output pane using the Foundation Framework `NSLog` function. When you compile and run the program, you should observe output similar to that shown in Figure 8-1.

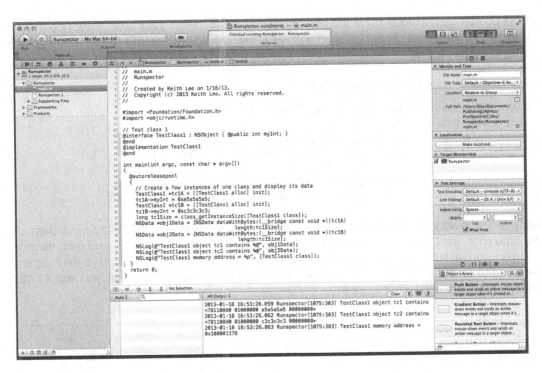

Figure 8-1. Runspector program, object inspection

In the output pane, the TestClass1 objects contain the data in Listing 8-4.

Listing 8-4. TestClass1 Output from Runspector Program

```
TestClass1 object tc1 contains <78110000 01000000 a5a5a5a5 00000000>
TestClass1 object tc2 contains <78110000 01000000 c3c3c3c3 00000000>
TestClass1 memory address = 0x100001178
```

Let's analyze this data. It was shown in Listing 8-2 that when the compiler parses an object, it generates an instance of an objc_object type whose contents consist of an isa pointer and the values of the object's instance variables. So, looking at the output from the program (see Listing 8-4), the data for TestClass1 object 1 (tc1) contains two items: an isa pointer (78110000 01000000) and the value assigned to its instance variable (a5a5a5a5 00000000). Similarly, the data for TestClass1 object 2 (tc2) contains an isa pointer (78110000 01000000) and the value assigned to its instance variable (c3c3c3c3 00000000). Notice that the first item in the object's objc_object data structure is its isa pointer. Also notice that the isa pointer for both instances is the same. This is as expected since they are instances of the same class and hence should have the same pointer value. Now an isa pointer points to the address in memory of a class, as shown by the last line of Listing 8-4.

```
TestClass1 memory address = 0x100001178
```

You may be thinking, "That memory address isn't the same as the value shown for the isa pointer!" Well actually it is: the Mac Pro computer on which this program was run is *little-endian*, which means that it reverses the order of bytes as stored in memory. Thus, the byte order of the address displayed by the isa pointer (0x78110000 01) is the reverse of the actual memory address. Well, hopefully this is all starting to make more sense. Let's go a little further. Update the main() function by adding the code shown in Listing 8-5.

Listing 8-5. Runspector main() Function, Class Data Type

```
// Retrieve and display the data for the TestClass1 class object
id testClz = objc_getClass("TestClass1");
long tcSize = class_getInstanceSize([testClz class]);
NSData *tcData = [NSData dataWithBytes:(__bridge const void *)(testClz)
                               length:tcSize];
NSLog(@"TestClass1 class contains %@", tcData);
NSLog(@"TestClass1 superclass memory address = %p", [TestClass1 superclass]);
```

In Listing 8-5, you added code to retrieve and display the data bytes for the TestClass1 class object. The runtime objc_getClass() function is used to retrieve the TestClass1 class, and then its data is displayed with an NSData instance and the NSLog function. The code also displays the memory address for the TestClass1 superclass. When you compile and run the program, you should observe output similar to that shown in Figure 8-2.

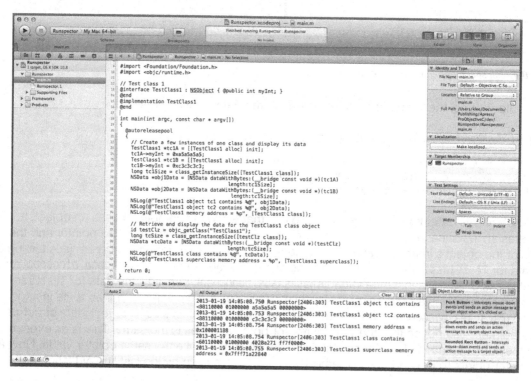

Figure 8-2. Runspector program, object and class inspection

The output pane displays the results shown in Listing 8-6.

Listing 8-6. TestClass1 Output from Runspector Program

```
TestClass1 object tc1 contains <88110000 01000000 a5a5a5a5 00000000>
TestClass1 object tc2 contains <88110000 01000000 c3c3c3c3 00000000>
TestClass1 memory address = 0x100001188
TestClass class contains <60110000 01000000 4028a271 ff7f0000>
TestClass1 superclass memory address = 0x7fff71a22840
```

The data of `TestClass1` objects are consistent with what you observed before—each contains an isa pointer and the value assigned to its instance variable. The data for the `TestClass1` class object consists of an isa pointer (`60110000  01000000`) and another value (`4028a271  ff7f0000`). This additional value is actually the pointer to the object's superclass. Earlier, you learned that the data structure for a class has an isa pointer (refer back to Listing 8-1), so this result is also consistent with the expected values. The memory address listed for the superclass confirms what you see in the data for the class object.

Well, you should now have a good understanding of the role of the compiler within the Objective-C runtime. You also implemented a program that used a few of the runtime APIs to inspect the data structures generated by the compiler. Great job! Now let's move on to runtime library and examine some of its implementation details.

Runtime Library

The Apple Objective-C runtime library implements the object-oriented features and dynamic properties of the Objective-C language. For the most part, the runtime library acts behind the scenes, but it also includes a public API that enables it to be used directly in your code.

This API is expressed in C and consists of a set of functions, data types, and language constants. You learned about some of the key runtime data types (e.g., `objc_object`, `objc_class`) and used a few of these functions in the previous section. Overall, the runtime library data types can be grouped as follows:

- Class definition data structures (`class`, `method`, `ivar`, `category`, `IMP`, `SEL`, etc.)
- Instance data types (`id`, `objc_object`, `objc_super`)
- Values (`BOOL`)

The functions fall into the following categories:

- Object messaging
- Class functions
- Instance functions
- Protocol functions
- Method functions
- Property functions
- Selector functions

The runtime library also defines several Boolean constants (YES, NO) and null values (NULL, nil, Nil).

The runtime library public API is declared in the runtime.h header file. Apple's runtime library is available for examination at http://opensource.apple.com. It incorporates a variety of design elements and system services to provide excellent performance and extensibility as the Objective-C language evolves over time. Later in this chapter, you'll look at elements of the runtime library implementation. For now, let's get a little hands-on experience by developing a program that uses these APIs.

Creating a Class Using the Runtime Library APIs

Now you are going to create a program that dynamically creates a class using the runtime APIs. In Xcode, create a new project by selecting **New ➤ Project ...** from the Xcode File menu. In the **New Project Assistant** pane, create a command-line application (choose **Command Line Tool** from the Mac OS X Application selection) and click **Next**. In the **Project Options** window, specify **DynaClass** for the Product Name, choose **Foundation** for the Project Type, select ARC memory management by checking the **Use Automatic Reference Counting** check box, and then click **Next**.

Specify the location in your file system where you want the project to be created (if necessary, select **New Folder** and enter the name and location for the folder), uncheck the **Source Control** check box, and then click the **Create** button.

OK, now let's implement the code. Select the **main.m** file in the navigator pane, and then add the code shown in Listing 8-7.

Listing 8-7. DynaClass main.m File

```
#import <Foundation/Foundation.h>
#import <objc/runtime.h>
#import <objc/message.h>

NSString *greeting(id self, SEL _cmd)
{
  return [NSString  stringWithFormat: @"Hello, World!"];
}

int main(int argc, const char * argv[])
{
  @autoreleasepool
  {
    // Dynamically create a class
    Class dynaClass = objc_allocateClassPair([NSObject class], "DynaClass", 0);

    // Dynamically add a method, use existing method (description) to retrieve signature
    Method description = class_getInstanceMethod([NSObject class], @selector(description));
    const char *types = method_getTypeEncoding(description);
    class_addMethod(dynaClass, @selector(greeting), (IMP)greeting, types);

    // Register the class
    objc_registerClassPair(dynaClass);
```

```
    // Now use the class - create an instance and send it a message
    id dynaObj = [[dynaClass alloc] init];
    NSLog(@"%@", objc_msgSend(dynaObj, NSSelectorFromString(@"greeting")));

  }
  return 0;
}
```

Note this additional import statement at the top of the file:

```
#import <objc/message.h>
```

This statement is required to include the runtime library messaging API (e.g., objc_msgSend()) in the file. Immediately after the import statements, the code defines the function greeting() that returns a simple greeting. This function will be used for the method implementation that will be dynamically added to the class. The main() function contains the logic for creating a new class using the runtime API. It creates a class pair (the class and its metaclass), adds a method to it that points to the greeting() function defined earlier, and then registers the class pair in the runtime, thereby enabling you to create instances of the class. Notice that the method signature is obtained by using that of a method (the NSObject description method) with the same signature. The next few lines create an instance of the class and send it a message, with the output from the method invocation logged to the output pane. When you compile and run the program, you should observe output similar to that shown in Figure 8-3.

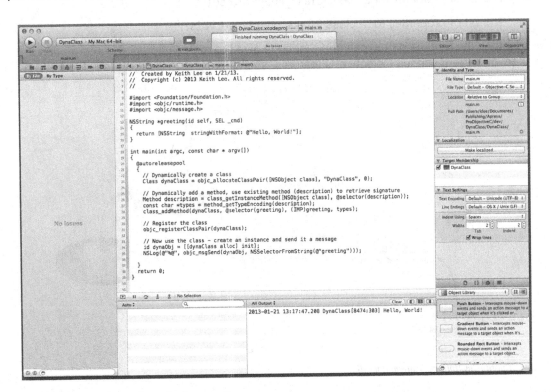

Figure 8-3. DynaClass program, dynamic class creation

Great job! You have now completed your overview of the runtime APIs and their usage. Please refer to the Apple Runtime Reference for a complete definition of these APIs. Now let's examine some of the runtime library design and implementation details.

Implementing Runtime Object Messaging

The runtime library includes functions that provide access to the following information (the functions are identified in parentheses):

- The class definition of an object (`objc_getClass`)
- The superclass for a class (`class_getSuperclass`)
- The metaclass definition of an object (`objc_getMetaClass`)
- The name of a class (`class_getName`)
- The version information for a class (`class_getVersion`)
- The size of a class in bytes (`class_getInstanceSize`)
- The list of instance variables for a class (`class_copyIvarList`)
- The list of methods for a class (`class_copyMethodList`)
- The list of protocols for a class (`class_copyProtocolList`)
- The list of properties for a class (`class_copyProperyList`)

Taken together, the runtime data types and functions give the runtime library the information it requires to implement various Objective-C features, such as object messaging (see Figure 8-4).

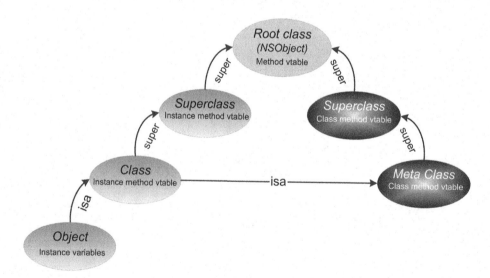

Figure 8-4. Runtime system messaging operation

When you send a message to an object, the runtime looks up the instance methods for the class via custom code that leverages the class method cache and its vtable. It searches the entire class hierarchy for the corresponding method, and when found, jumps to the method implementation. The runtime library includes numerous design mechanisms to implement object messaging. You'll look at a few of these, beginning with vtables.

Method Lookup via vtables

The runtime library defines a method data type (objc_method), as shown in Listing 8-7.

Listing 8-7. Runtime Library Method Data Type

```
struct objc_method
{
  SEL method_name;
  char * method_types;
  IMP method_imp;
};
typedef objc_method Method;
```

method_name is a variable of type SEL that describes the method name; method_types describe the data types of the parameters of the method; and method_imp is a variable of type IMP that provides the address of the function invoked when the method is selected for invocation (recall that Objective-C methods are, in fact, C functions that take at least two arguments: self and _cmd). Because method invocation occurs potentially millions of times during the execution of a program, the runtime system requires a fast, efficient mechanism for method lookup and invocation. A *vtable*, also called a *dispatch table*, is a mechanism commonly used in programming languages to support dynamic binding. The Objective-C runtime library implements a custom vtable dispatching mechanism designed to maximize both performance and flexibility. A *vtable* is an array of IMPs (Objective-C method implementations). Every runtime Class instance (objc_class) has a pointer to a vtable.

Each Class instance also includes a cache of pointers to recently used methods. This provides performance optimization for method calls. The logic implemented by the runtime library to perform method lookup is shown in Figure 8-5.

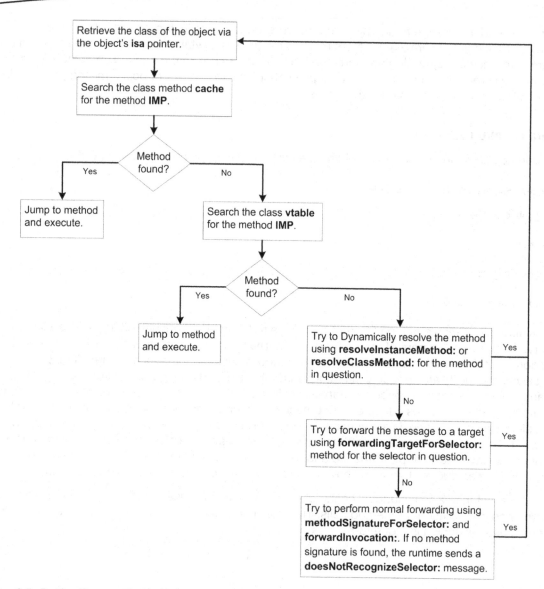

Figure 8-5. Runtime library method lookup

In Figure 8-5, the runtime library first searches the cache for the method IMP (pointer to the start of the method implementation). If not found, it then looks for the method IMP in its vtable, and if found, the IMP is then stored in the cache for future lookups. This design enables the runtime to perform a fast and an efficient method lookup.

Selector Uniquing via the dyld Shared Cache

The startup overhead for an Objective-C program is directly proportional to the amount of time required for *selector uniquing*. A selector name must be unique across an executable program, however, your custom classes and every shared library in your program contain their own copies of selector names, many of which may be duplicates (i.e., alloc, init, etc.). The runtime needs to choose a single canonical SEL pointer value for each selector name, and then update the metadata for every call site and method list to use the unique value. This process must be performed at application startup and uses up system resources (memory and program startup time). To make this process more efficient, the runtime performs selector uniquing through use of the dyld shared cache. *dyld* is a system service that locates and loads dynamic libraries. It includes a shared cache that enables these libraries to be shared across processes. The *dyld shared cache* also includes a selector table, thereby enabling selectors for shared libraries and your custom classes to be accessed from the cache. Thus, the runtime is able to retrieve selectors for shared libraries from the dyld shared cache, and only needs to update selectors for your app's custom classes.

Message Dispatching

Message invocation is ubiquitous in an Objective-C program. Just for application startup, objc_msgSend(), the runtime library function that performs object messaging, is called millions of times. Therefore, it is critical to optimize this code because even a slight change in its performance has a significant impact on the overall application performance. This method must look up the IMP corresponding to the message receiver and selector, and then jump to the IMP to begin its execution. In the last few sections, you learned how method caches and vtables are used to retrieve the IMP. Once this is accomplished, the runtime then dispatches the method using custom, optimized code written in assembly language. This code, referred to sometimes as a *trampoline*, looks up the right code and then jumps directly to it. This trampoline code works with any combination of parameters passed to it because they are just passed along for the method IMP to read. To handle the possible return value types, the runtime provides several different objc_msgSend() implementations.

Accessing Class Instance Methods

Now that you know how the runtime library looks up (and invokes) instance methods, you may be wondering how it does this for class methods (i.e., perform object messaging for class methods). Well, every Objective-C class is also, in fact, an object, hence it is capable of receiving messages, such as

```
[NSObject alloc]
```

So that explains how you can send messages to classes, but how does the runtime find and invoke class methods? Well, the runtime library implements this capability with metaclasses.

A *metaclass* is a special type of class object that stores information that enables the runtime to look up and invoke the class methods of an Objective-C class. There's a unique metaclass for every Objective-C class because every class potentially has a unique list of class methods. The runtime API provides functions for accessing metaclasses.

Class hierarchies are observed with metaclasses, as with regular classes. In the same way that a class points to a superclass with its superclass pointer, a metaclass points to the metaclass of a class's superclass using its own superclass pointer (refer back to Figure 8-4).

The base class's metaclass sets its superclass to the base class itself. The result of this inheritance hierarchy is that all instances, classes, and metaclasses in the hierarchy inherit from the hierarchy's base class.

The isa variable for an object points to a class that describes that instance, and can thus be used to access its instance methods, ivars, and so forth. The isa variable for an Objective-C class (object) points to a metaclass that describes the class (its class methods, etc.).

Putting this all together, the runtime performs messaging for both instance and class methods, as follows:

- When your source code sends a message to an object, the runtime retrieves the appropriate instance method implementation (via the corresponding class instance method vtable) and jumps to that method.

- When your source code sends a message to a class, the runtime retrieves the appropriate class method implementation (via its metaclass class method vtable) and jumps to that method.

Whew, that was a mouthful!! If necessary, take a moment to go over these concepts, and when you're ready, we'll attempt to clarify this with an example.

Examining Class Methods

Now you're going to code an example to see how the runtime data structures utilize metaclasses and the place of metaclasses in the overall class hierarchy. You'll do this by updating the Runspector program (developed earlier in this chapter) to retrieve metaclass information. Start Xcode (if not already started) and open the Runspector project by selecting **Open Recent ➤ Runspector.xcodeproj** from the Xcode File menu. Select the **main.m** file in the navigator pane and then add the code shown in Listing 8-8.

Listing 8-8. Runspector main() Function, Metaclass Data

```
// Retrieve and display metaclass data
id metaClass = objc_getMetaClass("TestClass1");
long mclzSize = class_getInstanceSize([metaClass class]);
NSData *mclzData = [NSData dataWithBytes:(__bridge const void *)(metaClass)
                                  length:mclzSize];
NSLog(@"TestClass1 metaclass contains %@", mclzData);
class_isMetaClass(metaClass) ?
  NSLog(@"Class %s is a metaclass", class_getName(metaClass)) :
  NSLog(@"Class %s is not a metaclass", class_getName(metaClass));
```

This code uses the runtime function objc_getMetaClass() to retrieve the metaclass definition for the named class, and then displays its associated data bytes. Next, the code uses the runtime function class_isMetaClass() to test whether the object is a metaclass and then logs a corresponding message to the console. You may be wondering about the use of the bridged cast (__bridge). Well, the NSData dataWithBytes:length: method takes as its first parameter a variable of type (const void *). You may recall from Chapter 4 that ARC memory management prohibits casts directly from Objective-C objects and (void *) types. A bridged cast (discussed in Chapter 6) enables the compiler to manage these scenarios. In this case, because there will be no transfer of ownership (i.e., the object assigned to the variable metaClass will still be managed by ARC), the __bridge annotation is used. On compiling and running the updated program, you should observe output similar to that shown in Figure 8-6.

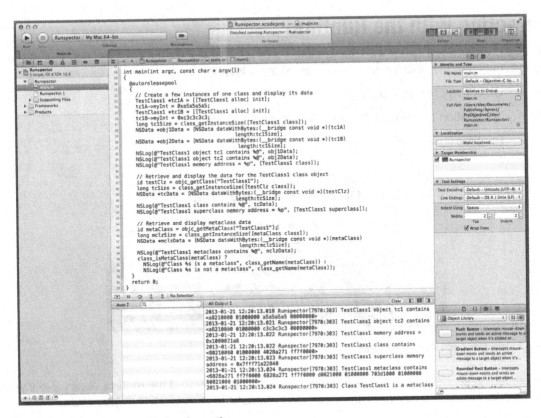

Figure 8-6. Runspector program, metaclass inspection

Note the metaclass information at the bottom of the output pane, as shown in Listing 8-9.

Listing 8-9. Runspector Program Metaclass Information

```
TestClass1 metaclass contains
<6828a271 ff7f0000 6828a271 ff7f0000 d0821000 01000000 703d1000 01000000 60821000 01000000>
Class TestClass1 is a metaclass
```

The metaclass data contains the isa pointer, the superclass pointer, and additional information. The superclass of TestClass1 is NSObject. Because this class defines no custom class methods, its isa pointer is also NSObject. Hence the metaclass isa pointer and superclass pointer should be identical. This is confirmed with the results displayed in Listing 8-9 (the value for each is 6828a271 ff7f0000).

This completes your review of the runtime library API and its implementation. In the next section, you'll look at the Objective-C APIs that you can use for directly interacting with the runtime system.

Interacting with the Runtime

Objective-C programs interact with the runtime system to implement the dynamic features of the language. In Figure 8-7, this interaction occurs at three levels:

- Objective-C source code
- Foundation Framework NSObject methods
- Runtime library API

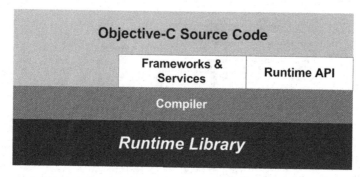

Figure 8-7. *Interacting with the runtime system*

In the preceding sections, you discussed the role of the compiler and the runtime library. Now you'll spend time looking at the runtime features of the Foundation Framework NSObject class.

NSObject Runtime Methods

As discussed throughout this chapter, the Objective-C language provides many dynamic programming capabilities. The runtime system provides a set of APIs that enable you to directly interact with the runtime; however, these are coded in C and thus mandate a procedural programming approach. As an alternative, the Foundation Framework NSObject class provides a set of methods that duplicate much of the functionality available from the runtime APIs. As your custom classes (and nearly all of the Cocoa framework classes) descend from NSObject, your code inherits these methods and thus can use them directly. The functionality provided by the NSObject runtime methods includes:

- Object introspection
- Message forwarding
- Dynamic method resolution
- Dynamic loading

Next, you'll demonstrate this with an example that uses NSObject runtime methods to perform object introspection.

Performing Object Introspection

You are now going to create a program that dynamically creates a class using the runtime APIs. In Xcode, create a new project by selecting **New ➤ Project ...** from the Xcode File menu. In the **New Project Assistant** pane, create a command-line application (choose **Command Line Tool** from the Mac OS X Application selection) and click **Next**. In the **Project Options** window, specify **Introspector** for the Product Name, choose **Foundation** for the Project Type, select ARC memory management by checking the **Use Automatic Reference Counting** check box, and then click **Next**.

Specify the location in your file system where you want the project to be created (if necessary, select **New Folder** and enter the name and location for the folder), uncheck the **Source Control** check box, and then click the **Create** button.

Now let's implement the code. Select the **main.m** file in the navigator pane, and then add the code shown in Listing 8-10.

Listing 8-10. Introspector main.m File

```
#import <Foundation/Foundation.h>

// Test class 1
@interface Greeter : NSObject
@property (readwrite, strong) NSString *salutation;
- (NSString *)greeting:(NSString *)recipient;
@end
@implementation Greeter
- (NSString *)greeting:(NSString *)recipient
{
  return [NSString stringWithFormat:@"%@, %@", [self salutation], recipient];
}
@end

int main(int argc, const char * argv[])
{
  @autoreleasepool
  {
    Greeter *greeter = [[Greeter alloc] init];
    [greeter setSalutation:@"Hello"];

    if ([greeter respondsToSelector:@selector(greeting:)] &&
        [greeter conformsToProtocol:@protocol(NSObject)])
    {
      id result = [greeter performSelector:@selector(greeting:) withObject:@"Monster!"];
      NSLog(@"%@", result);
    }
  }
  return 0;
}
```

Immediately after the import statement, the code defines the Greeter class. This class defines a property and a method that returns a simple greeting. In the main() function, you first create a Greeter instance and set the value of the property. Next, you use the NSObject runtime methods to perform object introspection. Specifically, you test the NSObject respondsToSelector: and conformsToProtocol: methods. If the result returned from these two conditional expressions is YES, the code sends a message to the Greeter instance using the NSObject runtime method performSelector:withObject:. Finally, the result returned from this method is logged to the output pane. When you compile and run the program, you should observe output similar to that shown in Figure 8-8.

Figure 8-8. *Introspector program output*

The complete list of NSObject runtime methods is defined in the NSObject class reference and the NSObject protocol reference. These are found in the Foundation Framework Reference Guide.

Roundup

In this chapter, you examined in detail the key components of the runtime system architecture. You should now have a good understanding of how the runtime system implements the object-oriented and dynamic features of the language. To recap, the following are the key takeaways:

- The Objective-C runtime system has two main components: the compiler and the runtime library. The compiler takes input Objective-C source code and generates code that is executed by the runtime library. This library is linked (during the linking phase) to all Objective-C programs. Together, they implement all of the object-oriented and dynamic features of the language.

- The runtime library APIs define a set of data types, functions, and constants. Many of these data types and functions map to corresponding Objective-C language elements (i.e., objects, classes, protocols, methods, instance variables, etc.). The runtime library public API is expressed in C.

- The runtime library implementation includes a variety of features and mechanisms to enhance application performance and extensibility. Examples of these include the method cache, vtable, and use of the dyld shared cache.

- The runtime library utilizes metaclasses to look up and invoke class methods. A metaclass is a special type of class object that stores information enabling the runtime to look up and invoke the class methods of an Objective-C class.

- The Foundation Framework NSObject class provides a set of methods for invoking runtime system functionality and behaviors. These methods perform object introspection, dynamic method resolution, dynamic loading, and message forwarding.

This completes your deep dive into the runtime system. Please feel free to review what you have gone over in the last two chapters and experiment with the example programs. Understanding the runtime system is very important for becoming proficient at developing Objective-C programs.

Chapter 9

Expert Section: Using the Runtime APIs

In Chapters 7 and 8, you learned about the dynamic features of Objective-C and the design and architecture of the runtime system that implements these features. In this Expert Section chapter, you are going to finish Part 2 of this book with several example programs that will enable you to get more hands-on experience with the runtime system features and its APIs. You'll create a dynamic proxy using the NSInvocation API, perform dynamic loading of your own custom framework bundle using the NSBundle API, and create a program that makes extensive use of the runtime library APIs. Believe me, after this chapter is done, you'll be well on your way to mastering the intricacies of the Objective-C runtime system!

Extending a Program with Loadable Bundles

Objective-C provides numerous dynamic programming features. These features increase the power and flexibility of the language, and enable you to modify a program during execution. In Chapter 7, you discussed dynamic loading and briefly described how the Foundation Framework NSBundle class can be used to manage bundles. Now you are going to create a program that utilizes these features to extend a running program using a loadable bundle.

Approach

For this example, you'll actually develop two projects. In one project, you'll code the program that uses a loadable bundle, and in the other project, you'll create the loadable bundle. You'll proceed as follows:

1. In Project 1, develop a protocol and a class that conforms to this protocol.

2. In Project 2, develop a loadable bundle comprised of a different class conforming to this protocol.

3. In Project 1, use the NSBundle class to find and load this bundle, create an object from a class in the bundle (developed in step 2), and then invoke a method on this object.

Sounds like fun, right? OK, let's get started!

Step 1: Laying the Foundation

In Xcode, create a new project by selecting **New ➤ Project …** from the Xcode File menu. In the **New Project Assistant** pane, create a command-line application. In the **Project Options** window, specify **DynaLoader** for the Product Name, choose **Foundation** for the Project Type, and select ARC memory management by selecting the **Use Automatic Reference Counting** check box. Specify the location in your file system where you want the project to be created (if necessary, select **New Folder** and enter the name and location for the folder), uncheck the **Source Control** check box, and then click the **Create** button.

Now you're going to create a protocol and a class that conforms to the protocol. You probably recall from Chapter 2 that a protocol declares methods and properties that can be implemented by any class. Combined with dynamic typing, this provides an idea mechanism for specifying a set of methods implemented by a class that is dynamically loaded from a bundle. Select **New ➤ File …** from the Xcode File menu, select the **Objective-C** protocol template, name the protocol **Greeter**, select the **DynaLoader** folder for the files location and the **DynaLoader** project as the target, and then click the **Create** button. A header file named `Greeter.h` has been added to the Xcode project navigator pane. Click this file to display the `Greeter` protocol (see Listing 9-1).

Listing 9-1. Greeter Protocol Template File

```
#import <Foundation/Foundation.h>

@protocol Greeter <NSObject>

@end
```

In the editor pane, update the `Greeter.h` file as shown in Listing 9-2.

Listing 9-2. Greeter Protocol Updates

```
#import <Foundation/Foundation.h>

@protocol Greeter <NSObject>

- (NSString *) greeting:(NSString *)salutation;

@end
```

This protocol declares a method named `greeting` that takes an `NSString` pointer as its parameter and returns an `NSString` pointer. Now let's implement a class that conforms to the `Greeter` protocol. Select **New ➤ File …** from the Xcode File menu, select the **Objective-C** class template, name the class **BasicGreeter** (select **NSObject** in the **Subclass of** drop-down list), select the **DynaLoader** folder for the files location and the **DynaLoader** project as the target, and then click the **Create** button. Next, in the Xcode project navigator pane, select the resulting header file named **BasicGreeter.h** and update the interface as shown in Listing 9-3.

Listing 9-3. BasicGreeter Interface

```
#import <Foundation/Foundation.h>
#import "Greeter.h"

@interface BasicGreeter : NSObject <Greeter>

@end
```

The template BasicGreeter interface has been updated to adopt the Greeter protocol; now select the **BasicGreeter.m** file and update the implementation as shown in Listing 9-4.

Listing 9-4. BasicGreeter Implementation

```
#import "BasicGreeter.h"

@implementation BasicGreeter

- (NSString *) greeting:(NSString *)salutation
{
   return [NSString stringWithFormat:@"%@, World!", salutation];
}

@end
```

The BasicGreeter implementation defines the greeting: method (and thus conforms to the Greeter protocol), returning a text string that begins with the method's input parameter. Now let's test this class. Select the **main.m** file and update the main() function, as shown in Listing 9-5.

Listing 9-5. BasicGreeter main() Function

```
#import <Foundation/Foundation.h>
#import "BasicGreeter.h"

int main(int argc, const char * argv[])
{
  @autoreleasepool
  {
    id<Greeter> greeter = [[BasicGreeter alloc] init];
    NSLog(@"%@", [greeter greeting:@"Hello"]);
  }
  return 0;
}
```

First, the function creates a BasicGreeter object and assigns it to a variable named greeter. This variable is declared to be of type id and conforms to the Greeter protocol. It then invokes the greeting: method on the object, and logs the result in the output pane. By declaring the variable as

```
id<Greeter> greeter
```

it can be assigned to any Objective-C object that conforms to the Greeter protocol. If you compile and run the program now, the output pane displays "Hello, World!" (see Figure 9-1).

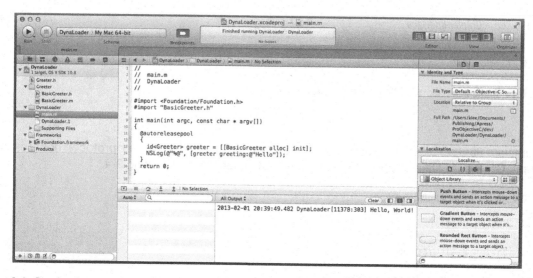

Figure 9-1. DynaLoader program output

Great! You have completed step 1. Now you will create another class that conforms to the Greeter protocol, this time packaged in a loadable bundle.

Step 2: Creating a Loadable Bundle

Xcode makes it easy to create a loadable bundle. It's simply another type of project. First, create a new project by selecting **New ➤ Project ...** from the Xcode File menu. In the **New Project Assistant** pane under OS X, select **Framework & Library**, and then select **Bundle** (see Figure 9-2).

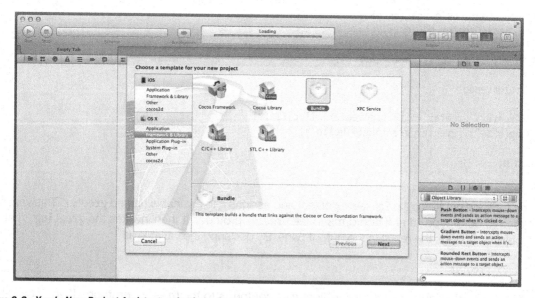

Figure 9-2. Xcode New Project Assistant, selecting a Bundle project template

Next, in the **Project Options** window, specify **CustomGreeter** for the Product Name, an **Organization Name** (optional value), and a **Company Identifier** (the default value is fine, but any name will suffice). Select **Cocoa** for the Framework the bundle will link against, and select ARC memory management by checking the **Use Automatic Reference Counting** check box. Specify the location in your file system where you want the project to be created (if necessary, select **New Folder** and enter the name and location for the folder), uncheck the **Source Control** check box, *do not* add to any project or workspace, and then click the **Create** button. The workspace window shown in Figure 9-3 is displayed.

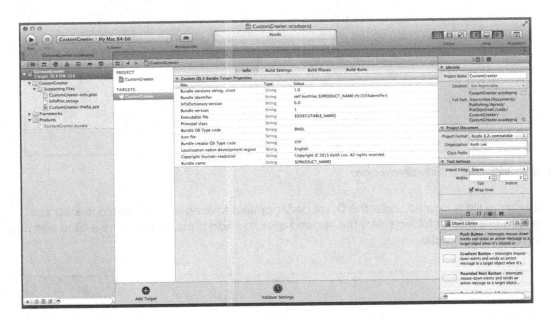

Figure 9-3. CustomGreeter bundle template

Cool. Xcode created an empty bundle. In the project navigator pane under the Products group, notice the CustomGreeter.bundle file. This is the bundle to which you'll add your code and resources. Also note the CustomGreeter-Info.plist file. It is a required file that contains information about the bundle's configuration. Now let's add a class to this bundle that implements the Greeter protocol. First, you need to include the Greeter.h header file in the bundle. Fortunately, Xcode provides a simple mechanism for importing files into a project. Hold down the Ctrl key and (from the Xcode project navigator pane) select the **CustomGreeter** project. A drop-down window then displays a set of options. Select the **Add Files to "CustomGreeter"** ... option (see Figure 9-4).

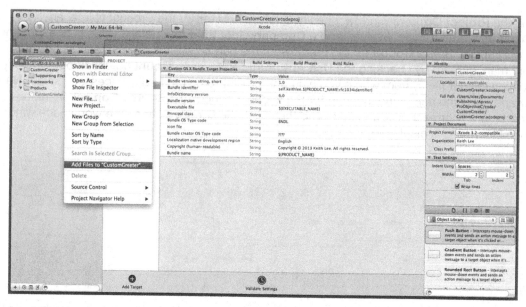

Figure 9-4. Adding files to CustomGreeter option

The `Greeter.h` file is located under the DynaLoader project folder that you created in step 1. Navigate to this project folder, select the file, and click the **Add** button (see Figure 9-5) to add it to the `CustomGreeter` bundle.

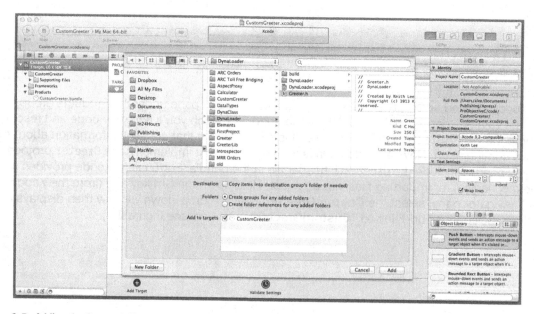

Figure 9-5. Adding the Greeter.h file to the CustomGreeter bundle

Now add a new class to the bundle that conforms to this protocol. Select **New ➤ File ...** from the Xcode File menu, select the **Objective-C** class template, name the class **CustomGreeter** (select NSObject in the **Subclass of** drop-down list), select the **CustomGreeter** folder for the files location and the **CustomGreeter** project as the target, and then click the **Create** button. In the Xcode project navigator pane, select the resulting header file named CustomGreeter.h and update the interface, as shown in Listing 9-6.

Listing 9-6. CustomGreeter Interface

```
#import <Foundation/Foundation.h>
#import "Greeter.h"

@interface CustomGreeter : NSObject <Greeter>

@end
```

As with the BasicGreeter class, the template CustomGreeter interface has been updated to adopt the Greeter protocol. Now select the CustomGreeter.m file and update the implementation as shown in Listing 9-7.

Listing 9-7. CustomGreeter Implementation

```
#import "CustomGreeter.h"

@implementation CustomGreeter

- (NSString *) greeting:(NSString *)salutation
{
    return [NSString stringWithFormat:@"%@, Universe!", salutation];
}

@end
```

The CustomGreeter implementation defines the greeting: method (and thus conforms to the Greeter protocol), returning a text string that begins with the method's input parameter. Now compile the bundle by selecting **Build** from the Xcode Product menu. And that's it—you've created a loadable bundle that includes a class (CustomGreeter) that conforms to the Greeter protocol. In the Xcode project navigator pane, note the CustomGreeter.bundle file in the Products group. Select this bundle file and note in the Xcode file inspector (on the right side of the Xcode workspace window) the full path shown in Figure 9-6. This indicates the path to the CustomGreeter.bundle file that you'll need when you load the bundle using the NSBundle class.

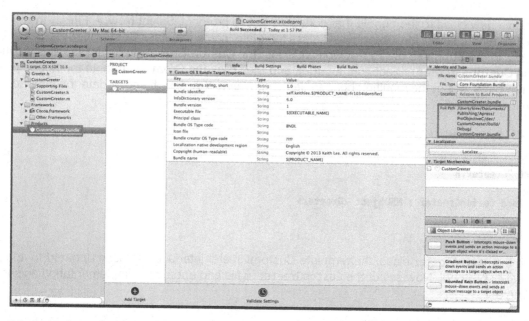

Figure 9-6. *CustomGreeter.bundle full path*

Step 3: Dynamically Loading the Bundle

Now that you have created a loadable bundle, let's use it to dynamically create an object (from a bundle class) and invoke a method on it. In Xcode, return to the DynaLoader project, select the **main.m** file in the project navigator pane, and update the main() function as shown in Listing 9-8.

Listing 9-8. Using NSBundle to Load a Bundle

```
#import <Foundation/Foundation.h>
#import "BasicGreeter.h"

int main(int argc, const char * argv[])
{
  @autoreleasepool
  {
    id<Greeter> greeter = [[BasicGreeter alloc] init];
    NSLog(@"%@", [greeter greeting:@"Hello"]);

    // Now create a bundle at the specified path (retrieved from input argument)
    NSString *bundlePath;
    if (argc != 2)
    {
      // No bundle path provided, exit
      NSLog(@"Please provide a path for the bundle");
    }
    else
    {
      bundlePath = [NSString stringWithUTF8String:argv[1]];
```

```objc
    NSBundle *greeterBundle = [NSBundle bundleWithPath:bundlePath];
    if (greeterBundle == nil)
    {
      NSLog(@"Bundle not found at path");
    }
    else
    {
      // Dynamically load bundle
      NSError *error;
      BOOL isLoaded = [greeterBundle loadAndReturnError:&error];
      if (!isLoaded)
      {
        NSLog(@"Error = %@", [error localizedDescription]);
      }
      else
      {
        // Bundle loaded, create an object using bundle and send it a message
        Class greeterClass = [greeterBundle classNamed:@"CustomGreeter"];
        greeter = [[greeterClass alloc] init];
        NSLog(@"%@", [greeter greeting:@"Hello"]);

        // Done with dynamically loaded bundle, now unload it
        // First release any objects whose class is defined in the bundle!
        greeter = nil;
        BOOL isUnloaded = [greeterBundle unload];
        if (!isUnloaded)
        {
          NSLog(@"Couldn't unload bundle");
        }
      }
    }
  }
  return 0;
}
```

I know, you added a lot of code here, but don't worry. You'll take this one step at a time. Functionally, the updates implement the following logic:

1. Retrieve the bundle path argument

2. Create an NSBundle object

3. Load the bundle

4. Get a bundle class

5. Unload the bundle

6. Set the bundle path argument

Let's discuss the code for each of these in turn.

Retrieving the Bundle Path Argument

As you've probably observed by now, an Objective-C `main()` function specifies two parameters: `argc` and `argv`. These parameters enable you to pass arguments to the program on execution.

```
int main(int argc, const char * argv[])
```

The parameter `argc` is the number of arguments to the program, and the space-separated argument values are stored in the `argv` array. The first argument in the `argv` array (`argv[0]`) is the name of the program executable, thus the value of the `argc` parameter is always one or more. Consider, for example, that the DynaLoader program was executed from the command line as follows:

```
> DynaLoader /CustomGreeter.bundle
```

The `main()` function variable `argc` would have a value of 2 and the `argv` array would have two elements: the value of the first would be DynaLoader and the second would be /CustomGreeter.bundle. The `main()` function has been updated to require that the bundle path be provided as an input argument to the program. The following code from Listing 9-8 verifies that the program has the correct number of arguments and then creates the path.

```
NSString *bundlePath;
if (argc != 2)
{
  // No bundle path provided, exit
  NSLog(@"Please provide a path for the bundle");
}
else
{
  bundlePath = [NSString stringWithUTF8String:argv[1]];
```

The conditional logic (**if (argc != 2)**) checks to make sure that the `argc` count is two (one for the program name and one for the bundle path). If the count is not equal to two, a message is logged to the output pane and the program exits; otherwise, the path is assigned to the proper input parameter (`argv[1]`) and the program continues.

Creating an NSBundle Object

The next set of statements creates an NSBundle object using the bundle path and verifies that the object was successfully created. The code uses an NSBundle convenience class method to create and initialize the class instance for the bundle at the specified path.

```
+ (NSBundle *) bundleWithPath:(NSString *) fullPath;
```

The code attempts to create a bundle object using the provided path; if it is not successful, it logs a message to the output pane.

```
bundlePath = [NSString stringWithUTF8String:argv[1]];
NSBundle *greeterBundle = [NSBundle bundleWithPath:bundlePath];
if (greeterBundle == nil)
{
  NSLog(@"Bundle not found at path");
}
```

Loading a Bundle

Now the code attempts to dynamically load the bundle. NSBundle provides several methods to load a bundle into the Objective-C runtime. The instance method used here loads a bundle and stores an error object in the parameter if any errors occurred.

```
- (BOOL)loadAndReturnError:(NSError **) error;
```

The method returns a Boolean value of YES if the bundle is successfully loaded or has already been loaded. Notice that the method takes a variable of type **NSError ** as its parameter; if the bundle is not successfully loaded, this enables the method to return an NSError object with error information (later in this book you'll learn all about error handling using the Foundation Framework NSError class). The code loads the bundle and performs a conditional check on the return value, logging an error message to the output pane if the bundle was not loaded successfully.

```
NSError *error;
BOOL isLoaded = [greeterBundle loadAndReturnError:&error];
if (!isLoaded)
{
  NSLog(@"Error = %@", [error localizedDescription]);
}
```

Getting a Bundle Class

Next, the code gets a bundle class, creates an instance of the class, and invokes a method on the object, logging the result returned by the method to the output pane.

```
Class greeterClass = [greeterBundle principalClass];
greeter = [[greeterClass alloc] init];
NSLog(@"%@", [greeter greeting:@"Hello"]);
```

The NSBundle instance method principalClass is used to retrieve the principal class of the bundle. The principal class controls all other classes in a bundle, and its classname is specified in the bundle's Info.plist file. If the name is not specified, the first class loaded in the bundle is the principal class. Because CustomGreeter.bundle contains only one class (CustomGreeter), the method loads a CustomGreeter class object. Next, an instance of the class is created and initialized. Note that this instance is assigned to the existing variable named greeter that was declared to be of type id<Greeter>. Because the CustomGreeter class also conforms to the Greeter protocol, this assignment is valid and causes neither a compile-time nor a runtime error.

Unloading a Bundle

Once the bundle is no longer needed, it can be unloaded, thereby conserving system resources. This is done with the following code from Listing 9-8.

```
greeter = nil;
BOOL isUnloaded = [greeterBundle unload];
if (!isUnloaded)
{
  NSLog(@"Couldn't unload bundle");
}
```

The runtime system requires that, prior to unloading a bundle, any objects created by a bundle class must be released; hence the greeter object is set to nil. The NSBundle unload method is used to unload a previously loaded bundle. In the preceding code, the result returned from the method invocation is tested to verify that the bundle was unloaded successfully; if not, a message is logged to the console.

Retrieving the Bundle Path Argument

As mentioned, the DynaLoader program takes an argument that specifies the full path of the bundle to be dynamically loaded. So prior to running the program, you have to identify the full path to the CustomGreeter.bundle and then run the program with this path set as its input argument. In step 2, you indicated how to view the full path of the CustomGreeter bundle (refer to Figure 9-6). In Xcode, open the **CustomGreeter** project (if not already opened), select **CustomGreeter.bundle** in the project navigator pane, and then note the bundle full path in the file inspector. Now add this path to the Xcode copy buffer by dragging and selecting it, and then selecting **Copy** from the Xcode Edit menu (see Figure 9-7).

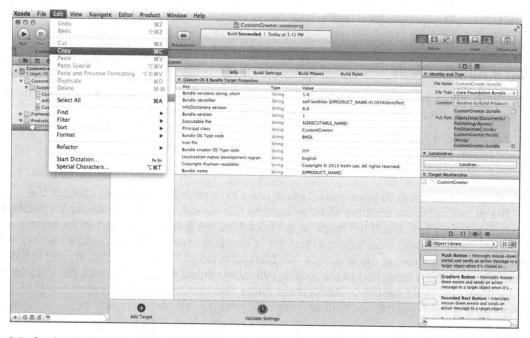

Figure 9-7. Copying the CustomGreeter.bundle full path

In Xcode, open the **DynaLoader** project, select DynaLoader from the **Scheme** button at the top of the toolbar, and then select **Edit Scheme ...** from the scheme drop-down (see Figure 9-8).

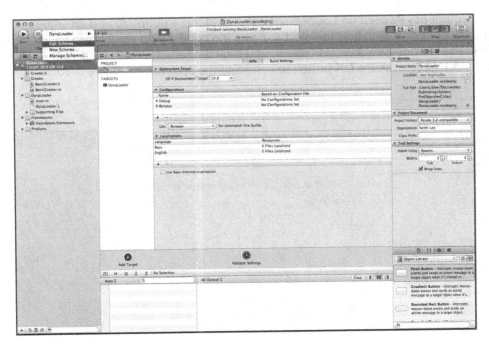

Figure 9-8. Edit CustomGreeter project scheme

A scheme defines build and test settings for an Xcode project or workspace. The build configuration information includes the arguments passed when the target program is executed, so this is where you'll specify the full path for the CustomGreeter bundle. In the Scheme editing dialog, select the **Arguments** tab to edit the arguments passed on program launch.

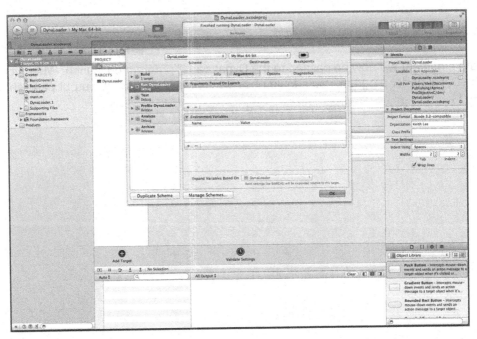

Figure 9-9. Scheme editing dialog Arguments tab

Under the **Arguments Passed on Launch** section, select the **+** button to add an argument. Now click inside the corresponding field to select it, paste the bundle path you copied earlier into the field by selecting **Paste** from the Xcode Edit menu, and click the Return button to store this value in the argument field. Finally, click the **OK** button to complete the update (see Figure 9-10).

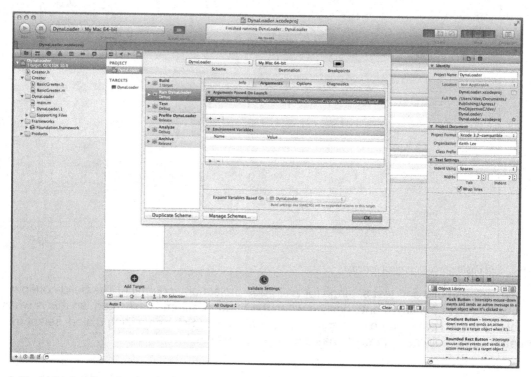

Figure 9-10. *Adding bundle path using the Scheme editor*

The file path argument will now be passed to the DynaLoader program on launch. When you compile and run the DynaLoader program, you should observe the messages in the output pane shown in Figure 9-11.

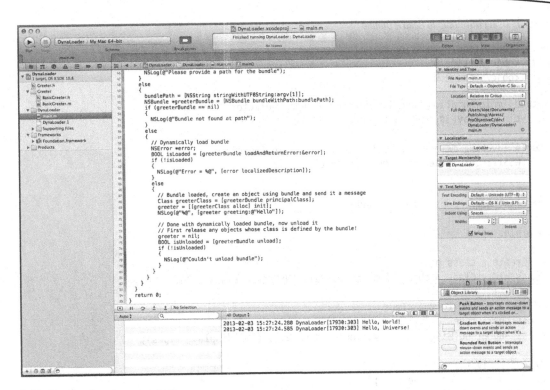

Figure 9-11. DynaLoader program output

As shown in the output pane, the `greeting:` method is first invoked on `BasicGreeter` object, and then it is invoked on a `CustomGreeter` object that is created from the dynamically loaded `CustomGreeter` bundle. This demonstrates how dynamic loading using the `NSBundle` class enables code and resources to be added to a running program.

Using the Runtime APIs

Now you'll create a program that uses the runtime APIs to dynamically create a class and a class instance, and then dynamically add a variable to the instance.

In Xcode, create a new project by selecting **New ➤ Project …** from the Xcode File menu. In the **New Project Assistant** pane, create a command-line application. In the **Project Options** window, specify **RuntimeWidget** for the Product Name, choose **Foundation** for the Project Type, and select ARC memory management by selecting the **Use Automatic Reference Counting** check box. Specify the location in your file system where you want the project to be created (if necessary, select **New Folder** and enter the name and location for the folder), uncheck the **Source Control** check box, and then click the **Create** button.

Now select the **main.m** file and add the code shown in Listing 9-9.

Listing 9-9. Using NSBundle to Load a Bundle

```objc
#import <Foundation/Foundation.h>
#import <objc/runtime.h>
#import <objc/message.h>

// Method implementation function for the display selector
static void display(id self, SEL _cmd)
{
  NSLog(@"Invoking method with selector %@ on %@ instance",
      NSStringFromSelector(_cmd), [self className]);
}

int main(int argc, const char * argv[])
{
  @autoreleasepool
  {
    // Create a class pair
    Class WidgetClass = objc_allocateClassPair([NSObject class], "Widget", 0);

    // Add a method to the class
    const char *types = "v@:";
    class_addMethod(WidgetClass, @selector(display), (IMP)display, types);

    // Add an ivar to the class
    const char *height = "height";
    class_addIvar(WidgetClass, height, sizeof(id), rint(log2(sizeof(id))),
              @encode(id));

    // Register the class
    objc_registerClassPair(WidgetClass);

    // Create a widget instance and set value of the ivar
    id widget = [[WidgetClass alloc] init];
    id value = [NSNumber numberWithInt:15];
    [widget setValue:value forKey:[NSString stringWithUTF8String:height]];
    NSLog(@"Widget instance height = %@",
        [widget valueForKey:[NSString stringWithUTF8String:height]]);

    // Send the widget a message
    objc_msgSend(widget, NSSelectorFromString(@"display"));

    // Dynamically add a variable (an associated object) to the widget
    NSNumber *width = [NSNumber numberWithInt:10];
    objc_setAssociatedObject(widget, @"width", width,
                      OBJC_ASSOCIATION_RETAIN_NONATOMIC);

    // Retrieve the variable's value and display it
    id result = objc_getAssociatedObject(widget, @"width");
    NSLog(@"Widget instance width = %@", result);
  }
  return 0;
}
```

Functionally, this code does the following:

- Define a method implementation function
- Create and register a class
- Create an instance of the class
- Dynamically add a variable to the instance

Next, you'll examine the code and we'll discuss how it implements this functionality.

Defining a Method Implementation

As you saw in Chapter 8, an Objective-C method is simply a C-language function that takes at least two arguments: self and _cmd. Immediately after the import statements, the code in Listing 9-9 defines a function that you'll use to add a method to a class.

```
// Method implementation function for the display selector
static void display(id self, SEL _cmd)
{
  NSLog(@"Invoking method with selector %@ on %@ instance",
      NSStringFromSelector(_cmd), [self className]);
}
```

Creating and Registering a Class

To dynamically create a class with the runtime APIs, you must perform the following steps:

1. Create a new class and metaclass.
2. Add methods and instance variables to the class (if any).
3. Register the newly created class.

This functionality is implemented with the following code from Listing 9-9.

```
// Create a class pair
Class WidgetClass = objc_allocateClassPair([NSObject class], "Widget", 0);

// Add a method to the class
const char *types = "v@:";
class_addMethod(WidgetClass, @selector(display), (IMP)display, types);

// Add an ivar to the class
const char *height = "height";
class_addIvar(WidgetClass, height, sizeof(id), rint(log2(sizeof(id))),
              @encode(id));

// Register the class
objc_registerClassPair(WidgetClass);
```

The runtime class_addMethod function takes as arguments the class to which the method should be added, the selector that specifies the name of the method being added, the function that implements the method, and a character string—known as *type encodings*—that describes the types of arguments and the return value of the method. Each possible type is represented by a type code; for example, the character "v" is the code for a void, "@" is the code for an object (whether a pointer to an Objective-C class or the id type), and ":" is the code for the SEL type. The complete list of type encodings are specified in the Apple Objective-C Runtime Programming Guide. The codes in the types parameter of the class_addMethod must be arranged in a defined order: the first code is for the return type, the second code is for method's implicit self parameter (the id type), the third code is for the type of the method's implicit _cmd parameter (the SEL type), and the remaining codes are for the types of each of the explicit parameters of the method. Thus for the display method, the corresponding types array has a value of "v@:."

Creating a Class Instance

The code creates an instance of the dynamically added class, sets its instance variable to a value, and then invokes the instance method. It also logs messages to the output pane to show the instance variable value and the method invocation.

Dynamically Adding a Variable to a Class Instance

Objective-C does not provide the capability for adding instance variables to an object; however, a feature of the runtime—associated objects—can be used to effectively mimic this functionality. An *associated object* is an object that is attached to a class instance, referenced by a key. This can be used in a variety of scenarios; for example, with Objective-C categories that don't permit instance variables. When you create an associated object, you specify the key mapped for the association, the memory management policy for the associated object, and its value. The following code from Listing 9-9 demonstrates use of the runtime APIs for associated objects.

```
// Dynamically add a variable (an associated object) to the widget
NSNumber *width = [NSNumber numberWithInt:10];
objc_setAssociatedObject(widget, @"width", width,
                    OBJC_ASSOCIATION_RETAIN_NONATOMIC);

// Retrieve the variable's value and display it
id result = objc_getAssociatedObject(widget, @"width");
NSLog(@"Widget instance width = %@", result);
```

The runtime APIs include an enum that lists the possible values for the memory management policy. In this policy, OBJC_ASSOCIATION_RETAIN_NONATOMIC, assigns a nonatomic strong reference to the associated object. This is similar to creating a property with the attributes nonatomic, strong. When you compile and run the RuntimeWidget program, you should observe the messages in the output pane shown in Figure 9-12.

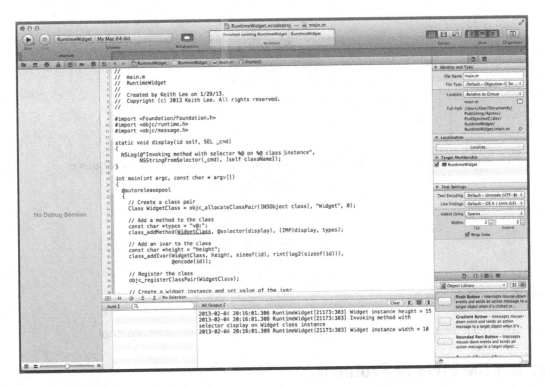

Figure 9-12. RuntimeWidget program output

This example demonstrates how to use the runtime APIs to dynamically create classes, class instances, and associated objects. Please refer to the Apple Objective-C Runtime Reference for the complete guide to the runtime APIs.

Creating a Dynamic Proxy

The final program demonstrates dynamic message forwarding using the Foundation Framework NSInvocation and NSProxy classes. In Chapter 3, you learned that Objective-C provides several types of message forwarding options: fast forwarding using the NSObject forwardingTargetForSelector: method and normal (full) forwarding using the NSObject forwardInvocation: method.

One of the benefits of normal forwarding is that it enables you to perform additional processing on an object message, its arguments, and return value. Used in conjunction with NSProxy, it provides an excellent mechanism for implementing *aspect-oriented programming* (AOP) in Objective-C. AOP is a programming paradigm that aims to increase program modularity by separating *cross-cutting* functionality (that rely on or affect many parts of a program) from its other parts. NSProxy is a Foundation Framework class specifically designed for proxying. It functions as the interface to the real class. Here, you create a subclass of NSProxy and implement the forwardInvocation: method, thereby enabling messages sent to the real (i.e., subject) class to be decorated with the desired cross-cutting functionality. An overall diagram of the components that you'll implement in this program and their interrelationships are depicted in Figure 9-13.

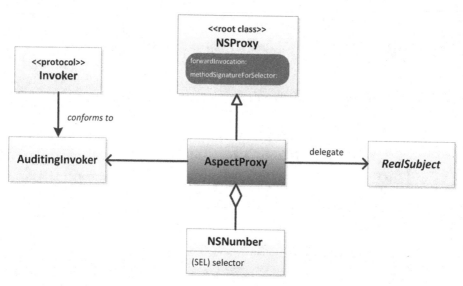

Figure 9-13. AspectProxy class diagram

Don't worry. You'll take it one step at a time. Let's begin with the `Invoker` protocol.

Creating the Invoker Protocol

In Xcode, create a new project by selecting **New ➤ Project ...** from the Xcode File menu. In the **New Project Assistant** pane, create a command-line application. In the **Project Options** window, specify **AspectProxy** for the Product Name, choose **Foundation** for the Project Type, and select ARC memory management by checking the **Use Automatic Reference Counting** check box. Specify the location in your file system where you want the project to be created (if necessary, select **New Folder** and enter the name and location for the folder), uncheck the **Source Control** check box, and then click the **Create** button.

Now you're going to create a protocol and a class that conforms to the protocol. Select **New ➤ File ...** from the Xcode File menu, select the **Objective-C** protocol template, name the protocol **Invoker**, select the **AspectProxy** folder for the files location and the **AspectProxy** project as the target, and then click the **Create** button. A header file named `Invoker.h` has been added to the Xcode navigator pane. In the editor pane, update the `Greeter.h` file, as shown in Listing 9-10.

Listing 9-10. Invoker Protocol

```
#import <Foundation/Foundation.h>

@protocol Invoker <NSObject>

// Required methods (must be implemented)
@required
- (void) preInvoke:(NSInvocation *)inv withTarget:(id) target;
// Optional methods
@optional
- (void) postInvoke:(NSInvocation *)inv withTarget:(id) target;

@end
```

This protocol declares two methods. preInvoke:withTarget: is a *required* method (it must be implemented by any class that conforms to this protocol) that implements cross-cutting functionality performed immediately prior to invoking the method on the real object. The method named preInvoke:withTarget: is an *optional* method that implements cross-cutting functionality performed immediately after invoking the method on the real object.

Now you'll implement a class that conforms to this protocol, implementing the desired cross-cutting functionality. Select **New ➤ File ...** from the Xcode File menu, select the **Objective-C** class template, name the class **AuditingInvoker** (select **NSObject** in the **Subclass of** drop-down list), select the **AspectProxy** folder for the files location and the **AspectProxy** project as the target, and then click the **Create** button. In the Xcode navigator pane, select the resulting header file named **AspectProxy.h** and update the interface as shown in Listing 9-11.

Listing 9-11. AuditingInvoker Interface

```
#import <Foundation/Foundation.h>
#import "Invoker.h"

@interface AuditingInvoker : NSObject <Invoker>

@end
```

The template AuditingInvoker interface has been updated to adopt the Invoker protocol. Now select the **AuditingInvoker.m** file and update the implementation as shown in Listing 9-12.

Listing 9-12. AuditingInvoker Implementation

```
#import "AuditingInvoker.h"

@implementation AuditingInvoker

- (void) preInvoke:(NSInvocation *)inv withTarget:(id)target
{
  NSLog(@"Creating audit log before sending message with selector %@ to %@ object",
       NSStringFromSelector([inv selector]), [target className]);
}

- (void) postInvoke:(NSInvocation *)inv withTarget:(id)target
{
  NSLog(@"Creating audit log after sending message with selector %@ to %@ object",
       NSStringFromSelector([inv selector]), [target className]);
}

@end
```

The AuditingInvoker implementation defines the preInvoke:withTarget: and the postInvoke:withTarget: methods, and thus it conforms to the Invoker protocol. The methods merely log appropriate messages to the Xcode output pane. OK, now that you're done implementing the cross-cutting functionality, let's tackle the NSProxy subclass.

Coding the Proxy Class

Now you're going to create the proxy class. It will subclass NSProxy and implement the message forwarding methods forwardInvocation: and methodSignatureForSelector:. Select **New ➤ File …** from the Xcode File menu, select the **Objective-C** class template, name the class **AspectProxy** (select **NSObject** in the **Subclass of** drop-down list), select the **AspectProxy** folder for the files location and the **AspectProxy** project as the target, and then click the **Create** button. In the Xcode navigator pane, select the resulting header file named **AspectProxy.h** and update the interface as shown in Listing 9-13.

Listing 9-13. AspectProxy Interface

```
#import <Foundation/Foundation.h>
#import "Invoker.h"

@interface AspectProxy : NSProxy

@property (strong) id proxyTarget;
@property (strong) id<Invoker> invoker;
@property (readonly) NSMutableArray *selectors;

- (id)initWithObject:(id)object andInvoker:(id<Invoker>)invoker;
- (id)initWithObject:(id)object selectors:(NSArray *)selectors
          andInvoker:(id<Invoker>)invoker;
- (void)registerSelector:(SEL)selector;

@end
```

The interface adds three properties and three methods. The proxyTarget property is the real object to which messages are forwarded through the NSProxy instance. The invoker property is an instance of a class (which conforms to the Invoker protocol) that implements the cross-cutting functionality desired. The selectors property is a collection of selectors that define the messages on which the cross-cutting functionality will be invoked. Two of the methods are initialization methods for an AspectProxy class instance, and the third method, registerSelector:, is used to add a selector to the current list. Now select the **AspectProxy.m** file and update the implementation as shown in Listing 9-14.

Listing 9-14. AspectProxy Implementation

```
#import "AspectProxy.h"

@implementation AspectProxy

- (id)initWithObject:(id)object selectors:(NSArray *)selectors
          andInvoker:(id<Invoker>)invoker
{
  _proxyTarget = object;
  _invoker = invoker;
  _selectors = [selectors mutableCopy];
  return self;
}
```

```objc
- (id)initWithObject:(id)object andInvoker:(id<Invoker>)invoker
{
  return [self initWithObject:object selectors:nil andInvoker:invoker];
}


- (NSMethodSignature *)methodSignatureForSelector:(SEL)sel
{
  return [self.proxyTarget methodSignatureForSelector:sel];
}


- (void)forwardInvocation:(NSInvocation *)inv
{
  // Perform functionality before invoking method on target
  if ([self.invoker respondsToSelector:@selector(preInvoke:withTarget:)])
  {
    if (self.selectors != nil)
    {
      SEL methodSel = [inv selector];
      for (NSValue *selValue in self.selectors)
      {
        if (methodSel == [selValue pointerValue])
        {
          [[self invoker] preInvoke:inv withTarget:self.proxyTarget];
          break;
        }
      }
    }
    else
    {
      [[self invoker] preInvoke:inv withTarget:self.proxyTarget];
    }
  }

  // Invoke method on target
  [inv invokeWithTarget:self.proxyTarget];

  // Perform functionality after invoking method on target
  if ([self.invoker respondsToSelector:@selector(postInvoke:withTarget:)])
  {
    if (self.selectors != nil)
    {
      SEL methodSel = [inv selector];
      for (NSValue *selValue in self.selectors)
      {
        if (methodSel == [selValue pointerValue])
        {
          [[self invoker] postInvoke:inv withTarget:self.proxyTarget];
          break;
        }
      }
    }
    else
```

```
    {
      [[self invoker] postInvoke:inv withTarget:self.proxyTarget];
    }
  }
}

- (void)registerSelector:(SEL)selector
{
  NSValue* selValue = [NSValue valueWithPointer:selector];
  [self.selectors addObject:selValue];
}

@end
```

The initialization methods initialize an AspectProxy object instance accordingly. Note that as NSProxy is a base class, there is no call to [super init] at the beginning of these methods. The registerSelector: method adds another selector to the collection, as mentioned earlier. The implementation of methodSignatureForSelector: returns an NSMethodSignature instance for the method to be invoked on the target object. The runtime system requires that this method be implemented when performing normal forwarding. The implementation of forwardInvocation: invokes the method on the target object and conditionally invokes the AOP functionality if the selector for the method invoked on the target object matches one of the selectors registered in the AspectProxy object. Whew. When you've had enough time to digest this, let's move on to the main.m file and test out your program!

Testing the AspectProxy

Let's test the AspectProxy, but first let's add a target class to the proxy. You'll use the Calculator class that you implemented in Chapter 7. It declares the following methods:

```
- (NSNumber *) sumAddend1:(NSNumber *)adder1 addend2:(NSNumber *)adder2;
- (NSNumber *) sumAddend1:(NSNumber *)adder1 :(NSNumber *)adder2;
```

As you learned earlier in this chapter, Xcode provides a simple mechanism for importing files into a project. Hold down the Ctrl key and (from the Xcode project navigator pane) select the AspectProxy project. A drop-down window displays a set of options. Select the **Add Files to "AspectProxy" ...** option. Navigate over to the Calculator project folder, select the **Calculator.h** and **Calculator.m** files, and click the **Add** button to add them to your AspectProxy project. OK, now with that done, let's update the main() function to create a calculator proxy and invoke its methods, causing the AOP AuditingInvoker methods to be invoked as well. In the project navigator pane, select the **main.m** file and update it as shown in Listing 9-15.

Listing 9-15. AspectProxy main() Function

```
#import <Foundation/Foundation.h>
#import "AspectProxy.h"
#import "AuditingInvoker.h"
#import "Calculator.h"
```

```
int main(int argc, const char * argv[])
{
  @autoreleasepool
  {
    // Create Calculator object
    id calculator = [[Calculator alloc] init];
    NSNumber *addend1 = [NSNumber numberWithInteger:-25];
    NSNumber *addend2 = [NSNumber numberWithInteger:10];
    NSNumber *addend3 = [NSNumber numberWithInteger:15];

    // Create proxy for object
    NSValue* selValue1 = [NSValue valueWithPointer:@selector(sumAddend1:addend2:)];
    NSArray *selValues = @[selValue1];
    AuditingInvoker *invoker = [[AuditingInvoker alloc] init];
    id calculatorProxy = [[AspectProxy alloc] initWithObject:calculator
                                                    selectors:selValues
                                                   andInvoker:invoker];

    // Send message to proxy with given selector
    [calculatorProxy sumAddend1:addend1 addend2:addend2];

    // Now send message to proxy with different selector, no special processing!
    [calculatorProxy sumAddend1:addend2 :addend3];

    // Register another selector for proxy and repeat message
    [calculatorProxy registerSelector:@selector(sumAddend1::)];
    [calculatorProxy sumAddend1:addend1 :addend3];

  }
  return 0;
}
```

First, the code creates a Calculator object and some data values. Next, it creates a proxy for the Calculator object, initializing it with a selector for the sumAddend1:addend2: method and an AuditingInvoker instance. Notice the following statement:

```
NSArray *selValues = @[selValue1];
```

The notation @[ ] is used to create an array literal. In Part 4 of this book, you'll examine Objective-C literals in depth. The sumAddend1:addend2: message is sent to the proxy. This causes the proxy to perform the AOP functionality of the AuditingInvoker instance in addition to the method on the Calculator object. Next, the sumAddend1:: message is sent to the proxy; because this method is not yet registered on the proxy when it is invoked, the AOP functionality is not performed. Finally, the sumAddend1:: selector is added to the proxy and the message is resent to the proxy; because the selector is now registered, the AOP functionality is now performed. When you compile and run the AspectProxy program, you should observe the messages in the output pane shown in Figure 9-14.

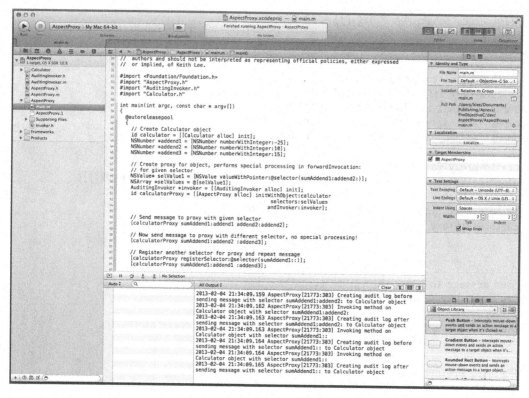

Figure 9-14. *AspectProxy program output*

Observe from the messages in the output pane that invoking the sumAddend1:addend2: method on the calculator proxy results in the proxy calling the preInvoke: method on the AuditorInvoker object, followed by the target method sumAddend1:addend2: method on the real subject (Calculator object), and finally the postInvoke: method on the AuditorInvoker object. Because the sumAddend1:addend2: method was registered with the calculator proxy, this matches the expected behavior. Next, the sumAddend1:: method is invoked on the calculator proxy. Because this method is not registered with the proxy, it only forwards this method call to the Calculator object, and does not call the AuditorInvoker methods. Finally, the sumAddend1:: method is registered with the proxy and the method is called again. This time, it calls the AOP methods on the AuditorInvoker object and the sumAddend1:: method on the real subject, as expected.

Roundup

In this chapter, you implemented three programs that together use numerous features of the Objective-C runtime system and its APIs. You also learned how to create loadable bundles and import code into a project using Xcode. You should now have a good understanding of the runtime system, its place in the Objective-C platform, and how to use its features and low-level APIs in your own programs. I recommend that you review these programs carefully, modify them to try out other features/behaviors, and become very familiar with the concepts demonstrated here. Now that you have these skills under you belt, why not take a break and give yourself a chance to let this all soak in. In Part 3, you'll explore the Foundation Framework.

Chapter 10

Foundation Framework General Purpose Classes

The Foundation Framework defines a base layer of APIs that can be used for any type of Objective-C program. It includes root object classes, classes for basic data types such as strings, wrapper classes for primitive data types, and collection classes for storing and manipulating other objects, as well as classes for system information, networking, and other functionality. Mastering the Foundation Framework APIs is one of the keys to becoming a proficient Objective-C programmer. Part 3 will help you get there as you examine these APIs in depth.

The Foundation Framework evolved from the NeXTSTEP OpenStep APIs, created in 1993. These APIs included application layer Objective-C libraries, divided into the Foundation Kit and the Application Kit. They also established the "NS" prefix-naming convention used for these APIs. When Apple acquired NeXT Software in 1996, the Foundation Kit served as the basis for the existing Foundation Framework.

In this chapter, you will explore Foundation Framework classes that provide common, general-purpose functionality required by most Objective-C programs. OK, let's get started!

Root Classes

A root, or base, class defines an interface and behaviors common to all classes below it in a class hierarchy. The Foundation Framework provides two root classes: NSObject and NSProxy. NSObject is the root class of most Objective-C class hierarchies, while NSProxy is a specialized class used to implement proxy objects. Both root classes adopt the NSObject protocol, which declares methods common to all Objective-C objects.

NSObject Protocol

The NSObject protocol specifies the basic API required for any Objective-C root class. As a protocol declares methods and properties that are not specific to any particular class, this design facilitates the definition of multiple root classes (even user-defined root classes). The methods declared by the NSObject protocol can be grouped into the following categories:

- Identifying classes and proxies
- Identifying and comparing objects
- Describing objects
- Object introspection
- Sending messages

The protocol also declares a set of obsolete methods used for manual memory management. Because ARC is the preferred memory management mechanism, these methods should no longer be used.

NSObject

The NSObject class is the root class of most Objective-C hierarchies; in fact, almost all of the Foundation Framework classes are subclasses of NSObject. It defines a set of class and instance methods that provide the following functionality:

- Basic object behaviors
- (Object, class) creation and initialization
- Dynamic (runtime system) features

You have used many of the NSObject methods in the preceding chapters, so by now you're probably pretty familiar with some of the functionality this class provides. What you'll do in the following paragraphs is examine some of the NSObject methods that I have yet to discuss in this book.

Basic Behaviors

The NSObject description class method returns a string that represents the contents of the class. The default implementation simply prints the name of the class. As an example, the following statement will display the string NSArray in the Xcode output pane.

```
NSLog(@"%@", [NSArray description]);
```

The NSObject protocol declares a description instance method; the default implementation (provided by the NSObject class) prints the object name and its address in memory. The debugDescription instance method returns a string that represents the contents of the object for presentation to the debugger; its default implementation is the same as that for the description instance method.

The `isEqual:` method returns a Boolean YES if the receiver and the input parameter (object) are equal. Two objects that are equal must have the same hash value. The default (NSObject) implementation returns YES if the receiver and the input parameter have the same memory address.

The `hash` method returns a value of type `NSUInteger` that can be used in a hash table structure. As noted earlier, two objects that are equal must have the same hash value. If hash values are used to determine the positions of objects in a collection, the value returned by the `hash` method of an object in a collection must not change while it is in the collection.

Sending Messages

NSObject defines a family of `performSelector:` instance methods used to send a message to an object. Each specifies a selector parameter identifying the message to send. The `performSelector:` method is equivalent to a standard Objective-C object message; for example, the following statements are equivalent:

```
[atom logInfo];
[atom performSelector:@selector(logInfo)];
```

The `performSelector:` method differs from a standard object message in that it enables you to send messages that are determined at runtime, as a variable selector value can be passed as the argument.

Several variations of the `performSelector:` method are declared in the NSObject protocol. These differ in the number of arguments (0–2) specified for the message (`performSelector:`, `performSelector:withObject:`, `performSelector:withObject:withObject:`). The NSObject class also defines multiple `performSelector:` methods. These provide additional functionality when sending a message to an object, specifically:

- Thread selection (current, background, user-specified)
- Method invocation semantics (synchronous, blocking)
- Event processing mode
- Method invocation delay

For example, the `performSelector:withObject:afterDelay:` method sends a message to an object after a specified delay. The following statement demonstrates use of this method to send a message to an object after a delay of 5 seconds.

```
[atom performSelector:@selector(logInfo) withObject:nil afterDelay:5.0];
```

Creation and Initialization

Now you're going to examine a few NSObject methods used for class loading and initialization. The `initialize` class method is used to initialize a class after it is loaded but before it is first used—that is, before it or any class that inherits from it is sent its first message. This method is called on a class at most once during program execution; in fact, if the class is not used, the method is not invoked. The `initialize` method is thread-safe and always sent to all of a class's superclasses before it is sent to the class itself. To prevent the possibility of the method being called twice (by a superclass in addition to the target class) the initialize method should be implemented using logic that verifies the caller is the target class, and not a superclass (as shown in Listing 10-1).

Listing 10-1. NSObject initialize Method Design

```
+ (void)initialize
{
  if (self == [MyClass class])
  {
    // Initilization logic
  }
}
```

Listing 10-1 shows that the conditional test verifies that the initialization logic is performed only on a receiver whose class is that for which the initialize method is implemented.

The NSObject load class method, if implemented, is also invoked one time, after a class is loaded. It differs from the initialize method in several ways:

- The load method is invoked very shortly after a class is loaded, prior to the initialize method. In fact, for classes that are statically linked (i.e., part of the program executable) the load method is called prior to the main() function. If the load method is implemented in a class packaged in a loadable bundle, it will be run when the bundle is dynamically loaded. Using the load method requires great care because it is called so early during application startup. Specifically, when this method is called, the program's autorelease pool is (usually) not present, other classes may not have been loaded, and so forth.

- The load method can be implemented for both classes and categories; in fact, every category of a class can implement its own load method. The initialize method should never be overriden in a category.

- The load method is invoked one time, if implemented, after a class is loaded. The initialize method is invoked one time, if implemented, when a class receives its first message; if the class is not used, the method is not invoked.

The NSObject new class method allocates a new instance of an object and then initializes it. It combines the alloc and init methods in a single method. The following two object creation and initialization statements are equivalent.

```
Atom *atom = [[Atom alloc] init];
Atom *atom = [Atom new];
```

The new method invokes a class's default init method; it does not invoke a custom init method.

NSProxy

The NSProxy class is an *abstract* root class used to implement the proxy pattern. It implements a minimal set of methods, thereby enabling almost all messages sent to it being captured and proxied to the target subject. NSProxy implements the methods declared by the NSObject protocol and declares two methods that must be implemented by subclasses:

- (void)forwardInvocation:(NSInvocation *)anInvocation;
- (NSMethodSignature *)methodSignatureForSelector:(SEL)aSelector;

> **Note**   An *abstract class* is defined as a class that cannot be directly instantiated; it may have either no implementation or an incomplete implementation. It may also have methods that are required to be implemented. Objective-C does not have language-level support for abstract classes; by convention, you specify an abstract class in Objective-C as one with no initializer and one or more methods that require implementation. Hence, a concrete subclass for an abstract class (e.g., NSProxy) must implement the unimplemented methods and at least one initializer (i.e., one init method).

Additionally, an NSProxy subclass (i.e., a *concrete subclass*) should declare and implement at least one init method to conform to Objective-C conventions for object creation and initialization. The Foundation Framework includes several concrete subclasses of NSProxy:

- NSDistantObject: Defines proxies for objects in other applications or threads.
- NSProtocolChecker: Defines an object that restricts the messages that can be sent to another object.

In Chapter 9, you implemented an NSProxy concrete subclass, AspectProxy, to provide cross-cutting (AOP) functionality around a proxied object. These examples illustrate just a few of the many uses for the NSProxy class.

Strings

The Foundation Framework includes a set of APIs used to manipulate character strings. The operations supported by these classes include:

- Creating, converting, and formatting strings
- Reading and writing strings to/from a file or resource
- String query, sorting, and comparison

In Objective-C a string is represented as an object. This means that strings can be used wherever other objects can be used (in collections, etc.). Each string object is composed of an array of Unicode (i.e., text) characters. The Foundation Framework NSString and NSMutableString classes provide the APIs for string objects. The classes NSAttributedString and NSMutableAttributedString manage strings that have associated attributes (e.g., font, paragraph style, foreground color, etc.). The attributes are identified by name and stored in a Foundation Framework NSDictionary object.

> **Note**   NSString and NSMutableString are members of the NSString class cluster. The *class cluster* design pattern is used extensively in the Foundation Framework for grouping a number of related classes with a common base interface. Likewise, NSAttributedString and NSMutableAttributedString are members of the NSAttributeString class cluster. In the case of these two class clusters, the mutable class of each pair declares additional methods that allow their (string) contents to be modified.

This family of classes supports the creation of immutable and mutable string objects, attributed strings, and Unicode characters.

NSString

NSString and NSMutableString provide the APIs for Objective-C objects that manage strings. The NSString class manages *immutable* strings, strings that are defined when they are created and, subsequently, can't be changed. NSMutableString is the *mutable* (its contents can be edited) subclass of NSString.

NSMutableString adds methods above those defined by its superclass (NSString) to create and initialize a (mutable) string, and to modify a string.

Creation and Initialization

The NSString class defines numerous methods for creating and initializing strings. The NSString init method returns an initialized NSString object with no characters. The NSString class also defines numerous initializers with parameters. These methods all begin with init and enable you to initialize an NSString object with characters, a byte buffer, contents of a file, contents of a URL, a C string, a UTF8 string, and so forth.

Scanning Values

The NSString class contains numerous methods for retrieving a primitive value from a string object. These methods support basic primitives (i.e., int, float, etc.) and the Foundation Framework NSInteger type. These methods follow a naming convention whereby the return type forms the prefix of the method name. The corresponding method signatures are shown in Listing 10-2.

Listing 10-2. NSString Methods for Retrieving Primitive Values

```
- (int) intValue;
- (float) floatValue;
- (double) doubleValue;
- (long long) longLongValue;
- (bool) boolValue;
- (NSInteger) integerValue;
```

The following example returns a result of type int assigned to the variable myValue for the string "17".

```
int myValue = [@"17" intValue];
```

Each of these methods returns a value of 0 if the string doesn't begin with a valid decimal text representation of a number. Also note that these methods don't support localization. The Foundation Framework NSScanner class provides additional functionality (including localization) for reading and converting NSString objects into numeric and string values. The following code fragment uses the NSScanner class to set the variable myValue (of type int) for the string "17".

```
NSScanner *scanner = [NSScanner scannerWithString:@"17"];
BOOL success = [scanner scanInt:&myValue];
```

The NSScanner scanInt: method returns a BOOL value of YES if the scanned string is numeric; if it returns NO, then the value stored in the variable myValue is not valid.

String Search and Comparison

The NSString class includes several methods to search for a substring within a string object. The rangeOfString: methods each return a *range* that identifies the first occurrence of an input string within the receiver object. The returned value is an NSRange instance, a Foundation Framework data type used to describe a portion of a series. NSRange is defined as a structure with two elements:

- *location*: An NSUInteger that specifies the start of the range.
- *length*: An NSUInteger that specifies the length of the range.

The following code fragment returns an NSRange instance assigned to the variable worldRange that identifies the first occurrence of the string "World" within the string "Hello, World!".

```
NSString *greeting = @"Hello, World!";
NSRange worldRange = [greeting rangeWithString:@"World"];
```

In the preceding example, the elements of worldRange have the values *six* (location) and 5 (length). Several of the rangeOfString: methods provide additional parameters that enable you to specify string comparison options, the range within the receiver object to search, and the locale to use for the search.

The NSString rangeOfCharacterFromSet: methods also perform range-based searches. They differ from the rangeOfString: methods in that they return a range that specifies the location (in the receiver string) of the first character found from a given character set. The character set input parameter is of type NSCharacterSet, a set of (Unicode-compliant) characters. The following code fragment returns an NSRange instance that identifies the first occurrence of a punctuation symbol (e.g., period, exclamation point, etc.) within the string "Hello, World!".

```
NSCharacterSet *chars = [NSCharacterSet punctuationCharacterSet];
NSRange charRange = [@"Hello, World!" rangeOfCharacterFromSet:chars];
```

In the preceding example, the elements of charRange have the values *eleven* (location) and 1 (length). As with the rangeOfString: methods, the rangeOfCharacterFromSet: methods provide additional parameters that enable you to specify string comparison options, and the range within the receiver object to search.

The NSString stringByReplacingOccurrencesOfString:withString: methods create a new string from an existing string, with all occurrences of a target (input) string in the receiver replaced by another (input) string. The following code fragment takes an initial string, "Hello, World!", and returns a new string, "Hello, Earthlings!", using this method.

```
NSString *greeting = @"Hello, World!";
NSString *newGreeting = [greeting stringByReplacingOccurrencesOfString:@"World!"
                     withString:@"Earthlings!"];
```

The NSString class contains several methods to compare a string to another string. The compare: methods return an NSComparisonResult instance, a Foundation Framework data type used to indicate how the items in a comparison are ordered a portion of a series. NSComparisonResult is defined as an enum with three constants:

- NSOrderedAscending: The left operand is less than the right.

- NSOrderedSame: The operands are equal.

- NSOrderedDescending: The left operand is greater than the right.

The following statement returns an NSComparisonResult assigned to the variable order that identifies the result of the ordered comparison between the strings "cat" and "dog".

```
NSComparisonResult order = [@"cat" compare:@"dog"];
```

The result of this comparison is NSOrderedAscending, indicating that the word *cat* is alphabetically ordered before the word *dog*. NSString contains additional comparison methods that enable you to perform localized comparisons, case insensitive comparisons, and other options.

String I/O

NSString includes methods for both reading and writing a string to/from a file or a URL. The writeToFile:atomically:encoding:error: method writes a string to a file at the specified path. This method also specifies the encoding to use if the file is written atomically (to prevent the file from being corrupted if the system crashes while the file is being written), and an error object that describes the problem if an error occurs while writing the file. The method returns YES if the string is written to the file successfully. The writeToURL:atomically:encoding:error: method writes a string to a given URL. The NSString stringWithContentsOfFile:, stringWithContentsOfURL:, initWithContentsOfFile:, and initWithContentsOfURL: methods create and initialize a string from a file or URL.

Introspection

The NSString class includes numerous methods for obtaining information about an NSString object. The following statement uses the NSString length method to retrieve the number of characters in the string "Hello, World!".

```
int len = [@"Hello, World!" length];
```

The following statement uses the NSString hasPrefix: method to return a Boolean value indicating whether the "Hello, World!" string has a prefix of "Hello".

```
BOOL hasPrefix = [@"Hello, World!" hasPrefix:@"Hello"];
```

Modifying a String

NSMutableString adds several methods to those provided by NSString for modifying a string. These methods enable you to append a string or a format string, to insert or delete characters in a string, to replace characters or a string within a string, or to set a string to a new value. The following code fragment creates a mutable string named "Hello" and then appends the string, "World!" to it.

```
NSMutableString *mgreet = [@"Hello" mutableCopy];
[mgreet appendString:@", World!"];
```

NSAttributedString

NSAttributedString and NSMutableAttributedString provide the APIs for Objective-C objects that manage strings and associated sets of attributes. The NSAttributedString class manages *immutable* strings, while the NSMutableAttributedString class manages *mutable* strings.

The methods provided for the NSAttributedString class enable the creation and initialization of strings, retrieval of string and attribute information, and enumerating over attributes in a string using a block object. The initWithString:attributes: method initializes an NSAttributeString instance with attributes, where the attributes are provided in an NSDictionary instance. The following code fragment creates and initializes an NSAttributedString with the string "Hello" and a single attribute (locale = en-US).

```
NSDictionary *attrs = @{@"locale":@"en-US"};
NSAttributedString *greeting = [[NSAttributedString alloc] initWithString:@"Hello"
                                                        attributes:attrs];
```

The next statement retrieves the value of the attribute (using the key "locale") from the attribute string and also sets the range of the attribute to the variable of type NSRange named range.

```
NSRange range;
id value = [greeting attribute:@"locale" atIndex:0 effectiveRange:&range];
```

NSString Literals

Objective-C provides language-level support for creating NSString literals using the @ symbol followed by a text string enclosed in double-quotes. The following statement creates an NSString object named book using an NSString literal.

```
NSString *book = @"Pro Objective-C";
```

NSString literals are compile-time constants. They are allocated at compile time and exist for the lifetime of the program.

Format Strings

The NSString class includes several methods for formatting string objects using a format string that is composed of ordinary text characters and zero or more format specifiers. A *format specifier* is a specification for converting an argument in a format string to a character string. Each format specifier begins with a % character that specifies a placeholder for an argument value, immediately followed by a character sequence that indicates the type of the argument. The list of format specifiers supported by the NSString formatting methods include those defined by the IEEE printf specification along with the format specifier '%@', which is used to format an Objective-C object. For example, the format string @"%d" expects an argument of integer type to be substituted for the format string. The NSString stringWithFormat: method and other related methods create and initialize NSString objects using format strings. The syntax for the stringWithFormat method is

```
+ (id)stringWithFormat:(NSString *)format, ...
```

Where format is the format string and ... specifies the comma-separated list of argument(s) to substitute into the format. The following example creates an NSString object assigned to the variable magicNumber with the text "Your number is 17".

```
NSString *magicNumber = [NSString stringWithFormat: @"Your number is %d", 17];
```

In this example the format string, @"Your number is %d", contains ordinary text and a single format specifier, %d, that is substituted for the argument 17. The next example creates a string formatted using the NSString object magicNumber.

```
NSString *description = [NSString stringWithFormat:
                    @"Description is %@", magicNumber];
```

The %@ format specifier substitutes the string returned by invoking either the descriptionWithLocale: (if available) or description method on the object.

The Foundation Framework includes several classes (NSFormatter, NSDateFormatter, NSNumberFormatter) that provide additional functionality for interpreting and creating NSString objects that represent other values.

Value Objects

The Foundation Framework value object classes implement object-oriented wrappers for primitive data types, along with general-purpose system information, tools, and locale support. The NSCalendar, NSDate, NSCalendarDate, NSDateComponents, and NSTimeZone classes provide support for date and time programming and formatting. The NSValue, NSNumber, NSDecimalNumber, and NSDecimalNumberHandler classes provide object-oriented wrappers for primitive data types, which can then be manipulated and/or added to collection objects. The NSData, NSMutableData, and NSPurgeableData classes provide object-oriented wrappers for byte buffers. NSValueTransformer is used to transform values from one representation to another. NSNull is a singleton object used to represent null values in collection objects that don't allow nil values. NSLocale provides support for *locales,* a collection of information used to adapt software for a specific region or language. NSCache provides an in-memory system cache for the temporary storage of objects that are expensive to re-create.

NSValue

The NSValue class is a container for a single data item. It can hold both C and Objective-C data types (including primitives) of constant length and is typically used to allow an item to be stored in a collection object (NSArray, NSSet, etc.), because these require their elements to be objects. The code fragment in Listing 10-3 creates an NSValue instance from a value of type int.

Listing 10-3. Creating an NSValue Instance

```
int ten = 10;
int *tenPtr = &ten;
NSValue *myInt = [NSValue value:&tenPtr withObjCType:@encode(int *)];
```

Note that the type is specified using an @encode directive. This value can now be stored in a collection object. The following statement retrieves the int value of the NSValue object and assigns this value to the variable result.

```
int result = *(int *)[myInt pointerValue];
```

NSNumber

The NSNumber class is a subclass of NSValue that functions as a container for primitive (scalar) types. It defines a set of methods for creating and accessing number objects as primitive types: signed/unsigned char, int, short int, long int, long long int, NSInteger, float, double, or BOOL types. NSNumber includes numerous class factory methods (whose names all begin with numberWith...) for creating and initializing an NSNumber with an input parameter of the specified primitive type. The following statement uses the numberWithDouble: method to create an NSNumber instance of type double and assign it to a variable named degrees2Radians.

```
NSNumber *degrees2Radians = [NSNumber numberWithDouble:(3.1415/180.0)];
```

NSNumber also includes initialization methods (whose names all begin with initWith...) to initialize an allocated NSNumber object with the input parameter value. The corresponding NSNumber ...Value methods (one for each of the supported types) can be used to retrieve a primitive value from an NSNumber object, for example:

```
double d2r = [degrees2Radians doubleValue];
```

NSNumber also includes a stringValue method to get the string representation of an NSNumber instance.

NSDecimalNumber

NSDecimalNumber is a subclass of NSNumber that is used to perform decimal arithmetic. It includes methods for creating and initializing decimal numbers, and methods for performing standard arithmetic operations (addition, subtraction, multiplication, division, etc.). It is especially useful for performing these operations on numbers where rounding errors can be significant (for example, with currency). Listing 10-4 adds two NSDecimalNumber objects and assigns the result to an NSDecimalNumber object named sum.

Listing 10-4. Adding Two Numbers Using NSDecimalNumber

```
NSDecimalNumber *num1 = [NSDecimalNumber decimalNumberWithString:@"2.56"];
NSDecimalNumber *num2 = [NSDecimalNumber decimalNumberWithString:@"7.78"];
NSDecimalNumber *sum = [num1 decimalNumberByAdding:num2];
```

The NSDecimalNumber methods that perform arithmetic operations include parameters that can be used to specify how calculation errors and rounding are handled.

NSNumber Literals

Objective-C provides language-level support for creating NSNumber literals. Any character, numeric, or Boolean literal that is prefixed with an @ character evaluates to an NSNumber object initialized to that value. The following statements are equivalent:

```
NSNumber *num = [NSNumber numberWithInt:17];
NSNumber *num = @17;
```

NSNumber literals are created from scalar values, not expressions. In addition, NSNumber literals are evaluated at runtime; they are not compile-time constants and thus cannot be used to initialize static variables. In essence, the literal @17 is actually shorthand for the expression [NSNumber numberWithInt:17], an object message that is evaluated at runtime. More information on NSNumber literals is provided in Chapter 16, which explores Objective-C literals in depth.

Date and Time Support

The NSCalendar, NSDate, NSCalendarDate, NSDateComponents, and NSTimeZone classes provide support for date and time programming and formatting. An NSDate instance represents an absolute timestamp. The following statement creates a date that represents the current time.

```
NSDate *now = [[NSDate alloc] init];
```

The following statements compare two dates and return an NSComparisonResult that indicates whether the input date is later, the same, or earlier than the receiver's dates.

```
NSTimeInterval secondsPerDay = 24 * 60 * 60;
NSDate *tomorrow = [now dateByAddingTimeInterval:secondsPerDay];
NSComparisonResult *result = [now compare:tomorrow];
```

The NSCalendar class encapsulates calendar information used to organize periods of time. It provides an implementation for several different calendars, including the Buddhist, Gregorian, Hebrew, Islamic, and Japanese calendars. The following statement returns a calendar for the current user's chosen locale.

```
NSCalendar *currentCalendar = [NSCalendar currentCalendar];
```

The following statement creates a Gregorian calendar.

```
NSCalendar *gregorianCalendar = [[NSCalendar alloc]
                      initWithCalendarIdentifier:NSGregorianCalendar];
```

NSCalendar provides methods for retrieving the component elements of a date in a calendar, represented as NSDateComponents objects.

The NSDateComponents class represents the component elements of a date/time. It is used to set/get these elements, and also specify a time interval. The following statements retrieve date components from a current calendar object with monthly calendar units.

```
NSDate *date = [NSDate date];
NSDateComponents *components = [currentCalendar components:NSMonthCalendarUnit
                                      fromDate:date];
```

NSCache

In computer programming, a cache is a mechanism that stores data so that future requests for the same data can be retrieved more quickly. They are commonly used to store objects that are expensive to re-create. The Foundation Framework NSCache class provides an in-memory system cache for the temporary storage of objects that are expensive to re-create. In addition to managing cache values, the class includes methods for managing the cache size, managing discarded objects, and managing the cache delegate. A cache delegate conforms to the NSCacheDelegate protocol, and is sent messages when an object is about to be evicted or removed from the cache. An NSCache instance stores key-value pairs, similar to an NSDictionary (to be discussed later in this chapter). It differs in that it provides autoremoval policies, and thus manages memory utilization. The following code fragment creates an NSCache instance, sets the number of objects the cache can hold, and then adds an object to the cache.

```
NSCache *cache = [[NSCache alloc] init];
[cache setCountLimit:500];
[cache setObject:@"Hello, World!" forKey:@"greeting"];
```

Collections

The Foundation Framework collections classes manage collections of objects. Most collection classes have both an immutable and a mutable version. NSArray and NSMutableArray manage arrays, ordered collections of objects that can be of any type; the elements of an NSArray do not have to be of the same type. NSDictionary and NSMutableDictionary are used for groups of key-value pairs. NSSet, NSMutableSet, and NSCountedSet are used to manage unordered collections of objects. The NSEnumerator and NSDirectoryEnumerator classes enumerate collections of other objects, such as arrays and dictionaries. NSIndexSet and NSMutableIndexSet manage collections of *index sets* (collections of unique unsigned integers used to store indexes into another data structure). NSHashTable, NSMapTable, and NSPointerArray are mutable collections that support weak relationships when using the garbage collector.

The NSHashTable, NSMapTable, and NSPointerArray classes are available for use on the Apple OS X platform only (i.e., these classes are not available for the iOS platform).

NSArray

NSArray and NSMutableArray manage ordered collections of objects that do not have to be of the same type. NSArray is immutable (the objects assigned to the array at initialization cannot be removed, although there contents can be changed). NSMutableArray allows adding or removing objects in a collection. The operations supported by NSArray include array creation and initialization, query (obtaining information about the array or retrieving its elements), finding an object in an array, object messaging to array elements, comparing arrays, and sorting an array. Many NSArray and NSMutableArray operations are executed in constant time (accessing an element, adding/removing on ends, replacing an element), whereas inserting an element in the middle of an NSMutableArray takes linear time. The following statement uses the NSArray arrayWithObjects: convenience constructor to create an NSArray object assigned to the variable myArray initialized with NSNumber literals.

```
NSArray *myArray = [NSArray arrayWithObjects:@1, @2, nil];
```

Notice that the arrayWithObjects: method requires parameters with a comma-separated list of objects ending with nil. The next statement retrieves the first element of this NSArray object using the NSArray indexOfObject: method.

```
id num0 = [myArray objectAtIndex:0];
```

The following statement returns the index of the NSNumber object (with a value of 2) in the preceding NSArray object.

```
NSUInteger index = [myArray indexOfObject:@2];
```

NSArray also includes the following methods to persist the contents of an array to a property list and initialize an NSArray object from a property list:

- writeToFile:atomically:
- writeToURL:atomically:
- initWithContentsOfFile:
- initWithContentsOfURL:

When persisting an array (via the `writeTo...` methods), its contents must all be property list objects (i.e., NSString, NSData, NSDate, NSNumber, NSArray, NSDictionary objects).

NSArray Literals

Objective-C provides language-level support for creating NSArray literals. The array is defined by a comma-separated list of objects between square brackets, prefixed by an @ character. Unlike the NSArray arrayWithObjects: and initWithObjects: methods, the list of objects used to define an NSArray literal is not required to end with a nil. The following statements are equivalent:

```
NSArray *myArray = [NSArray arrayWithObjects:@1, @2, nil];
NSArray *myArray = @[@1, @2];
```

As with NSNumber literals, NSArray literals are not compile-time constants; they are evaluated at runtime.

NSPointerArray

NSPointerArray is a mutable collection similar to NSMutableArray that can hold arbitrary pointers and NULL values. It also allows you to manage the collection by setting the count for the array, such that if the number of elements in the collection is less than the count, then the collection is padded with NULL values; or if the number of elements in the collection is greater than the count, then the elements in the collection above the count value are removed.

NSDictionary

The NSDictionary and NSMutableDictionary classes manage collections of key/value (object) pairs. Within a collection, the value of a key is unique (i.e., it must be an object that adopts the NSCopying protocol and implements the hash and isEqual: methods). The operations supported by these classes include object creation and initialization, query, finding objects in the collection, filtering, comparing, and sorting the collection. The sorting options include sorting with selectors (using the keySortedByValueUsingSelector: method), and sorting with blocks (using the keySortedByValueUsingComparator: method). For keys with good hash functions (for example, NSString), NSDictionary operations take constant time (accessing, setting, removing an element from an NSDictionary or NSMutableDictionary). The code fragment shown in Listing 10-5 creates and initializes an NSDictionary object with two elements.

Listing 10-5. Creating and Initializing an NSDictionary Object

```
NSArray *objects = @[@1, @2];
NSArray *keys = @[@"one", @"two"];
NSDictionary *myDi = [NSDictionary dictionaryWithObjects:objects];
                   withKeys:keys];
```

The next statement retrieves the value from the preceding NSDictionary object that has the key "one".

```
id value = [myDi objectForKey:@"one"];
```

As with NSArray, NSDictionary includes methods to persist the contents of a dictionary to a property list and initialize an NSDictionary object from a property list:

- writeToFile:atomically:
- writeToURL:atomically:
- initWithContentsOfFile:
- initWithContentsOfURL:

When persisting a dictionary (via the writeTo... methods), its contents must all be property list objects (NSString, NSData, NSDate, NSNumber, NSArray, and NSDictionary objects).

NSDictionary Literals

Objective-C provides language-level support for creating NSDictionary literals. The dictionary is defined by a comma-separated list of key-value pairs between curly braces, prefixed by an @ character. In each key-value pair, a colon separates the key and value. The following statements are equivalent:

```
NSArray *objects = @[@1, @2];
NSArray *keys = @[@"one", @"two"];
NSDictionary *myDi = [NSDictionary dictionaryWithObjects:objects];

NSDictionary *myDi = @{@"one":@1, @"two":@2};
```

As with NSNumber literals, NSDictionary literals are not compile-time constants; they are evaluated at runtime.

NSMapTable

NSPointerArray is a mutable collection similar to NSDictionary that provides additional storage options. Specifically, it can store arbitrary pointers. It can also store weakly referenced keys and/or values.

NSSet

NSSet and NSMutableSet manage unordered collections of objects that do not have to be of the same type. The objects stored in an NSSet are unique. The operations supported by NSSet include creation and initialization, finding an object in a set, comparing, and sorting (using the NSSet sortedArrayUsingDescriptors: method). If the objects in the set have a good hash function, accessing an element, setting an element, and removing an element all take constant time. With a poor hash function (one that causes frequent hash collisions), these operations take up linear time.

Sets, excluding NSCountedSets, ensure that no object is represented more than once, and there is no net effect for adding an object more than once. The following statement uses the NSSet setWithObjects: convenience constructor to create an NSSet object assigned to the variable mySet initialized with NSNumber literals.

```
NSSet *mySet = [NSSet setWithObjects:@1, @2, nil];
```

NSCountedSet

NSCountedSet is a mutable set that allows an object to be added multiple times (i.e., its elements aren't required to be distinct). Each distinct object has an associated counter. An NSSet object keeps track of the number of times each distinct object is inserted and requires a corresponding object(s) to be removed the same number of times.

NSHashTable

NSHashTable is a mutable collection similar to NSSet that provides different options. Specifically, it can store arbitrary pointers. It can also store weakly referenced keys and/or values.

NSPointerFunctions

The NSPointerFunctions class defines functions for managing pointer functions. An NSHashTable, NSMapTable, or NSPointerArray object typically uses an NSPointerFunctions instance to define behavior for the pointers it manages.

XML Processing

The Foundation Framework XML processing classes support general-purpose XML document management and parsing functionality. The classes logically represent an XML document as a hierarchical tree structure and support the query and manipulation of XML document nodes. These classes support several XML-related technologies and standards, such as XQuery, XPath, XInclude, XSLT, DTD, and XHTML.

Classes NSXMLDTD and NSXMLDTDNode are used for creating and modifying XML Document Type Definitions (DTDs). NSXMLDocument, NSXMLNode, and NSXMLElement are used for tree-based processing of XML documents. Instances of NSXMLParser are used to parse XML documents in an event-driven manner.

XML DTD Processing

The NSXMLDTD classes (NSXMLDTD and NSXMLDTDNode) represent a Document Type Definition (DTD). They are used for creating and modifying DTDs. The XML DTD processing classes (NSXMLDTD, NSXMLDTDNode) are available for use on the Apple OS X platform only (i.e., these classes are not available for the iOS platform).

Tree-Based XML Processing

The Foundation NSXML classes enable you to create, manipulate, modify, and query XML documents. These classes employ a Document Object Model (DOM) styled, tree-based data model that represents an XML document as a tree of nodes. Each node of the tree corresponds to an XML construct—an Element, an Attribute, Text, a Comment, a Processing Instruction, or a Namespace. An NSXMLDocument object represents an entire XML document as a logical tree structure. The code fragment shown in Listing 10-6 creates an NSXMLDocument for the URL http://www.apress.com/proobjectivec.xml.

Listing 10-6. Creating an NSXMLDocument Object

```
NSURL *url = [NSURL URLWithString:@"http://www.apress.com/proobjectivec.xml"];
NSError *err;
NSXMLDocument *xmlDoc = [[NSXMLDocument alloc]
                          initWithContentsOfURL:url
                                    options:NSXMLDocumentValidate
                                      error:&err];
```

NSXMLNode, the superclass of NSXMLDocument, includes methods for navigating a tree of nodes from an XML document. The following code fragment uses an NSXMLNode method, nextNode, to retrieve the next node in an XML document.

```
NSXMLNode *node = [xmlDoc nextNode];
```

NSXMLElement, a subclass of NSXMLNode, represents element nodes in an XML tree structure. It includes methods for managing child elements and attributes of an XML document. The following code fragment gets the NSXMLElement object with the given tag name of "test" and then uses this object to retrieve the child element nodes (an NSArray object) that have the specified name.

```
NSXMLElement *testElem = [NSXMLNode elementWithName:@"test"];
NSArray *children = [noteElem elementsForName:@"item"];
```

The XML processing classes (NSXMLDocument, NSXMLNode, NSXMLElement) are available for use on the Apple OS X platform only (i.e., these classes are not available for the iOS platform).

Event-Driven XML Processing

The NSXMLParser class is used to parse XML documents, including DTD documents, in an event-driven manner. An NSXMLParser instance is configured with a *delegate*, an object that implements certain methods that are invoked on it while the NSXMLParser instance is processing an XML document. The delegate must conform to the NSXMLParserDelegate protocol, thereby enabling it to respond to events (i.e., method invocations) when the parser begins/ends processing the document, processes XML elements and attributes, and so forth. The method shown in Listing 10-7 demonstrates the creation, initialization, and use of an NSXMLParser instance to parse an XML document.

Listing 10-7. Parsing an XML Document

```
- (void) parseXMLInfoset:(NSString *)file
{
  NSURL *infoset = [NSURL fileURLWithPath:file];
  NSXMLParser *parser = [[NSXMLParser alloc]
    initWithContentsOfURL:infoset];
  [parser setDelegate:self];
  [parser setShouldResolveExternalEntities:YES];
  [parser parse];
}
```

As mentioned earlier, a delegate object must conform to the NSXMLParserDelegate protocol to be able to process document parsing events (e.g., begin parsing a document, end parsing a document, start parsing an element, start mapping a namespace prefix, end mapping a namespace prefix) from an NSXMLParser instance. Unlike the NSXML (tree-based XML processing classes), the event-driven XML parser classes enable you to read XML documents but not create or update them.

The NSXMLParser class is available for use on both the Apple OS X and iOS platform. The other XML processing classes mentioned here are only available for use on the OS X platform.

Predicates

This collection of classes provides a general means of specifying queries using predicates and expressions. A *predicate* is a logical operator that returns either a true or false value and is composed of one or more *expressions*. Predicates are used to constrain a search for a query or to provide filtering of returned results. The NSExpression class is used to represent expressions in a predicate, and it supports multiple expression types. NSPredicate, NSComparisonPredicate, and NSCompoundPredicate are used to create predicates. The code fragment shown in Listing 10-8 creates and initializes an array, then creates a predicate that searches for elements in the array with a value greater than 1, and then creates a new, filtered array using this predicate.

Listing 10-8. Creating a Filtered Array Using a Predicate

```
NSArray *nArray = @[@1, @2];
NSPredicate *pred = [NSPredicate predicateWithFormat: @"SELF > 1"];
NSArray *filteredArray = [nArray filteredArrayUsingPredicate:pred];
```

Roundup

In this chapter, you began your review of the Foundation Framework, focusing on classes that provide common, general-purpose functionality required for most Objective-C programs. You should now be familiar with Foundation Framework classes that provide the following functionality:

- Root classes
- Working with strings
- Numbers and value objects
- Collections
- XML processing

Chapter 11

Foundation Framework System Services

In this chapter, you will learn about Foundation Framework classes that provide system services. These classes implement a variety of operating system services for networking, file management, interprocess communication, system information retrieval, text processing, threading, and concurrency.

Network Services

The Foundation Framework includes various APIs to support network services. In the next few chapters, you'll learn about APIs used to access network host information, and explore how to utilize the Bonjour network protocol to publish and discover network services.

NSHost

The NSHost class contains methods to access information for a *network host*, which is a collection of network names and addresses for a computer or device connected to a network. An NSHost object represents an individual network host. Its methods can be used to look up the network name and address information for the host or other objects on a network. The code in Listing 11-1 uses the NSHost currentHost and name methods to retrieve the NSHost object for the host the program is running on, and then logs the host name to the console.

Listing 11-1. Retrieving the Network Host Name Using NSHost

```
NSHost myHost = [NSHost currentHost];
NSLog(@"Host name is %@", [myHost name]);
```

Listing 11-2 uses the NSHost hostWithName: and address methods to create an NSHost object with the domain name www.apress.com, and then logs the host address to the console.

Listing 11-2. Retrieving a Host Address Using NSHost

```
NSHost *apress = [NSHost hostWithName:@"www.apress.com"];
NSLog(@"Apress host address is %@", [apress address]);
```

Bonjour Network Services

Bonjour is a protocol that automatically creates a functional IP network without the need for configuration or manual intervention, also known as *zero configuration networking*. Bonjour is designed to enable devices, such as computers and printers, to connect to a network automatically. It performs a variety of functions, including service discovery, address assignment, and hostname resolution.

The NSNetService and NSNetServiceBrowser classes provide functionality to manage Bonjour network services. The NSNetService class represents a network service that an application publishes or uses as a client. A service can be either a local service that your application is publishing or a remote service that your application wants to use. The NSNetServiceBrowser class is used to find published network services. Each class must provide a delegate object that performs processing upon completion of method invocation. The methods for each class are invoked asynchronously and performed within a *run loop*. Later in this chapter, you'll learn how to use the NSRunLoop class to manage run loops.

Application Services

These classes consist of several general-purpose APIs used to retrieve and/or set information associated with an application process. The NSProcessInfo class is used to retrieve information about the currently executing program (i.e., process). The class method processInfo retrieves the single NSNProcessInfo object for the current process. NSProcessInfo includes instance methods used to retrieve process information, such as its command-line arguments, environment variables, host name, process name, and so forth. The following statement uses the processInfo and processName methods to retrieve the name of the current process.

```
NSString *name = [[NSProcessInfo processInfo] processName];
```

The NSUserDefaults class provides an API for managing *user preferences*, information stored persistently on the local file system and used to configure an application. An application provides preferences to enable users to customize its behavior. NSUserDefaults includes methods to both set and retrieve preferences, and manage other aspects of the preferences system. The set and retrieve methods support primitive types along with objects that are property list types (i.e., objects of type NSData, NSString, NSNumber, NSDate, NSArray, or NSDictionary). Preferences are stored in a user's defaults database as key-value pairs.

The code in Listing 11-3 uses the standardUserDefaults, setObject:forKey: and objectForKey: methods to set a user preference, and then retrieve and log the value set to the console.

```
NSUserDefaults *defaults = [NSUserDefaults standardUserDefaults];
[defaults setObject:@"Hello" forKey:@"USER_SALUTATION"];
NSLog(@"Salutation is %@", [defaults objectForKey:@" USER_SALUTATION"]);
```

Regular Expressions and Text Processing

NSRegularExpression is used to apply *regular expression* processing on strings. A regular expression is a pattern that provides a means of both specifying and identifying text. The class includes methods to create and initialize an NSRegularExpression object, and methods to perform a variety of regular expression operations (find matches, number of matches, etc.).

The Foundation Framework NSOrthography, NSSpellServer, and NSTextCheckingResult classes are primarily used for text processing. NSOrthography describes the linguistic content of text (the scripts the text contains, the dominant language and possibly other languages for the scripts, the dominant script and language for the text overall). NSSpellServer provides a mechanism for making an application's spell checker available to any application as a spelling service. It includes methods for configuring a spelling server, providing spelling services, and managing the spell-checking process. The NSSpellServer class is available for use on the OS X platform only. The NSTextCheckingResult class is used to describe the items located by text checking. Each object represents the occurrence of the requested text found during the analysis of a block of text. The code in Listing 11-4 uses an NSRegularExpression object to retrieve an NSTextCheckingResult object and display its data.

Listing 11-4. Retrieving an NSTextCheckingResult from a Regular Expression

```
NSError *error;
NSRegularExpression *regex = [NSRegularExpression
  regularExpressionWithPattern:@"World"
                    options:NSRegularExpressionCaseInsensitive
                      error:&error];
NSString *greeting = @"Hello, World!";
NSTextCheckingResult *match = [regex
  firstMatchInString:greeting
            options:0
              range:NSMakeRange(0, [greeting length])];
NSRange range = [match range];
NSLog(@"Match begins at %ldth character in string",
  (unsigned long)range.location);
```

As shown in Listing 11-4, a regular expression is created using the NSRegularExpression regularExpressionWithPattern: method. Next, the code uses the firstMatchInString:options: range: method to retrieve the result of the regular expression query as an NSTextCheckingResult. The pattern located by the query is then logged to the console with the NSTextCheckingResult range method.

File System Utilities

The File I/O classes consist of a collection of APIs for using files and directories. The classes enable you to represent file paths, perform basic operations with files and directories, find directories on the system, and use streams to perform input/output (I/O) operations with files, in-memory, or to/from a network resource.

Application Bundles

The NSBundle class groups code and resources that can be used in a program. They are used to locate program resources, dynamically load and unload executable code, and assist in localization. The NSBundle class includes methods that enable you to create and initialize a bundle, retrieve a bundle or bundle class, load a bundle's code, find resources in a bundle, retrieve bundle information, and manage localization. In Chapters 7 and 9, you learned about loadable bundles and used the NSBundle class to dynamically load a bundle and create an object from a bundle class, so you can refer to these chapters for further information and code examples.

File Management

The NSFileHandle class provides low-level file management utilities. An NSFileHandle class instance is an object-oriented wrapper for a file descriptor. It includes methods for creating and initializing file handlers, retrieving a file descriptor, performing file I/O using a file handler, and closing a file when you are done. It also supports asynchronous file operations. Many of the NSFileHandle creation methods also acquire ownership of the file descriptor, and automatically close the file when the object is deallocated. The class also includes methods to create an NSFileHandle object with an input file descriptor. In these scenarios, the closeFile method can be used to close the descriptor. Listing 11-5 demonstrates the use of NSFileHandle APIs to read a file named Example.txt from the system's default location to store temporary files.

Listing 11-5. Using NSFileHandle to Read a File

```
NSString *tmpDir = NSTemporaryDirectory();
NSString *myFile = [NSString stringWithFormat:@"%@/%@", tmpDir,
                    @"Example.txt"];
NSFileHandle *fileHandle = [NSFileHandle fileHandleForReadingAtPath:myFile];
if (fileHandle)
{
  NSData *fileData = [fileHandle readDataToEndOfFile];
  NSLog(@"%lu bytes read from file %@", [fileData length], myFile);
}
```

The NSFileManager class provides general-purpose methods for performing basic file-system operations. It includes methods to create a file manager, locate directories, query directory contents, manage file and directory items, create soft/hard links to files, query file access, get/set file system attributes, and even manage iCloud-storage items. Listing 11-6 uses the NSFileManager APIs to list the contents at the current directory path, and then query whether the first file found in this directory is executable.

Listing 11-6. Using NSFileManager to List the Contents of a Directory

```
NSFileManager *filemgr = [NSFileManager defaultManager];
NSString *currentPath = [filemgr currentDirectoryPath];
NSArray *contents = [filemgr contentsOfDirectoryAtPath:currentPath error:&error];
NSLog(@"Contents: %@", contents);
if (contents)
{
  NSString *file = [NSString stringWithFormat:@"%@/%@", currentPath, contents[0]];
  if ([filemgr isExecutableFileAtPath:file])
  {
    NSLog(@"%@ is executable", file);
  }
}
```

Stream Input-Output

Streams provide a convenient mechanism for reading and writing data sequentially, whether that data be located in memory, a file, or over a network. The NSStream, NSInputStream, and NSOutputStream classes provide functionality for reading from/writing to streams. NSStream is an abstract class, and NSInputStream and NSOutputStream are its concrete subclasses. A stream can be read/written asynchronously (usually the preferred approach) or synchronously by polling. To access a stream asynchronously, a delegate object is set for the stream (i.e., an NSInputStream or NSOutputStream object) and the stream is then scheduled in a run loop. The delegate conforms to the NSStreamDelegate protocol. The run loop invokes its stream:handleEvent: to handle stream events (status, data available, error conditions). Listing 11-7 demonstrates use of the NSInputStream APIs to create an input stream from a file, and then synchronously read data from a file named Example.txt (stored in the current directory) into a buffer.

Listing 11-7. Using NSInputStream to Read a File

```
NSString *currentPath = [[NSFileManager defaultManager] currentDirectoryPath];
NSString *myFile = [NSString stringWithFormat:@"%@/%@", currentPath,
                    @"Example.txt"];
NSInputStream *ins = [NSInputStream inputStreamWithFileAtPath:myFile];
[ins open];
if (ins && [ins hasBytesAvailable])
{
  uint8_t buffer[1024];
  NSUInteger len = [ins read:buffer maxLength:1024];
  NSLog(@"Bytes read = %lu", len);
}
```

After creating the input stream, the stream is opened. Next, the NSInputStream hasBytesAvailable method is used to determine whether the stream has any bytes to read, and if so, the NSInputStream read method is used to read the data into a buffer. Finally, the number of bytes read is logged to the console.

Metadata Queries

The NSMetadataItem and NSMetadataQuery set of classes provide APIs for metadata queries that enable an application to search for files based on data that is part of the file or file system. Together they provide a programmatic way to perform file searches using file metadata, as provided with the Apple desktop Spotlight search tool.

The NSMetadataItem and NSMetadataQuery classes are available for use on the OS X platform only (i.e., this class is not available for the iOS platform).

Concurrency and Threading

The concurrency and threading support classes implement functionality that both manage threads and support the concurrent execution of multiple sections of code using threads. The following paragraphs provide a general introduction to these classes, refer to Chapter 17 for an in-depth guide to concurrent programming with the Objective-C platform.

Thread Management

The NSTask and NSThread classes are used to manage threads and processes. NSTask enables the creation and management of processes within the Objective-C runtime. An NSTask instance operates as a separate process that does not share memory space with another process, including the process that created it. An NSTask object can only be run once and its environment is configured prior to the task being started. The launchedTaskWithLaunchPath:arguments: method is used to create and start a new task that executes the program named greeting in the current directory, as shown in the following statement.

```
NSTask *hello = [NSTask launchTaskWithLaunchPath:@"./greeting"
                                        arguments:nil];
```

The init method can be used to create a new task; subsequently, the methods setLaunchPath:, setArguments:,(if the method has arguments) and launch would then be used to start the task.

```
NSTask *hello = [[NSTask alloc] init];
[hello setLaunchPath:@"./greeting"];
[hello launch];
```

The isRunning method can be used to query the state of a task, as shown in the following statement.

```
BOOL running = [hello isRunning];
```

A thread is an operating system mechanism that enables the concurrent execution of multiple sequences of instructions. A thread is typically implemented as a lightweight process, in that multiple threads can exist concurrently within the same process. Threads within a process can share computer memory and other resources. NSThread is used to create and control threads. The class includes methods to create and initialize an NSThread object, start and stop a thread, configure a thread, and query a thread and its execution environment. The NSThread class method detachNe wThreadSelector:toTarget:withObject: is used to create and start a new thread. The following statement uses this method to create and start a new thread on the execute: method of an object named processEngine, with an input parameter of myData.

```
NSThread *myThread = [NSThread detachNewThreadSelector:@selector(execute:)
                                              toTarget:processEngine
                                            withObject:myData];
```

The thread priority can be set with the setThreadPriority: method, as shown in the following statement which sets the thread myThread to a priority of 1.0, the highest priority.

```
[myThread setThreadPriority:1.0];
```

A thread can be signaled to cancel with cancel method; the following statement sends this message to the thread myThread.

```
[myThread cancel];
```

Concurrent Operations

NSOperation, NSBLockOperation, and NSInvocationOperation are used to manage concurrent execution of one or more operations, code, and data associated with a single task. An operation queue is an Objective-C object that provides the ability to execute tasks concurrently. Each task (i.e., operation) defines the work to be performed, along with its associated data, and is encapsulated in either a block object or a concrete subclass of NSOperation. NSOperation is an abstract class that encapsulates the code and data associated with a single task. For nonconcurrent tasks, a concrete subclass typically only needs to override the main method. For concurrent tasks, you must override at a minimum the methods start, isConcurrent, isExecuting, and isFinished. Listing 11-8 provides an implementation of the class GreetingOperation, a concrete subclass of NSOperation that logs a simple greeting to the output pane.

Listing 11-8. GreetingOperation Class

```
@interface GreetingOperation : NSOperation
@end

@implementation GreetingOperation
- (void)main
{
  NSLog(@"Hello, world!");
}
@end
```

NSOperationQueue controls the execution of NSOperation objects through a queuing system. Operation queues may employ threads to execute their operations; however, this implementation detail is hidden, thereby simplifying application development and reducing the potential for errors. Listing 11-9 creates an instance of a GreetingOperation, and then submits it to an NSOperationQueue to execute concurrently.

Listing 11-9. Submitting GreetingOperation Instance to a Queue

```
NSOperation *greetingOp = [[GreetingOperation alloc] init];
[[NSOperationQueue mainQueue] addOperation:greetingOp];
```

Operation queues provide a simpler, more efficient mechanism for implementing concurrency and are therefore recommended in lieu of threads for implementing concurrent programming.

Locking

NSLock, NSDistributedLock, NSConditionLock, and NSRecursiveLock are used to create locks for synchronizing code execution. NSLock implements a basic mutual exclusion (mutex) lock for concurrent programming. It conforms to the NSLocking protocol and thus implements the lock and unlock methods to acquire and release a lock accordingly.

The NSDistributedLock class defines a lock that can be used by multiple applications on multiple hosts to control access to a shared resource.

The NSConditionLock class defines a lock that can be acquired and released only under certain conditions.

The NSRecursiveLock class defines a lock that can be acquired multiple times by the same thread without causing deadlock. It keeps track of the number of times it was acquired, and must be balanced by corresponding calls to unlock the object before the lock is released.

Timers and Run Loops

A *run loop* is a thread-based mechanism used to schedule work and coordinate the receipt of input events. If a program thread needs to respond to incoming events, you need to attach it to a run loop in order to wake up this thread when new events arrive. The run method of the iOS UIApplication class (or NSApplication in OS X) starts an application's main loop as part of the normal startup sequence; hence, if you use the Xcode template projects for creating iOS or OS X programs, you typically won't need to create a run loop in your code. In other scenarios—when creating a command-line program, for example—you need to create a run loop if your program needs to respond to events from input sources. The Foundation Framework includes numerous classes that provide inputs asynchronously (for example, the networking, URL handling, and stream I/O APIs), so you would use a run loop in conjunction with instances of these classes.

The NSRunLoop class provides the API for managing run loops. This class includes methods to access run loops and modes, manage timers and ports, run a loop, and manage messages. The NSRunLoop currentRunLoop method retrieves the current run loop, the NSRunLoop object for the current thread. If a run loop doesn't already exist for the thread, it is created and returned. The following statement retrieves the run loop for the current thread.

```
NSRunLoop *loop = [NSRunLoop currentRunLoop];
```

The run mode defines the set of input sources for a run loop. The Foundation Framework defines a set of constants that specify the available run loop modes. The constant NSDefaultRunLoopMode is the most commonly used run-loop mode.

There are several NSRunLoop methods used to run a loop. The run method puts the thread in a permanent loop in the NSDefaultRunLoopMode, during which it processes events from all input sources. If you want a run loop to terminate, you shouldn't use this method, but rather one of the other methods used to conditionally run a loop based on receipt of input and/or a specified amount of time has elapsed.

The `runMode:beforeDate:` method runs the loop once in the `NSDefaultRunLoopMode`, blocking for input until an event is received from an attached input source or the date specified by the `beforeDate:` parameter arrives. The following statement invokes this method, waiting indefinitely until input is received.

```
[loop runMode: NSDefaultRunLoopMode beforeDate:[NSDate distantFuture]];
```

Providing a date parameter value of [`NSDate distantFuture`] evaluates to an infinite wait until input is received.

The `NSTimer` class is used to create timers that send a specified message to a target object after a certain time has elapsed. They work in conjunction with `NSRunLoop` objects to provide synchronous delivery of events to a thread. An `NSTimer` determines the maximum amount of time a run loop object should wait for input. `NSTimer` includes methods to create and initialize a timer, fire a timer, stop a timer, and retrieve information about a timer. The `scheduledTimerWithTimeInterval:invocation:repeats:` method creates a timer that fires after the specified interval, using the invocation specified, and repeating the timer if requested. The `invalidate` method stops a timer from firing again. The `isValid` method returns a Boolean value indicating whether or not the timer is currently valid.

Creating a Bonjour Network Service Client

Now you're going to create a program that demonstrates the use of the Bonjour network services APIs and run loops. This program will create a service browser that asynchronously looks for registered services of specified types.

In Xcode, create a new project by selecting **New ➤ Project ...** from the Xcode File menu. In the **New Project Assistant** pane, create a command-line application. In the **Project Options** window, specify **BonjourClient** for the Product Name, choose **Foundation** for the Project Type, and select ARC memory management by selecting the **Use Automatic Reference Counting** check box. Specify the location in your file system where you want the project to be created (if necessary, select **New Folder** and enter the name and location for the folder), uncheck the **Source Control** check box, and then click the **Create** button.

Now you're going to create a class that downloads a URL resource using the URL loading APIs. Select **New ➤ File ...** from the Xcode File menu, then select the Objective-C class template, and name the class **BonjourClient**. Then select the **BonjourClient** folder for the files location and the **BonjourClient** project as the target, and then click the **Create** button. Next, in the Xcode project navigator pane, select the resulting header file named **BonjourClient.h** and update the interface, as shown in Listing 11-10.

Listing 11-10. BonjourClient Interface

```
#import <Foundation/Foundation.h>

@interface BonjourClient : NSObject <NSNetServiceBrowserDelegate>

@property (retain) NSNetServiceBrowser *serviceBrowser;
@property BOOL finishedLoading;

@end
```

The BonjourClient interface adopts the NSNetServiceBrowserDelegate protocol, thereby enabling it to asynchronously load data from an NSNetServiceBrowser instance. The serviceBrowser property is the NSNetServiceBrowser instance. The finishedLoading property is used to indicate when the NSNetServiceBrowser instance is finished loading data. Now select the **BonjourClient.m** file and update the implementation, as shown in Listing 11-11.

Listing 11-11. BonjourClient Implementation

```objc
#import "BonjourClient.h"

@implementation BonjourClient

- (id)init
{
  if ((self = [super init]))
  {
    _finishedLoading = NO;
    _serviceBrowser = [[NSNetServiceBrowser alloc] init];
    [_serviceBrowser setDelegate:self];
}

  return self;
}

#pragma mark -
#pragma mark NSNetServiceBrowserDelegate methods

- (void)netServiceBrowserWillSearch:(NSNetServiceBrowser *)netServiceBrowser
{
  NSLog(@"Beginning search");
}

- (void)netServiceBrowser:(NSNetServiceBrowser *)sb
           didFindService:(NSNetService *)ns
               moreComing:(BOOL)moreComing
{
  NSLog(@"Found service: %@", ns);
  if (!moreComing)
  {
    // No more services, stop search
    [self.serviceBrowser stop];
  }
}

- (void)netServiceBrowserDidStopSearch:(NSNetServiceBrowser *)netServiceBrowser
{
  // Stopped search, set flag to exit run loop
  NSLog(@"Stopped search");
  self.finishedLoading = YES;
}

@end
```

All right, let's analyze this code one method at a time. The init method initializes the finishedLoading property to a value of NO to indicate that the BrowserClient instance has not finished browsing for services. It then creates a service browser instance and assigns it to the corresponding property, setting itself as the delegate object. This means that the BrowserClient instance will implement the necessary NSNetServiceBrowserDelegate protocol methods, thereby responding to asynchronous events when its service browser instance is searching for registered services.

The netServiceBrowserWillSearch: message is sent to the delegate by the service browser instance when it begins searching for services. The implementation here just logs a message to the output pane, indicating that the browser is beginning a search for services.

The netServiceBrowser:didFindService:moreComing: message is sent to the delegate by the service browser instance when it finds a registered service. The method implementation here just logs the method found to the output pane, and then performs a conditional check to see if the service browser is waiting for additional services. If there are no more services available, the browser is sent a stop message with the following statement.

```
[self.serviceBrowser stop];
```

The netServiceBrowserDidStopSearch: message is sent to the delegate by the service browser instance when a search for services is stopped. The implementation logs a message to the output pane, indicating that the search was stopped, and then sets the finishedLoading property to YES.

OK, now that you have implemented the BonjourClient class, let's use this to search for registered services using the Bonjour protocol. In the Xcode project navigator, select the **main.m** file and update the main() function, as shown in Listing 11-12.

Listing 11-12. BonjourClient main() Function

```
#import <Foundation/Foundation.h>
#import "BonjourClient.h"

int main(int argc, const char * argv[])
{
  @autoreleasepool
  {
    // Retrieve the current run loop for browsing
    NSRunLoop *loop = [NSRunLoop currentRunLoop];

    // Create a browser client and add its service browser to the current run loop
    BonjourClient *client = [[BonjourClient alloc] init];

    // Browse for the specified service types
    [client.serviceBrowser searchForServicesOfType:@"_ipp._tcp."
                                          inDomain:@"local."];
```

```
    // Loop until the browser is stopped
    while (!client.finishedLoading &&
            [loop runMode:NSDefaultRunLoopMode beforeDate:[NSDate distantFuture]]);
  }
  return 0;
}
```

The main() function begins by retrieving the current run loop, required for asynchronous URL loading with NSNetServiceBrowser objects. Next, a BonjourClient instance is created and initialized. Then the service browser begins browsing for registered services using the searchForServicesOfType :inDomain: method. Here you specify as types services those that use the IPP (internet printing protocol, used for printers) and TCP (transport control protocol) protocols, and are registered in the local domain. The next statement is a run loop used to keep the application running until the service browser has finished searching for registered services.

```
while (!client.finishedLoading &&
        [loop runMode:NSDefaultRunLoopMode beforeDate:[NSDate distantFuture]]);
```

The *while* loop has a conditional expression composed of two parts, and is followed by a semicolon, signifying an empty statement. Thus there is no logic executed within the body of the while loop; it is used just to keep the application running until the asynchronous search being performed by the service browser has finished. The first part of the conditional expression, !client.finishedLoading, checks the value of this Boolean property. If it is YES, then the while loop is exited; otherwise, you continue on to process the remainder of the expression.

Next, the expression [[NSRunLoop currentRunLoop] runMode:NSDefaultRunLoopMode beforeDate:[NSDate distantFuture]] executes the run loop once, blocking for input from an input source (for example, receipt of an NSNetServiceBrowser message). Once the input is received, the message is processed on the current thread (i.e., the corresponding delegate method is invoked) and the loop begins again. Thus the while loop will not be exited until the finishedLoading property is set. As shown in Listing 11-10, this property is set by the BonjourClient delegate method netServiceBrowserDidStopSearch:, the matching message is sent by the service browser when it has finished the search.

Earlier in this chapter, you learned that the Bonjour protocol enables the detection of devices (such as computers and printers) connected on a network. Hence, if possible, make sure that you have one or more devices connected to your local area network when you test this program. Once you have performed these configuration steps and compiled and run the BonjourClient program, you should observe messages in the output pane similar to those shown in Figure 11-1.

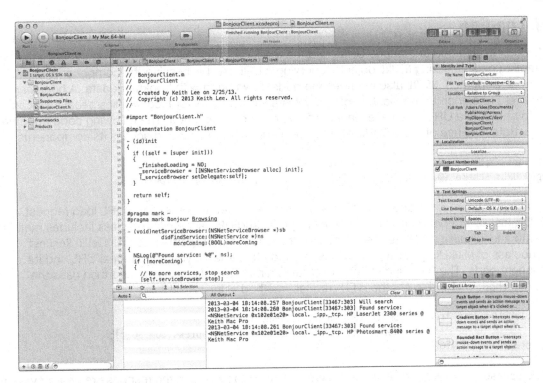

Figure 11-1. BonjourClient program output

As shown in Figure 11-1, the services retrieved are listed in the output pane, along with messages indicating the beginning and end of the search. And that's it. This hands-on exercise showed you how to write a program that uses the Foundation Framework APIs to asynchronously find registered services. Feel free to take some time to review this program and the key features covered here—using run loops and the Bonjour network protocol. Once you're done, let's move on to URL handling!

URL Handling

The URL handling classes are used for interacting with URLs and communicating with resources using standard Internet protocols (ftp, http, https, local files). The classes provide the following functionality:

- URL loading
- Cache management
- Authentication and credentials management
- Cookie management
- Protocol support

These classes also support proxy servers and SOCKET Secure (SOCKS) gateways per the user's system preferences.

URL Loading

NSURL objects are used to manage URLs and the resources they refer to. The class includes methods for creating and initializing NSURL objects, querying a URL, and accessing the components of a URL (e.g., host, port, etc.). NSURL also provides methods for working with bookmark data. A *bookmark* is a persistent reference to the location of a file. It is a valuable tool for locating files because it can be used to re-create a URL to a file, even if the file is moved or renamed. The following code fragment demonstrates the use of the NSURL APIs to create an NSURL object and access its components.

```
NSURL *url = [NSURL URLWithString:@"http://www.apress.com:80"];
NSLog(@"URL: scheme %@, host %@, port %@", url.scheme, url.host, url.port);
```

The classes NSURLRequest and NSMutableURLRequest are used to represent a URL load request. NSURLRequest is independent of the network protocol and URL scheme. The class includes methods to create and initialize a URL request, and to retrieve request properties. NSMutableURLRequest is a subclass of NSURLRequest that provides methods that enable you to change a URL and its component parts. The following statement creates a mutable URL request, and then uses the setHTTPMethod: method to set the HTTP request method value.

```
NSMutableURLRequest *req = [NSMutableURLRequest requestWithURL:
                        [NSURL URLWithString:@"http://www.apress.com:80"]];
[req setHTTPMethod:@"GET"];
```

NSURLResponse and NSHTTPURLResponse classes are used to represent the response returned by a URL request. An NSURLConnection object is created by either an object that performs a synchronous load of a URL request (sendSynchronousRequest:returningResponse:error:) or objects that conform to the NSURLConnectionDataDelegate protocol. The NSHTTPURLResponse class is a subclass of NSURLResponse that provides methods for accessing HTTP-specific information returned by a URL request.

The NSURLConnection and NSURLDownload classes are used to download the contents of a resource identified by a URL. NSURLConnection supports synchronous and asynchronous resource loading, starting and stopping a connection, and managing a delegate object used to control various aspects of a URL connection (i.e., cache management, authentication and credentials, protocol support, and cookie management). For asynchronous loading, a delegate object must be set. This object must conform to the NSURLConnectionDelegate protocol and thus implement, at a minimum, the following methods:

- connection:didReceiveData: (to retrieve data loaded)
- connection:didFailWithError: (to handle connection errors
- connection:didFinishLoading: (to perform processing after a connection has finished loading data)

Listing 11-13 demonstrates use of various URL loading APIs to synchronously load the data from a URL.

Listing 11-13. Using NSURLConnection to Synchronously Load the Contents of a URL

```
NSURL *url = [NSURL URLWithString:@"http://www.apress.com/index.html"];
NSURLRequest *request = [NSURLRequest requestWithURL:url];
NSURLResponse *response;
```

```
NSError *aerror;
NSData *data = [NSURLConnection sendSynchronousRequest:request
                                    returningResponse:&response
                                                error:&aerror];
NSLog(@"Expected content length = %lld; loaded %lu bytes",
     [response expectedContentLength], [data length]);
```

As shown in Listing 11-13, the code creates an NSURL instance and then a corresponding NSURLRequest. It then creates a connection and loads the data using the NSURLConnection sendSynchronousRequest:returningResponse:error: method. The result is returned in an NSData object.

The NSURLDownload class is used to asynchronously download the contents of a URL to a file. It includes methods to initialize a download (set request and delegate), set the destination path, resume a partial download, and cancel loading the request. The class also provides support for decoding files stored in the MacBinary, BinHex, and gzip formats. The delegate object must conform to the NSURLDownloadDelegate protocol and thus implement, at a minimum, the following methods:

- download:didFailWithError: (to handle connection errors)
- downloadDidFinish: (to perform processing after a connection has finished loading data)

The NSURLDownload class is available for use on the OS X platform only (i.e., this class is not available for the iOS platform).

Cache Management

The cache management classes (NSURLCache and NSCachedURLResponse) provide a cache memory for responses to URL requests. The NSURLCache class provides a general-purpose cache for URLs, whereas the NSCachedURLResponse encapsulates a URL response (NSURLResponse object) and the data loaded from the URL (an NSData object). An NSURLConnection delegate object implements the connection:willCacheResponse: method, providing a NSCachedURLResponse object initialized with an NSURLCache, to manage caching. How this works is best illustrated by an example; so now you'll create a program that uses the URL loading classes to download a resource. Let's begin!

Downloading a Resource with the URL Loading APIs

In Xcode, create a new project by selecting **New ➤ Project ...** from the Xcode File menu. In the **New Project Assistant** pane create a command-line application. In the **Project Options** window, specify **NetConnector** for the Product Name, choose **Foundation** for the Project Type, and select ARC memory management by selecting the **Use Automatic Reference Counting** check box. Specify the location in your file system where you want the project to be created (if necessary select **New Folder** and enter the name and location for the folder), uncheck the **Source Control** check box, and then click the **Create** button.

Now you're going to create a class that downloads a URL resource using the URL loading APIs. Select **New ➤ File ...** from the Xcode File menu, select the **Objective-C** class template, and name the class **NetConnector**. Select the **NetConnector** folder for the files location and the **NetConnector** project as the target, and then click the **Create** button. Next, in the Xcode project navigator pane, select the resulting header file named **NetConnector.h** and update the interface, as shown in Listing 11-14.

Listing 11-14. NetConnector Interface

```
#import <Foundation/Foundation.h>
#define HTTP_SCHEME        @"http"
#define CACHE_MEMORY_SIZE (4 * 1024 * 1024)

@interface NetConnector : NSObject <NSURLConnectionDelegate>

@property (readonly) BOOL finishedLoading;

- (id) initWithRequest:(NSURLRequest *)request;
- (void) reloadRequest;

@end
```

The NetConnector interface adopts the NSURLConnectionDelegate protocol, thereby enabling it to asynchronously load data from an NSURLConnection instance. The property finishedLoading is used to indicate when the NSURLConnection instance is finished loading data. The initWithRequest: method initializes a NetConnector object and loads a URL using the input NSURLRequest. The reloadRequest method is used to reload the input NSURLRequest. Now select the **NetConnector.m** file and update the implementation, as shown in Listing 11-15.

Listing 11-15. NetConnector Implementation

```
#import "NetConnector.h"

// Extension to declare provide properties
@interface NetConnector()

@property NSURLRequest *request;
@property BOOL finishedLoading;
@property NSURLConnection *connector;
@property NSMutableData *receivedData;

@end

@implementation NetConnector

- (id) initWithRequest:(NSURLRequest *)request
{
  if ((self = [super init]))
  {
    _request = request;

    // Create URL cache with appropriate in-memory storage
    NSURLCache *URLCache = [[NSURLCache alloc] init];
    [URLCache setMemoryCapacity:CACHE_MEMORY_SIZE];
    [NSURLCache setSharedURLCache:URLCache];
```

```
    // Create connection and begin downloading data from resource
    _connector = [NSURLConnection connectionWithRequest:request delegate:self];
  }
  return self;
}

- (void) reloadRequest
{
  self.finishedLoading = NO;
  self.connector = [NSURLConnection connectionWithRequest:self.request
                                          delegate:self];

}

#pragma mark -
#pragma mark Delegate methods

- (void)connection:(NSURLConnection *)connection
didReceiveResponse:(NSURLResponse *)response
{
  if (self.receivedData != nil)
  {
    [self.receivedData setLength:0];
  }
}

- (NSCachedURLResponse *)connection:(NSURLConnection *)connection
                  willCacheResponse:(NSCachedURLResponse *)cachedResponse
{
  NSURLResponse *response = [cachedResponse response];
  NSURL *url = [response URL];
  if ([[url scheme] isEqualTo:HTTP_SCHEME])
  {
    NSLog(@"Downloaded data, caching response");
    return cachedResponse;
  }
  else
  {
    NSLog(@"Downloaded data, not caching response");
    return nil;
  }
}

- (void)connection:(NSURLConnection*)connection didReceiveData:(NSData*)data
{
    if (self.receivedData != nil)
    {
      [self.receivedData appendData:data];
    }
    else
    {
      self.receivedData = [[NSMutableData alloc] initWithData:data];
    }
}
```

```objc
- (void)connectionDidFinishLoading:(NSURLConnection *)connection
{
  NSUInteger length = [self.receivedData length];
  NSLog(@"Downloaded %lu bytes from request %@", length, self.request);

  // Loaded data, set flag to exit run loop
  self.finishedLoading = YES;
}

- (void)connection:(NSURLConnection *)connection didFailWithError:(NSError *)error
{
  NSLog(@"Error loading request %@", [error localizedDescription]);
  self.finishedLoading = YES;
}

@end
```

OK, so I know that this is a lot of code, but don't worry, you'll take it one step at a time!. The file begins with a category extension that declares private properties used within the NetConnector implementation. The implementation defines both the methods declared by the interface and methods declared by the NSURLConnectionDelegate protocol. The initWithRequest: method assigns the input NSURLRequest to the private NetConnector request property, creates and initializes an NSURLCache instance for caching responses, and ends by creating an NSURLConnection object and starting the download of the URL. The following statements from Listing 11-15 create the cache, configure it with in-memory storage, and then set it to be the shared cache used with the connection.

```objc
NSURLCache *URLCache = [[NSURLCache alloc] init];
[URLCache setMemoryCapacity:CACHE_MEMORY_SIZE];
[NSURLCache setSharedURLCache:URLCache];
```

The reloadRequest method reloads the URL. It first resets the finishedLoading flag, and then creates a new NSURLConnection object with the saved request and downloads the URL.

The remaining methods implemented here are NSURLConnectionDelegate protocol methods. The connection:didReceiveResponse: message is sent when a connection is able to send a response to the request. As shown in Listing 11-15, this method sets the receivedData object to a length of zero, thereby discarding data received from previous requests.

The connection:willCacheResponse: message is sent before a connection stores the response in the cache. This enables the method implementation to modify the response or prevent it from being cached. As shown in Listing 11-15, the method performs conditional logic that enables/disables caching of the response based on whether or not the scheme for the URL is http.

The connection:didReceiveData: message is sent as the data is received from the resource. This method may be called multiple times during a single request if the data is received incrementally. As shown in Listing 11-15, the method appends the received data to the receivedData object.

The connectionDidFinishLoading: message is sent when a connection has finished loading the data successfully. The method implementation here just logs a message to the output pane, indicating that the connection has finished loading the resource, and then sets the finishedLoading flag used to exit the run loop.

Finally, the connection:didFailWithError: message is sent when a connection fails to load a request successfully. Here you just log a message to the output pane, indicating the error that occurred, and set the finishedLoading flag.

OK, now that you have implemented the NetConnector class, let's use this to load a URL. In the Xcode project navigator, select the **main.m** file and update the main() function, as shown in Listing 11-16.

Listing 11-16. NetConnector main() Function

```
#import <Foundation/Foundation.h>
#import "NetConnector.h"

#define INDEX_URL        @"http://www.wikipedia.com/index.html"

int main(int argc, const char * argv[])
{
  @autoreleasepool
  {
    // Retrieve the current run loop
    NSRunLoop *loop = [NSRunLoop currentRunLoop];

    // Create the request with specified cache policy, then begin downloading!
    NSURLRequest *request = [NSURLRequest
                              requestWithURL:[NSURL URLWithString:INDEX_URL]
                                 cachePolicy:NSURLRequestReturnCacheDataElseLoad
                              timeoutInterval:5];
    NetConnector *netConnect = [[NetConnector alloc] initWithRequest:request];

    // Loop until finished loading the resource (Note the empty statement!)
    while (!netConnect.finishedLoading &&
           [loop runMode:NSDefaultRunLoopMode beforeDate:[NSDate distantFuture]]);

    // Log the amount of memory being used by the cache
    NSLog(@"Cache memory usage = %lu bytes", [[NSURLCache sharedURLCache]
                                               currentMemoryUsage]);

    // Reload data from request, this time it will be retrieved from the cache!
    [netConnect reloadRequest];
    while (!netConnect.finishedLoading &&
           [loop runMode:NSDefaultRunLoopMode beforeDate:[NSDate distantFuture]]);

    // Zero out cache
    [[NSURLCache sharedURLCache] removeAllCachedResponses];
  }
  return 0;
}
```

The main() function begins by retrieving the current run loop, required for asynchronous URL loading with NSURLConnection objects. Next, an NSURLRequest instance is created using the convenience constructor requestWithURL:cachePolicy:timeoutInterval:. This constructor enables you to select the cache policy for the request. The policy NSURLRequestReturnCacheDataElseLoad specifies that a cache value should be used (even if out of date) if available; otherwise, the data should be loaded from the resource. Note that if a URL does not support caching, the data will not be loaded from the cache, even if the policy specifies otherwise. A NetConnector instance is then created using the request and its NSURLConnection object begins downloading the resource. The next statement is a loop used to keep the application running until the connection has finished loading the resource.

```
while (!netConnect.finishedLoading &&
       [loop runMode:NSDefaultRunLoopMode beforeDate:[NSDate distantFuture]]);
```

Looks familiar, doesn't it? This loop is identical to the one used for the Bonjour service browser program that you implemented earlier in this chapter. It runs the loop, receiving events from its input sources and executing any corresponding delegate methods, until the connection has finished loading the resource. The next statement logs the cache memory usage to the output pane, enabling us to view cache utilization. Then you reload the request. As shown in Listing 11-16, the next set of statements reloads the URL. As the data is already stored in the cache and the cache policy specifies that a cache value should be used, it is immediately retrieved without being loaded from the URL. Finally, the in-memory cache is zeroed out, thereby freeing this memory. Now when you compile and run the NetConnector program, you should observe the messages in the output pane, as shown in Figure 11-2.

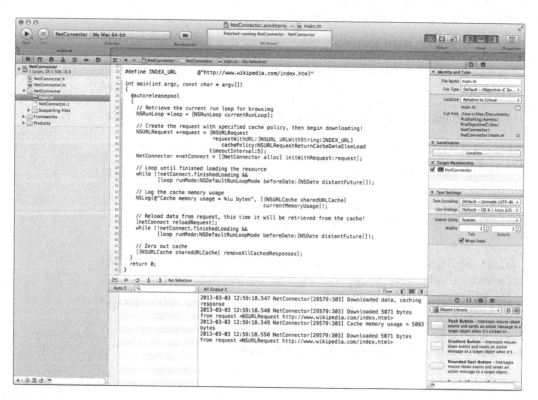

Figure 11-2. NetConnector program output

As shown in the output pane, the response is cached after the data is downloaded. The total amount of data is then logged to the console, along with the URL of the request. Next, the cache memory utilization is output. This is identical to the data downloaded. The request is then reloaded. Because the response is already in the cache, it is retrieved from there (notice that the delegate method `connection:willCacheResponse:` is not invoked). OK, that was pretty involved, wasn't it? Well, you now have a pretty good handle on the use of the URL loading APIs to asynchronously download a URL. Once you're ready, let's move on and look into handling authentication challenges when trying to load a resource.

Authentication and Credentials Management

The authentication and credentials classes (`NSURLProtectionSpace`, `NSURLCredentialStorage`, `NSURLCredential`, `NSURLAuthenticationChallenge`, and `NSURLAuthenticationChallengeSender`) provide support for authenticating users requesting access to protected URLs. A resource that requires authentication requests credentials from a client attempting to load the resource. The Foundation Framework `NSURLAuthenticationChallenge` class encapsulates a challenge from a server that requires authentication from the client. `NSURLCredential` represents an authentication credential returned by a user in response to an authentication challenge. The delegate protocols for `NSURLConnection` and `NSURLDownload` instances are sent messages when a connection request issues an authentication challenge. The corresponding methods should be implemented to return the appropriate credential.

For the `NSURLConnectionDelegate` protocol, the message `connection:willSendRequestForAuth enticationChallenge:` should be implemented to return the appropriate credential. An example implementation of this method for the NetConnector program is shown in Listing 11-17.

Listing 11-17. Handling Authentication Challenges

```
- (void)connection:(NSURLConnection *)connection
willSendRequestForAuthenticationChallenge:(NSURLAuthenticationChallenge *)challenge
{
  NSURLCredential *credential =
    [NSURLCredential credentialWithUser:@"TestUser"
                               password:@"TestPassword"
                            persistence:NSURLCredentialPersistenceForSession];
  [[challenge sender] useCredential:credential
        forAuthenticationChallenge:challenge];
}
```

As shown in Listing 11-17, the method creates a credential with a user name of `TestUser` and a password of `TestPassword;`. The `useCredential:forAuthenticationChallenge:` message uses this credential to respond to an authentication challenge for the connection.

Cookie Management

The Foundation Framework classes NSHTTPCookie and NSHTTPCookieStorage facilitate the creation and management of *HTTP cookies*, which are used to provide persistent storage of data across URL requests. An NSHTTPCookie instance represents a cookie, and NSHTTPCookieStorage is a singleton object used to manage cookies. For OS X applications, cookies are shared and kept in sync across processes. Session cookies are local to a single process and not shared between programs. The NSHTTPCookie class provides methods to create cookies, convert cookies to request headers, and retrieve cookie properties. The NSHTTPCookieStorage class provides methods for retrieving the shared cookie storage instance, managing the cookie accept policy, and managing (i.e., adding, removing, retrieving) cookies.

Protocol Support

The Foundation Framework classes NSURLProtocol and NSURLProtocolClient enable the creation of custom protocols for loading data from a URL. NSURLProtocol is an abstract class that provides the basic structure to perform protocol-specific URL loading. It includes methods for creating NSURLProtocol objects, registering/unregistering protocol classes, request management, retrieving protocol attributes, and starting/stopping downloads. NSURLProtocolClient is a protocol used by NSURLProtocol subclasses to communicate with the URL loading system.

Interprocess Communication

The Foundation Framework includes a collection of classes that support process-to-process communication. Specifically, they provide facilities for creating and using communication channels.

Communication via Pipes

The NSPipe class encapsulates a *pipe*, a one-way channel for communication between processes. The API includes methods to create and initialize a pipe, and retrieve the corresponding NSFileHandle instance for a pipe. The NSTask class provides several methods for setting the input and output channels for a process (setStandardOutput:, setStandardInput:). Listing 11-18 demonstrates the use of the NSTask and NSPipe APIs to create and launch a task (the Unix command /bin/ls simply lists the files in the current directory), set the task's standard output, and then retrieve and log the standard output written to the pipe after task completion.

Listing 11-18. Using NSPipe and NSTask to Invoke a Process

```
NSTask *task = [[NSTask alloc] init];
[task setLaunchPath:@"/bin/ls"];
NSPipe *outPipe = [NSPipe pipe];
[task setStandardOutput:outPipe];
[task launch];
```

```
NSData *output = [[outPipe fileHandleForReading] readDataToEndOfFile];
NSString *lsout = [[NSString alloc] initWithData:output
                                      encoding:NSUTF8StringEncoding];
NSLog(@"/bin/ls output:\n%@", lsout);
```

Communication via Ports

NSPort, NSMachPort, NSMessagePort, and NSSocketPort provide low-level mechanisms for communication between threads or processes, typically via NSPortMessage objects.

NSPort is an abstract class. It includes methods to create and initialize a port, create connections to a port, set port information, and monitor a port. NSMachPort, NSMessagePort, and NSSocketPort are concrete subclasses of NSPort used for specific types of communication ports. NSMachPort and NSMessagePort allow local (on the same machine) communication only. In addition, NSMachPort is used with Mach ports, the fundamental communication port in OS X. NSSocketPort allows both local and remote communication, but may be less efficient than the others when used for local communication. Port instances can be supplied as parameters when creating an NSConnection instance (using the initWithReceivePort:sendPort: method). You can also add a port to a run loop via the NSPort scheduleInRunLoop:forMode: method.

As ports are a very low-level interprocess communication mechanism, you should implement interapplication communication using distributed objects whenever possible and use NSPort objects only when necessary. In addition, when you are finished using a port object, you must explicitly invalidate the object via the NSPort invalidate method.

The NSSocketPort and NSPortMessage classes are only available for use on the OS X platform.

Port Registration

NSPortNameServer, NSMachBootstrapServer, NSMessagePortNameServer, and NSSocketPortNameServer provide an interface to the port registration service, used to retrieve instances of NSMachPort, NSMessagePort, and NSSocketPort.

NSPortNameServer provides an object-oriented interface to the port registration service used by the distributed objects system. NSConnection objects use it to contact each other and to distribute objects over the network. You should rarely need to interact directly with an NSPortNameServer instance. NSMachBootstrapServer, NSMessagePortNameServer, and NSSocketPortNameServer are subclasses of NSPortNameServer that return corresponding port instances (NSMachPort, NSMessagePort, NSSocketPort).

The NSPortNameServer, NSMachBootstrapServer, NSMessagePortNameServer, and NSSocketPortNameServer classes are only available for use on the OS X platform.

Roundup

In this chapter, you began your review of the Foundation Framework, focusing on classes that provide common, general-purpose functionality required for most Objective-C programs. You should now be familiar with Foundation Framework classes that provide the following functionality:

- Network services
- Application services
- File system utilities
- URL handling
- Interprocess communication
- Concurrency and threading

Chapter 12

Foundation Framework Specialized Services

In this chapter, you will explore several Foundation Framework classes that provide specialized system services. These classes implement functionality to support event-driven programming via notifications, object persistence via archiving and serialization, and distributed programming with distributed objects.

Notifications

The Foundation Framework includes a collection of APIs—the *notifications support classes*—that provide a powerful mechanism for event-driven programming. A *notification* encapsulates information about an event. It can be sent to one or more observing objects in response to an event that occurs within a program. The notifications architecture follows a broadcast model; hence objects receiving events are decoupled from those sending them. The notification support classes enable the creation and posting of notifications, sending and receiving notifications, and asynchronous posting of notifications via queues. The APIs also support registering for notifications and the delivery of notifications to specific threads.

NSNotification encapsulates the information sent by a notification object. It consists of a unique name, the posting object, and (optionally) a dictionary of supplementary information. The class includes methods for creating and initializing notifications, and retrieving notification information. Listing 12-1 creates a notification named ApplicationDidHandleGreetingNotification for a simple greeting.

Listing 12-1. Retrieving the Network Host Name Using NSHost

```
NSString *nName = @"ApplicationDidHandleGreetingNotification";
NSNotification *notif = [NSNotification notificationWithName:nName
                                            object:@"Hello, World!"];
```

So you may be wondering, why the long name for the notification? Well, Apple has provided some guidelines for the names of notifications. It recommends that a notification name be composed of the following elements:

- Name of the associated class
- The word *Did* or *Will*
- Unique part of the name
- The word *Notification*

These guidelines are designed to facilitate the creation of unique notification names that are self-descriptive.

The NSNotificationCenter and NSDistributedNotificationCenter classes provide the mechanisms for broadcasting notifications to interested observers. They include methods for getting the notification center instance, adding and removing notification observers, and posting notifications. NSDistributedNotificationCenter is a subclass of NSNotificationCenter that provides a mechanism for broadcasting notifications to other processes. The class method defaultCenter is used to retrieve the default notification center instance associated with an application, as shown in the following statement.

```
[NSNotificationCenter defaultCenter];
```

NSNotificationCenter provides several methods for posting notifications. The following statement uses the postNotification: method to post the notification created in Listing 12-1.

```
[[NSNotificationCenter defaultCenter] postNotification:notif];
```

NSNotificationCenter also provides methods to create and post a notification with a single method. The following statement uses the postNotificationName:object: method to create and post a notification using the notification name created in Listing 12-1.

```
[[NSNotificationCenter defaultCenter] postNotificationName:nName
                                      object:@"Salut!"];
```

NSNotificationCenter includes several methods for managing notification observers. You can register an object to receive a notification using the addObserver:selector:name:object: method. This method takes parameters that specify the observer object to receive a notification, the message to send to the observer, the name of the notification for which to register the observer, and the sender from which the observer wants to receive notifications. Listing 12-2 registers an object named handler (an instance of the Greeter class) to receive notifications from the variable named nName (see Listing 12-1), sending the message handleGreeting: to the observer.

Listing 12-2. Registering a Notification Observer

```
Greeter *handler = [Greeter new];
[[NSNotificationCenter defaultCenter] addObserver:handler
                       selector:@selector(handleGreeting:)
                             name:nName
                          object:nil];
```

Classes that receive notification events must implement a notification handler method with the following signature.

```
- (void) methodName:(NSNotification *)notification;
```

methodName is the name of the method. In Listing 12-2, the Greeter class implements a notification handler method named handleGreeting:.

NSNotificationCenter also provides methods to remove an observer; the removeObserver: method unregisters an observer from notifications that it had previously registered for. The method removeObserver:name:object: is more fine-grained. It removes entries that match a specified observer, notification name, and sender. The following statement removes the notification with variable name nName for the observer named handler.

```
[[NSNotificationCenter defaultCenter] removeObserver:handler
                                 name:uName
                              object:nil];
```

The NSNotificationQueue class provides a queue for notification centers, thereby enabling asynchronous posting and/or the coalescing of notifications. *Coalescing* is a process that enables you to filter (from a queue) notifications that are similar in some way to a notification that was queued earlier. The class includes methods to retrieve a notification queue instance, and add/remove notifications on the queue. The class method defaultQueue is used to retrieve the default notification queue instance for the current thread, as shown in the following statement.

```
[NSNotificationQueue defaultQueue];
```

The method initWithNotificationCenter: provides the capability to create a notification queue for a specified notification center. Listing 12-3 retrieves the default notification center and then creates a notification queue associated with it.

Listing 12-3. Creating a Notification Queue for a Specified Notification Center

```
NSNotificationCenter *notifier = [NSNotificationCenter defaultCenter];
NSNotificationQueue *queue = [[NSNotificationQueue alloc]
                        initWithNotificationCenter:notifier];
```

NSNotificationQueue includes two methods for posting notifications. The enqueueNotification:postingStyle:coalesceMask:forModes: method enables you to specify the posting style, coalescing option, and supported run modes for posting the notification. The coalescing options are constant values defined as follows:

- NSNotificationNoCoalescing: Do not coalesce notification, post all.

- NSNotificationCoalescingOnName: Coalesce notifications with the same name, such that only one is posted.

- NSNotificationCoalescingOnSender: Coalesce notifications with the same sender, such that only one is posted.

The posting style defines the interaction mode (synchronous/asynchronous, when idle/as soon as possible) used to queue the notification. These options are specified as constant values, as follows:

- NSPostASAP: Asynchronously posts as soon as possible, when the current iteration of the corresponding run loop completes.

- NSPostWhenIdle: Asynchronously posts when the run loop is waiting for input source or timer events.

- NSPostNow: The notification queued is posted immediately (after coalescing), effectively providing synchronous behavior. This behavior does not require a run loop.

Listing 12-4 synchronously queues the notification assigned to the variable named notif (see Listing 12-1), coalescing notifications with the same name.

Listing 12-4. Posting a Notification to a Queue with Coalescing

```
[[NSNotificationQueue defaultQueue]
    enqueueNotification:notif
            postingStyle:NSPostNow
            coalesceMask:NSNotificationCoalescingOnName
                forModes:nil];
```

NSNotificationQueue also includes a method to remove notifications from the queue. The following statement uses the dequeueNotificationsMatching:coalesceMask: method to dequeue notifications assigned to the variable named notif with no coalescing.

```
[[NSNotificationQueue defaultQueue]
    dequeueNotificationsMatching:notif
                    coalesceMask:NSNotificationNoCoalescing];
```

Archives and Serialization

The Foundation Framework archives and serialization classes implement mechanisms for converting an object (i.e., an object graph) into an architecture-independent byte buffer. This data can then be written to a file or transmitted to another process, potentially over a network. Later, the data can be converted back into objects, preserving the associated object graph. In this way, these classes provide a lightweight means of data persistence. The serialization process preserves the data and the positions of objects in an object hierarchy, whereas the archiving process is more general purpose—it preserves the data, data types, and the relations between the objects in an object hierarchy.

Archiving

NSCoder is an abstract class that declares the interface used to both *marshal* and *unmarshall* object graphs. The marshalling process converts an object's information into a series of bytes, and the unmarshalling process creates an object from a (previously marshalled) series of bytes. NSCoder includes methods for encoding and decoding data of various types, testing an NSCoder instance, and provides support for secure coding. The Foundation Framework includes four concrete subclasses of NSCoder: NSArchiver, NSUnarchiver, NSKeyedArchiver, and NSKeyedUnarchiver.

Sequential Archives

NSArchiver and NSUnarchiver are used to create *sequential* archives, which means that the objects and values of a sequential archive must be decoded in the same order that they were encoded. In addition, when decoding a sequential archive, the entire object graph must be decoded. NSArchiver is used to encode objects for writing to a file or some other use, and NSUnarchiver is used to decode objects from an archive. NSArchiver includes methods for initialization, archiving data, retrieving archived data, and substituting classes or objects in an archive. NSUnarchiver includes methods for initialization, decoding objects, substituting classes or objects, and management.

Keyed Archives

Whereas NSArchiver and NSUnarchiver are sequential archives, NSKeyedArchiver and NSKeyedUnarchiver are keyed archives—each value in the archive can be individually named/keyed. The key must be unique within the scope of the object in which the value is being encoded/decoded. When decoding a keyed archive, the values can be decoded out of sequence or not at all. Hence, keyed archives provide better support for forward and backward compatibility and are recommended over the sequential archiving classes. NSKeyedArchiver includes methods for initialization, archiving data, encoding data and objects, and management. NSKeyedUnarchiver includes methods for initialization, unarchiving data, decoding objects, and management.

The code shown in Listing 12-5 uses the NSKeyedArchiver archiveRootObject: method to archive an NSString instance named greeting to a file in the current directory named greeting.archive.

Listing 12-5. Archiving an Object with NSKeyedArchiver

```
NSString *greeting = @"Hello, World!";
NSString *cwd = [[NSFileManager defaultManager] currentDirectoryPath];
NSString *archivePath = [cwd stringByAppendingString:@"/greeting.archive"];
BOOL result = [NSKeyedArchiver archiveRootObject:greeting toFile:archivePath];
```

The next code fragment uses the NSKeyedUnarchiver unarchiveObjectWithFile: method to decode an NSString object named greeting from an archive stored in the file archivePath.

```
NSString *greeting = [NSKeyedUnarchiver unarchiveObjectWithFile:archivePath];
```

Encoding and Decoding Objects

While the NSKeyedArchiver and NSKeyedUnarchiver classes are responsible for the archiving process, a class must conform to the NSCoding protocol to support enconding/decoding of class instances. This protocol declares two methods, encodeWithCoder: and initWithCoder:, that encode/decode an object's state (e.g., its properties and instance variables). When a *coder object* (i.e., an NSKeyedArchiver or NSKeyedUnarchiver instance) archives an object, it instructs the object to encode its state by invoking its encodeWithCoder: method. Hence, a class must implement the appropriate encode and decode method(s) because these will be called by the selected coder object. Listing 12-6 depicts an implementation of a class named MyType that conforms to the NSCoding protocol.

Listing 12-6. Implementing the NSCoding Protocol Methods

```
@interface MyType : NSObject <NSCoding>

@property NSString *type;

@end

@implementation MyType

- (void)encodeWithCoder:(NSCoder *)coder
{
  [coder encodeObject:self.type forKey:@"TYPE_KEY"];
}

- (id)initWithCoder:(NSCoder *)coder
{
  if ((self = [super init]))
  {
    type = [coder decodeObjectForKey:@"TYPE_KEY"];
  }
  return self;
}

@end
```

Property List Serialization

Property list serialization provides a means of converting a *property list*, a structured collection of data organized as name-value pairs, to/from an architecture-independent byte stream. The Foundation Framework NSPropertyListSerialization class provides methods to serialize and deserialize property lists directly and validate a property list. It also supports conversion of property lists to/from XML or an optimized binary format. In contrast to archiving, basic serialization does not record the data type of the values nor the relationships between them; only the values themselves are recorded. Hence, you must write your code to deserialize data with the proper types and in the proper order.

A property list organizes data as named values and collections of values. They are frequently used to store, organize, and access standard types of data. Property lists can be created programmatically, or more commonly, as XML files.

XML Property Lists

Property lists are most commonly stored in XML files, referred to as *XML plist* files. The NSArray and NSDictionary classes both have methods to persist themselves as XML property list files and to create class instances from XML plists.

NSPropertyListSerialization

The NSPropertyListSerialization class enables the programmatic creation of property lists. This class supports the following Foundation data types (the corresponding Core Foundation toll-free bridged data types are provided in parentheses):

- NSData (CFData)

- NSDate (CFDate)

- NSNumber: integer, float, and Boolean values (CFNumber, CFBoolean)

- NSString (CFString)

- NSArray (CFArray)

- NSDictionary (CFDictionary)

Because the supported data types include the collection classes NSArray and NSDictionary, each of which can contain other collections, an NSPropertyListSerialization object can be used to create hierarchies of data. As a property list is structured as a collection of name-value pairs, a dictionary is used to programmatically create property list data. Listing 12-7 demonstrates the use of the instance method dataWithPropertyList:format:options:error: to serialize an NSDictionary property list collection of name-value pairs to a data buffer named plistData.

Listing 12-7. Property List Serialization of Name-Value Pairs

```
NSError *errorStr;
NSDictionary *data = @{ @"FirstName" : @"John", @"LastName" : @"Doe" };
NSData *plistData = [NSPropertyListSerialization dataWithPropertyList:data
                    format:NSPropertyListXMLFormat_v1_0
                    options:0
                    error:&errorStr];
```

The format: parameter specifies the property list format, of type enum NSPropertyListFormat. The allowed values are as follows:

- NSPropertyListOpenStepFormat: Legacy ASCII property list format.

- NSPropertyListXMLFormat_v1_0: XML property list format.

- NSPropertyListBinaryFormat_v1_0: Binary property list format.

The options: parameter is meant to specify the selected property list write option. This parameter is currently unused and should be set to 0. If the method does not complete successfully, an NSError object is returned in the error: parameter that describes the error condition. Listing 12-8 demonstrates use of the propertyListWithData:options:format:error: method to deserialize a property list from the plistData data buffer of Listing 12-7.

Listing 12-8. Property List Deserialization

```
NSError *errorStr;
NSDictionary *plist = [NSPropertyListSerialization
                        propertyListWithData:plistData
                        options:NSPropertyListImmutable
                        format:NULL
                        error:&errorStr];
```

The `options:` parameter specifies the property list read option. This value can be any of those for the enum type `NSPropertyListMutabilityOptions`. The possible values are as follows:

- `NSPropertyListImmutable`: The returned property list contains immutable objects.

- `NSPropertyListMutableContainers`: The returned property list has mutable containers but immutable leaves.

- `NSPropertyListMutableContainersAndLeaves`: The returned property list has mutable containers and mutable leaves.

The `format:` parameter contains the format that the property list was stored in. If the value `NULL` is provided, then it is not necessary to know the format. The possible non-`NULL` values for the format are of enum type `NSPropertyListFormat`.

Property list serialization does not preserve the full class identity of its objects, only its general kind. In other words, a property list object may be any of the preceding supported types. When a collection class is stored as a property list, its elements must also be in the list of supported property list data types. In addition, the keys for `NSDictionary` property list objects must be of type string (`NSString`). As a result, if a property list is serialized and then deserialized, the objects in the resulting property list might not be of the same class as the objects in the original property list. In particular, when a property list is serialized, the mutability of the container objects (i.e., `NSDictionary` and `NSArray` objects) is not preserved. When deserializing, though, you can choose to have all container objects created mutable or immutable.

Property list serialization also does not track the presence of objects referenced multiple times. Each reference to an object within the property list is serialized separately, resulting in multiple instances when deserialized.

Archiving an Object Graph

OK, now that you have a good handle on the archiving and serialization classes, you're going to create a program that demonstrates use of the Foundation Framework Archiving APIs. This program will create an object graph from a class hierarchy and then encode and decode the object graph from an archive. The classes that you'll develop are diagrammed in Figure 12-1.

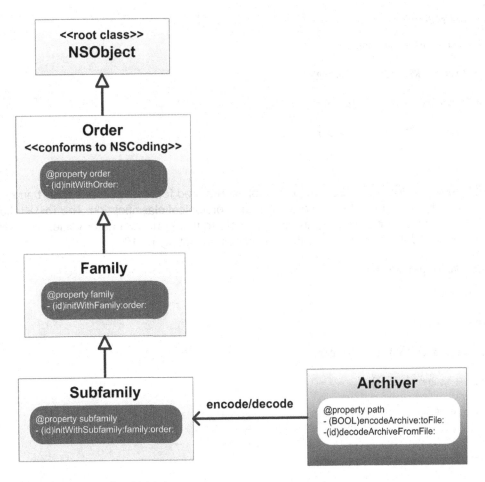

Figure 12-1. ArchiveCat program class hierarchy

As shown in Figure 12-1, the program consists of a class hierarchy (the Subfamily-Family-Order classes) and a class (Archiver) that's used to archive instances of this hierarchy. In Xcode, create a new project by selecting **New ➤ Project ...** from the Xcode File menu. In the **New Project Assistant** pane, create a command-line application. In the **Project Options** window, specify **ArchiveCat** for the Product Name, choose **Foundation** for the Project Type, and select ARC memory management by selecting the **Use Automatic Reference Counting** check box. Specify the location in your file system where you want the project to be created (if necessary, select **New Folder** and enter the name and location for the folder), uncheck the **Source Control** check box, and then click the **Create** button.

Next, you're going to create the class hierarchy for the object graph. You'll start with the base class and then successively implement the remaining subclasses. Select **New ➤ File ...** from the Xcode File menu, select the **Objective-C** class template, and name the class **Order**. Select the **ArchiveCat** folder for the files location and the **ArchiveCat** project as the target, and then click the **Create** button. Next, in the Xcode project navigator pane, select the resulting header file named **Order.h** and update the interface, as shown in Listing 12-9.

Listing 12-9. Order Interface

```
#import <Foundation/Foundation.h>

@interface Order : NSObject <NSCoding>

@property (readonly) NSString *order;

- (id)initWithOrder:(NSString *)order;

@end
```

The Order interface adopts the NSCoding protocol, as required for classes that support archiving. The read-only property order identifies the order group in biological classification. The initWithOrder: method initializes an Order object, setting the property to the input parameter value. Now select the **Order.m** file and update the implementation, as shown in Listing 12-10.

Listing 12-10. Order Implementation

```
#import "Order.h"

@implementation Order

- (id)initWithOrder:(NSString *)order
{
  if ((self = [super init]))
  {
    _order = order;
  }

  return self;
}

- (id)initWithCoder:(NSCoder *)coder
{
  if ((self = [super init]))
  {
    _order = [coder decodeObjectForKey:@"ORDER_KEY"];
  }
  return self;
}

- (void)encodeWithCoder:(NSCoder *)coder
{
  [coder encodeObject:self.order forKey:@"ORDER_KEY"];
}

- (NSString *) description
{
  return [NSString stringWithFormat:@"Order:%@", self.order];
}

@end
```

The initWithOrder: implementation is very similar to init methods you've developed elsewhere in this book. It simply assigns the order input parameter to the order property's backing instance variable.

The initWithCoder: method, declared by the NSCoding protocol, initializes the object using the archived state. Its input parameter, coder, is the NSCoder instance used to decode the Order instance archive. The superclass of Order is NSObject; because NSObject doesn't adopt the NSCoding protocol, the self variable is assigned the returned value of the superclass init call.

```
self = [super init]
```

Next, the Order class state (represented by its properties and instance variables) is decoded and initialized. As the Order class has a single property named order, the property's instance variable is assigned to the value decoded by the decodeObjectForKey: method, where the key is named ORDER_KEY.

The encodeWithCoder: method is used to archive the Order class state, its input parameter, coder, is the NSCoder instance used to encode the Order instance archive. Because the superclass of Order doesn't adopt the NSCoding protocol, this method doesn't invoke the superclass's encodeWithCoder: method, but just encodes the Order class state. Specifically, the method invokes the encodeWithCoder: method on the coder for each property/variable that needs to be archived.

```
[coder encodeObject:self.order forKey:@"ORDER_KEY"];
```

Finally, the class overrides the description method (inherited from its superclass) to return a text string listing the value for the order property.

Now you'll implement the next class in the hierarchy. Select **New ➤ File ...** from the Xcode File menu, select the **Objective-C** class template, and name the class **Family**. Select the **ArchiveCat** folder for the files location and the **ArchiveCat** project as the target, and then click the **Create** button. Next, in the Xcode project navigator pane, select the resulting header file named **Family.h** and update the interface, as shown in Listing 12-11.

Listing 12-11. Family Interface

```
#import "Order.h"

@interface Family : Order

@property(readonly) NSString *family;

- (id)initWithFamily:(NSString *)family order:(NSString *)order;

@end
```

The Family interface subclasses the Order class, and hence adopts the NSCoding protocol. The read-only property family specifies the family group in a biological classification. The initWithFamily:order: method initializes a Family object, setting the family and order properties to the input parameter values provided. Now select the **Family.m** file and update the implementation, as shown in Listing 12-12.

Listing 12-12. Family Implementation

```objc
#import "Family.h"

@implementation Family

- (id)initWithFamily:(NSString *)family order:(NSString *)order
{
  if ((self = [super initWithOrder:order]))
  {
    _family = family;
  }

  return self;
}

- (id)initWithCoder:(NSCoder *)coder
{
  if ((self = [super initWithCoder:coder]))
  {
    _family = [coder decodeObjectForKey:@"FAMILY_KEY"];
  }
  return self;
}

- (void)encodeWithCoder:(NSCoder *)coder
{
  [super encodeWithCoder:coder];
  [coder encodeObject:self.family forKey:@"FAMILY_KEY"];
}

- (NSString *) description
{
  return [NSString stringWithFormat:@"Family:%@, %@", self.family,
        [super description]];
}

@end
```

This implementation is very similar to that of the Order class, so you'll just focus on the key differences. The initWithFamily:order: invokes the superclass initWithOrder: method to initialize the superclass state properly, and then assigns the family input parameter to the property's backing instance variable.

The initWithCoder: method is very similar to that provided for the Order class (as shown in Listing 12-10). However, as the superclass of the Family class (Order) adopts the NSCoding protocol, the *self* variable is assigned the returned value of the superclass initWithCoder: call.

```objc
self = [super initWithCoder:coder]
```

In this way, the superclass state (the order property) is initialized properly. Next, the Family class state (represented by its properties and instance variables) is decoded and initialized. As the Family class has a single property named family, the property's instance variable is assigned to the value decoded by the coder's decodeObjectForKey: method, where the key is named FAMILY_KEY.

The encodeWithCoder: method is used to archive the Family class state. Because the superclass of Family (the Order class) adopts the NSCoding protocol, this method first invokes invoke the superclass's encodeWithCoder: method. Next, it invokes the encodeWithCoder: method on the coder for each property/variable that needs to be archived; in this case, the family property.

As with the Order class, the description method returns a text string consisting of the value of the family property concatenated with the value of the description for its superclass.

```
return [NSString stringWithFormat:@"Family:%@, %@", self.family,
        [super description]];
```

Now you'll implement the final class in the hierarchy. Select **New ➤ File ...** from the Xcode File menu, select the **Objective-C** class template, and name the class **Subfamily**. Select the **ArchiveCat** folder for the files location and the **ArchiveCat** project as the target, and then click the **Create** button. Next, in the Xcode project navigator pane, select the resulting header file named **Subfamily.h** and update the interface, as shown in Listing 12-13.

Listing 12-13. Subfamily Interface

```
#import "Family.h"

@interface Subfamily : Family

@property(readonly) NSString *genus;
@property(readonly) NSString *species;

- (id)initWithSpecies:(NSString *)species
                genus:(NSString *)genus
               family:(NSString *)family
                order:(NSString *)order;

@end
```

The Subfamily interface subclasses the Family class. The read-only properties genus and species specifies the genus and species for an animal group in a biological classification. The initWithSpecies:family:order: method initializes a Subfamily object, similar to the corresponding methods for the Family and Order classes. Now select the **Subfamily.m** file and update the implementation, as shown in Listing 12-14.

Listing 12-14. Subfamily Implementation

```
#import "Subfamily.h"

@implementation Subfamily

- (id)initWithSpecies:(NSString *)species
                genus:(NSString *)genus
```

```objectivec
                  family:(NSString *)family
                   order:(NSString *)order
{
  if ((self = [super initWithFamily:family order:order]))
  {
    _species = species;
    _genus = genus;
  }

  return self;
}

- (id)initWithCoder:(NSCoder *)coder
{
  if ((self = [super initWithCoder:coder]))
  {
    _species = [coder decodeObjectForKey:@"SPECIES_KEY"];
    _genus = [coder decodeObjectForKey:@"GENUS_KEY"];
  }
  return self;
}

- (void)encodeWithCoder:(NSCoder *)coder
{
  [super encodeWithCoder:coder];
  [coder encodeObject:self.species forKey:@"SPECIES_KEY"];
  [coder encodeObject:self.genus forKey:@"GENUS_KEY"];
}

- (NSString *) description
{
  return [NSString stringWithFormat:@"Animal - Species:%@ Genus:%@, %@",
          self.species, self.genus, [super description]];
}

@end
```

This implementation is very similar to that of the Family class, differing primarily in the Subfamily class state (the genus and species properties). In all other respects, the logic is identical, as you'll see if you compare Listing 12-12 and Listing 12-14. Now you'll implement the class used to archive the hierarchy. Select **New ➤ File ...** from the Xcode File menu, select the **Objective-C** class template, and name the class **Archiver**. Select the **ArchiveCat** folder for the files location and the **ArchiveCat** project as the target, and then click the **Create** button. Next, in the Xcode project navigator pane, select the resulting header file named **Archiver.h** and update the interface, as shown in Listing 12-15.

Listing 12-15. Archiver Interface

```
#import <Foundation/Foundation.h>

@interface Archiver : NSObject

@property (readwrite) NSString *path;

- (BOOL) encodeArchive:(id)data toFile:(NSString *)file;
- (id) decodeArchiveFromFile:(NSString *) file;

@end
```

The Archiver interface has a single property, path, which defines the path for the file the archive is written to. The methods encodeArchive:toFile: and decodeArchiveFromFile: are used to encode/decode an archive to/from a file on the file system. Now select the **Archiver.m** file and update the implementation, as shown in Listing 12-16.

Listing 12-16. Archiver Implementation

```
#import "Archiver.h"

@implementation Archiver

- (id) init
{
  if ((self = [super init]))
  {
    _path = NSTemporaryDirectory();
  }

  return self;
}

- (BOOL) encodeArchive:(id)objectGraph toFile:(NSString *)file
{
  NSString *archivePath = [self.path stringByAppendingPathComponent:file];

  // Create an archiver for encoding data
  NSMutableData *mdata = [[NSMutableData alloc] init];
  NSKeyedArchiver *archiver = [[NSKeyedArchiver alloc]
                             initForWritingWithMutableData:mdata];

  // Encode the data, keyed with a simple string
  [archiver encodeObject:objectGraph forKey:@"FELINE_KEY"];
  [archiver finishEncoding];

  // Write the encoded data to a file, returning status of the write
  BOOL result = [mdata writeToFile:archivePath atomically:YES];
  return result;
}
```

```
- (id) decodeArchiveFromFile:(NSString *) file
{
  // Get path to file with archive
  NSString *archivePath = [self.path stringByAppendingPathComponent:file];

  // Create an unarchiver for decoding data
  NSData *data = [[NSMutableData alloc] initWithContentsOfFile:archivePath];
  NSKeyedUnarchiver *unarchiver = [[NSKeyedUnarchiver alloc]
                                   initForReadingWithData:data];

  // Decode the data, keyed with simple string
  id result = [unarchiver decodeObjectForKey:@"FELINE_KEY"];
  [unarchiver finishDecoding];

  // Return the decoded data
  return result;
}

@end
```

As shown in Listing 12-16, the init method sets the value for the path property. It uses the Foundation NSTemporaryDirectory() function to create a path to the user's temporary directory on the file system, and assigns that value to the property's backing instance variable.

The encodeArchive:toFile: method encodes an object graph to a file. It creates a file path by prepending the path property to the input file string. It then creates a mutable data object for archiving the graph. Next, it creates an NSKeyArchiver instance to perform the archiving, initialized with the data object. It encodes the graph to the data object with the key FELINE_KEY, and then finishes the encoding. Finally, it writes the archived data object to the file, returning a Boolean that indicates the success/failure of the write.

The decodeArchiveFromFile: method decodes an archive from a file, returning the initialized object graph. It creates a file path by prepending the path property to the input file string. It then creates a data object for unarchiving the graph. Next, it creates an NSKeyUnarchiver instance to perform the unarchiving, initialized with the data object. It decodes the graph to a data object with the key FELINE_KEY, finishes the decoding, and then returns the initialized data object.

And that's it! Now that you have implemented the class hierarchy and the archiver class, let's use this to archive an object graph. In the Xcode project navigator, select the **main.m** file and update the main() function, as shown in Listing 12-17.

Listing 12-17. ArchiveCat main() Function

```
#import <Foundation/Foundation.h>
#import "Archiver.h"
#import "Subfamily.h"
```

```
int main(int argc, const char * argv[])
{
  @autoreleasepool
  {
    // Create an Archiver to encode/decode an object graph
    Archiver *archiver = [[Archiver alloc] init];

    // Create an object graph and archive it to a file
    id animal = [[Subfamily alloc] initWithSpecies:@"Lion"
                                             genus:@"Panther"
                                            family:@"Felid"
                                             order:@"Carnivore"];
    NSLog(@"\n%@", [animal description]);
    NSString *file = @"data.archive";

    // Display results
    if ([archiver encodeArchive:animal toFile:file])
    {
      NSLog(@"You encoded an archive to file %@",
            [[archiver path] stringByAppendingString:file]);
    }

    // Decode object graph from archive and log its description
    id data = [archiver decodeArchiveFromFile:file];
    if ([archiver decodeArchiveFromFile:file])
    {
      NSLog(@"You decoded an archive from file %@\n%@",
            [[archiver path] stringByAppendingString:file], [data description]);
    }

  }
  return 0;
}
```

As shown in Listing 12-17, the main() function begins by creating an Archiver object. It then creates an object graph, logs its description to the output pane, and names the archive file. Next, the graph is archived to the named archive file, and if successful, a message is logged to the console.

The next set of statements decodes an object graph from the archive. First, it decodes the archive using the Archiver decodeArchiveFromFile: method. It then performs a condition check on the result of the method call, and if it returns an object graph (meaning the operation completed successfully), it logs a description of the object graph to the output pane. Now when you compile and run the ArchiveCat program, you should observe messages in the output pane comparable to those shown in Figure 12-2.

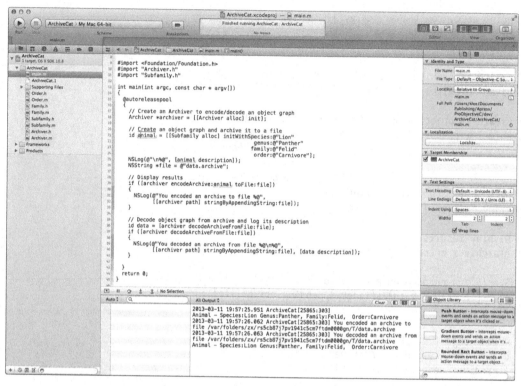

Figure 12-2. ArchiveCat program output

As shown in the output pane, a Subfamily object (i.e., object graph) is created and initialized with its input parameters, and its description is logged to the output pane. Next, the object is archived to the specified file, and the full path of the archive file is logged to the output pane. A corresponding object is then decoded from the archive and its description is logged to the output pane. As the description for the initially created object and the object decoded from the archive is identical, this validates that the archive was correctly encoded and decoded. This demonstrates use of the Archiving APIs to encode/decode an archive. Look this code over for a while and make sure that you have a good handle on the archiving process. When you're ready, let's move on to distributed objects.

Distributed Objects

The Distributed Objects classes provide functionality for distributed object communication; in essence, an object in one process sending a message to an object in a different process. The NSConnection class manages connections between distributed objects in different threads and/or processes. NSDistantObject is a subclass of NSProxy that defines proxies for distributed objects in other threads or processes. The NSProtocolChecker, also a subclass of NSProxy, defines an object that restricts the messages that can be sent to another object (its delegate). A protocol checker acts as a type of proxy that only forwards the messages it receives to its target if they are in its designated protocol.

To *vend* an object (i.e., to make an object instance distributed so that it can be invoked by other applications over a network), the object should first be configured as the root object of an NSConnection instance and the connection should then be registered on the network. Listing 12-18 vends an object named helloServiceObj and registers it under the name HelloService.

Listing 12-18. Registering the HelloService Distributed Object

```
NSConnection *connection = [NSConnection defaultConnection];
[connection setRootObject:helloServiceObj];
[connection registerName:@"HelloService"];
```

Registration makes the distributed object available to remote clients. The connection must be started within a run loop (i.e., an NSRunLoop instance) to capture incoming requests for the distributed object.

A client can invoke methods on a distributed object by obtaining a proxy for it. The following statement obtains a proxy on the local host for the distributed object shown in Listing 12-18.

```
NSDistantObject *helloProxy =
    [NSConnection rootProxyForConnectionWithRegisteredName:@"HelloService"
                                               host:nil];
```

The NSDistantObject setProtocolForProxy: method is used to set the methods handled by the distributed object. If the distributed object from Listing 12-18 adopts a protocol named HelloProtocol and its methods comprise those available for clients, and then the following statement can be used to configure the proxy named helloProxy to support this protocol.

```
[helloProxy setProtocolForProxy: @protocol (HelloProtocol)];
```

The NSInvocation and NSMethodSignature classes are used to support the Foundation Framework's distributed object system. The NSInvocation class was introduced in Chapter 9, where you learned that an NSInvocation object is composed of all the elements of an Objective-C message: the receiving (target) object, selector, parameters, and return value. NSMethodSignature is used to forward messages that a receiving (distributed) object does not respond to. It contains type information for the arguments and return value of a method.

The distributed object classes are only available for use on the Mac OS X platform.

Scripting

The Foundation Framework scripting classes support the creation of *scriptable applications,* that is, applications that can be controlled with AppleScript—a scripting language that makes possible direct control of scriptable applications and scriptable parts of Apple OS X.

NSScriptCommand and its subclasses implement standard AppleScript commands. NSScriptObjectSpecifier and its subclasses locate scriptable objects. NSScriptCoercionHandler and NSScriptKeyValueCoding perform essential functions related to scripting.

The scripting classes are only available for use on the OS X platform.

Roundup

In this chapter, you continued your review of the Foundation Framework, focusing on classes that provide specialized system services for Objective-C programs. You should now be familiar with Foundation Framework classes that provide the following functionality:

- Notifications
- Archives and Serialization
- Distributed Objects
- Scripting

Chapter 13

Foundation Functions and Data Types

The Foundation Framework is not only composed of classes, it also includes numerous functions, data types, and constants. Now you may be thinking, "Why do I need these additional APIs? After all, Objective-C is an object-oriented programming language and the Foundation Framework provides a complete set of classes." Well, these APIs are, in fact, an important part of the Foundation Framework, and together they provide a variety of essential functionality for Objective-C software development. In this chapter, you will explore these APIs and the provided sample code to learn how they can be used in your programs.

Foundation Functions

The Foundation Framework defines a number of functions and function-like macros. The Apple Foundation Functions Reference provides a definitive guide for these functions. Here you'll examine Foundation functions that perform the following tasks:

- Assertions and logging
- String localization
- Numerical operations and byte ordering
- Runtime operations

Assertions

An assertion is a statement placed in code to check the existence of a condition. Assertions are used to provide runtime verification of assumptions that, if not present, should cause the program to terminate. Coding with assertions is one of the quickest and most effective ways to detect and correct bugs. Assertions can also document the logic of your program, thereby enhancing maintainability.

Each assertion contains a Boolean expression that you believe will be true when the assertion executes. If it is not true, the system will throw an error. By verifying that the expression is indeed true, the assertion confirms your assumptions about the behavior of your program, increasing your confidence that the program is free of errors.

The following are examples of situations where you would use assertions:

- *Internal invariant*: An assumption concerning program behavior. This assumption is often indicated with comments in code, but it can be documented and validated at runtime with an assertion.

- *Control-flow invariant*: An assumption concerning control flow, specifically locations in your code that should not be reached.

- *Precondition*: A condition that must be true before a method is invoked.

- *Postcondition*: A condition that must be true after a method is invoked.

- *Class invariant*: A condition that must be true for each class instance.

An example of an *internal invariant* is the conditional expression in Listing 13-1.

Listing 13-1. Example of a Conditional Expression with an Internal Invariant

```
if (value >= 0)
{
  ...
}
else
{
  // value must be negative
  ...
}
```

As shown in Listing 13-1, these assumptions are often indicated with comments in code, but can be documented and validated at runtime with an assertion. The code excerpt from Listing 13-1 is updated in Listing 13-2 to express the invariant with an assertion.

Listing 13-2. Example of an Internal Invariant Expressed with an Assertion

```
if (value >= 0)
{
  ...
}
else
{
  NSAssert((value < 0), @"Value not valid here, should be negative");
  ...
}
```

A common type of precondition is a conditional check of the input parameters for a method (or function). For public methods, preconditions are explicitly checked in code and throw the appropriate exception if the condition is not satisfied, hence they should not be checked with assertions. Assertions can be used to check preconditions for private methods and functions.

Assertions can be used to test postconditions for both public and private methods/functions.

A *class invariant* constrains the properties (i.e., internal state) and behavior of each instance of a class. Assertions can be used to define class invariants in a manner similar to that used to express the other situations discussed earlier.

Assertion Macros

The Foundation assertion functions are, in fact, macros that enable the creation of assertions in Objective-C code. Each assertion macro evaluates a condition and, if the condition evaluates to false, passes a string (and possibly additional printf-style arguments formatted into the string) describing the failure to an NSAssertionHandler instance. NSAssertionHandler is a Foundation Framework class used to handle false assertions, and each program thread has its own NSAssertionHandler object. So, when the condition of a Foundation assertion macro evaluates to false, it passes the condition describing the error to the NSAssertionHandler object for the current thread. This object in turn logs the error and then raises an exception (specifically, an NSInternalIncosistencyException) that causes the program to terminate. NSAssertionHandler instances are generally not created programmatically, but rather by an assertion function.

There are multiple Foundation assertion macros to support the creation of assertions within Objective-C methods and functions. Each assertion macro has at least one argument: a conditional expression that evaluates to true or false. Most also include an argument that contains a format string describing the error condition. The assertion macros support the substitution of zero to five arguments in a format string. The complete list of Foundation assertions functions is provided in Table 13-1.

Table 13-1. Foundation Assertion Functions

Foundation Function	Description
NSAssert	Generates an assertion for an Objective-C method if a given condition evaluates to NO (false). Its arguments include the conditional expression and a format string (with no format specifier) that describes the error.
NSAssert1	Similar to NSAssert, its arguments include the conditional expression, a format string (with one format specifier), and an argument to be inserted into the format string.
NSAssert2, NSAssert3, NSAssert4, NSAssert5	Similar to NSAssert, its arguments include the conditional expression, a format string (with two, three, four, or five format specifiers), and two, three, four, or five arguments to be inserted into the format string.
NSParameterAssert	Generates an assertion for the parameter of an Objective-C method. Its arguments are the conditional expression for a parameter.
NSCAssert	Generates an assertion for an Objective-C function: if a given condition evaluates to NO (false). Its arguments include the conditional expression and a format string (with no format specifier) that describes the error.
NSCAssert1	Similar to NSCAssert, its arguments include the conditional expression, a format string (with one format specifier), and an argument to be inserted into the format string.

(continued)

Table 13-1. *(continued)*

Foundation Function	Description
NSCAssert2, NSCAssert3, NSCAssert4, NSCAssert5	Similar to NSCAssert, its arguments include the conditional expression, a format string (with two, three, four, or five format specifiers), and two, three, four, or five arguments to be inserted into the format string.
NSCParameterAssert	Generates an assertion for the parameter of an Objective-C function. Its arguments are the conditional expression for a parameter.

The following statement uses the NSAssert function to assert that the value of the variable named age is within the prescribed range.

```
NSAssert((age > 0) && (age <=18), @"Variable age not within prescribed range");
```

In the next statement, the same assertion is performed again, this time using the NSAssert1 function to log the value of the variable if the assertion fails.

```
NSAssert1((age > 0) && (age <=18),
    @"Value %d for age not within prescribed range", age);
```

Assertions can be used to check parameters of private methods or functions. Parameter checking for public methods/functions is normally part of the corresponding published API; hence, these should be checked whether or not assertions are enabled. Listing 13-3 uses the NSParameterAssert function to assert that the parameters for the method encodeArchive:toFile: have valid values.

Listing 13-3. Asserting Method Parameter Values Using NSParameterAssert

```
- (BOOL) encodeArchive:(id)objectGraph toFile:(NSString *)file
{
  NSParameterAssert(file != nil);
  NSParameterAssert([objectGraph conformsToProtocol:@protocol(NSCoding)]);
  ...
}
```

You can disable assertions in your code by defining the preprocessor macro; NS_BLOCK_ASSERTIONS, for example.

```
#define NS_BLOCK_ASSERTIONS
```

Logging

The Foundation Framework includes two functions, NSLog and NSLogv, for logging output to the system log facility. In Xcode, error messages from these functions are displayed in the Xcode output pane. By now you have become familiar with the NSLog function through the example source code provided in this book, so here you'll examine the NSLogv function.

NSLogv, as with NSLog, logs an error message to the system log facility. It differs from NSLog in that it supports a variable argument list. The declaration for the NSLog function is

void NSLogv(NSString *format, va_list args);

The variable format is a format string, and the variable args is a data type used for providing a list of (variable) arguments to functions. So you may be wondering, when would you use NSLogv? If you have a method or function that takes a variable argument list, then NSLogv can be used to log messages with this list. For example, the variadic function printArgs declared as follows:

void printArgs(int numArgs, ...);

logs a number of function arguments to the system log facility, where the arguments are a variable list (specified by the ... variable argument symbol) and the number of arguments from this list to be logged (specified by the numArgs function argument). Given this function declaration, Listing 13-4 demonstrates how this function is implemented using the NSLogv function.

Listing 13-4. Using NSLogv to Log a variadic Argument List

```
void printArgs(int numArgs, ...)
{
  va_list args;
  va_start(args, numArgs);
  va_end(args);
  NSMutableString *format = [[NSMutableString alloc] init];
  [format appendString:@"Arguments: "];
  for (int ii=0; ii<numArgs-1; ii++)
  {
    [format appendString:@"%@, "];
  }
  if (numArgs > 1)
  {
    [format appendString:@"%@"];
  }
  NSLogv(format, args);
}
```

If this function is invoked as follows:

printArgs(3, @"Hello", @"Objective-C", @"World!");

It logs to the console the following message:

```
Arguments: Hello, Objective-C, World!
```

Bundles

The Foundation Framework includes several function macros for retrieving localized strings. They are used to load strings from a program's strings files. Before you begin examining these macros, let's take a moment to discuss internationalization and localization.

Internationalization is the process of designing an application so that it can serve different languages and regions (i.e., locales) without being changed. *Localization* is the adaptation of an internationalized application to a local market. Localization can be applied to many parts of an application, including its visible text, icons and graphics, views, and data.

Localizing Strings

Localizing visible text is a key part of the localization process. Strings in code that require localization must be extracted, localized, and reinserted back in the code in order to display properly in the specified locale. Apple provides a tool, *genstrings*, which can be used to facilitate text localization. The genstrings tool searches your code for uses of the localization function macros and uses the information they contain to build the initial set of *strings* files (resource files that contain localizable strings) for your application. For example, if your source code contains a statement that utilizes the localization function macro NSLocalizedString to return a localized version of the string Yes, as follows:

```
NSString *yes = NSLocalizedString(@"Yes", @"Word for yes");
```

the genstrings tool will parse this statement and use it to build a strings file. The genstrings tool can parse C and Objective-C source code files with the .c or .m filename extensions. You can also specify the output directory where genstrings places the resulting strings files. In most cases, you would want to specify the directory containing the project resources for your development language.

The following example uses the genstrings tool to parse all Objective-C source files in the current directory and store the resulting strings file in the en.lproj subdirectory, which must already exist.

```
genstrings -o en.lproj *.m
```

The first time you run the genstrings tool, it creates a set of new strings files for you. Subsequent executions on the sme file(s) replace the contents of those strings files with the current string entries found in your source code.

Localized Strings Functions

Once you have localized strings in a strings file, the Foundation localized string function macros can be used to retrieve the appropriate localized string for a specified locale. The Foundation Framework defines four function macros for getting localized strings, shown in Table 13-2.

Table 13-2. Foundation Localized String Functions

Foundation Function	Description
NSLocalizedString	Retrieves a localized version of a string on the main application bundle in the default strings table.
NSLocalizedStringFromTable	Retrieves a localized version of a string on the main application bundle in the specified strings table.
NSLocalizedStringFromTableInBundle	Retrieves a localized version of a string on the specified application bundle and strings table.
NSLocalizedStringWithDefaultValue	Retrieves a localized version of a string on the specified application bundle and strings table, using the default value if the key is not found.

The localized string functions depend on an NSBundle class instance. Each function invokes an NSBundle object's localizedStringForKey:value:table: method, providing the function arguments as parameters for the method.

So, the localization functions both provide expressions that can be parsed by the genstrings tool to create an application's strings file, and retrieve a localized version of a string. They also let you associate translation comments with each entry.

For example, if your program has a strings table in a file named Localizable.strings that includes the following strings:

```
"Yes" = "Yes"
"No" = "No"
```

the NSLocalizedStringFromTable function would retrieve the string Yes with the following statement.

```
NSString *yes = NSLocalizedStringFromTable(@"Yes", @"Localizable.strings",
            @"Word for yes");
```

Conversely, if the Localizable.strings file for the French locale contained the values

```
"Yes" = "Oui"
"No" = "Non"
```

Then the preceding statement would retrieve the string Oui.

Decimal Numbers and Byte Ordering

The Foundation Framework includes functions for performing decimal number operations. The arithmetic operations supported include decimal arithmetic, rounding, comparison, copy, normalizing, and string representations.

The functions take one or more NSDecimal numbers as arguments, along with (potentially) other parameters. NSDecimal is a Foundation data type used to describe a decimal number.

NSDecimalAdd, NSDecimalSubtract, NSDecimalMultiply, and NSDecimalDivide perform the associated arithmetic operations on NSDecimal instances. NSDecimalMultiplyByPowerOf10 multiplies a number by an input power of 10. Each takes as an input argument an NSRoundingMode Foundation constant that specifies how the result is rounded. The available rounding modes are:

- NSRoundDown: Rounds the returned value down.

- NSRoundUp: Rounds the returned value up.

- NSRoundPlain: Rounds to the closest possible return value. When the value is halfway between two positive numbers, it rounds up. When the value is halfway between two negative numbers, it rounds down.

- NSRoundBankers: Rounds to the closest possible return value. When the value is halfway between two numbers, it returns the value whose last digit is even.

Rounding can be explicitly performed using the NSDecimalRound function, or automatically performed for the NSDecimal arithmetic functions if the result has more digits than the maximum number of significant digits allowed (38).

NSDecimalPower raises a number to the specified power. NSDecimalNormalize and NSDecimalCompact both change the representation of a decimal number. NSDecimalCompact formats a decimal so that it takes up the minimum amount of memory. All of the NSDecimal functions expect compact decimal arguments. NSDecimalNormalize updates the format of its two decimal arguments such that they have the same exponent. NSDecimalAdd and NSDecimalSubtract invoke NSDecimalNormalize. NSDecimalRound rounds the input decimal according to the input NSRoundingMode constant.

NSDecimalCopy copies the value of a decimal number to another NSDecimalNumber instance. NSDecimalCompare compares two decimal numbers, returning the result of the comparison as an NSComparisonResult value (a Foundation constant) that can have one of the following values:

- NSOrderedDescending: The left operand is greater than the right operand.

- NSOrderedAscending: The left operand is less than the right operand.

- NSOrderedSame: The two operands are equal.

Using the NSDecimal Functions

Now you'll create a program that demonstrates the use of the Foundation decimal arithmetic functions. In Xcode, create a new project by selecting **New ➤ Project ...** from the Xcode File menu. In the **New Project Assistant** pane, create a command-line application. In the Project Options window, specify **DecimalAddition** for the Product Name, choose **Foundation** for the Project Type, and select ARC memory management by selecting the **Use Automatic Reference Counting** check box. Specify the location in your file system where you want the project to be created (if necessary select **New Folder** and enter the name and location for the folder), uncheck the **Source Control** check box, and then click the **Create** button.

OK, the DecimalAddition project is created. Now select the **main.m** file and update the main() function, as shown in Listing 13-5.

Listing 13-5. Performing Decimal Arithmetic Using the NSDecimalAdd and NSDecimalRound Functions

```
#import <Foundation/Foundation.h>

int main(int argc, const char * argv[])
{
  @autoreleasepool
  {
    // Create two NSDecimal numbers using the NSDecimalNumber class
    NSDecimal dec1 = [[NSDecimalNumber decimalNumberWithString:@"1.534"]
                    decimalValue];
    NSDecimal dec2 = [[NSDecimalNumber decimalNumberWithString:@"2.011"]
                    decimalValue];

    // Declare result and rounded result variables for the calculations
    NSDecimal result;
    NSDecimal roundedResult;
```

```
    // Now perform the decimal addition
    NSDecimalAdd(&result, &dec1, &dec2, NSRoundPlain);
    NSLog(@"Sum = %@", NSDecimalString(&result, nil));

    // Demonstrate rounding the result using the available rounding modes
    NSDecimalRound(&roundedResult, &result, 2, NSRoundUp);
    NSLog(@"Sum (round up) = %@", NSDecimalString(&roundedResult, nil));
    NSDecimalRound(&roundedResult, &result, 2, NSRoundDown);
    NSLog(@"Sum (round down) = %@", NSDecimalString(&roundedResult, nil));
    NSDecimalRound(&roundedResult, &result, 2, NSRoundPlain);
    NSLog(@"Sum (round plain) = %@", NSDecimalString(&roundedResult, nil));
    NSDecimalRound(&roundedResult, &result, 2, NSRoundBankers);
    NSLog(@"Sum (round bankers) = %@", NSDecimalString(&roundedResult, nil));
  }
  return 0;
}
```

As shown in Listing 13-5, the NSDecimalNumber class is used to create two decimal numbers of the Foundation type NSDecimal. The NSDecimalAdd function is then used to add the two numbers. Because the number of digits in the result is less than the maximum allowed, no rounding is performed and the result printed by the NSLog function is 3.545. Next, the NSDecimalRound function is used to explicitly round the result to two digits after the decimal point; each of the available rounding modes is used to demonstrate how they affect the result. When you compile and run the program, you should observe messages in the output pane comparable to those shown in Figure 13-1.

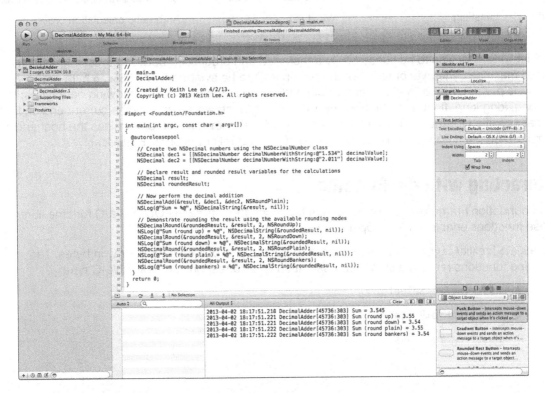

Figure 13-1. DecimalAddition program output

As you can see in Figure 13-1, the selected rounding mode affects the result as explained earlier.

The NSDecimalNumber class provides methods that duplicate much of the functionality of the NSDecimal functions; hence, you have the choice of which to use to perform decimal arithmetic. The NSDecimal functions provide better performance and lower memory utilization than the NSDecimalNumber class. However, the NSDecimalNumber class performs these decimal operations using objects, and enables you to directly store the results of these operations in an object-oriented collection like an instance of NSArray or NSDictionary.

Byte Ordering

The Foundation Framework includes a set of functions that perform byte ordering; specifically, these functions can be used to swap the order of bytes of a number as stored in memory. Byte ordering is important when a binary file created on one computer is read on another computer with a different byte order. Big endian machines (such as a Motorola 680x0 CPU) store data with the most significant byte in the lowest memory address. A little endian machine (such as an Intel CPU) stores the most significant byte in the highest memory address. For example, the decimal value of 4132 (hexadecimal 1024) would be stored as shown in Table 13-3.

Table 13-3. Byte Ordering for Big Endian and Little Endian Machines

Endian	First Byte	Middle Bytes	Last Byte	Hex Value	Description
Big	Most sig.	...	Least sig.	10 24	Similar to a number written on paper.
Little	Least sig.	...	Most sig.	24 10	Arithmetic calculation order.

In order for binary files to be successfully transferred and processed between these big and little endian machines, the byte ordering of the data needs to be swapped. The NSSwap byte ordering functions perform big to little and little to big endian byte ordering for the following data types: short, int, long, long long, float, and double. The NSSwapHost functions swap from the current endian format to that specified for the input data type. The NSHostByteOrder function determines the host endian format. It returns a Foundation constant value of NS_LittleEndian or NS_BigEndian.

Interacting with the Runtime

The Foundation Framework includes several functions that utilize the Objective-C runtime library. These functions enable dynamic operations.

The NSGetSizeAndAlignment function is used to get the size of a character array in bytes. The following functions retrieve a string representation of a corresponding Objective-C type:

- NSStringFromSelector
- NSStringFromProtocol
- NSStringFromClass

The following statement retrieves a text string (sayHello:) for a selector specified with the @selector directive, and assigns this string to the variable methodName.

```
NSString *methodName = NSStringFromSelector(@selector(sayHello:));
```

The next set of functions perform the converse operation; they retrieve an Objective-C type from a string representation:

- NSSelectorFromString
- NSProtocolFromString
- NSClassFromString

The following statement dynamically retrieves a selector from the input string.

```
SEL methodSel = NSSelectorFromString(@"sayHello:");
```

File Paths

A set of Foundation functions provides operations for managing file paths, including retrieving the user name, home directory, temporary directory, and directory search paths. The following statement demonstrates use of the NSFullUserName function to retrieve the full name of the current user.

```
NSString *fullName = NSFullUserName();
```

The NSUserName function, in comparison, returns the logon name of the current user.

The following statement demonstrates use of the NSHomeDirectory function to retrieve the home directory for the current user.

```
NSString *homeDir = NSHomeDirectory();
```

The NSHomeDirectoryForUser function retrieves the home directory for the user specified in the input argument.

The NSTemporaryDirectory function retrieves the full path to the temporary directory for the current user.

The NSSearchPathForDirectoriesInDomains function returns a list of directory search paths for the specified directories in the specified domains. The syntax for the function is

```
NSSearchPathForDirectoriesInDomains(
  NSSearchPathDirectory directory,
  NSSearchPathDomainMask domainMask,
  BOOL expandTilde);
```

The NSSearchPathDirectory is a Foundation constant that specifies a variety of directories in the file system, for example the Documents directory. The NSSearchPathDomainMask is a Foundation constant used to specify the domain for the search; for example, the user's home directory. The BOOL argument is set to YES if the paths returned should be expanded. Listing 13-6 demonstrates the use of the function to retrieve the documents directory for the current user.

Listing 13-6. Retrieving the Documents Directory Using the NSSearchPathForDirectoriesInDomains Function

```
NSArray *paths = NSSearchPathForDirectoriesInDomains(NSDocumentDirectory,
                                           NSUserDomainMask, YES);
NSString *documentsDirectory = paths[0];
```

Geometry

The Foundation Framework includes functions that assist in the performance of geometric calculations on points, ranges, rectangles, and sizes. A point represents a location in two-dimensional Euclidean geometry with x and y coordinates. A range represents a one-dimensional quantity beginning at a specified location of a specified length. A size represents a two-dimensional quantity of specified width and height. The point, range, and size Foundation functions perform operations to create, retrieve, test for equality, and return string representations of these quantities. The Foundation data types NSPoint represents points, NSRange represents ranges, and NSSize represents sizes. The following statement creates a new NSPoint from the specified values.

```
NSPoint point = NSMakePoint(0, 5);
```

The Foundation framework also includes numerous functions for manipulating rectangles, including operations to create, get, get components, query, test for equality, and return string representations. There are also functions that perform geometric operations (test for intersection, union, divide, point in rectangle, etc.). The Foundation data type NSRect represents rectangles. The following statement creates a rectangle at point {0, 0} and size [5, 10].

```
NSRect rect1 = NSMakeRect(0.0, 0.0, 5.0, 10.0);
```

The next set of statements creates a new rectangle at point {2.5, 5} and size [5, 10], and then calculates the intersection of the two rectangles.

```
NSRect rect2 = NSMakeRect(2.5, 5.0, 5.0, 10.0);
NSRect rect3 = NSIntersectionRect(rect1, rect2);
```

Data Types

The Foundation Framework defines a number of custom data types, many of which are used in conjunction with the Foundation functions. These include data types that represent numbers, geometric concepts, and general structures. These data types are primarily C structures. Some of the more common are listed in Table 13-4.

Table 13-4. Common Foundation Data Types

Foundation Function	Description
NSInteger	Data type used to represent an integer value across different processor architectures. On 32-bit machines, NSInteger is a 32-bit integer; whereas on 64-bit machines, it is a 64-bit integer.
NSUInteger	Data type used to represent an unsigned integer value across different processor architectures.
NSDecimal	C struct data type used to represent a decimal number.
NSPoint	C struct data type used to represent a point in two-dimensional Euclidean space.
NSRange	C struct data type used to represent a range, a one-dimensional quantity beginning at a specified location of a specified length.
NSSize	C struct data type used to represent a size, two-dimensional quantity of specified width and height.
NSRect	C struct data type used to represent a rectangle in two-dimensional Euclidean space.
NSComparator	A block object data type used for comparison operations. The block returns a Foundation constant NSComparisonResult that indicates the ordering of the two objects compared.
NSTimeInterval	A Foundation type (of type double) used to specify a time interval, in seconds.
NSStringEncoding	A Foundation type (of type NSUInteger) used to represent string encoding values.

Constants

The Foundation constants include enumerations, global variables, geometric and numeric constants, exceptions, and Foundation framework version numbers. The enumerations define enumerations used by the Foundation Framework APIs. The global variables define general constants. The geometric constants define alignment options and minimum/maximum edges for rectangles. The numeric constants define constants for NSDecimal, NSInteger, NSUInteger, and NSMapTable data types. The exception constants define standard exceptions. The version number constants define the list of version numbers for the Foundation Framework. The definitive reference for the Foundation constants is the Foundation Constants Reference.

Roundup

In this chapter, you examined the Foundation functions, data types, and constants, and learned how they can be used to develop Objective-C programs. You also became familiar with some of the trade-offs involved in choosing the appropriate API when multiple choices are available (e.g., Foundation class versus function). You should now be familiar with the following Foundation Framework APIs:

- Foundation functions
- Foundation data types
- Foundation constants

The definitive reference for these APIs is provided in the Apple Foundation Functions Reference.

14

Expert Section: Error Handling

How your code deals with errors is critical to implementing quality software. Runtime errors that impact the operation and/or performance of a program can be due to a variety of causes, such as incorrect user input, system issues, or programming errors. The Foundation Framework includes several APIs for handling runtime error conditions. In this Expert Section chapter, you will examine these APIs in depth. The chapter explores the causes of runtime errors, the programming options for error handling, and the Foundation Framework APIs for handling errors and exception conditions. After completing this chapter, you will be able to use the Foundation Framework error handling and exception processing APIs to write programs that respond properly to errors as they arise, and even provide support for error recovery.

Runtime Error Conditions

A *runtime error* is an error that occurs while a program is running; it contrasts with other categories of program errors, such as syntax and linking errors, which occur prior to program execution. Runtime errors are generally due to the following types of conditions:

- *Logical error*: An error due to the fact that the code doesn't correctly implement the corresponding program logic. This type of error is manifested during program execution when it doesn't produce the expected output.

- *Semantic error*: An error due to the improper use of program statements (for example, performing division by zero or the improper initialization of a variable).

- *User input error*: An error due to invalid user input.

If any of these conditions occurs and is not handled, it can result in a variety of adverse consequences, including program termination or improper operation. As a result, a variety of mechanisms have been developed in computer programming to detect and respond to errors. For Objective-C, the Foundation Framework includes several APIs for error handling, grouped into the following categories:

- Assertions
- Error codes
- Error objects
- Exceptions

Before examining these APIs in detail, let's briefly review each of these error types and how they are used.

Assertions

An assertion is used to provide a runtime check of a condition that, if not present, should cause the program to terminate. Assertions can be disabled via a compiler directive; hence, they should only be used to detect programming logic and semantic errors, not runtime errors due to invalid user input, and so forth. In Chapter 13, you learned about the Foundation Framework assertion functions. These support the creation of assertions for both Objective-C methods and functions.

Error Codes

Error codes are unique integer values used to identify and perhaps convey information about a particular error that occurs during program execution. Error codes are a simple mechanism for reporting errors but are limited in the amount of information they can provide for error handling.

Error Objects

Error objects are used to both encapsulate and convey information about runtime errors that users need to know about. An error object is made up of an error code and additional information related to the error, some of which can potentially be used for recovering from the error. Because they are objects, error objects also benefit from the basic properties of OOP (encapsulation, inheritance, subclassing, etc.). The Foundation Framework includes several APIs to support error objects: the NSError class for creating and manipulating error objects, and a set of standard error codes.

Exceptions

In computer programming, an exception is an anomalous, unexpected event that occurs during program execution and requires special processing. Exception handling typically changes program flow, with control being passed to special code designated for this purpose. Exception processing logic varies depending upon the severity of the event, ranging from simple logging to attempting recovery and to program termination. The Foundation Framework includes several APIs to support exception processing: the NSException class for creating and manipulating exceptions, and a set of standard exception names. The Objective-C language includes a set of directives that are used with the Foundation Framework exception APIs to perform exception processing.

NSError

The Foundation Framework NSError class is used to create error objects. The properties of this class are an error code, the error domain, and a dictionary of user information. The class includes methods for creating and initializing error objects, retrieving error properties, getting a localized error description, and facilitating error recovery.

An error domain is a mechanism used to organize error codes according to a system, subsystem, framework, and so forth. Error domains enable you to identify the subsystem, framework, and so forth, that detected the error. They also help prevent naming collisions between error codes, because error codes between different domains can have the same value. The user info dictionary is an NSDictionary instance that holds error information beyond the code and domain. The types of information that can be stored in this dictionary include localized error information and references to supporting objects. The following statement creates an error object using the NSError class factory method errorWithDomain:code:userInfo:.

```
NSError *err = [NSError errorWithDomain:NSCocoaErrorDomain
                            code:NSFileNoSuchFileError
                        userInfo:nil];
```

This particular error would be created if, for example, a file is not found at the path specified. Notice that the user info dictionary is not provided (the userInfo parameter is set to nil). Listing 14-1 creates the same error object, this time with a user info dictionary.

Listing 14-1. Creating an NSError Object

```
NSString *desc = NSLocalizedString(@"FileNotFound", @"");
NSDictionary *info = @{NSLocalizedDescriptionKey:desc};
NSError *err = [NSError errorWithDomain:NSCocoaErrorDomain
                            code:NSFileNoSuchFileError
                        userInfo:info];
```

Listing 14-1 shows the user info dictionary for this example consists of one entry, the key-value pair for a localized description. The localized string is created using the Foundation NSLocalizedString function. The constant NSLocalizedDescriptionKey is a standard user info dictionary key defined in the NSError class.

The Foundation Framework declares four major error domains:

- NSMachErrorDomain: OS kernel error codes.

- NSPOSIXErrorDomain: Error codes derived from standard POSIX-conforming versions of Unix, such as BSD.

- NSOSStatusErrorDomain: Error codes specific to Apple OS X Core Services and the Carbon framework.

- NSCocoaErrorDomain: All of the error codes for the Cocoa frameworks (this includes the Foundation Framework and other Objective-C frameworks).

In addition to the major error domains presented here, there are also error domains for frameworks, groups of classes, and even individual classes. The NSError class also enables you to create your own error domain when creating and initializing an NSError object. As mentioned previously, Listing 14-1 uses the constant NSLocalizedDescriptionKey. The NSError class defines a set of common user info dictionary keys that can be used to create the key-value pairs for the user info dictionary. These keys are listed in Table 14-1.

Table 14-1. NSError Standard User Info Dictionary Keys

Key	Value Description
NSLocalizedDescriptionKey	Localized string representation of the error.
NSFilePathErrorKey	The file path of the error.
NSStringEncodingErrorKey	An NSNumber object containing the string encoding value.
NSUnderlyingErrorKey	The error encountered in an underlying implementation (which caused this error).
NSURLErroKey	An NSURL object.
NSLocalizedFailureReasonErroryKey	Localized string representation of the reason that caused the error.
NSLocalizedRecoverySuggestionErrorKey	Localized recovery suggestion for the error.
NSLocalizedRecoveryOptionsErrorKey	NSArray containing the localized titles of buttons for display in an alert panel.
NSRecoveryAttempterErrorKey	An object that conforms to the NSErrorRecoveryAttempting protocol.
NSHelpAnchorErrorKey	Localized string representation of help information for a help button.
NSURLErrorFailingURLString	NSURL object containing the URL that caused the load to fail.
NSURLErrorFailingURLStringErrorKey	String for the URL that caused the load to fail.
NSURLErrorFailingURLPeerTrustErrorKey	SecTrustRef object representing the state of a failed SSL handshake.

Using Error Objects

OK, so now you know how to create NSError objects, but how do you use them? In general, there are two scenarios for obtaining NSError objects:

- Delegation: An error object passed as a parameter to a delegation method that you implement.

- Indirection: An error object retrieved via indirection from a method that your code invokes.

The delegation pattern is a design pattern whereby an object (the delegator) delegates one or more tasks to another delegate object. The tasks are encapsulated in the method(s) of the delegate object. When necessary, the delegator invokes the appropriate method on the delegate object, providing any required parameters. Many Foundation Framework classes implement the delegation pattern to enable custom error handling. The delegating Foundation object invokes a method on a delegate object (custom code that you implement) that includes an error object as a parameter.

The NSURLConnectionDelegate protocol declares a delegation method (connection:didFailWithError:) that returns an error object:

```
- (void)connection:(NSURLConnection *)connection didFailWithError:(NSError *)error;
```

This protocol is used for asynchronously loading a URL request via an NSURLConnection object. Your code implements a delegate object that conforms to this protocol and sets it as the delegate of the NSURLConnection object. Your code then loads the URL request asynchronously, and if an error occurs, the delegating (NSURLConnection) object invokes the connection:didFailWithError: method on your delegate object.

A common Objective-C programming convention for methods that return an error object is to make this the last parameter of the method and to specify the type of this parameter as a pointer to an error object pointer (also known as *double-indirection*). The following example declares a method named getGreeting that has an error object of type NSError as its parameter.

```
- (NSString *)getGreeting(NSError **error);
```

This approach enables the called method to modify the pointer the error object points to, and if an error occurs, return an error object specific to the method call.

A return value for the method is required. It is either an object pointer or a Boolean value. Your code invokes such a method by including a reference to an error object as its last parameter, or providing NULL as the last parameter if you don't need to access the error. After the method is invoked, the result is inspected. If the value is NO or nil, then the error object should be processed; else no error object was returned. Many Foundation classes have methods that return an error object by indirection. In addition, your classes can use this convention to implement methods that return an error object.

Listing 14-2 depicts a class named FileWriter, which declares a method that (indirectly) returns an error object.

Listing 14-2. FileWriter Interface with Method That Returns an NSError Object

```
@interface FileWriter : NSObject
+ (BOOL) writeData:(NSData *)data toFile:(NSString *)path error:(NSError **)err;
@end
```

For your code to call this method on a FileWriter object, it must first declare an NSError object, as shown in Listing 14-3, and then check the return value to see if an error occurred.

Listing 14-3. Invoking FileWriter Method That Returns an NSError Object

```
NSError *writeErr;
NSData *greeting = [@"Hello, World" dataUsingEncoding:NSUTF8StringEncoding];
BOOL success = [FileWriter writeData:greeting
                             toFile:NSTemporaryDirectory()
                              error:&writeErr];
if (!success)
{
  // Process error
  ...
}
```

Now you'll create a couple of example programs that perform error handling for error objects passed by delegation methods and error objects obtained via indirection.

Handling Delegation Method Errors

Now you'll implement a program that performs error handling for a delegate method. In Chapter 11, you implemented a program, NetConnector, which demonstrates URL loading using the Foundation Framework NSURLConnection class. Here you'll update this program to handle errors when loading a URL.

In Xcode, open the NetConnector project by selecting **Open ➤ NetConnector.xcodeproj** from the Xcode File menu. The source code for the project consists of three files that implement the NetConnector class and the main function. Let's start by making some updates to the NetConnector class. Select the **NetConnector.m** file in the navigator pane, and then update the NetConnector implementation (updates in **bold**), as shown in Listing 14-4.

Listing 14-4. NetConnector Class Implementation, Updated to Handle Errors

```
#import "NetConnector.h"

@interface NetConnector()

@property NSURLRequest *request;
@property BOOL isFinished;
@property NSURLConnection *connector;
@property NSMutableData *receivedData;

@end

@implementation NetConnector

- (id) initWithRequest:(NSURLRequest *)request
{
  if ((self = [super init]))
  {
    _request = request;
    _finishedLoading = NO;
```

```objc
    // Create URL cache with appropriate in-memory storage
    NSURLCache *URLCache = [[NSURLCache alloc] init];
    [URLCache setMemoryCapacity:CACHE_MEMORY_SIZE];
    [NSURLCache setSharedURLCache:URLCache];

    // Create connection and begin downloading data from resource
    _connector = [NSURLConnection connectionWithRequest:request delegate:self];
  }
  return self;
}

- (void) reloadRequest
{
  self.finishedLoading = NO;
  self.connector = [NSURLConnection connectionWithRequest:self.request
                                                 delegate:self];

}

#pragma mark -
#pragma mark Delegate methods

- (void)connection:(NSURLConnection *)connection didFailWithError:(NSError *)error
{
  NSString *description = [error localizedDescription];
  NSString *domain = [error domain];
  NSInteger code = [error code];
  NSDictionary *info = [error userInfo];
  NSURL *failedUrl = (NSURL *)[info objectForKey:NSURLErrorFailingURLErrorKey];
  NSLog(@"\n*** ERROR ***\nDescription-> %@\nURL-> %@\nDomain-> %@\nCode-> %li",
        description, failedUrl, domain, code);
  self.finishedLoading = YES;
}

- (void)connection:(NSURLConnection *)connection
didReceiveResponse:(NSURLResponse *)response
{
  if (self.receivedData != nil)
  {
    [self.receivedData setLength:0];
  }
}

- (NSCachedURLResponse *)connection:(NSURLConnection *)connection
                  willCacheResponse:(NSCachedURLResponse *)cachedResponse
{
  NSURLResponse *response = [cachedResponse response];
  NSURL *url = [response URL];
  if ([[url scheme] isEqualTo:HTTP_SCHEME])
  {
    NSLog(@"Downloaded data, caching response");
    return cachedResponse;
  }
```

```
  else
  {
    NSLog(@"Downloaded data, not caching response");
    return nil;
  }
}

- (void)connection:(NSURLConnection*)connection didReceiveData:(NSData*)data
{
  if (self.receivedData != nil)
  {
    [self.receivedData appendData:data];
  }
  else
  {
    self.receivedData = [[NSMutableData alloc] initWithData:data];
  }
}

- (void)connectionDidFinishLoading:(NSURLConnection *)connection
{
  NSUInteger length = [self.receivedData length];
  NSLog(@"Downloaded %lu bytes from request %@", length, self.request);

  // Loaded data, set flag to exit run loop
  self.finishedLoading = YES;
}

@end
```

An NSURLConnection sends the connection:didFailWithError: message to its delegate object if the connection doesn't load its request successfully. As shown in Listing 14-4, the NetConnector class is set as the delegate for its NSURLConnection object, and hence its connection:didFailWithError: method will be invoked on request load errors. The method implementation retrieves the properties of the NSError object: description, domain, code, and user info. The URL of the failed load request is stored in the user info dictionary. Its key is NSURLErrorFailingURLErrorKey, one of the NSError standard user info dictionary keys listed in Table 14-1. The method logs the values of this data to the output pane.

Next, you will update the main() function, but before you do that, you need to create a page with a valid URL that cannot be loaded. Doing this forces an error to occur when you attempt to load the page using an NSURLConnection object. Open an OS X terminal window and enter the Unix commands shown in Listing 14-5.

Listing 14-5. Using the Mac OS X Terminal Utility to Create a File

```
touch /tmp/ProtectedPage.html
chmod u-r /tmp/ProtectedPage.html
```

The touch command creates a new, empty file. As shown in Listing 14-6, the full path for the file is /tmp/ProtectedPage.html. The chmod u-r command removes read access to the file for the current user. The corresponding URL for this resource is file:///tmp/ProtectedPage.html. OK, now that this resource is configured properly, let's update the main() function. Select the **main.m** file in the navigator pane, and then update the main() function, as shown in Listing 14-6.

Listing 14-6. NetConnector main() Function Implementation

```
#import <Foundation/Foundation.h>
#import "NetConnector.h"

#define INDEX_URL        @"file:///tmp/ProtectedPage.html"

int main(int argc, const char * argv[])
{
  @autoreleasepool
  {
    // Retrieve the current run loop for the connection
    NSRunLoop *loop = [NSRunLoop currentRunLoop];

    // Create the request with specified cache policy, then begin downloading!
    NSURLRequest *request = [NSURLRequest
                        requestWithURL:[NSURL URLWithString:INDEX_URL]
                            cachePolicy:NSURLRequestReturnCacheDataElseLoad
                        timeoutInterval:5];
    NetConnector *netConnect = [[NetConnector alloc] initWithRequest:request];

    // Loop until finished loading the resource
    while (!netConnect.finishedLoading &&
            [loop runMode:NSDefaultRunLoopMode beforeDate:[NSDate distantFuture]]);

    // Zero out cache
    [[NSURLCache sharedURLCache] removeAllCachedResponses];
  }
  return 0;
}
```

The key change in the main() function is the URL. It is updated to the URL for the resource that you created earlier, file:///tmp/ProtectedPage.html. The code will attempt to asynchronously load this resource (with an NSURLConnection object) using the NetConnector initWithRequest: method. As shown in Listing 14-4, the NetConnector class implements the connection:didFailWithError: method to handle errors loading a URL.

Now save, compile, and run the updated NetConnector program and observe the messages in the output pane (as shown in Figure 14-1).

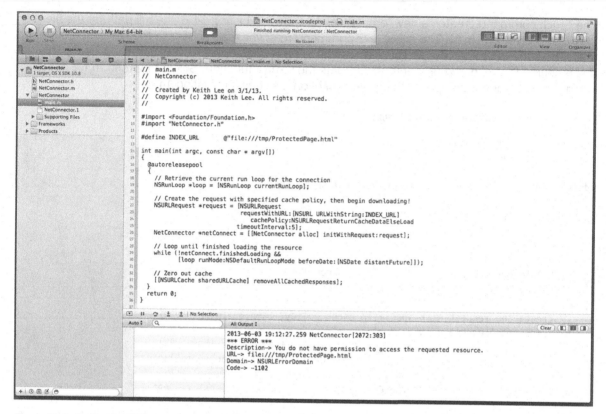

Figure 14-1. *Testing the NSError portion of the updated NetConnector project*

The messages in the output pane show that the NSURLConnection failed to load the URL, and hence sent the connection:didFailWithError: message to its delegate object—in this case, the NetConnector instance. As shown in the method implementation of Listing 14-4, the error description, failed URL, error code, and domain are logged to the output pane. OK, great. Now that you've got that under your belt, let's implement a program that returns an error object via indirection.

Creating Errors Objects via Indirection

Now you will create a program that demonstrates error handling for a Foundation Framework object. In Xcode, create a new project by selecting **New Project ...** from the Xcode File menu. In the **New Project Assistant** pane, create a command-line application. In the **Project Options** window, specify **FMErrorObject** for the Product Name, choose **Foundation** for the Project Type, and select ARC memory management by selecting the **Use Automatic Reference Counting** check box. Specify the location in your file system where you want the project to be created (if necessary select **New Folder** and enter the name and location for the folder), uncheck the **Source Control** check box, and then click the **Create** button.

In the Xcode project navigator, select the **main.m** file and update the main() function, as shown in Listing 14-7.

Listing 14-7. FMErrorObject main() Function Implementation

```objectivec
#import <Foundation/Foundation.h>

#define FILE_PATH        @"/tmp/NoSuchFile.txt"

int main(int argc, const char * argv[])
{
  @autoreleasepool
  {
    NSFileManager *fileMgr = [NSFileManager defaultManager];
    NSError *fileErr;
    BOOL success = [fileMgr removeItemAtPath:FILE_PATH error:&fileErr];
    if (!success)
    {
      NSString *description = [fileErr localizedDescription];
      NSString *domain = [fileErr domain];
      NSInteger code = [fileErr code];
      NSDictionary *info = [fileErr userInfo];
      NSURL *failedPath = (NSURL *)[info objectForKey:NSFilePathErrorKey];
      NSLog(@"\n*** ERROR ***\nDescription-> %@\nPath-> %@\nDomain-> %@\nCode-> %li",
            description, failedPath, domain, code);
    }
  }
  return 0;
}
```

Logically, the code uses an NSFileManager instance method to remove a file from the file system. If an error occurs when invoking the method, it returns an error object via indirection that describes the error, along with an appropriate return result. As shown in Listing 14-7, the file begins by defining a variable, FILE_PATH, which represents the full path of a file on the local file system (in order to test error object creation and processing make sure that this file, /tmp/NoSuchFile.txt, doesn't exist). The main() function begins by creating a FileManager object and an NSError pointer. It then attempts to delete the file by invoking the NSFileManager removeItemAtPath:error: method. As the error parameter is not NULL, an NSError object will be returned if an error occurs when invoking this method.

Next, a conditional expression is performed using the Boolean result of this method; if the returned value is NO, then an error occurred trying to remove the file and the body of the conditional expression is executed. This code retrieves the properties of the NSError object: description, domain, code, and user info. The full path of the file that couldn't be removed is stored in the user info dictionary. Its key is NSFilePathErrorKey, one of the NSError standard user info dictionary keys listed in Table 14-1. The method logs the values of this data to the output pane.

Now save, compile, and run the FMErrorObject program and observe the messages in the output pane (as shown in Figure 14-2).

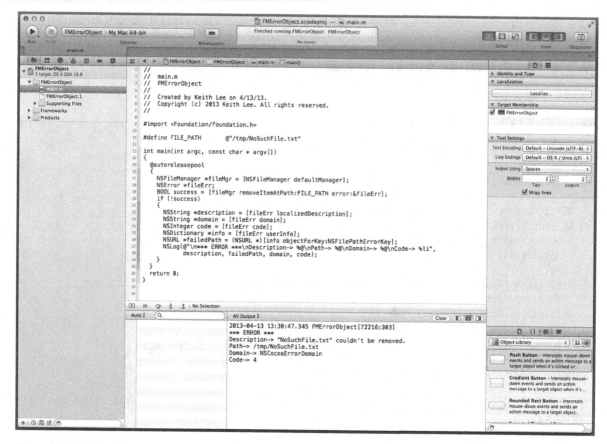

Figure 14-2. Testing NSError by indirection in the FMErrorObject project

The messages in the output pane show that the NSFileManager object failed to remove the file, and hence set an error object (via indirection) in the error parameter of the removeFileWithPath:error: method, and set its return result to NO. The error description, file path, error code, and domain are logged to the output pane. Perfect. Now that you understand how to retrieve and process error objects, let's examine the Foundation Framework support for error recovery.

Error Recovery

The NSError class provides a mechanism for recovering from errors. The NSErrorRecoveryAttempting informal protocol provides methods that are implemented to perform error recovery. An object that adopts this protocol must implement at least one of its two methods for attempting recovery from errors. The user info dictionary of an NSError object that supports error recovery must contain, at a minimum, the following three entries:

- The recovery attempter object (retrieved using the key NSRecoveryAttempterErrorKey)

- The recovery options (retrieved using the key NSLocalizedRecoveryOptionsErrorKey)

- A localized recovery suggestion string (retrieved using the key NSLocalizedRecoverySuggestionErrorKey)

The recovery attempter may implement any logic appropriate for error recovery. Note that the error recovery functionality is only available on the Apple OS X platform.

Error Responders

The Application Kit provides APIs and mechanisms that can be used to respond to errors encapsulated in NSError objects. The NSResponder class defines an error responder chain used to pass events and action messages up the view hierarchy. It includes methods to display information in the associated NSError object, and then forwards the error message to the next responder. This enables each object in the hierarchy to handle the error appropriately, perhaps by adding additional information pertaining to the error. Note that the error responder functionality is available only on the Apple OS X platform.

NSError Codes

The Foundation Framework defines a number of standard NSError codes as Foundation constants. These errors are enumerations defined for the following NSError class error domains, as follows:

- Cocoa (NSErrorCocoaDomain)
- URL Loading System (NSURLDomain)

Exception Processing

Objective-C provides mechanisms for handling exception conditions during program execution. An exception condition can be defined as an unrecoverable programming or runtime error. Examples include errors such as an unimplemented (abstract) method, or runtime errors such as an out-of-bounds collection access. The compiler directives @try, @catch(), @throw, and @finally provide runtime support for exception handling, and the NSException class encapsulates information pertinent to an exception.

When an exception is raised, program control flow transfers to the local exception handler. The program stack frame is also unwound between where the exception was raised and where it was caught and handled. As a result, resources that are not automatically managed (e.g., Foundation Framework objects, objects created using manual reference counting, and any C language–specific resources, such as structures) may not be cleaned up properly. Specifically, the Foundation Framework APIs are not exception-safe; thus if used within an exception-handling domain and an exception is thrown, they may leak memory and/or have corrupted content. Thus, the general rule is that when an exception is raised, no attempt at recovery should be made and the application should be exited promptly.

The @try, @catch, and @finally directives make up a control structure for code that executes within the boundaries of the exception handling logic. The @try directive defines a statement block (also referred to as an exception-handling domain) that can potentially throw an exception. The @catch() directive defines a statement block containing code for handling an exception thrown within the preceding @try block. The parameter of the @catch() directive is the exception object thrown locally, usually an NSException object. A @finally directive defines a statement block (after the preceding @try block) that is subsequently executed whether or not the associated exception is thrown. The @finally block is commonly used to perform any cleanup actions for its corresponding @try and @catch() blocks (e.g., releasing resources, etc.). The syntax for code that uses the exception compiler directives is depicted in Listing 14-8.

Listing 14-8. Exception Handling Using Compiler Directives

```
@try
{
  // Code implementing solution logic (may throw exceptions)
  ...
}
@catch (NSException *exception)
{
  // Exception handling code
  ...
}
@finally
{
  // Cleanup code
  ...
}
```

The @throw directive is used to throw an exception, usually an NSException object but may, in fact, be other types of objects. When an exception is thrown within the body of a @try block, the program jumps immediately to the nearest @catch() block to handle the exception (if one exists).

The Cocoa frameworks come with a large set of predefined exception names that describe specific error states. These should be used (where applicable) when creating an exception.

NSException

The NSException class supports exception management. Its methods provide functionality for creating NSException instances, querying an instance, raising exceptions, and retrieving exception stack frames. The following statement uses the exceptionWithName:reason:userInfo: factory method to create an NSException object.

```
NSException *exception = [NSException exceptionWithName:NSGenericException
                                   reason:@"Test exception"
                                   userInfo:nil];
```

The parameters for this method are the name of the exception (exceptionWithName:), the reason for the exception (reason:), and a dictionary (userInfo:) containing user-defined information relating to the exception. In the preceding example, the exception name is NSGenericException, one of the Foundation Constants general exception names. Listing 14-9 creates and raises an exception using the raise:format: class method. This exception is caught and handled within the body of the corresponding @catch() block.

Listing 14-9. Creating and Raising an NSException Instance

```
@try
{
  [NSException raise:NSGenericException format:@"My Generic Exception"];
}
@catch (NSException *exception)
{
  NSLog(@"EXCEPTION\nName-> %@\nDescription-> %@", [exception name],
        [exception description]);
}
```

Listing 14-9 shows the argument to the @catch() directive is an NSException object, the exception raised in the corresponding exception-handling domain. Exceptions can also be nested, thereby enabling an exception to be processed by the local exception handler domain and any surrounding handlers. Listing 14-10 modifies the example shown in Listing 14-9 to demonstrate the use of nested exception handlers.

Listing 14-10. Nested Exception Handlers

```
@try
{
  @try
  {
    [NSException raise:NSGenericException format:@"My Generic Exception"];
  }
  @catch (NSException *exception)
  {
    NSLog(@"EXCEPTION handling in domain 2\nName-> %@\nDescription-> %@",
          [exception name], [exception description]);
    @throw;
  }
  @finally
  {
    NSLog(@"Cleanup for exception domain 2");
  }
}
@catch (NSException *exception)
{
  NSLog(@"EXCEPTION handling in domain 1\nName-> %@\nDescription-> %@",
        [exception name], [exception description]);
}
@finally
{
  NSLog(@"Cleanup for exception domain 1");
}
```

If an exception is not caught by your code, it is caught by the uncaught exception handler function. The default implementation of this function logs a message to the output pane, and then exits the program. The Foundation function NSSetUncaughtExceptionHandler() can be used to set a custom uncaught exception handler.

Exceptions and Memory Management

Memory management must be carefully considered when handling exceptions, particularly when using Manual Retain Release (MRR) memory management. As exception processing changes program flow control, Listing 14-11 demonstrates how an exception in a method (when using MRR memory management) may cause an object to leak memory.

Listing 14-11. Exception Handling and Memory Leaks

```
- (void) processOrderWithItem:(OrderItem *)item
{
  Order *order = [[Order alloc] initWithItem:item];
  [order process];
  [order release];
}
```

If the process method throws an exception, the Order object will not be released, and hence it leaks memory. To prevent this, the solution is to enclose the method statements within an exception-handling domain and to release the allocated object within its @finally block, as shown in Listing 14-12.

Listing 14-12. Preventing Memory Leaks with an Exception Handling Domain

```
- (void) processOrderWithItem:(OrderItem *)item
{
  Order *order = nil;
  @try
  {
    order = [[Order alloc] initWithItem:item];
    [order process];
    [order release];
  }
  @finally
  {
    [order release];
  }
}
```

By default, ARC memory management is not exception-safe. A program using ARC can be made exception-safe if it is compiled with the -fobjc-arc-exceptions option. This will increase program resource utilization and also slightly decrease performance, and hence its use must be carefully considered.

Performing Exception Handling

Now you will create a program that demonstrates exception handling for a Foundation Framework object. In Xcode, create a new project by selecting **New Project ...** from the Xcode File menu. In the **New Project Assistant** pane, create a command-line application. In the **Project Options** window, specify **XProcessor** for the Product Name, choose **Foundation** for the Project Type, and select ARC memory management by selecting the **Use Automatic Reference Counting** check box. Specify the location in your file system where you want the project to be created (if necessary select **New Folder** and enter the name and location for the folder), uncheck the **Source Control** check box, and then click the **Create** button.

In the Xcode project navigator, select the **main.m** file and update the main() function, as shown in Listing 14-13.

Listing 14-13. XProcessor main() Function Implementation

```
#import <Foundation/Foundation.h>

int main(int argc, const char * argv[])
{
  @autoreleasepool
  {
    NSArray *words = @[@"Hello", @"Bonjour", @"Guten Tag", @"Hola"];
    @try
    {
      int count = 0;
      NSLog(@"Salutation = %@", words[count]);
    }
    @catch (NSException *exception)
    {
      NSLog(@"EXCEPTION\nName-> %@\nDescription-> %@", [exception name],
            [exception description]);
    }
  }
  return 0;
}
```

The main() function first creates an NSArray object with four entries. Then an entry from the array is retrieved and logged to the output pane. Because the NSArray method for retrieving an object at a specified index will throw an NSRangeException (one of the Foundation standard exception names) if the index is beyond the end of the array, this statement is placed within an exception-handling domain. If an exception is thrown, it is logged to the output pane.

Now save, compile, and run the XProcessor program and observe that the expected message (Hello) is displayed in the output pane (as shown in Figure 14-3).

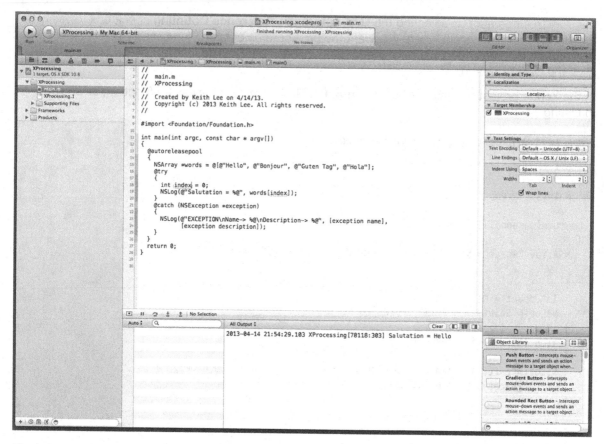

Figure 14-3. Testing the XProcessor project, no exception raised

No exception was thrown because the value set for the index was within range. Now change the value for the count variable to four.

```
int index = 0;
```

Then recompile and run the program. Observe that because the index exceeded the range, an exception was thrown and handled within the @catch() block (as shown in Figure 14-4).

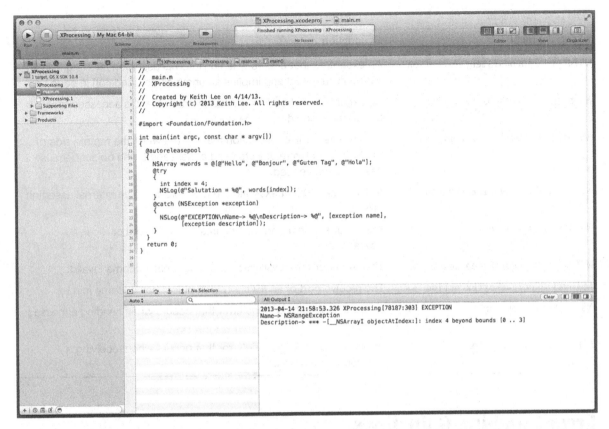

Figure 14-4. Testing the XProcessor project, exception raised

This example demonstrates exception handling for Foundation Framework APIs. Let's continue on with the Foundation constants that define a set of standard exception names.

Foundation Standard Exception Names

The Foundation Framework defines a set of standard exception names. These general exception names are listed and described in Table 14-2.

Table 14-2. Foundation Constants General Exception Names

Exception Name	Description
NSGenericException	A generic name for an exception.
NSRangeException	An exception that occurs when attempting access outside the bounds of some data, such as an array or a string.
NSInvalidArgumentException	An exception that occurs when you pass an invalid argument to a method.

(continued)

Table 14-2. (continued)

Exception Name	Description
NSInternalInconsistencyException	An exception that occurs when an internal assertion fails (e.g., via an NSAssert function) and implies an unexpected condition in code.
NSObjectInaccessibleException	An exception that occurs when a remote object is accessed from a thread that should not access it.
NSObjectNotAvailableException	A distributed object exception that occurs when the remote side of the NSConnection refuses to send a message to the object because it has not been vended.
NSDestinationInvalidException	A distributed object exception that occurs when an internal assertion fails.
NSPortTimeoutException	A timeout set on a port that expires during a send or receive operation.
NSInvalidSendPortException	The send port of an NSConnection object has become invalid.
NSInvalidRecievePortException	The receive port of an NSConnection object has become invalid.
NSPortSendException	An NSPort-specific generic error that occurs when sending a message to a port.
NSPortReceiveException	An NSPort-specific generic error that occurs when receiving a message from a port.

Error Handling Guidelines

You now have a good understanding of error objects and exceptions, along with the corresponding Foundation Framework APIs. So now you may be wondering, "Which do I use for detecting and handling errors?" Before I provide guidelines and recommendations, let's begin by reviewing some of the key points regarding error objects and exceptions.

Error Objects

- Pros:
  - Encapsulates error info (code, domain, user info)
  - Provides infrastructure for recovery
  - Supported by the Cocoa frameworks
- Cons:
  - Couples error-handling logic with business logic
  - Labor intensive, difficult to understand
  - Difficult to maintain and/or modify

Exceptions

- Pros:

    - Decouples detection and handling of exception conditions, thereby improving program design and maintenance.

    - Automates propagation from the point of detection to handling.

- Cons:

    - Unwinds stack, resulting in a performance hit.

    - Uses more resources (slightly increases the size of the executable).

    - Still requires parameter/result checks.

    - Cocoa frameworks (including the Foundation Framework) are not exception-safe.

Guidelines and Recommendations

Error objects should be used to detect and handle expected errors within an Objective-C program that can (potentially) be recovered from. Assertions should be used as a programming aid to check program invariants, conditions, assumptions, and so forth. Note that because assertions may be disabled prior to compilation (as is often the case for production releases), they should not be used for parameter checking of public APIs. Exceptions should only be used to detect programming or unexpected runtime errors that cannot be recovered from, and which should be handled by immediately terminating the application.

Roundup

In this chapter, you examined the Foundation Framework APIs for error handling and exception processing. You should now be familiar with Foundation Framework classes that provide the following functionality:

- Error handling using error objects

- Exception processing

- Guidelines for using assertions, error objects, and exceptions

Now that you have concluded this review of the Foundation Framework APIs, it's time to move on to Part 4 of this book, which focuses on new and advanced topics in Objective-C. Before you do that, however, perhaps now's a good time to review what you've covered so far and then give yourself a well-deserved break. When you're ready, turn the page and dive in!

Chapter 15

Blocks

Welcome back. Congratulations on making it to this point! So far, you have covered all the fundamental elements of the Objective-C platform. But guess what? You haven't reached the finish line just yet! That's because Objective-C has a variety of additional, advanced features that, once mastered, will enable you to take your programming to the next level. In Part 4 of this book, you will explore several of these features and learn how to use them in your programs.

In this chapter, you will learn how to program with *blocks*, a powerful feature available for the Objective-C language. The chapter explores block syntax and semantics, memory management, how to develop blocks in your own code, and how to use blocks in existing APIs (such as the Foundation Framework).

Simply put, blocks provide a way to create a group of statements (i.e., a block of code) and assign those statements to a variable, which can subsequently be invoked. In this way, they are similar to functions and methods, but in addition to executable code, they may also contain variable bindings to stack or heap memory. A block is an implementation of a *closure,* a function that allows access to variables outside its typical scope. In addition, an Objective-C block is actually an object; it is a subclass of NSObject and has all of its associated properties (you can send messages to it, etc.). Apple developed blocks as an extension to the C family of programming languages (C, Objective-C, and C++). They are available for use with Mac OS X v10.6 and later, as well as iOS 4.0 and later.

Block Syntax

One of the most difficult things about learning how to program with blocks is mastering their syntax. This section explains block syntax in depth and provides numerous examples to illustrate their application in code.

The syntactic features added to support blocks enable the declaration of variables of block type and the definition of block literals.

The *block type* consists of a return value type and a list of parameter types. A caret symbol (^) operator is used to declare a variable of block type. Figure 15-1 illustrates the syntax for a block type declaration.

Return Type	Block Name	Parameter Type(s)
returnType	(^blockName)	(parameterType, parameterType, …)

Figure 15-1. Block type declaration syntax

Figure 15-1 shows that the returnType is the type of the value returned by the block when it is invoked. The block variable named blockName is preceded by a caret and enclosed in parentheses. As mentioned previously, a variable of block type may have parameters. The list of parameter types is enclosed in parentheses and follows the block name, where the parameterTypes are each separated by a comma. If a block variable declaration has no parameters, its list of parameter types should be specified as void (enclosed in parentheses). OK, that summarizes the syntax for declaring variables of block type. Now let's look at some examples. The following statement declares a block variable named oneParamBlock that has a single parameter of type int and returns a value of type int.

```
int (^oneParamBlock)(int);
```

As stated, a block variable with no return value has its return type specified as void in its declaration. The next example declares a block variable named twoParamsBlock that takes two parameters of type int and returns nothing.

```
void (^twoParamsBlock)(int, int);
```

A block declaration can also include parameter names, similar to an Objective-C method declaration. The following shows the previous example with named input parameters.

```
void (^twoParamsBlock)(int parm1, int parm2);
```

The next example declares a block variable named noParamsBlock with no parameters and that returns a value of type int.

```
int (^noParamsBlock)(void);
```

Because variables can be declared with block type, a block variable can serve as a function argument or method parameter. In these cases, it is common to create a type definition (via a typedef statement) to provide an alternate name for a block type, thereby simplifying its subsequent usage in your code. Listing 15-1 demonstrates the declaration of a method that takes a block as a method parameter.

Listing 15-1. Block Variable in a Method Declaration

```
typedef int (^AdderBlock)(int);
@interface Calculator : NSObject
- (int)process:(int)count withBlock:(AdderBlock)adder;
@end
```

Listing 15-1 shows that a `typedef` statement is used to create a block type named `AdderBlock`. This type is subsequently used as the parameter type in a method declaration.

A block literal expression defines a reference to a block. It begins with the caret operator, followed by a return type, the list of parameters, and then a collection of statements (the block statement body) enclosed in braces. The syntax for a block literal expression is shown in Figure 15-2.

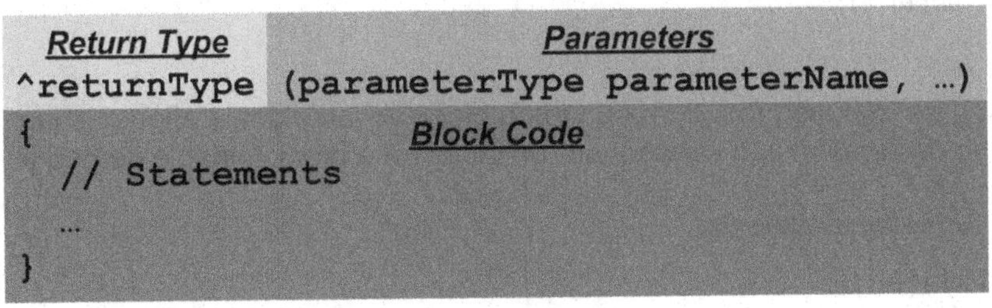

Figure 15-2. Block literal expression syntax

As you see in Figure 15-2, the caret symbol at the beginning of the expression indicates the beginning of a block literal expression, with the optional `returnType` specifying the type of the return value of the statement body. The block parameters (passed into the body of the block) are enclosed in parentheses with a type and a name for each, separated by commas. The block code (enclosed within braces) comprises the *statements* executed when the block is invoked. If the block definition specifies a return type, the code includes a `return` statement with a value of the specified `returnType`. If there are multiple return statements in a block literal expression, the return type specified must be identical for each. Now let's examine a few simple block literal expressions. Listing 15-2 takes a single parameter of type `int` and returns a value that equals its input parameter incremented by 1.

Listing 15-2. Block Literal Expression

```
^int (int addend)
{
  return addend + 1;
}
```

As mentioned previously, it is not required to specify the return type for a block definition, because the compiler will infer it from the return statement within the body of the block. Listing 15-3 modifies Listing 15-2 by not specifying the return type in the expression.

Listing 15-3. Block Literal Expression, No Return Type

```
^(int addend)
{
  return addend + 1;
}
```

If a block literal expression has no parameters, then the parenthesized parameter list is not required. Listing 15-4 provides an example of a block literal with no parameters and no return value, and that logs a greeting to the console.

Listing 15-4. Block Literal Definition, No Parameters

```
^{
  NSLog(@"Hello, World!");
}
```

A block literal can be assigned to a corresponding block variable declaration. Listing 15-5 demonstrates the declaration and subsequent definition of a block variable named oneParamBlock.

Listing 15-5. Block Declaration and Definition

```
int (^oneParamBlock)(int);
oneParamBlock = ^(int param1)
{
  return param1 * param1;
};
```

As you would expect, the block declaration and definition can be combined into one statement. Listing 15-6 demonstrates the compound declaration and definition of a block variable named incBlock.

Listing 15-6. Compound Block Declaration and Definition

```
int (^incBlock) (int) = ^(int addend)
{
  return addend + 1;
};
```

As shown in Listing 15-6, the block literal expression parameter type(s) and return type must conform to the corresponding block variable declaration.

Comparing Figures 15-1 and 15-2, you will note that there are several differences between the syntax of a block variable declaration and a block literal expression. For example, a block variable parameter types list is not optional; if there are no parameters, then a single void parameter type must be provided. Contrast that with a block literal expression for which the parameter list is optional—if there are no parameters, then the list may be omitted. Table 15-1 summarizes key differences in the syntax of block variable declarations and block literal expressions.

Table 15-1. *Comparison of Block Syntactic Elements*

Block Syntactic Element	Block Variable Declaration	Block Literal Expression
Caret operator	Begins a block variable declaration. The caret precedes the variable name, both of which are enclosed in parenthesis.	Begins a block literal expression.
Name	The block variable name is required.	Block literal expressions are nameless.
Return type	The return type is required in a block variable declaration. A block variable with no return value has a declared return type of void.	The return type is optional in a block literal expression because the compiler will infer it from the type of the return value in the expression statement body. If the expression statement body has more than one return statement, they all must be of the same type.
Parameters	The parameter type list is mandatory in a block variable declaration. If the block variable has no parameters, then the declared parameter type list is void.	A parameter list is not required in a block literal expression that has no parameters.

Once a variable of block type has been declared and assigned to a conforming block literal expression, it can be invoked directly with the invoke operator. This syntax is similar to a C function call syntax, with a list of parameters corresponding to the block declaration. (The type of the return value, if any, also corresponds to the block type declaration.) The following statement invokes the block in Listing 15-6 and assigns the result to the variable myValue.

```
int myValue = incBlock(5);
```

A block expression can also be defined and invoked in a single statement. Recall that a block expression is anonymous; hence, the invoke operator takes an anonymous (i.e., nameless) function followed by a parameter list that corresponds to the block expression. Listing 15-7 defines a block expression and invokes it in a single statement that logs the message "Greetings, Earthling!" to the console.

Listing 15-7. Block Expression Definition and Invocation

```
^(NSString *user)
{
  NSLog(@"Greetings, %@!", user);
}(@"Earthling");
```

A block expression can also be defined inline as an *anonymous function*, thereby serving as a parameter of a function or method invocation. The recommended practice in these scenarios is to use only one block literal as a parameter to a function or method, and that it be the last parameter in the list (if the function/method has other parameters). Listing 15-8 invokes an instance method (from the class interface shown in Listing 15-1) that creates a block literal expression and uses it as a parameter to a method invocation.

Listing 15-8. Block Literal Expression in a Method Invocation

```
Calculator calc = [Calculator new];
int value = [calc process:2
            withBlock:^(int addend)
            {
              return addend + 1;
            }];
```

Many Objective-C APIs, including the Foundation Framework, contain methods that take a block as a parameter. Later in this chapter, you will develop several programs with blocks, so take your time and review this material as long as necessary until you thoroughly grasp the syntax.

Blocks Are Closures!

As stated earlier in this chapter, a block is an implementation of a *closure,* a function that allows access to local variables declared outside of its typical scope. To understand what this means, let's take a moment to understand scope and visibility rules. The *visibility* of a variable refers to the portion(s) of a program in which it can be accessed; this is also referred to as a variable's *scope*. For example, variables declared within a C function definition have local scope, meaning that they are visible and accessible within the function, and not accessible elsewhere. (Note that a function can also reference global variables.) A block augments the visibility of variables compared to C functions through several features, as follows:

- Support for *lexical scope*. This is the ability to reference local variables and parameters from an enclosing scope.

- __block variables. The __block keyword, applied to a variable outside a block but within the same lexical scope, enables this variable to be modified within a block.

- Instance variable access. A block defined within an object's method implementation can access the object's instance variables.

- const imports. Constant variables imported through a header file (via an #import or #include directive) are visible within a block literal expression.

Lexical Scope

One of the unique features of blocks is its support for lexical scoping. In contrast, C functions do not have access to local variables declared outside of their definition. The example shown in Listing 15-9 will not compile because the local variable myVar is not visible within the logValue function definition.

Listing 15-9. C Function Attempting to Access a Local Variable Outside Its Scope

```
void logValue()
{
  // ERROR, illegal access of myVar, not within scope
  NSLog(@"Variable value = %d", myVar);
}
```

```
int main(int argc, const char * argv[])
{
  @autoreleasepool
  {
    int myVar = 10;
    logValue();
  }
  return 0;
}
```

A block supports lexical scoping, thus a block literal expression has access to variables declared within the same lexical scope. In addition, blocks can be defined anywhere other variables can; for example, within other blocks, functions, and methods. C functions, on the other hand, cannot be defined within other functions or methods. Listing 15-10 compiles and runs successfully because the variable myVar is declared within the same lexical scope as the block logValueBlock.

Listing 15-10. Block Accessing Local Variable Through Lexical Scoping

```
{
  int myVar = 10;
  void (^logValueBlock)(void) = ^{
    NSLog(@"Variable value = %d", myVar);
  };
  logValueBlock();
}
```

Listing 15-10 shows that a block has access to local variables declared outside its definition. Specifically, these local variables are declared (and initialized) within an enclosing scope, *prior to* the block literal expression. Braces delimit a local scope; in addition scopes may be nested. Referring again to Listing 15-10, the variable myVar is declared at the same scope as the block definition assigned to logValueBlock, prior to the literal expression, and thus can be used within the expression. On the other hand, Listing 15-11 will not compile, because the local variable myVar is declared and initialized after the block literal expression.

Listing 15-11. Illegal Access of Local Variable in Block, Declared After Block Literal Expression

```
void (^logValueBlock)(void) = ^{
  // ERROR, illegal access of myVar, declared after literal expression
  NSLog(@"Variable value = %d", myVar);
};
int myVar = 10;
logValueBlock();
```

Local variables accessed through lexical scoping behave as constant values (for primitive types) or by reference variables (for objects) within a block literal expression. Listing 15-12 will not compile because a primitive variable accessed through lexical scoping cannot be modified within a block literal.

Listing 15-12. Block Attempting to Modify a Local Variable Accessed Through Lexical Scoping

```
int myVar = 10;
void (^logValueBlock)(void) = ^{
  // ERROR, lexical scope variable not assignable
  myVar = 5;
  NSLog(@"Variable value = %d", myVar);
};
logValueBlock();
```

As local scopes can be nested, a block can capture local variables within multiple (nested) scopes. This is demonstrated in the code from Listing 15-13.

Listing 15-13. Block Capturing Local Variables Within Multiple Nested Scopes

```
for (int ii=0; ii<2; ii++)
{
  for (int jj=0; jj<3; jj++)
  {
    void (^logValueBlock)(void) = ^{
      NSLog(@"Variable values = %d, %d", ii, jj);
    };
    logValueBlock();
  }
}
```

Mutable __block Variables

By default, block local variables accessed through lexical scoping are visible but not writeable within a block literal expression. The __block storage type modifier can be used to make these variables read-write (i.e., mutable). The __block modifier can be used on all supported Objective-C types, except for C variable-length arrays (an array with a length that is not a constant expression) and C structures that contain variable-length arrays. Its use cannot be combined with the existing local storage modifiers auto, register, and static. Listing 15-14 illustrates the use of a __block variable.

Listing 15-14. Correct Use of __block Storage

```
__block int myVar = 10;
void (^incBlock)(int) = ^(int amount){
  myVar += amount;
  NSLog(@"New value = %d", myVar);
};
incBlock(5);
```

Variables qualified with the __block storage type are copied to the heap if the referencing block is copied to heap storage. This last point brings up the topic of memory management with blocks, the subject of the next section.

Memory Management with Blocks

At runtime, a block literal expression is allocated on the stack and thus has the same lifetime as a local variable. As a result, it must be copied to permanent storage (i.e., onto the heap) to be used outside of the scope in which it is defined. For example, if you want to return a block literal from a method or save it for later use, then the block must be copied onto the heap and subsequently released when no longer in use. Listing 15-15 illustrates a block literal that's used outside its scope. This may result in a dangling pointer that causes the program to crash.

Listing 15-15. Block Literal Used Outside of Its Lexical Scope

```
void (^greetingBlock)(void);
{ // scope begins, local variables pushed onto stack
  greetingBlock = ^{
    NSLog(@"Hello, World!");
  };
} // scope ends, stack variables (e.g. the block literal) popped off stack
greetingBlock(); // Block invocation may cause the program to crash!
```

Listing 15-15 shows that the block literal expression assigned to the variable greetingBlock has the same lifetime as a local variable; it thus no longer exists outside of its lexical scope. Objective-C includes copy (Block_copy()) and release (Block_release()) operations that provide memory management for block literals.

The Block_copy() operation copies a block literal onto the heap. It is implemented as a function that takes a block literal reference as its parameter and returns a block reference of the same type.

The Block_release() operation releases a block literal from the heap so that its memory is reclaimed. It is implemented as a function that takes a block reference as its parameter. A block reference is released from the heap if it matches a corresponding block reference that was copied to the heap; otherwise, the function call has no effect. In order to avoid a memory leak, a Block_copy() call must be balanced by a corresponding Block_release(). The Foundation Framework defines copy and release methods for blocks that are the functional equivalent of the Block_copy() and Block_release() functions. Listing 15-16 updates the code in Listing 15-15 with the appropriate block copy operations.

Listing 15-16. Using the Block Copy and Release Methods

```
void (^greetingBlock)(void);
{
  greetingBlock = [^{
    NSLog(@"Hello, World!");
  } copy];
}
greetingBlock();            // Block invocation works (uses heap storage)
[greetingBlock release];    // released block to prevent memory leak
```

With ARC memory management, the compiler automatically performs the block copy and release operations as long as the block does not return an id type or pass an id type as a parameter. In either case, the copy and release operations must be performed manually, as with MRR memory management. Listing 15-17 demonstrates the use of these operations for a block that passes an id type as a parameter.

Listing 15-17. Using the Block_copy and Block_release Functions for Blocks with an id Type Parameter

```
void (^greetingBlock)(id salutation);
{
  greetingBlock = Block_copy(^(id salutation){
  NSLog(@"%@, World!", salutation);
  });
}
greetingBlock(@"Hello");
Block_release(greetingBlock);
```

Variables declared with the __block storage type have different semantics, depending on whether or not MRR or ARC memory management is in use. Under MRR, __block variables *are not* retained if used within a block literal; however, under ARC, __block variables *are* retained if used within a block literal. What this means is that if you are using ARC memory management and don't want a __block variable to be retained (for example, to avoid circular references), the __weak storage type should also be applied to the variable.

Using Blocks

Now that you understand the syntax for coding blocks and some of the key concerns with respect to their semantics and memory management, you can begin exploring how to best use blocks in your code. Apple developed blocks for use with Grand Central Dispatch (GCD) to support concurrent programming, and these APIs use blocks to schedule code for execution (GCD is covered in more detail in Chapter 17). However, there are many other ways to use blocks, both within existing APIs and in your own classes. In general, blocks are most naturally used to implement small, self-contained pieces of code that encapsulate units of work. They are typically executed concurrently (for example, via GCD) over the items of a collection or as a callback when an operation has finished. Because blocks can be defined inline, they can eliminate the need to create entirely separate classes and methods for context-sensitive code, such as asynchronous completion handlers. They also enable related code to be kept together, and not scattered among multiple files. As noted before, many Apple APIs (and an increasing number of third-party APIs) now use blocks. The next few sections will demonstrate these common usage scenarios as you implement several programs that use blocks.

Sorting an Array Using Blocks

Now you will create a program that demonstrates array sorting using blocks. In Xcode, create a new project by selecting **New ➤ Project ...** from the Xcode File menu. In the **New Project Assistant** pane, create a command-line application. In the **Project Options** window, specify **BlockArraySorter** for the Product Name, choose **Foundation** for the Project Type, and select ARC memory management by checking the **Use Automatic Reference Counting** check box. Specify the location in your file system where you want the project to be created (if necessary, select **New Folder** and enter the name and location for the folder), uncheck the **Source Control** check box, and then click the **Create** button.

In the Xcode project navigator, select the **main.m** file and update the file, as shown in Listing 15-18.

Listing 15-18. BlockArraySorter main.m File

```objc
#import <Foundation/Foundation.h>
#include <stdlib.h>

#define ArrayElements 10

int main(int argc, const char * argv[])
{
  @autoreleasepool
  {
    // Create an array of numbers with random values (0-99)
    NSMutableArray *numbers = [NSMutableArray arrayWithCapacity:ArrayElements];
    for (int elem=0; elem<ArrayElements; elem++)
    {
      unsigned int value = arc4random() % 100;
      [numbers addObject:[NSNumber numberWithUnsignedInt:value]];
    }
    NSLog(@"Values: %@", numbers);       // Log the numbers unsorted

    // Sort the array of numbers in ascending order
    [numbers sortUsingComparator:^(id obj1, id obj2){
      if ([obj1 integerValue] > [obj2 integerValue])
      {
        return (NSComparisonResult)NSOrderedDescending;
      }
      if ([obj1 integerValue] < [obj2 integerValue])
      {
        return (NSComparisonResult)NSOrderedAscending;
      }
      return (NSComparisonResult)NSOrderedSame;
    }];
    NSLog(@"Values: %@", numbers);       // Log the numbers sorted
  }
  return 0;
}
```

First, the file imports the stdlib.h header file via an #include preprocessor directive. This header file is required for the arc4random() function used later in the code. Next, the file defines a constant value, ArrayElements, which is used to control the number of elements in an array.

The main() function contains the body of the program logic. It first creates an NSMutableArray object and then adds 10 elements to the array; each element is an NSNumber object with a random number. The random number, obtained using the arc4random() function, is constrained to a value between 0–99 (inclusive) with the following statement.

```objc
unsigned int value = arc4random() % 100;
```

The values of the array are then logged to the output pane. Because the numbers were randomly selected and the array has not been sorted, the order of the values displayed in the output pane is random. Next, the array is sorted using the NSMutableArray sortUsingComparator: method. This method sorts the array using the comparison method specified by the block literal input parameter. The full method signature is

```
- (void)sortUsingComparator:(NSComparator)cmptr
```

Thus the block literal expression is of block type NSComparator, a Foundation Framework data type whose type definition is

```
typedef NSComparisonResult (^NSComparator)(id obj1, id obj2);
```

So an NSComparator is a block type that takes two parameters of type id and returns a value of type NSComparisonResult. NSComparisonResult is a Foundation Framework enumeration used to indicate the ordering of items in a request, its values are as follows:

- NSOrderedAscending (the left operand is smaller than the right)

- NSOrderedSame (the left and right operands are equal)

- NSOrderedDescending (the left operand is larger than the right)

The block literal performs a comparison between array element values and returns the appropriate NSComparisonResult to sort the array elements based on ascending (numerical) order, as shown in Listing 15-18.

```
[numbers sortUsingComparator:^(id obj1, id obj2){
  if ([obj1 integerValue] > [obj2 integerValue])
  {
    return (NSComparisonResult)NSOrderedDescending;
  }
  if ([obj1 integerValue] < [obj2 integerValue])
  {
    return (NSComparisonResult)NSOrderedAscending;
  }
  return (NSComparisonResult)NSOrderedSame;
}];
```

Now save, compile, and run the BlockArraySorter program and observe the messages in the output pane (as shown in Figure 15-3).

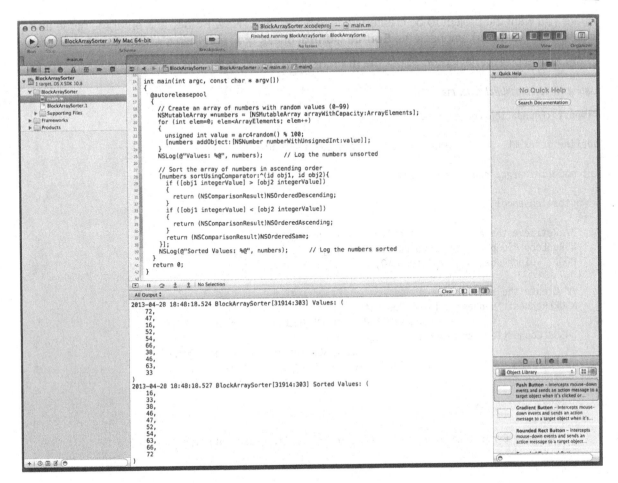

Figure 15-3. Testing the BlockArraySorter project

The messages in the output pane show that the array was correctly sorted using the block literal expression. It first displays the values for the unsorted array elements and then redisplays the array elements, this time sorted based on the numeric value of each element. Many of the Foundation Framework collection classes (NSArray, NSDictionary) contain methods that use a block literal to sort their elements, so this demonstrates a common use of blocks that you will encounter. Perfect. Now that you have one example under your belt, let's develop another program that uses a block to perform an asynchronous callback function.

Loading a URL Using Blocks

Next, you will create a program that uses a block to asynchronously load a URL request, executing the block when the request has finished loading. In Xcode, create a new project by selecting **New ➤ Project ...** from the Xcode File menu. In the **New Project Assistant** pane, create a command-line application. In the **Project Options** window, specify **BlockURLLoader** for the Product Name, choose **Foundation** for the Project Type, and select ARC memory management by checking the **Use Automatic Reference Counting** check box. Specify the location in your file system where you want the project to be created (if necessary, select **New Folder** and enter the name and location for the folder), uncheck the **Source Control** check box, and then click the **Create** button.

In the Xcode project navigator, select the **main.m** file and update the file, as shown in Listing 15-19.

Listing 15-19. BlockURLLoader main.m File

```
#import <Foundation/Foundation.h>

#define IndexURL        @"http://www.wikipedia.com/index.html"

int main(int argc, const char * argv[])
{
  @autoreleasepool
  {
    // Retrieve the current run loop for the connection
    NSRunLoop *loop = [NSRunLoop currentRunLoop];
    BOOL __block downloadComplete = NO;

    // Create the request
    NSURLRequest *request = [NSURLRequest
                               requestWithURL:[NSURL URLWithString:IndexURL]];
    [NSURLConnection sendAsynchronousRequest:request
                                       queue:[NSOperationQueue currentQueue]
                           completionHandler:^(NSURLResponse *response,
                                               NSData *data, NSError *error)
    {
      if (data == nil)
      {
        NSLog(@"Error loading request %@", [error localizedDescription]);
      }
      else
      {
        NSLog(@"\n\tDownloaded %lu bytes from request %@",
              [data length], [request URL]);
      }
      downloadComplete = YES;
    }];

    // Loop until finished downloading the resource
    while ( !downloadComplete &&
           [loop runMode:NSDefaultRunLoopMode beforeDate:[NSDate distantFuture]]);
  }
  return 0;
}
```

After the Foundation Framework import, the file defines a constant value, IndexURL, for the URL to be downloaded.

The main() function contains the body of the program logic. It begins by retrieving the current run loop, required for asynchronous URL loading with NSURLConnection objects. It also declares and initializes a BOOL variable named downloadComplete. This variable is declared with __block storage type, thereby enabling its value to be changed within a block literal of the same scope. Next, an NSURLRequest instance is created (its URL is specified by the #define constant) using the convenience constructor requestWithURL:. Then the code creates an NSURLConnection object to load the request. It uses the sendAsynchronousRequest:queue:completionHandler: method. The completion handler is the handler block literal that is executed. The queue is an NSOperationQueue instance to which the handler block is dispatched when the request completes or fails. It is used to enable the execution of asynchronous operations. The block literal checks the return value of the download request (NSData *). If its value is nil, then an error occurred during the download and this is logged to the console; otherwise, the download was successful and the number of bytes downloaded is logged to the console.

```
if (data == nil)
{
  NSLog(@"Error loading request %@", [error localizedDescription]);
}
else
{
  NSLog(@"\n\tDownloaded %lu bytes from request %@",
        [data length], [request URL]);
}
downloadComplete = YES;
```

The next statement is a loop used to keep the application running until the connection has finished loading the resource.

```
while (!downloadComplete &&
       [loop runMode:NSDefaultRunLoopMode beforeDate:[NSDate distantFuture]]);
```

This statement was used in examples in previous chapters. To summarize, it runs the loop, receiving events from its input sources and executing any corresponding delegate or callback methods until the connection has finished loading the resource.

Now save, compile, and run the BlockURLLoader program and observe the messages in the output pane (as shown in Figure 15-4).

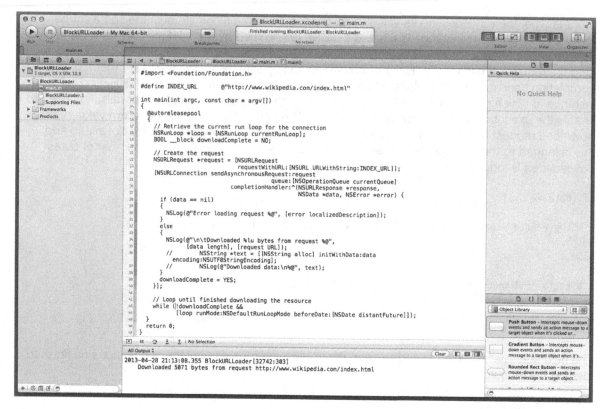

Figure 15-4. *Testing the BlockURLLoader project*

The messages in the output pane show that the URL was successfully downloaded and processed using the block literal expression. It displays the number of bytes downloaded and the URL for the request. Several Foundation Framework classes (e.g., NSURLConnection), Cocoa Framework classes, and various third-party APIs contain methods that use a block literal to perform callback functions, so it is very important to become familiar with this programming model. All right, enough said. Now let's conclude this whirlwind tour with another program that uses a block to perform concurrent programming.

Concurrent Programming Using Blocks

You'll finish this chapter with a program that uses a block to perform concurrent programming. This program employs GCD to concurrently execute several tasks defined with blocks. In Xcode, create a new project by selecting **New ➤ Project ...** from the Xcode File menu. In the **New Project Assistant** pane, create a command-line application. In the **Project Options** window, specify **BlockConcurrentTasks** for the Product Name, choose **Foundation** for the Project Type, and select ARC memory management by checking the **Use Automatic Reference Counting** check box. Specify the location in your file system where you want the project to be created (if necessary, select **New Folder** and enter the name and location for the folder), uncheck the **Source Control** check box, and then click the **Create** button.

In the Xcode project navigator, select the **main.m** file and update it, as shown in Listing 15-20.

Listing 15-20. BlockConcurrentTasks main.m File

```objc
#import <Foundation/Foundation.h>
#define YahooURL        @"http://www.yahoo.com/index.html"
#define ApressURL       @"http://www.apress.com/index.html"

typedef void (^DownloadURL)(void);

/* Retrieve a block used to download a URL */
DownloadURL getDownloadURLBlock(NSString *url)
{
  NSString *urlString = url;
  return ^{
    // Downloads a URL
    NSURLRequest *request = [NSURLRequest
                             requestWithURL:[NSURL URLWithString:urlString]];

    NSError *error;
    NSDate *startTime = [NSDate date];
    NSData *data = [NSURLConnection sendSynchronousRequest:request
                                    returningResponse:nil
                                                error:&error];

    if (data == nil)
    {
      NSLog(@"Error loading request %@", [error localizedDescription]);
    }
    else
    {
      NSDate *endTime = [NSDate date];
      NSTimeInterval timeInterval = [endTime timeIntervalSinceDate:startTime];
      NSLog(@"Time taken to download %@ = %f seconds", urlString, timeInterval);
    }
  };
}

int main(int argc, const char * argv[])
{
  @autoreleasepool
  {
    // Create queues for tasks
    dispatch_queue_t queue1 =
    dispatch_get_global_queue(DISPATCH_QUEUE_PRIORITY_DEFAULT, 0);
    dispatch_queue_t queue2 =
    dispatch_get_global_queue(DISPATCH_QUEUE_PRIORITY_DEFAULT, 0);

    // Create a task group
    dispatch_group_t group = dispatch_group_create();

    // Get current time for metrics
    NSDate *startTime = [NSDate date];
```

```
    // Now create and dispatch async tasks
    dispatch_group_async(group, queue1, getDownloadURLBlock(YahooURL));
    dispatch_group_async(group, queue2, getDownloadURLBlock(ApressURL));

    // Block until all tasks from group are completed
    dispatch_group_wait(group, DISPATCH_TIME_FOREVER);

    // Retrieve time taken for concurrent execution and log
    NSDate *endTime = [NSDate date];
    NSTimeInterval timeInterval = [endTime timeIntervalSinceDate:startTime];
    NSLog(@"Time taken to download URLs concurrently = %f seconds", timeInterval);
  }
  return 0;
}
```

Listing 15-20 includes, in addition to the main() function, a function named getDownloadURLBlock that returns a block literal used to download a URL. The file begins by defining two constants, YahooURL and ApressURL, which name the URLs to be downloaded. Next, a type definition is provided for the block type to be used. The file then defines the getDownloadURLBlock() function. This function returns a block literal used to synchronously download a URL via the NSURLConnection method sendSynchronousRequest:returningResponse:error. It also computes the amount of time taken to download the URL using several NSDate APIs. The interval is computed as an NSTimeInterval value. Note that the block captures the URL string (provided as an argument to the function) using lexical scoping.

The main() function uses GCD APIs to create and dispatch two tasks for concurrent execution. It first creates two global concurrent dispatch queues for executing tasks in parallel.

```
dispatch_queue_t queue1 =
  dispatch_get_global_queue(DISPATCH_QUEUE_PRIORITY_DEFAULT, 0);
dispatch_queue_t queue2 =
  dispatch_get_global_queue(DISPATCH_QUEUE_PRIORITY_DEFAULT, 0);
```

Next, it creates a *task group*, which is used to group tasks and is useful for queuing tasks to perform asynchronous execution, waiting on a group of queued tasks, and so forth. The code then dispatches the two tasks to the task group.

```
dispatch_group_async(group, queue1, getDownloadURLBlock(YahooURL));
dispatch_group_async(group, queue2, getDownloadURLBlock(ApressURL));
```

Notice that the task to be executed is specified by a block literal retrieved by the getDownloadURLBlock() function; one using the Yahoo URL and the other using the Apress URL. The GCD dispatch_group_async() function causes these tasks to be performed concurrently. Next, the GCD dispatch_group_wait() function is used to block the main thread until both concurrent tasks complete.

```
dispatch_group_wait(group, DISPATCH_TIME_FOREVER);
```

Finally, the amount of time taken to complete the two concurrent tasks is computed and logged to the console. Now save, compile, and run the BlockConcurrentTasks program and observe the messages in the output pane (as shown in Figure 15-5).

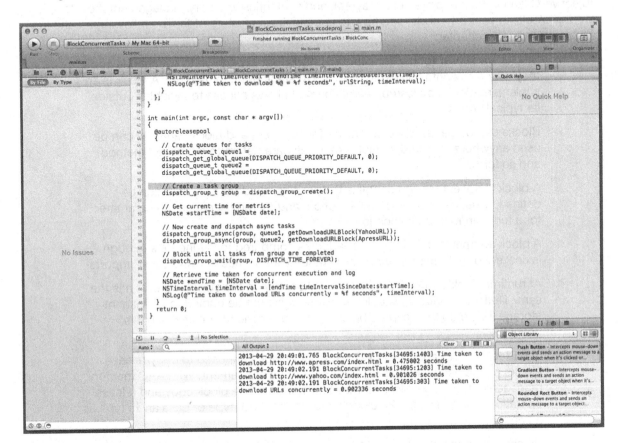

Figure 15-5. Testing the BlockConcurrentTasks project

The messages in the output pane show that the concurrent tasks were performed successfully. It also shows that the elapsed time to perform the tasks concurrently was less than what would have been taken to perform them sequentially. Cool. You just learned how to use blocks to perform concurrent programming and also received a brief introduction to the Grand Central Dispatch system. Note that Chapter 17 provides a complete introduction on the use of GCD to perform concurrent programming.

Roundup

In this chapter, you learned how to program with blocks, a powerful feature now available for the Objective-C language. It explored block syntax and semantics, memory management, how to develop blocks in your own code, and how to use blocks in existing APIs. The following are the key takeaways from this chapter:

- Blocks are similar to functions and methods, but in addition to executable code, they may also contain variable bindings to stack or heap memory. A block is an implementation of a *closure,* a function that allows access to variables outside its typical scope.

- Blocks can be declared as variables of block type, and block variables can be used anywhere standard variables can—as parameters to a function/method, and so forth.

- A block literal expression contains the code invoked by a block. It can be defined inline, as an anonymous function, and thereby serve as the parameter for a function/method invocation.

- A block augments the visibility of variables compared to C functions through lexical scoping, __block variables, instance variable access, and const imports.

- At runtime, a block literal expression is allocated on the stack and thus has the same lifetime as a local variable. As a result, it must be copied to permanent storage (i.e., onto the heap) to be used outside of the scope in which it is defined.

- The Block_copy() and Block_release() operations are used to copy/release blocks on the heap when using MRR memory management. With ARC memory management, the compiler automatically performs the block copy and release operations as long as the block does not return an id type or pass an id type as a parameter.

- Blocks are most naturally used to implement small, self-contained pieces of code that encapsulate units of work. They are typically executed concurrently over the items of a collection or as a callback when an operation has finished. Because blocks can be defined inline, they can eliminate the need to create entirely separate classes and methods for context-sensitive code, such as asynchronous completion handlers. They also enable related code to be kept together, and not scattered among multiple files.

This was a detailed chapter that exposed you to a variety of advanced topics: blocks, concurrent programming, and the GCD APIs. Spend a little time to go over everything covered here. Feel free to modify the examples to learn more about these concepts. In the next chapter, you will learn all about Objective-C literals, another recent addition to the Objective-C language.

Chapter 16

Objective-C Literals

Since its inception, the Objective-C language has provided support for *programming literals*, notations that represent fixed values in the source code. Until recently, literal notation was confined to scalar types. In this chapter, you will learn all about one of the more recent additions to the language, *Objective-C Literals*, which provides support for object literals. You will learn their syntax, associated semantics, and guidelines for their usage. The chapter will also cover object subscripting, another recent addition to the language.

Literals

In computer-programming, a *literal* is a notation for representing a fixed value in source code. As its name implies, literal notation enables you to write, in code, the literal symbol for a datatype. This is important because without literal notation it would be very tedious and error-prone to write constant values in code. For example, consider the following assignment statement.

```
int luckyNumber = 7;
```

The symbol 7 represents literal notation for an integer value of seven. Without literal notation, you would have to construct the value of seven in code, perhaps as shown in Listing 16-1.

Listing 16-1. Creating an Integer Value in Code Without Literals

```
static int zero;                          // Statics are initialized to 0
int one = zero++;
int two = one++;
int luckyNumber = (two * two) + two + one;   // 7 = 4 + 2 + 1
```

Having to go through all of this trouble to code values for simple datatypes would quickly discourage you from programming. Thus the advantages of literal notation are self-evident. Now this may seem pretty obvious to you. After all, don't all programming languages support coding literal values? Well, in fact, the extent of support for literal notation differs among the various languages.

Traditionally, the Objective-C language has provided support for literal notation of primitive/scalar types (i.e., `int`, `float`, `Boolean` types), along with text strings (`NSString` instances). Objective-C Literals enable the creation of object literals; specifically, NSNumber literals, collection literals, (boxed) expression literals, and (boxed) C-string literals. In the next few sections, you will learn how to use these object literals in code.

NSNumber Literals

You may recall that Chapter 10 provided a brief overview of NSNumber literals. To recap, the Foundation Framework class `NSNumber` is a container for primitive (i.e., scalar) types. An instance of `NSNumber` provides an object wrapper of a scalar value (integer value, floating-point value, or Boolean value). NSNumber objects are useful in a variety of scenarios; for example, with the Foundation Framework collection classes that can't hold primitive types. However, the creation and initialization of an `NSNumber` requires the use of the `NSNumber` APIs, which can be tedious for cases with a lot of objects (e.g., a collection class initialized with many `NSNumber` objects).

An NSNumber literal uses a simple notation for creating and initializing an `NSNumber` object from a scalar literal expression, its syntax is

```
@ScalarValue
```

The literal begins with the ampersand (@) symbol, followed by a `ScalarValue` that represents any character, numeric, or Boolean literal value. Listing 16-2 demonstrates the use of NSNumber literals in a statement that creates an `NSArray` object named `numbers`.

Listing 16-2. Creating an NSArray Instance Using NSNumber Literals

```
NSArray *numbers = [NSArray arrayWithObjects:@'A', @YES, @-3, @21U, @250L,
                @9876543210LL, @3.14F, @-52.687, nil];
```

The use of NSNumber literals in the preceding statement greatly simplifies the amount of code you have to write, thereby reducing the chance for errors. So that's all well and good, but you may be wondering, how does this all work? Well, the compiler translates each NSNumber literal into a convenience constructor that creates the corresponding NSNumber instance at runtime. In effect, the following two expressions are equivalent:

```
@17
[NSNumber numberWithInt:17]
```

The same is true for scalar data types with modifiers; the next two expressions are also equivalent:

```
@3.14f
[NSNumber numberWithFloat:3.14]
```

So when you write the NSNumber literal `@17` in code, the compiler translates that into the expression `[NSNumber numberWithInt:17]`. In effect, the literal notation is a shortcut for an NSNumber object creation.

As NSNumber literals are, in effect, `NSNumber` objects, they have available the full range of `NSNumber` APIs; for example, the following statement compares the values of two NSNumber literals.

```
NSComparisonResult comparison = [@17 compare:@16];
```

Note that NSNumber literal objects are created from scalar values, not expressions. Also be aware that NSNumber literals are evaluated at runtime; as such, they are not compile-time constants and hence cannot be used to initialize static or global variables. The following statement will not compile:

```
static NSNumber *badNumber = @0;            // ERROR!
```

Container Literals

Objective-C provides support for the creation of a variety of container literals; specifically, literal notation for arrays and dictionaries (i.e., `NSArray` and `NSDictionary` objects).

NSArray Literals

Chapter 10 provided a brief overview of NSArray literals. This notation simplifies the creation of NSArray instances. The syntax for an array literal is

```
@[firstObj, secondObj, ...]
```

An NSArray literal begins with an ampersand (@) symbol, followed by a comma-separated list of objects enclosed in brackets. The list of objects *is not* terminated with a `nil`. As with the `NSArray` APIs, the objects of the array must be Objective-C object pointer types, including other Objective-C Literals (NSNumber literals, NSArray literals, etc.). Listing 16-3 modifies the example shown in Listing 16-2, this time using array literal notation to create an NSArray object.

Listing 16-3. Creating an NSArray Literal

```
NSArray *numbers = @[@'A', @YES, @-3, @21U, @250L,
                     @9876543210LL, @3.14F, @-52.687];
```

Array literals can be nested, thereby enabling the creation of arrays within arrays. Listing 16-4 demonstrates the creation of a nested NSArray literal.

Listing 16-4. Nested NSArray Literals

```
NSArray *groups = @[@[@0, @1, @2], @[@"alpha", @"beta"]];
```

As the previous examples demonstrate, NSArray literal notation both simplifies the creation of arrays and reduces programmer errors.

The compiler translates each NSArray literal into the NSArray convenience constructor `arrayWithObjects:count:`. This method is invoked at runtime to create the corresponding NSArray instance. In effect, the NSArray literal

```
@[@"Hello", @"World"];
```

is equivalent to the code fragment shown in Listing 16-5.

Listing 16-5. Creating an NSArray Instance (Without Array Literal Notation)

```
NSString *strings[2];
strings[0] = @"Hello";
strings[1] = @"World";
[NSArray arrayWithObjects:strings count:2];
```

Array literal notation is used to create immutable array instances. You can create a mutable array
(e.g., an NSMutableArray) from an array literal by sending it a `mutableCopy` message, as follows.

```
NSMutableArray *mutableWords = [@[@"Hello", @"World"] mutableCopy];
```

NSDictionary Literals

Objective-C also provides support for creating NSDictionary literals. The syntax for a dictionary literal is

```
@{keyObj:valueObj, ...}
```

An NSDictionary literal begins with an ampersand symbol, followed by one or more comma-separated
key-value pairs, all enclosed in braces. For each key-value pair, a colon is placed between the key and its
corresponding value. Each key must be an object pointer type that conforms to the NSCopying protocol,
and each value must be an object pointer type. Neither keys nor values in a dictionary literal can have a
nil value; NSNull must be used to represent null objects in a container. Listing 16-6 creates a simple
dictionary literal with two entries—an order for one cheeseburger and an order for two hot dogs.

Listing 16-6. Creating an NSDictionary Literal

```
NSDictionary *orders = @{@1111:@"1 Cheeseburger",
                         @1112:@"2 Hot dogs"};
```

Notice that the NSDictionary literal syntax for key-value pairs is key:value, whereas the standard
NSDictionary APIs use a value, key syntax for creating a dictionary instance (e.g., the NSDictionary
method `dictionaryWithObjects:forKeys:`). As with array literals, dictionary literals can be nested;
that is, the value in the key-value pair can be a container instance (including another NSDictionary
literal). Listing 16-7 demonstrates the creation of a nested NSDictionary literal (`currentOrders`) with
two entries, where the value for each entry is an NSDictionary literal.

Listing 16-7. Nested NSDictionary Literal

```
NSDictionary *order1 = @{@1111:@"1 Cheeseburger",
                         @1112:@"2 Hot dogs"};
NSDictionary *order2 = @{@1113:@"1 large cheese pizza"};
NSDictionary *currentOrders = @{@"table1":order1, @"table2":order2};
```

The compiler translates each NSDictionary literal expression into the NSDictionary convenience
constructor `dictionaryWithObjects:forKeys:count:`. This method is invoked at runtime to create the
corresponding NSDictionary instance—in effect, the following dictionary literal:

```
@{@1111:@"1 Cheeseburger"}
```

is equivalent to the code fragment shown in Listing 16-8.

Listing 16-8. Creating an NSDictionary Instance (Without Dictionary Literal Notation)

```
NSString *values[1];
values[0] = @"1 Cheeseburger";
NSNumber *keys[1];
keys[0] = @1111;
[NSDictionary dictionaryWithObjects:values forKeys:keys count:1];
```

Dictionary literal notation is used to create immutable dictionary instances. As specified with array literals, you can create a mutable dictionary (e.g., an NSMutableDictionary) from a dictionary literal by sending it a mutableCopy message.

Expression Literals

Expression literals, also known as *boxed expressions*, enable you to create literals from parentheses-enclosed expressions. The syntax of an expression literal is

```
@( <expression> )
```

The expression evaluates to either a scalar (numeric, enumerations, BOOL) or C-string pointer type. The type of the resultant object corresponds to the type of the expression. Scalar types produce NSNumber instances and C strings produce NSString objects using UTF-8 character encoding. The following statement creates an NSNumber instance using a boxed expression.

```
NSNumber *degrees2Radians = @( M_PI / 180.0 );
```

In the preceding example, the arithmetic expression M_PI/180.0 is evaluated and the result is *boxed*; that is, it is used to create an NSNumber instance. The equivalent statement for this boxed expression is

```
NSNumber *degrees2Radians = [NSNumber numberWithDouble:(M_PI / 180.0)];
```

The next example creates an NSString instance using a boxed expression.

```
NSString *currentUser = @(getenv("USER"));
```

The getenv() function retrieves the value of an environment variable, where the input parameter is the name of the variable to be retrieved. The return value to the function is a pointer to a C string.

Although enumerations are typically used to define constant scalar values, they cannot be used directly to create NSNumber literals; for example, the following attempt to create an NSNumber literal from an enum (shown in Listing 16-9) will not compile.

Listing 16-9. Attempt to Create an NSNumber Literal from an enum

```
enum
{
  Zero = 0,
  One
};
NSNumber *zeroNumber = @Zero;       // Error!
```

Instead, an enum value must be placed inside an expression literal (i.e., a *boxed enum*) to create an NSNumber instance. Listing 16-10 corrects the example shown in Listing 16-9 to create an NSNumber instance from a boxed enum.

Listing 16-10. Creating an NSNumber from a Boxed enum

```
enum
{
  Zero = 0,
  One
};
NSNumber *zeroNumber = @(Zero);      // Correct!
```

If an enum has a *fixed underlying type* (i.e., it specifies the type used to store its values), the NSNumber instance will be created with the corresponding type. The example shown in Listing 16-11 creates an NSNumber instance from a boxed enum; as the enumeration is of type unsigned int, the NSNumber instance is created with the corresponding type.

Listing 16-11. Creating an NSNumber from a Boxed enum with a Fixed Underlying Type

```
enum : unsigned int
{
  Zero = 0,
  One
};
NSNumber *zeroNumber = @(Zero);      // invokes [NSNumber numberWithUnsignedInt:]
```

Object Subscripting

Object subscripting is a recent addition to the Objective-C language that enables Objective-C objects to be used with the C subscripting operator ([ ]). It provides a clean, concise syntax for getting and setting the elements of a Foundation Framework array and dictionary (e.g., NSArray and NSDictionary). In addition, the subscripting operators are generic, and thus enable the corresponding methods to be implemented by any class to provide custom subscripting.

NSArray Subscripting

When applied to NSArray and NSMutableArray objects, the subscript operand has an integral type. NSArray supports getting the elements of an array using the subscript operand. The example shown in Listing 16-12 creates an NSArray literal and then retrieves an element from the resultant array using subscripting.

Listing 16-12. Retrieving an NSArray Element Using Subscripting

```
NSArray *words = @[@"Hello", @"World"];
NSString *word = words[0];
```

NSMutableArray supports both getting and setting the elements of an array using the subscript operand. Listing 16-13 creates a mutable array from an NSArray literal, and then sets an element of the array to a new value.

Listing 16-13. Setting an NSMutableArray Element Using Subscripting

```
NSMutableArray *words = [@[@"Hello", @"World"] mutableCopy];
words[1] = @"Earthlings";
```

The NSArray and NSMutableArray classes use the subscript operand (i.e., an index) to access the appropriate element from its collection. The subscripting operator does not allow you to add elements to a mutable array; it only allows you to replace existing elements. For either NSArray or NSMutableArray instances, if the subscripting operand is outside of the array bounds, an NSRangeException is thrown. In addition, when setting an NSMutableArray element using subscripting, the object the array element is being set to must not be nil.

When the subscript operand is applied on an NSArray or NSMutableArray object, the expression is rewritten to use one of two different selectors, depending on whether the element is being read or written. For read (i.e., get) operations, the compiler translates this into an expression using the NSArray method objectAtIndexedSubscript:. In effect, the following two expressions are equivalent:

```
NSString *word = words[0]
NSString *word = [words objectAtIndexedSubscript:1]
```

For write (i.e., set) operations, the compiler translates this into an expression that uses the NSMutableArray method setObject:atIndexedSubscript:. In effect, the following two expressions are equivalent:

```
words[1] = @"Earthlings";
[words setObject:@"Earthlings" atIndexedSubscript:1];
```

The NSArray method objectAtIndexedSubscript: takes an NSUInteger (e.g., an unsigned integer) as its input parameter and returns a value of some Objective-C object pointer type. The NSMutableArray method setObject:atIndexedSubscript: takes an Objective-C pointer type as its first parameter and an NSUInteger as its second parameter.

NSDictionary Subscripting

When applied to NSDictionary and NSMutableDictionary objects, the subscript operand has an Objective-C pointer type. NSDictionary supports getting the elements of a dictionary using the subscript operand. The example shown in Listing 16-14 creates an NSDictionary literal, and then retrieves an element from the resultant array using subscripting.

Listing 16-14. Retrieving an NSDictionary Element Using Subscripting

```
NSDictionary *order1 = @{@1111:@"1 Cheeseburger",
                         @1112:@"2 Hot dogs"};
NSString *order = order1[@1111];
```

NSMutableDictionary supports both getting and setting the elements of an array using the subscript operand. Listing 16-15 creates a mutable dictionary from an NSDictionary literal, and then sets an element of the array to a new value.

Listing 16-15. Setting an NSMutableDictionary Element Using Subscripting

```
NSMutableDictionary *order1 = [@{@1111:@"1 Cheeseburger",
                                 @1112:@"2 Hot dogs"} mutableCopy];
order1[@1112] = @"1 Cheese pizza";
```

The NSDictionary and NSMutableDictionary classes use the subscript operand (i.e., a key) to access the appropriate element from its collection. The subscripting operator does not allow you to add elements to a mutable array; it only allows you to replace existing elements. For NSDictionary or NSMutableDictionary instances, attempting to retrieve an element via subscripting returns nil if there is no value associated with the input key. When setting an NSMutableDictionary element using subscripting, the method raises an NSInvalidArgument exception if the key or object is nil.

When the subscript operand is applied on an NSDictionary or NSMutableDictionary object, the expression is rewritten to use one of two different selectors, depending on whether the element is being read or written. For read (i.e., get) operations, the compiler translates this into an expression using the NSDictionary method objectForKeyedSubscript:. In effect, the following two expressions are equivalent:

```
NSString *order = order1[@1111];
NSString *order = [order1 objectForKeyedSubscript:@1111];
```

For write (i.e., set) operations, the compiler translates this into an expression that uses the NSMutableDictionary method setObject:forKeyedSubscript:. In effect, the following two expressions are equivalent:

```
order[@1111] = @"1 Cheeseburger";
[order setObject:@"1 Cheeseburger" forKeyedSubscript:@1111];
```

The NSDictionary method objectForKeyedSubscript: takes an Objective-C pointer type that conforms to the NSCopying protocol as its input parameter and returns a value of some Objective-C object pointer type. The NSMutableDictionary method setObject:forKeyedSubscript: takes an Objective-C pointer type as its first parameter and an Objective-C pointer type that conforms to the NSCopying protocol as its second parameter.

As with Objective-C Literals, the object subscripting operations are evaluated at runtime; as such, they are not compile-time constants and cannot be used to initialize static or global variables.

Custom Subscripting

As noted earlier, the object subscripting operators support any type of Objective-C object. The compiler translates these operators into message selectors, and your code implements one or more of the corresponding methods to support object subscripting. In effect, there are two types of subscript expressions: *array-style* and *dictionary-style*. You were introduced to this with the NSArray and NSDictionary subscripting operations presented earlier. In sum, array-style subscript expressions use integer typed subscripts, and dictionary-style subscript expressions use Objective-C object pointer typed subscripts (i.e., a key). Each type of subscript expression is mapped to a message send operation using a predefined selector.

The instance methods for array-style subscripting are

```
- (id)objectAtIndexedSubscript:(NSUInteger)index
- (void)setObject:(id)anObject atIndexedSubscript:(NSUInteger)index
```

The `objectAtIndexedSubscript:` method retrieves the value at the specified index, whereas the `setObject:atIndexedSubscript:` method sets the value at the specified index. As an example, given a class named `Hello` that supports array-style subscripting, an array-style subscript expression is used to return a value in the following assignment statement.

```
id value = helloObject[2];          // helloObject is a Hello class instance
```

In this case (i.e., retrieving a value for an associated index), the subscript expression (`helloObject[2]`) is translated by the compiler into a message send with the selector `objectAtIndexedSubscript:`, and is thus equivalent to the statement

```
id value = [helloObject objectAtIndexedSubscript:2];
```

In the next example, an array-style subscript expression is used to set a value in an assignment statement.

```
helloObject[2] = @"Howdy";
```

When setting a value via an array-style subscript expression, the expression (in this case `helloObject[2]`) is translated by the compiler into a message send with the selector `setObject:atIndexedSubscript:`, and is thus equivalent to the statement

```
[helloObject setObject:@"Howdy" atIndexedSubscript:2];
```

The message-send operations are type-checked and performed just like explicit Objective-C message sends. The implementing class determines the meaning of the index.

The instance methods for dictionary-style subscripting are

```
- (id)objectForKeyedSubscript:(id)key
- (void)setObject:(id)anObject forKeyedSubscript:(id<NSCopying>)key
```

These methods are analogous to the array-style subscripting methods, using a key (of type `id`—i.e., an object pointer) instead of an index to get or set the associated value. Given a class named `Order` that supports dictionary-style subscripting, a dictionary-style subscript expression is used to return a value in the following statement.

```
id item = orderObject[@"1234"];     // orderObject is an Order class instance
```

In this case, the subscript expression (`orderObject[@"1234"]`) is translated by the compiler into a message send with the selector `objectForKeyedSubscript:`, and is thus equivalent to the statement

```
id item = [orderObject objectForKeyedSubscript:@"1234"];
```

Conversely, a dictionary-style subscript expression is used to set a value in the following assignment statement.

```
orderObject[@"1234"] = @"Cheeseburger";
```

In this case, the subscript expression (orderObject[@"1234"]) is translated by the compiler into a message send with the selector setObject:forKeyedSubscript:, and is thus equivalent to the statement.

```
[orderObject setObject:@"Cheeseburger" forKeyedSubscript:@"1234"];
```

As shown in these examples, the custom subscripting operations should be used to get and set the elements of an object, and not for other purposes (e.g., appending or deleting objects, etc.). This enables the syntax to remain consistent with its intent, and thus identical to that employed for the Foundation Framework array and dictionary subscript operations.

Editing Register Values Using Custom Subscripting

Now you will create a program that demonstrates the use of custom subscripting. In addition, it also features extensive use of several Foundation Framework APIs presented in earlier chapters. The program you'll create is called *RegEdit* and consists of a header file along with two classes. RegEdit simulates a 32-bit wide computer memory register. It supports operations for setting and manipulating the register's contents. The program has three command-line inputs: the initial register settings (a 32-bit hexadecimal value), the selected register byte to get/set, and the (optional) register (hexadecimal) byte value to set.

In Xcode, create a new project by selecting **New ➤ Project ...** from the Xcode File menu. In the **New Project Assistant** pane, create a command-line application. In the **Project Options** window, specify **RegEdit** for the Product Name, choose **Foundation** for the Project Type, and select ARC memory management by checking the **Use Automatic Reference Counting** check box. Specify the location in your file system where you want the project to be created (if necessary, select **New Folder** and enter the name and location for the folder), uncheck the **Source Control** check box, and then click the **Create** button.

First, you're going to create a header file that defines several constants used in other classes. Select **New ➤ File ...** from the Xcode File menu, select **Header File template** (from the OS X C and C++ selection), and name the header file **RegEditConstants**. Select the **RegEdit** folder for the files location and the **RegEdit** project as the target, and then click the **Create** button. Next, in the Xcode project navigator pane, select the resulting header file named **RegEditConstants.h** and update the interface, as shown in Listing 16-16.

Listing 16-16. RegEditConstants Interface

```
#ifndef RegEdit_RegEditConstants_h
#define RegEdit_RegEditConstants_h

#define kByteMultiplier  0xFF
#define kRegisterSize (sizeof(uint32))

#endif
```

Listing 16-16 shows that the include guard prevents recursive inclusion of the header file (necessary if the file is imported using the #include directive). The header file defines two constants: kByteMultiplier is used to perform register bit manipulation operations, and kRegisterSize defines the width (in bits) of the register. Next, you're going to create a class used to parse command-line inputs for the program. Select **New ➤ File ...** from the Xcode File menu, select the **Objective-C** class template, and name the class **CLIParser**. Make the class a subclass of **NSObject**, select the **RegEdit** folder for the files location and the **RegEdit** project as the target, and then click the **Create** button. In the Xcode project navigator pane, select the resulting header file named **CLIParser.h** and update the interface, as shown in Listing 16-17.

Listing 16-17. CLIParser Interface

```
#import <Foundation/Foundation.h>

@interface CLIParser : NSObject

- (id) initWithCount:(int)argc arguments:(const char *[])argv;
- (BOOL) parseWithRegister:(uint32 *)registerValue
               byteNumber:(NSInteger *)byteN
                doSetByte:(BOOL *)doSet
                byteValue:(unsigned int *)byteValue
                    error:(NSError **)anError;

@end
```

The initWithCount:arguments: method initializes a CLIParser object, setting its state to the input parameter values. The parseWithRegister:byteNumber:doSetByte: method parses the command-line inputs, setting the value of the input parameters by indirection. The actual implementation of the class will be discussed later, but for now let's create the actual RegEdit class. Select **New ➤ File ...** from the Xcode File menu, select the **Objective-C** class template, and name the class **RegEdit**. Make the class a subclass of **NSObject**, select the **RegEdit** folder for the files location and the **RegEdit** project as the target, and then click the **Create** button. Next, in the Xcode project navigator pane, select the resulting header file named **RegEdit.h** and update the interface, as shown in Listing 16-18.

Listing 16-18. RegEdit Interface

```
#import <Foundation/Foundation.h>

@interface RegEdit : NSObject

@property (readonly) uint32 regSetting;

- (id) initWithValue:(uint32)value;
- (id) objectAtIndexedSubscript:(NSInteger)index;
- (void) setObject:(id)newValue atIndexedSubscript:(NSInteger)index;

@end
```

The interface begins by declaring a read-only property named regSetting. It is used to store the binary value (1/0) of each bit of a register. The property is of type uint32, a standard C type for an unsigned, (exactly) 32-bit wide integer; hence the register is 32-bits wide. The initWithValue: method initializes a RegEdit instance with the desired initial register settings. The objectAtIndexedSubscript: and setObject:atIndexedSubscript: methods are used to implement custom subscripting of RegEdit objects.

Now select the **RegEdit.m** file and update the implementation, as shown in Listing 16-19.

Listing 16-19. RegEdit Implementation

```objc
#import "RegEdit.h"
#import "RegEditConstants.h"

@interface RegEdit()

@property (readwrite) uint32 regSetting;

@end

@implementation RegEdit

- (id) initWithValue:(uint32)value
{
  if ((self = [super init]))
  {
    _regSetting = value;
  }
  return self;
}

- (id) objectAtIndexedSubscript:(NSInteger)index
{
  NSUInteger byteNumber = index * 8;
  if ((1 << byteNumber) > self.regSetting)
  {
    [NSException raise:NSRangeException
              format:@"Byte selected (%ld) exceeds number value", index];
  }
  unsigned int byteValue =
    (self.regSetting & (kByteMultiplier << byteNumber)) >> byteNumber;
  return [NSNumber numberWithUnsignedInt:byteValue];
}

- (void) setObject:(id)newValue atIndexedSubscript:(NSInteger)index
{
  if (newValue == nil)
  {
    [NSException raise:NSInvalidArgumentException
              format:@"New value is nil"];
  }
```

```
    NSUInteger byteNumber = index * 8;
    if ((1 << byteNumber) > self.regSetting)
    {
      [NSException raise:NSRangeException
                  format:@"Byte selected (%ld) exceeds number value", index];
    }
    uint32 mask = ~(kByteMultiplier << byteNumber);
    uint32 tmpValue = self.regSetting & mask;
    unsigned char newByte = [newValue unsignedCharValue];
    self.regSetting = (newByte << byteNumber) | tmpValue;
}
9
@end
```

The RegEdit class extension at the beginning of the file makes the regSetting property writeable
in order to enable its value to be updated by other methods within the class implementation. The
RegEdit implementation begins by defining the initWithValue: method. This method initializes
the regSetting property with the input parameter value. Next, the implementation defines the
objectAtIndexedSubscript: method. This method retrieves the value of a byte from the register,
where the byte retrieved is that specified by the input parameter (index). The RegEdit register
represents a *little-endian* machine; hence the least significant byte has the lowest memory address
(i.e., byte 0). The selected register byte is returned as an unsigned integer wrapped in an NSNumber
instance. The method also includes logic that checks the input parameter value and raises an
exception if the byte selected exceeds the register value.

```
if ((2 << (byteNumber-1)) > self.regSetting)
{
  [NSException raise:NSRangeException
              format:@"Byte selected (%ld) exceeds number value",
    (unsigned long)index];
}
```

The setObject:atIndexedSubscript: method implementation begins by executing logic that verifies
the selected register is within range and the input value is not nil, raising an exception if either
condition is not true. The method then sets the value of the selected register byte to the input value.

```
uint32 mask = ~(kByteMultiplier << byteNumber);
uint32 tmpValue = self.regSetting & mask;
unsigned char newByte = [newValue unsignedCharValue];
self.regSetting = (newByte << byteNumber) | tmpValue;
```

Notice that both custom subscripting methods perform bit-level operations to get/set the register's
values at the level of its individual bits. The bitwise left-shift (<<) and right-shift (>>) operators are
used to move each bit in a number the specified number of bits to the left or right. The bitwise
complement operator (~) is used to flip the bits of a number. The bitwise OR operator (|) performs
a bit-by-bit, logical OR operation on two numbers, whereas the bitwise AND operator (&) performs a
bit-by-bit, logical AND operation on two numbers.

OK, that summarizes the key details of the RegEdit class implementation. Now you will implement the CLIParser class, select the CLIParser.m file, and update the CLIParser class implementation, as shown in Listing 16-20.

Listing 16-20. CLIParser Implementation

```objc
#import "CLIParser.h"
#import "RegEditConstants.h"

NSString *HelpCommand =
@"\n  RegEdit -n [Hex initial register settings] -b [byte number] -v [hex byte value]";
NSString *HelpDesc = @"\n\nNAME\n  RegEdit - Get/set selected byte of a register.";
NSString *HelpSynopsis = @"\n\nSYNOPSIS";
NSString *HelpOptions = @"\n\nOPTIONS";
NSString *HelpRegValue = @"\n  -n\tThe initial register settings.";
NSString *HelpRegByte = @"\n  -b\tThe byte to retrieve from the register.";
NSString *HelpByteValue = @"\n  -v\tValue to set for the selected register byte.";

@implementation CLIParser

// Private instance variables
{
  const char **argValues;
  int argCount;
}

- (id) initWithCount:(int)argc arguments:(const char *[])argv
{
  if ((self = [super init]))
  {
    argValues = argv;
    argCount = argc;
  }
  return self;
}

- (BOOL) parseWithRegister:(uint32 *)registerValue
                byteNumber:(NSInteger *)byteN
                 doSetByte:(BOOL *)doSet
                 byteValue:(unsigned int *)byteValue
                     error:(NSError **)anError
{
  // Retrieve command line arguments using NSUserDefaults
  NSUserDefaults *defaults = [NSUserDefaults standardUserDefaults];
  NSString *numberString = [defaults stringForKey:@"n"];
  NSString *byteString = [defaults stringForKey:@"b"];
  NSString *valueString = [defaults stringForKey:@"v"];
```

```objective-c
// Display help message if register value or byte number not provided
if (!numberString || !byteString)
{
  NSString *help = [NSString stringWithFormat:@"%@%@%@%@%@%@%@",
                     HelpDesc, HelpSynopsis, HelpCommand,
                     HelpOptions, HelpRegValue, HelpRegByte,
                     HelpByteValue];
  printf("%s\n", [help UTF8String]);
  return NO;
}

// Scan input register value
NSScanner *scanner = [NSScanner scannerWithString:numberString];
if (!numberString ||
    ([numberString length] == 0) ||
    ([numberString length] > kRegisterSize*2) ||
    ![scanner scanHexInt:registerValue])
{
  // Create error and return NO
  if (anError != NULL)
  {
    NSString *msg =
    [NSString stringWithFormat:
     @"ERROR!, Register value must be from 1-%ld hexadecimal characters",
     kRegisterSize*2];
    NSString *description = NSLocalizedString(msg, @"");
    NSDictionary *info = @{NSLocalizedDescriptionKey:description};
    int errorCode = 1;
    *anError = [NSError errorWithDomain:@"CustomErrorDomain"
                                    code:errorCode
                                userInfo:info];
  }
  return NO;
}

// Scan input register byte number
scanner = [NSScanner scannerWithString:byteString];
if (!byteString ||
    ([byteString length] == 0) ||
    [scanner scanInteger:byteN])
{
  unsigned int numberLength = (unsigned int)(ceil([numberString length] * 0.5));
  if ((*byteN < 0) || (*byteN > (numberLength - 1)))
  {
    // Create error and return NO
    if (anError != NULL)
    {
      NSString *msg = [NSString stringWithFormat:
                        @"ERROR!, Register byte number must be from 0-%d",
                        numberLength-1];
      NSString *description = NSLocalizedString(msg, @"");
      NSDictionary *info = @{NSLocalizedDescriptionKey:description};
```

```
            int errorCode = 2;
            *anError = [NSError errorWithDomain:@"CustomErrorDomain"
                                            code:errorCode
                                        userInfo:info];
        }
        return NO;
      }
    }

    // Scan input value to set register byte
    if (valueString)
    {
      *doSet = YES;
      scanner = [NSScanner scannerWithString:valueString];
      if ([scanner scanHexInt:byteValue])
      {
        if (*byteValue > UCHAR_MAX)
        {
          if (anError != NULL)
          {
            NSString *msg =
            [NSString stringWithFormat:
             @"ERROR!, Register byte value must be 1-2 hexadecimal characters"];
            NSString *description = NSLocalizedString(msg, @"");
            NSDictionary *info = @{NSLocalizedDescriptionKey:description};
            int errorCode = 3;
            *anError = [NSError errorWithDomain:@"CustomErrorDomain"
                                            code:errorCode
                                        userInfo:info];
          }
          return NO;
        }
      }
    }
  }

  return YES;
}

@end
```

Listing 16-20 shows that the parseWithRegister:byteNumber:doSetByte: method contains quite a few lines of code. However, it doesn't introduce many new ideas; just about all of the code here is based on concepts and/or APIs that you encountered earlier in this book. Let's begin with the NSUserDefaults class. It is used here to retrieve command-line arguments when the program is run.

```
NSString *numberString = [defaults stringForKey:@"n"];
NSString *byteString = [defaults stringForKey:@"b"];
NSString *valueString = [defaults stringForKey:@"v"];
```

Next, an NSScanner object is used to scan the input values retrieved using the NSUserDefaults object, converting these values into the appropriate type and format, as shown in the following excerpt from Listing 16-20.

```
NSScanner *scanner = [NSScanner scannerWithString:numberString];
[scanner scanHexInt:registerValue]
```

The code also validates each command-line input value. It creates an NSError object to return to the caller if the value fails the validation checks, as follows.

```
if (anError != NULL)
{
  NSString *msg =
  [NSString stringWithFormat:
   @"ERROR!, Register value must be from 1-%ld hexadecimal characters",
   kRegisterSize*2];
  NSString *description = NSLocalizedString(msg, @"");
  NSDictionary *info = @{NSLocalizedDescriptionKey:description};
  int errorCode = 1;
  *anError = [NSError errorWithDomain:@"CustomErrorDomain"
                                  code:errorCode
                              userInfo:info];
}
```

As shown in Listing 16-20, this logic is used to retrieve the command-line inputs and format them appropriately for use as inputs to the appropriate RegEdit instance method. OK, now that you have finished examining these two classes, let's move on to the main() function. In the Xcode project navigator, select the **main.m** file and update the main() function, as shown in Listing 16-21.

Listing 16-21. RegEdit main() Function

```
#import <Foundation/Foundation.h>
#import "RegEdit.h"
#import "CLIParser.h"

int main(int argc, const char * argv[])
{
  @autoreleasepool
  {
    // First retrieve command line arguments using CLI parser
    CLIParser *parser = [[CLIParser alloc] initWithCount:argc arguments:argv];
    uint32 registerValue;
    NSInteger registerByte;
    unsigned int byteValue;
    BOOL isSetByte;
    NSError *error;
    BOOL success = [parser parseWithRegister:&registerValue
                                  byteNumber:&registerByte
                                   doSetByte:&isSetByte
                                   byteValue:&byteValue
                                       error:&error];
```

```
    if (!success)
    {
      // log error and quit
      if (error)
      {
        NSLog(@"%@", [error localizedDescription]);
        return -1;
      }
    }
    else
    {
      // Now create a RegEdit instance and set its initial value
      RegEdit *regEdit = [[RegEdit alloc] initWithValue:registerValue];
      NSLog(@"Initial register settings -> 0x%X", (uint32)[regEdit regSetting]);

      // Get selected register byte using custom subscripting
      NSNumber *byte = regEdit[registerByte];
      NSLog(@"Byte %ld value retrieved -> 0x%X", (long)registerByte,
            [byte intValue]);

      // Set selected register byte to input value using custom subscripting
      if (isSetByte)
      {
        NSLog(@"Setting byte %d value to -> 0x%X", (int)registerByte, byteValue);
        regEdit[registerByte] = [NSNumber numberWithUnsignedInt:byteValue];
        NSLog(@"Updated register settings -> 0x%X", [regEdit regSetting]);
      }
    }
  }
  return 0;
}
```

The `main()` function begins by creating `CLIParser` object. It parses the command-line arguments, logging an error if the arguments are not parsed successfully. It then creates a `RegEdit` instance and gets/sets a byte in the register as specified by the command-line arguments.

Now you will edit the project scheme (as you did earlier in an example from Chapter 9) to set the values for the program's command-line arguments. In Xcode, select **RegEdit** in the **Scheme** button at the top of the toolbar, and then select **Edit Scheme ...** from the scheme drop-down (as shown in Figure 16-1).

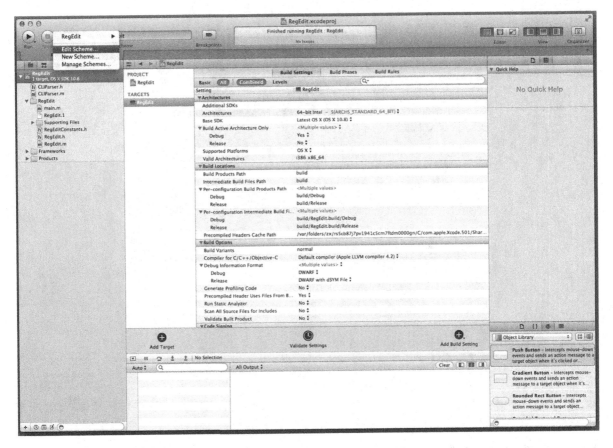

Figure 16-1.   Edit RegEdit project scheme

In the Scheme editing dialog, select the **Arguments** tab to edit the arguments passed on program launch. Under the **Arguments Passed on Launch** section, select the **+** button to add the argument values. As shown in Figure 16-2, the initial register setting is specified with a -n argument, the register byte with a -b argument, and the byte value with a -v argument.

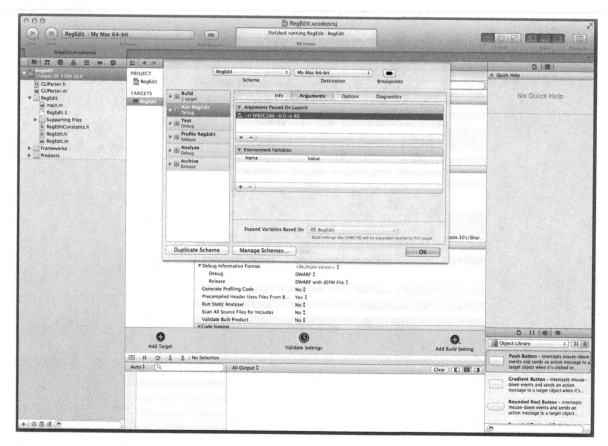

Figure 16-2. Adding command-line arguments using Scheme editor

The command-line argument settings provided in Figure 16-2 are

```
-n 1FB2C3A6 -b 0 -v A5
```

Hence, the initial register setting is 0x1FB2C3A6, the register byte selected is 0, and the value of that byte will be updated to 0xA5.

The command-line arguments will now be passed to the RegEdit program on launch. When you compile and run the program, you should observe the messages in the output pane shown in Figure 16-3.

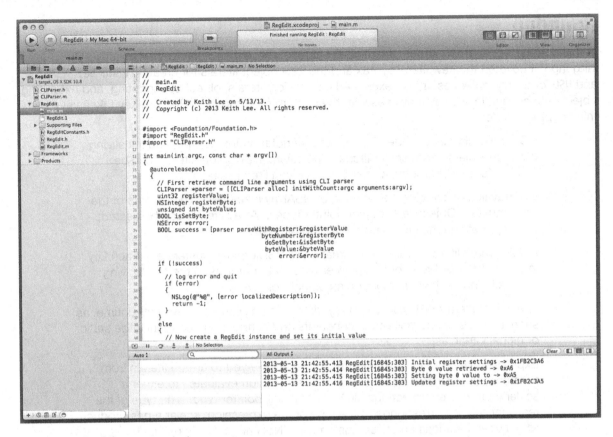

Figure 16-3. RegEdit program output

The output pane shows that initial register settings, the retrieved byte, and the updated register settings (with the new byte value) are displayed appropriately. Try running the program with different inputs to observe how it operates, and once you become comfortable with custom subscripting, feel free to add other features to enhance it. Cool. Great job making it this far! This program demonstrates the use of Objective-C Literals and object subscripting.

Roundup

In this chapter, you learned about Objective-C Literals, a recent addition to the Objective-C language. It covered the new literal syntax and the new object literals for creating NSNumber, NSArray, and NSDictionary instances. It also examined expression literals, object subscripting, and extending object subscripting in your own classes with the custom subscripting APIs. The key takeaways from this chapter include:

- NSNumber literals provide simple, concise notation for creating and initializing NSNumber objects from scalar literal expression. NSNumber literals can be created for any character, numeric, or Boolean literal value.

- NSArray literals simplify the creation of NSArray instances. The objects of the array must be Objective-C object pointer types. Array literals can be nested, thereby enabling the creation of arrays within arrays.

- NSDictionary literals simplify the creation of NSDictionary instances. Each key in the literal must be an object pointer type that conforms to the NSCopying protocol, and each value must be an object pointer type.

- The object literals (NSNumber, NSArray, NSDictionary) are evaluated at runtime; as such, they are not compile-time constants and cannot be used to initialize static or global variables.

- Expression literals (i.e., boxed expressions) enable you to create literals from parentheses-enclosed expressions. The expression evaluates to either a scalar (numeric, enumerations, BOOL) or C-string pointer type. The type of the resultant object corresponds to the type of the expression; scalar types produce NSNumber instances and C strings produce NSString objects using UTF-8 character encoding.

- Object subscripting provides a simple, concise syntax for getting and setting the elements of a Foundation Framework array and dictionary (e.g., NSArray and NSDictionary). In addition, the subscripting operators are generic, and thus enable the corresponding methods to be implemented by any class to provide custom subscripting.

- The custom subscripting operations should be used to get and set the elements of an object, and not for other purposes (e.g., appending or deleting objects, etc.). This enables the syntax to remain consistent with that employed for the Foundation Framework array and dictionary subscript operations, and thus provide ease of use.

Now you should be well on your way to mastering Objective-C object literals and object subscripting. Feel free to review the material of this chapter and tinker with the program and examples to let it all sink in. The topic of the next chapter is concurrent programming, so when you're ready, turn the page to begin.

Chapter 17

Concurrent Programming

In computer science, *concurrent processing* refers to logical control flows (implemented in software) whose execution overlaps in time. Concurrent processing can occur at many different levels of a computer system, from the hardware level up to and including the application layer. From a programmer perspective, application-level concurrency enables you to develop applications that perform numerous operations in parallel, including responding to asynchronous events, accessing I/O devices, servicing network requests, parallel computing, and so forth.

The Objective-C platform provides a variety of language extensions, APIs, and operating system services that are designed to enable you to safely and efficiently implement concurrent programming. In this chapter, you will explore this technology in depth and apply what you learn with several example programs.

Concurrent Programming Fundamentals

Concurrent programming is a broad field with many concepts and ideas that have various interpretations. Therefore, it's important to understand some basic terminology, along with identifying some of the benefits and design concepts for concurrent programming.

Let's begin by differentiating concurrent from sequential processing. Basically, sequential processing refers to logical control flows that execute sequentially (i.e., one after the other), as shown in Figure 17-1.

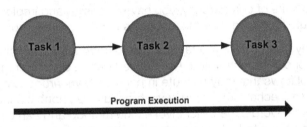

Figure 17-1. Sequential processing of control flows

This contrasts with the concurrent processing, which refers to logical control flows that may execute in parallel, as depicted in Figure 17-2.

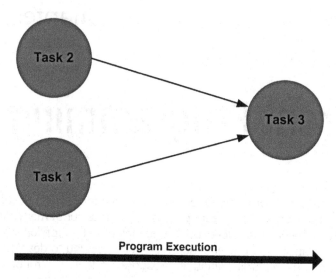

Figure 17-2. Concurrent processing of control flows

So, concurrent computing implies the simultaneous execution of multiple tasks. But in fact, whether a program designed to take advantage of concurrency actually executes multiple tasks in parallel is a function of the computer system on which it runs. This brings up another distinction that should be pointed out, and that's the difference between concurrent and parallel computing. Broadly speaking, concurrent computing is a function of design, whereas parallel computing is a function of hardware.

Parallel computing refers to software that executes multiple operations or tasks simultaneously. The ability to perform parallel computing (i.e., parallel processing) is directly a function of the computer system hardware. For example, most modern computers have multiple cores (CPUs) and/or multiple processors. This enables them to simultaneously execute multiple instructions. On the other hand, concurrent computing refers to software that is designed and implemented to be able to perform multiple operations or tasks simultaneously. If your software is designed and implemented using *concurrent programming* principles and mechanisms, then some/all of its component parts may execute concurrently depending upon the capabilities of the underlying computer system. Therefore, in order to realize the benefits of concurrency, you have to design and implement your software appropriately, and execute it on hardware that supports parallel processing.

Finally, before you go any further, it's important for you to understand the difference between concurrent and asynchronous programming. As I defined earlier, concurrent processing refers to multiple logical control flows that may execute in parallel. *Asynchronous processing*, on the other hand, is effectively a mechanism for the asynchronous (i.e., nonblocking) invocation of methods/functions. In other words, the caller invokes the method and can continue processing while the method is being executed. This approach can improve application responsiveness, system throughput, and so forth, while abstracting the underlying implementation mechanisms. Asynchronous processing can be implemented using a variety of devices, including concurrent programming APIs and services.

Benefits of Concurrency

Application-level concurrent processing enables you to develop programs that can perform multiple operations in parallel. However, these features do not come for free; concurrency must be factored into both software design and implementation, given the capabilities of the underlying computing system. Now this may sound like a burden when it comes to developing programs, however, the motivations for concurrent processing are numerous, some of which include the following:

- *Increased application throughput.* As concurrent processing enables the parallel execution of tasks, overall *application throughput*, defined as the number of tasks that an application can execute over time, is increased compared to sequential processing.

- *Improved system utilization.* The execution of multiple tasks in parallel enables system resources to be more consistently and efficiently utilized.

- *Improved overall application responsiveness.* Concurrent execution of tasks enables other tasks to continue running if one is waiting (for input, etc.) Thus overall application idle time decreases and application responsiveness is increased.

- *Better mapping to the problem domain.* Certain problems, particularly in the scientific, mathematical, and artificial intelligence fields, can be modeled as a collection of simultaneously executing tasks. This makes solution implementation (in code) with concurrent programming the more natural, preferred approach.

Implementing Concurrency

OK, so now that you are (hopefully) convinced of the benefits of concurrent processing, the next question is: How do you do it? Well, there are numerous ways to implement concurrency in computer systems, from specialized programming languages up to and including parallelized computer systems. Some of the more common approaches include the following:

- *Distributed computing*: In this form of concurrent processing, a number of tasks are distributed to and executed on multiple, networked computers that communicate by message passing.

- *Parallel programming*: In this form of concurrent processing, a number of calculations are performed simultaneously, typically on multicore CPUs and programmable GPUs. This approach utilizes parallel computing to improve performance and deliver features made possible by compute-intensive algorithms.

- *Multiple processes*: In this form of concurrent processing a number of tasks is distributed to multiple software processes on a single computer for concurrent execution. Each process has separate resources and a separate address space, managed by the operating system.

■ *Multiple threads*: Also known as *multithreading*, in this approach tasks are mapped to multiple threads, which are configured to execute concurrently. The threads execute within the context of a single program (i.e., process) and thus share its resources (address space, memory, etc.).

Note   The term *thread* refers to a sequence of instructions that can be executed independently. A thread is sometimes referred to as a lightweight process, and multiple threads may share an address space. A *process* is a running computer program with its own address space and allocation of system resources. A process may have multiple threads that execute sequentially, concurrently, or a combination of the two. A *task* refers to a logical unit of work. A task may be executed by a thread or a process.

Each of these approaches has its specific applications and usage scenarios. Whereas OS X and iOS both support (to different extents) each of the concurrent computing approaches presented earlier, the concurrent programming mechanisms that you will examine in this chapter are all based on the multithreading approach, so that's what you'll be exploring here.

Challenges with Concurrency

For all of its benefits, concurrent programming is difficult to implement correctly. This is primarily due to the challenges of synchronizing operations and sharing information between concurrently executing *threads of control* (i.e., logical control flows). Synchronization is required to control the relative order in which operations occur in different threads, while information sharing enables communication between threads. In addition, the overall program execution order is nondeterministic due to the simultaneous execution of multiple threads of control. Thus, different executions of the same program may produce different results. As a result, bugs in concurrent programs may be difficult to detect and reproduce. Furthermore, the complexity introduced by multiple threads and their potential interactions makes these programs much more difficult to analyze and reason.

There are a variety of mechanisms used to address these challenges; two of the more common are shared memory and message passing. The shared-memory programming model implies *shared state*—that is, some of the program data is accessible to multiple threads. As the threads of a program utilize a common address space, shared memory is a natural mechanism for information sharing. It's also fast and efficient.

Shared Data

The shared-memory model requires a mechanism to coordinate shared data access between the threads. This is commonly implemented using a synchronization mechanism; for example, a lock or a condition. A *lock* is a mechanism used to control access to data or a resource shared by multiple threads. A thread acquires a lock to a shared resource, performs operations on the resource, and then releases the lock, thereby enabling other threads to access the resource. A *condition* variable is a synchronization mechanism that causes a thread to wait until a specified condition occurs. Condition variables are commonly implemented using locks.

The Problems with Locks

Locks are one of the most common mechanisms used for controlling access to shared data. They enforce a *mutual exclusion* policy, thereby preventing concurrent access to the protected data/resource. Unfortunately, using locks to coordinate access to shared data introduces the possibility of deadlock, live-lock, or resource starvation—any of which can halt program execution. A *deadlock* is a situation in which two or more threads are each blocked, waiting to acquire a resource locked by another, thus preventing the blocked threads from finishing. An example of a deadlock condition is a circular wait. Figure 17-3 illustrates a deadlock condition that can occur between concurrent threads accessing shared data.

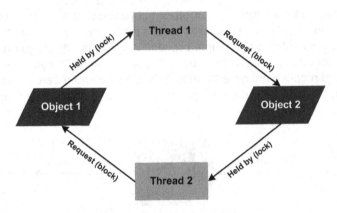

Figure 17-3. A deadlock condition between two threads accessing shared data

A *live-lock* is a situation where a thread is unable to progress because it is responding to the action of another thread(s). A live-locked thread is not blocked. It is spending all of its computing time responding to other threads to resume normal execution.

Resource starvation is a condition where a thread is not able to gain regular access to a shared resource, typically because it is being used by other threads and thus cannot execute as intended. This can happen if one or more other threads hold onto shared resources for an inordinate amount of time. In effect, you can look at live-lock as a form of resource starvation.

As you develop larger and more complex concurrent programs that use shared data, the potential for your code to cause a deadlock condition increases. The following are some of the most common recommendations for preventing these conditions:

■ *Implement a total ordering on lock acquisition.* Make sure that locks are acquired and released in a fixed order. This approach requires detailed knowledge of the threaded code, and may not even be feasible for third-party software.

■ *Prevent hold and wait conditions.* Acquire all locks at once, atomically. This requires that any time any thread grabs a lock, it first acquires the global *prevention* lock. This approach eliminates the possibility of hold-and-wait scenarios, but potentially decreases concurrency and also requires detailed knowledge of the threaded code.

- *Provide preemption*. Use locks that provide a *trylock* or similar mechanism to grab a lock, if available, or return an appropriate result if not. This approach has the potential of causing livelock, and still requires detailed knowledge of how the code is using locks.

- *Provide timeouts on waits*. Use locks that provide a timeout feature, thereby preventing indefinite waits on a lock.

Message Passing

In the message passing, model state is not shared; instead, the threads communicate by exchanging messages. This approach enables threads to both synchronize and communicate information through message exchanges. Message passing avoids the issues surrounding mutual exclusion and it maps naturally to multiple core, multiple processor systems. Message passing can be used to perform both synchronous and asynchronous communication. With synchronous message passing, the sender and receiver are directly linked; the sender and receiver block while the message exchange is performed. Asynchronous message passing utilizes queues for message transfer, as shown in Figure 17-4.

Figure 17-4. *Message passing using queues*

Messages are not sent directly between threads, but rather are exchanged through message queues. Hence, the sender and receiver are decoupled and the sender does not block when it posts a message to the queue. Asynchronous message passing can be used to implement concurrent programming. In fact, the next section will cover several frameworks that do just that.

Concurrent Programming with Objective-C

Now that you understand some of the key issues regarding concurrent programming, you can begin to explore the mechanisms available to implement concurrent programming in Objective-C. This ranges from language features to APIs and system services, and includes the following:

- *Language features*: The Objective-C language includes several language features to support concurrent programming. The @synchronized directive is used to create locks in Objective-C code. Thread-safe access to Objective-C properties can be specified declaratively using the atomic property qualifier.

- *Message passing*: The Foundation Framework NSObject class includes several methods that deliver messages to other threads. These methods queue the messages on the run loop of the target thread and can be performed synchronously or asynchronously.

- *Threads*: The Foundation Framework provides a complete set of APIs for directly creating and managing threads. It also includes a set of Foundation Framework APIs for performing synchronized access to data shared by multiple threads.

- *Operation queues*: These are Objective-C based message-passing mechanisms that utilize an asynchronous design approach to perform concurrent programming.

- *Dispatch queues*: These are a C-based set of language features and runtime services used to perform tasks asynchronously and concurrently.

Language Features

The @synchronized directive provides a simple mechanism for creating locks in Objective-C code, thereby enabling concurrent threads to synchronize access to shared state. The syntax for using this directive in your code is shown in Listing 17-1.

Listing 17-1. Syntax for the @synchronized Directive

```
@synchronized(uniqueObj)
{
  // Critical section - code protected by the directive
}
```

Listing 17-1 shows that the @synchronized directive is followed by a unique identifier in parentheses and a protected block of code surrounded by braces. The unique identifier is an object used to distinguish the protected block. If multiple threads attempt to access this critical section with the same unique identifier, one of the threads would acquire the lock first and the other(s) would block until the first thread finished executing the critical section.

Note that the @synchronized block implicitly adds an exception handler to the protected code. This handler automatically releases the lock in the event that an exception is thrown. Hence, you must enable Objective-C exception handling in your code in order to use this directive.

The Objective-C language also includes a feature that is intended to provide atomic access to properties. The atomic property qualifier is an Objective-C language feature that is designed to provide atomic access to a property, even when its accessor methods are called concurrently from different threads. *Atomic* means that a property's accessor methods always set/get a complete (consistent) value, regardless of whether the property is being accessed concurrently. The following statement declares an atomic, read-write property named greeting.

```
@property (atomic, readwrite) NSString *greeting;
```

By default, an Objective-C property is atomic, hence the use of the atomic keyword in the preceding property declaration is not necessary.

Note that the atomic property qualifier provides atomic access for a property, but not thread safety. Listing 17-2 depicts a class named Person whose interface declares atomic properties named firstName and lastName.

Listing 17-2. Person Class Atomic Properties

```
@interface Person : NSObject
@property (readwrite) NSString *firstName;
@property (readwrite) NSString *lastName;
@end
```

Although the properties firstName and lastName are atomic, as specified earlier, a Person object is *not* thread-safe. Hence, if two different threads accessed the same Person object, access to each of the individual properties within the object would be atomic, but the names could be inconsistent relative to each other, depending upon the order of access and the (get/set) operations performed. For example, the following statement declares a Person property.

```
@property (readwrite) Person *person;
```

The property is itself composed of two properties (firstName and lastName) that can be accessed atomically, but the person property itself is not thread-safe. This is due to the fact that there is no mechanism provided to collectively synchronize concurrent access to its components (i.e., firstName and lastName could be modified independently). This can be accomplished using the @synchronized directive or a synchronization primitive, which you will learn about shortly.

Message Passing

The Foundation Framework NSObject class includes a collection of methods that use the message-passing paradigm to invoke a method on an object with a thread. The thread can be an existing secondary thread or the main application thread. The method selectors are

- performSelector:onThread:withObject:waitUntilDone:

- performSelector:onThread:withObject:waitUntilDone:modes:

- performSelectorOnMainThread:withObject:waitUntilDone:

- performSelectorOnMainThread:withObject:waitUntilDone:modes:

Each method specifies a selector for a method on the receiver object that will be invoked with a thread. This method is also known as a *thread entry-point routine*. The selector message is queued on the run loop of the thread, and the method is executed on the thread as part of the run loop's standard processing. These message-passing methods enable you to specify whether the thread is invoked asynchronously or synchronously. Synchronous invocation results in the current thread blocking until the method finishes execution. Because these methods are defined for the NSObject class, they are provided for all classes that descend from NSObject (i.e., the majority of the Foundation Framework APIs and most of the custom classes that you will implement). Listing 17-3 depicts use of the performSelector:onThread: method to asynchronously invoke the downloadTask method on a thread named secondaryThread, where this method is defined for a custom class named ConcurrentProcessor.

Listing 17-3. NSObject performSelector:onThread:withObject:waitUntilDone: Method Invocation

```
ConcurrentProcessor *processor = [ConcurrentProcessor new];
[processor performSelector:@selector(downloadTask)
                  onThread:secondaryThread
                withObject:nil
             waitUntilDone:NO];
```

As shown in Listing 17-3, the `waitUntilDone:` parameter specifies asynchronous/synchronous operation. In this example, the input value is set to NO, thus the current thread returns immediately.

When you create a thread, you can configure portions of its runtime environment (e.g., stack size, thread-local storage, thread priority, etc.). It is also important to configure the thread context appropriately by implementing the thread entry-point routine with the following functionality (as necessary):

- *An autorelease pool*: An autorelease pool should be created at the beginning of the entry-point routine, and destroyed at the end of the routine.

- *An exception handler*: If the application catches and handles exceptions, the entry-point routine should be configured to catch any exceptions that can occur. Chapter 14 discusses the Objective-C mechanisms for exception handling.

- *A run loop*: In order to have a thread process requests dynamically as they arrive, you can setup a run loop in the entry-point routine. Chapter 11 covers the use of the Foundation Framework NSRunLoop class.

Listing 17-4, the `ConcurrentProcessor` `downloadTask` method, demonstrates implementation of an entry-point routine per the guidelines documented earlier.

Listing 17-4. ConcurrentProcessor downloadTask Method

```
@implementation ConcurrentProcessor
...
- (void)downloadTask
{
  @autoreleasepool
  {
    NSURL *url = [NSURL URLWithString:@"http://www.apress.com"];
    NSString *str = [NSString stringWithContentsOfURL:url
                                             encoding:NSUTF8StringEncoding
                                                error:nil];
    NSLog(@"URL Contents:\n%@", str);
    self.isLoaded = YES;
  }
}
@end
```

The NSObject `performSelectorOnMainThread:` methods are typically used to return values (status, results, etc.) from secondary thread objects to main (application) thread objects. This enables the implementation of communication between secondary threads and the main thread. This API is especially important for objects (such as those of the UIKit) that should only be used from the application's main thread.

Threads

As mentioned earlier in this chapter, a thread is a logical control flow that executes within the context of a single process. The Apple OS X and iOS operating systems provide direct support for the creation, management, and execution of threads. At the application layer, the Foundation Framework provides APIs for creating and managing threads, and also a collection of APIs to synchronize shared data access between concurrent threads.

NSObject Threads

The NSObject method performSelectorInBackground:withObject: enables you to implicitly create and start a new thread that is used to execute a method on an object. The thread begins immediately as a secondary background thread, and the current thread returns immediately.

Listing 17-5 depicts use of the performSelectorInBackground:withObject: method to asynchronously invoke the downloadTask method, on an instance of the ConcurrentProcessor class.

Listing 17-5. NSObject performSelectorInBackground:withObject: Method Invocation

```
ConcurrentProcessor *processor = [ConcurrentProcessor new];
[processor performSelectorInBackground:@selector(downloadTask)
                            withObject:nil];
while (!processor.isLoaded)
  ;
```

This method provides a simple mechanism for executing a method on an object with a new background thread. As noted earlier, the thread instance is created implicitly, hence you do not use the thread APIs directly. The thread's context should be configured in the method (the thread's entry-point routine), with an autorelease pool, an exception handler, and a run loop, as necessary.

NSThread

The NSThread class provides APIs that can be used to *explicitly* create and manage threads. The class includes methods to create and initialize an NSThread object (attached to an object instance method), start and stop a thread, configure a thread, and query a thread and its execution environment.

The NSThread APIs to create and initialize a thread are

- detachNewThreadSelector:toTarget:withObject:
- initWithTarget:selector:object:

The detachNewThreadSelector:toTarget:withObject: class method creates and starts a new thread. Its input parameters are the selector to use as the thread entry-point and the target of the selector on the new thread. Listing 17-6 modifies the code in Listing 17-5 to invoke the downloadTask method on a thread using the detachNewThreadSelector:toTarget:withObject: method.

Listing 17-6. Using the NSThread detachNewThreadSelector:toTarget:withObject: Method

```
ConcurrentProcessor *processor = [ConcurrentProcessor new];
[NSThread detachNewThreadSelector:@selector(downloadTask)
                         toTarget:processor
                       withObject:nil];
```

This method both creates the new thread and invokes the receiver's entry-point routine (i.e., the method mapped to its selector). The detachNewThreadSelector:toTarget:withObject: method is functionally equivalent to the NSObject performSelectorInBackground:withObject: method. The NSThread initWithTarget:selector:object: method, by contrast, creates a new thread object but does not start it. The NSThread start instance method is invoked on an initialized thread to begin executing the receiver's entry-point routine, as shown in Listing 17-7.

Listing 17-7. Using the NSThread initWithTarget:selector:object: Method

```
ConcurrentProcessor *processor = [ConcurrentProcessor new];
NSThread *computeThread = [[NSThread alloc] initWithTarget:processor
                                      selector:@selector(computeTask:)
                                        object:nil];
[computeThread setThreadPriority:0.5];
[computeThread start];
```

Listing 17-7 shows that the initialization method creates and initializes a new NSThread instance. It sets the selector, the target receiver instance, and an object that can be passed as a parameter to the entry-point routine. The initWithTarget:selector:object: method returns the initialized NSThread instance, hence it can be used to configure the thread prior to invoking the start method. Also shown in Listing 17-7, prior to starting the thread its priority is set using the instance method setThreadPriority:.

As noted previously, the NSThread API includes a number of methods for configuring a thread, determining its execution state, and querying its environment. These enable you to set the thread priority, stack size, and thread dictionary; retrieve the current thread and call stack information; pause the thread, and a variety of other operations. As an example, the following statement pauses the current thread for 5 seconds.

```
[NSThread sleepForTimeInterval:5.0];
```

Thread Synchronization

If you decide to use threads for concurrent programming, the Objective-C platform provides several mechanisms to manage shared state and perform synchronization between threads. Specifically, the Foundation Framework includes a set of lock and condition variable APIs that provide object-oriented implementations of these mechanisms, as you will see next.

Locks

The Foundation Framework includes several classes (NSLock, NSRecursiveLock, NSConditionLock, NSDistributedLock) that implement various types of locks for synchronizing access to shared state. A lock is used to protect a *critical section*, that is, a section of code that accesses shared data or a resource, which must not be concurrently executed by multiple threads.

NSLock implements a basic mutual exclusion (mutex) lock for concurrent programming. It conforms to the NSLocking protocol and thus implements the lock and unlock methods to acquire and release a lock accordingly. Earlier in this chapter, you learned about the @synchronized primitive, an Objective-C language feature that implements a mutex lock comparable to NSLock. Key differences between the two is that 1) the @synchronized directive implicitly creates the lock, whereas the NSLock API directly creates the lock, and 2) the @synchronized directive implicitly provides an exception handler for the critical section, whereas the NSLock class does not provide this functionality. Listing 17-8 illustrates use of the NSLock APIs to protect a critical section.

Listing 17-8. Using an NSLock Instance to Protect a Critical Section

```
NSLock *computeLock = [NSLock new];
...
[computeLock lock];
// Critical section code
...
[computeLock unlock];
```

The NSDistributedLock class defines a lock that can be used by multiple applications on multiple hosts to control access to a shared resource. Unlike the NSLock class, an NSDistributedLock instance doesn't enforce mutual exclusion, but rather it reports when the lock is busy and it is up to the code using the lock to proceed appropriately based on the lock status. Listing 17-9 creates a distributed lock using the path of a file (named /hello.lck) that you would like to use as the locking system object.

Listing 17-9. Using an NSDistributedLock Instance to Control Access to a Resource

```
NSDistributedLock *fileLock = [NSDistributedLock lockWithPath:@"/hello.lck"];
// Access resource
...
...
// Unlock resource
[fileLock unlock];
```

The NSDistributedLock does not conform to the NSLocking protocol. Also, because this lock is implemented using the file system, the lock must be released explicitly. If an application terminates while holding a distributed lock, other clients must use the NSDistributedLock breakLock method to break a lock in this scenario.

The NSConditionLock class defines a mutex lock that can be acquired and released only under certain conditions, where the condition is an integer value that you define. Condition locks are normally used to ensure that tasks are performed in a specific order; for example, in a producer-consumer flow between threads. Listing 17-10 creates a conditional lock that is used to acquire a lock when a specified condition occurs.

Listing 17-10. Using an NSConditionLock Instance to Control Access to a Resource

```
NSConditionLock *datalock = [[NSConditionLock alloc] initWithCondition:NO];
...
// Acquire lock - no data in buffer
[dataLock lock];
// Add data to buffer
...
// Unlock with condition - data in buffer
[dataLock unlockWithCondition:YES];
```

The NSRecursiveLock class defines a lock that can be acquired multiple times by the same thread without causing deadlock. It keeps track of how many times it was acquired and must be balanced by corresponding calls to unlock the object before the lock is released.

Conditions

Condition variables are a type of lock that can be used to synchronize the order in which operations proceed. In contrast to a lock, a thread trying to acquire a condition remains blocked until that condition is explicitly signaled by another thread. In addition, a thread waiting on a condition remains blocked until that condition is explicitly signaled by another thread. In effect, condition variables allow threads to synchronize based upon the actual value of data.

The Foundation Framework NSCondition class implements a condition variable. The logic for using a condition object is as follows:

1. Lock the condition object and check its corresponding BOOL conditional expression.

2. If the conditional expression evaluates to YES, perform associated task and then go to step 4.

3. If the conditional expression evaluates to NO, block the thread using the condition object's wait or waitUntilDate: methods, then retest (step 2).

4. Optionally, signal the condition object again using its signal or broadcast methods, or change the value of the conditional expression.

5. Unlock the condition object.

Listing 17-11 provides the template for an entry-point routine that uses an NSCondition object named condition to consume and process data.

Listing 17-11. Using an NSCondition Instance to Synchronize Consumer Operations on Shared Data

```
- (void)consumerTask
{
  @autoreleasepool
  {
    // Acquire lock for condition and test boolean condition
    [condition lock];
    while (!self.dataAvailable)
```

```
   {
     [condition wait];
   }

   // Data available, now process it (code not provided here)
   ...

   // Finished processing, update predicate value and signal condition
   self.dataAvailable = NO;
   [condition signal];

   // Unlock condition
   [condition unlock];
  }
}
```

The corresponding entry-point routine that produces data for processing by the consumerTask method is shown in Listing 17-12.

Listing 17-12. Using an NSCondition Instance to Synchronize Producer Operations on Shared Data

```
- (void)producerTask
{
  @autoreleasepool
  {
    // Acquire lock for condition and test boolean condition
    [condition lock];
    while (self.dataAvailable)
    {
      [condition wait];
    }

    // Retrieve data for processing (code not provided here)
    ....

    // Finished retrieving data, update predicate value and signal condition
    self.dataAvailable = YES;
    [condition signal];

    // Unlock condition
    [condition unlock];
  }
}
```

As shown in Listings 17-11 and 17-12, condition variables provide an effective mechanism to both control access to shared data and to synchronize operations on that data.

Using Threads for Concurrency

Now that you have learned about threads and synchronization, you will implement an example program that performs concurrent processing using threads and these synchronization mechanisms. In Xcode, create a new project by selecting **New ➤ Project ...** from the Xcode File menu. In the **New Project Assistant** pane, create a command-line application. In the **Project Options** window, specify **ConcurrentThreads** for the Product Name, choose **Foundation** for the Project Type, and select ARC memory management by checking the **Use Automatic Reference Counting** check box. Specify the location in your file system where you want the project to be created (if necessary, select **New Folder** and enter the name and location for the folder), uncheck the **Source Control** check box, and then click the **Create** button.

Next, you will create the class with a method that will be executed in a separate thread. Select **New ➤ File ...** from the Xcode File menu, select the **Objective-C** class template, and name the class **ConcurrentProcessor**. Select the **ConcurrentThreads** folder for the files location and the **ConcurrentThreads** project as the target, and then click the **Create** button. In the Xcode project navigator pane, select the **ConcurrentProcessor.h** file and update the class interface, as shown in Listing 17-13.

Listing 17-13. ConcurrentProcessor Interface

```
#import <Foundation/Foundation.h>

@interface ConcurrentProcessor : NSObject

@property (readwrite) BOOL isFinished;
@property (readonly) NSInteger computeResult;

- (void)computeTask:(id)data;

@end
```

The interface declares two properties and a single method. The method `computeTask:` is the method that will be executed in a separate thread. This method performs computations, where its input parameter is the number of computations to perform. The property `isFinished` is used to signal completion of the computations in the thread(s) that execute the method. The property `computeResult` contains the results of the computation. OK, now using the Xcode project navigator, select the **ConcurrentProcessor.m** file and update it as shown in Listing 17-14.

Listing 17-14. ConcurrentProcessor Implementation

```
#import "ConcurrentProcessor.h"

@interface ConcurrentProcessor()
@property (readwrite) NSInteger computeResult;
@end
```

```objc
@implementation ConcurrentProcessor
{
  NSString *computeID;        // Unique object for @synchronize lock
  NSUInteger computeTasks;    // Count of number of concurrent compute tasks
  NSLock *computeLock;        // lock object
}

- (id)init
{
  if ((self = [super init]))
  {
    _isFinished = NO;
    _computeResult = 0;
    computeLock = [NSLock new];
    computeID = @"1";
    computeTasks = 0;
  }
  return self;
}

- (void)computeTask:(id)data
{
  NSAssert(([data isKindOfClass:[NSNumber class]]), @"Not an NSNumber instance");
  NSUInteger computations = [data unsignedIntegerValue];
  @autoreleasepool
  {
    @try
    {
      // Obtain lock and increment number of active tasks
      if ([[NSThread currentThread] isCancelled])
      {
        return;
      }
      @synchronized(computeID)
      {
        computeTasks++;
      }

      // Obtain lock and perform computation in critical section
      [computeLock lock];
      if ([[NSThread currentThread] isCancelled])
      {
        [computeLock unlock];
        return;
      }
      NSLog(@"Performing computations");
      for (int ii=0; ii<computations; ii++)
      {
        self.computeResult = self.computeResult + 1;
      }
```

```
    [computeLock unlock];
    // Simulate additional processing time (outside of critical section)
    [NSThread sleepForTimeInterval:1.0];

    // Decrement number of active tasks, if none left update flag
    @synchronized(computeID)
    {
      computeTasks--;
      if (!computeTasks)
      {
        self.isFinished = YES;
      }
    }
  }
  @catch (NSException *ex) {}
  }
}

@end
```

The file begins by declaring a class extension that enables write access for the computeResult property. Next, the implementation begins by declaring several private instance variables used for thread management and synchronization. Of note is the computeTasks variable; it contains a count of the number of threads concurrently executing the computeTask: method. The init method initializes ConcurrentProcessor objects, setting variables to the appropriate initial values.

Now let's examine the computeTask: method. First, observe that the method is surrounded by an autorelease pool and a try-catch exception block. These are required to ensure that objects are not leaked from the thread in which the method executes and that it handles any thrown exceptions (each thread is responsible for handling its own exceptions). Because this method can be executed concurrently by multiple threads and it also accesses and updates shared data, access to this data must be synchronized. The code uses the @synchronized directive to control access to the computeTasks variable, thereby enabling it to be updated by one thread at a time.

```
@synchronized(computeID)
{
  computeTasks++;
}
```

The method is also implemented to support thread cancellation, and thus periodically checks the state of the thread and exits if it is cancelled.

```
if ([[NSThread currentThread] isCancelled])
{
  return;
}
```

Next, the method contains code to perform its computations. This simple computation merely increments the value of the computeResult property the number of times specified by the method's input parameter. This code must be performed within a critical section to enforce synchronized access to its shared data. The code acquires a lock to the NSLock instance. Once the lock is obtained, it tests to see if the thread has been cancelled, and if so, it releases the lock and exits the thread without performing its computations.

```
[computeLock lock];
if ([[NSThread currentThread] isCancelled])
{
  [computeLock unlock];
  return;
}
```

The code then performs its computations and releases the lock. Next, the thread pauses for one second to simulate additional processing performed outside of the critical section (hence concurrently).

```
[computeLock unlock];
[NSThread sleepForTimeInterval:1.0];
```

The method concludes by decrementing the number of threads executing it, and setting the isFinished property if none remain. This logic is all implemented within a synchronized block to ensure access by only one thread at a time.

```
@synchronized(computeID)
{
  computeTasks--;
  if (!computeTasks)
  {
    self.isFinished = YES;
  }
}
```

Now that you have finished implementing the ConcurrentProcessor class, let's move on to the main() function. In the Xcode project navigator, select the **main.m** file and update the main() function, as shown in Listing 17-15.

Listing 17-15. ConcurrentThreads main() Function

```
#import <Foundation/Foundation.h>
#import "ConcurrentProcessor.h"

int main(int argc, const char * argv[])
{
  @autoreleasepool
  {
    ConcurrentProcessor *processor = [ConcurrentProcessor new];
    [processor performSelectorInBackground:@selector(computeTask:)
                            withObject:[NSNumber numberWithUnsignedInt:5]];
    [processor performSelectorInBackground:@selector(computeTask:)
                            withObject:[NSNumber numberWithUnsignedInt:10]];
    [processor performSelectorInBackground:@selector(computeTask:)
                            withObject:[NSNumber numberWithUnsignedInt:20]];
```

```
    while (!processor.isFinished)
        ;
    NSLog(@"Computation result = %ld", processor.computeResult);
  }
  return 0;
}
```

The main() function begins by creating a ConcurrentProcessor object. It then executes its computeTask: method with a new background thread using its performSelectorInBackground: method. This method is executed with three separate threads, each time providing a different input value for the number of computations performed. The function then uses a conditional expression to test if all of the threads have finished executing the computeTask: method. Once this occurs, the result of the computation is logged to the output pane.

When you compile and run the program, you should observe the messages in the output pane shown in Figure 17-5.

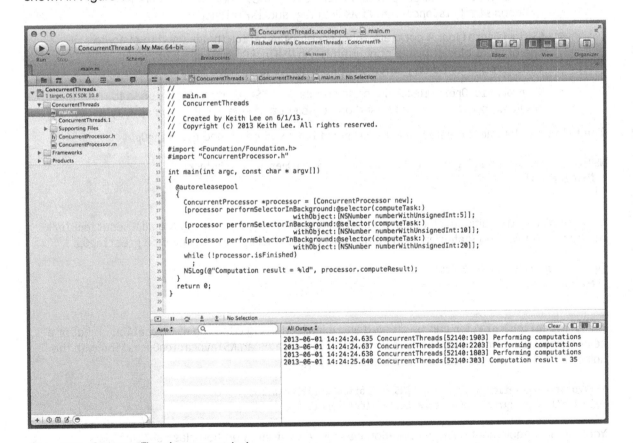

Figure 17-5. ConcurrentThreads program output

This program demonstrates the use of threads to perform concurrent programming. It also illustrates some of the complexities involved with thread management and synchronization. In the next section, you will learn about a different mechanism for concurrent programming, operations and operation queues.

Operations and Operation Queues

In Chapter 11, you learned about operation objects, instances of the NSOperation class (and its subclasses) that encapsulate the code and data for a single task. As an operation object encapsulates a single unit of work, it is an ideal vehicle for implementing concurrent programming. The Foundation Framework includes the following three operation classes:

- NSOperation: The base (abstract) class for defining operation objects. For nonconcurrent tasks, a concrete subclass typically only needs to override the main method. For concurrent tasks, you must override at a minimum the methods start, isConcurrent, isExecuting, and isFinished.

- NSBlockOperation: A concrete subclass of NSOperation that is used to execute one or more block objects concurrently. An NSBlockOperation object is considered finished only when all of its block objects have finished execution.

- NSInvocationOperation: A concrete subclass of NSOperation that is used to create an operation object based on an object and selector that you specify.

The following statement creates an NSBlockOperation instance named greetingOp.

```
NSBlockOperation* greetingOp = [NSBlockOperation blockOperationWithBlock: ^{
  NSLog(@"Hello, World!");
}];
```

You can also add additional blocks to an NSBlockOperation instance using the addExecutionBlock: method. The following statement adds a block to the NSBlockOperation instance greetingOp.

```
[greetingOp addExecutionBlock: ^{
  NSLog(@"Goodbye");
}];
```

An NSInvocationOperation can be created and initialized using either an NSInvocation object or a selector and receiver object. The following statement creates an NSInvocationOperation with the selector hello and a receiver object named greetingObj.

```
NSInvocationOperation invokeOp = [[NSInvocationOperation alloc]
  initWithTarget:greetingObj selector:@selector(hello)];
```

You can also implement custom operation classes. A custom operation class subclasses NSOperation and must implement, at a minimum, the main method to perform the desired task. Optionally, it can also provide the following functionality:

- Custom initialization methods

- Custom helper methods (invoked via the main method)

- Accessor methods for setting data values and accessing the results of the operation

- Methods that conform the class to the NSCoding protocol (to support archiving the object)

Operation objects support a variety of features that facilitate concurrent programming, several of which are

- Establishing dependencies between operation objects, thereby enabling you to control their order of execution.

- Creating a completion block that is executed after an operation's main task has finished.

- Retrieving an operation's execution state.

- Prioritizing operations in an operation queue.

- Cancelling operations.

An operation object is executed by invoking its start method. The default implementation of this method executes the operation's task (implemented by its main method) synchronously. Hence, you may be wondering how operation objects support concurrent programming. Well, operation objects are typically executed by adding them to operation queues, which provide built-in support for executing operations concurrently. Specifically, operation queues provide threads for executing operations.

An operation queue is a mechanism that provides the capability to execute operations concurrently. The Foundation Framework NSOperationQueue class is an Objective-C implementation of an operation queue. An operation can be added to an NSOperationQueue instance as a block object or an instance of a subclass of NSOperation. An operation queue manages the execution of operations. Thus it includes methods to manage operations in the queue, manage the number of running operations, suspend operations, and retrieve specific queues. Listing 17-16 creates and initializes an NSOperationQueue instance and then uses its addOperationWithBlock: method to submit a block object to the queue.

Listing 17-16. Adding a Block Object to an Operation Queue

```
NSOperationQueue *queue = [NSOperationQueue new];
[queue addOperationWithBlock: ^{
  NSLog(@"Hello, World!");
  }];
[queue waitUntilAllOperationsAreFinished];
```

Once an operation is added to a queue, it remains in the queue until it is explicitly cancelled or finishes executing its task. You can cancel an (NSOperation) object added to an operation queue by invoking its cancel method or by invoking the cancelAllOperations method on the queue.

The execution order of operations within a queue is a function of the priority level of each operation and the interoperation object dependencies. The current implementation of NSOperationQueue uses Grand Central Dispatch to initiate execution of their operations. As a result, each operation in the queue is executed in a separate thread.

Operation objects and operation queues provide an object-oriented mechanism for performing asynchronous, concurrent programming. They eliminate the need for low-level thread management, and simplify synchronization and coordination of execution for multiple interdependent tasks. Because they utilize system services that can scale dynamically in response to resource availability and utilization, they ensure that tasks are executed as quickly and as efficiently as possible.

Executing Operation Objects Manually

Although operation objects are typically executed using operation queues, it is possible to start an operation object manually (i.e., not add it to a queue). To do this, you must code the operation as a *concurrent operation* in order to have it execute it asynchronously. This is accomplished by performing the following steps:

- *Override the start method.* This method should be updated to execute the operation asynchronously, typically by invoking its main method in a new thread.

- *Override the main method (optional).* In this method, you implement the task associated with the operation. If preferred, you can skip this method and implement the task in the start method, but overriding the main method provides a cleaner design that is consistent with the intent.

- *Configure and manage the operation's execution environment.* Concurrent operations must set up their environment and report its status to clients. Specifically, the isExecuting, isFinished, and isConcurrent methods must return appropriate values relative to the operation's state, and these methods must be thread-safe. These methods must also generate the appropriate key-value (KVO) observer notifications when these values change.

> **Note**   Key-value observing is an Objective-C language mechanism that enables objects to be notified of changes to specified properties of other objects. Chapter 18 examines key-value programming in depth.

To highlight the differences between a nonconcurrent operation object (typically executed via an operation queue) versus a concurrent operation object, let's look at some code. Listing 17-17 illustrates the implementation of a custom, nonconcurrent operation class named GreetingOperation.

Listing 17-17. Minimal Implementation of a Custom, Nonconcurrent Operation Class

```
@implementation GreetingOperation

- (void)main
{
  @autoreleasepool
  {
    @try
    {
      if (![self isCancelled])
```

```
    {
        // Insert code to implement the task below
        NSLog(@"Hello, World!");
        [NSThread sleepForTimeInterval:3.0];
        NSLog(@"Goodbye, World!");
    }
    }
    @catch (NSException *ex) {}
    }
}

@end
```

As shown in Listing 17-17, the code to perform the task is implemented in the main method. Note that this method includes an autorelease pool and a try-catch block. The autorelease pool prevents memory leaks from the associated thread, while the try-catch block is required to prevent any exceptions from leaving the scope of this thread. The main method also checks if the operation is cancelled in order to quickly terminate its execution if it is no longer needed. To invoke this operation asynchronously, you can add it to an operation queue, as shown in Listing 17-18.

Listing 17-18. Executing a Custom Operation in an Operation Queue

```
NSOperationQueue *queue = [NSOperationQueue new];
GreetingOperation *greetingOp = [GreetingOperation new];
[greetingOp setThreadPriority:0.5];
[queue addOperation:greetingOp];
[queue waitUntilAllOperationsAreFinished];
```

This demonstrates the steps required to implement a nonconcurrent operation and submit it to an operation queue for execution. In the next section, you will implement a concurrent operation to understand the differences between the two options.

Implementing Concurrent Operations

Now you will create a program that implements a custom, concurrent operation. It will provide the same functionality as the program shown in Listing 17-14 and enable you to compare the differences between the two implementations. In Xcode, create a new project by selecting **New ➤ Project ...** from the Xcode File menu. In the **New Project Assistant** pane, create a command-line application. In the **Project Options** window, specify **GreetingOperation** for the Product Name, choose **Foundation** for the Project Type, and select ARC memory management by checking the **Use Automatic Reference Counting** check box. Specify the location in your file system where you want the project to be created (if necessary, select **New Folder** and enter the name and location for the folder), uncheck the **Source Control** check box, and then click the **Create** button.

Next you will create the custom operation class. Select **New ➤ File ...** from the Xcode File menu, select the **Objective-C** class template, and name the class **GreetingOperation**. Make the class a subclass of **NSOperation**, select the **GreetingOperation** folder for the files location and the **GreetingOperation** project as the target, and then click the **Create** button. In the Xcode project navigator pane, select the **GreetingOperation.m** file and update the class implementation, as shown in Listing 17-19.

Listing 17-19. GreetingOperation Implementation

```objc
#import "GreetingOperation.h"

@implementation GreetingOperation
{
  BOOL finished;
  BOOL executing;
}

- (id)init
{
  if ((self = [super init]))
  {
    executing = NO;
    finished = NO;
  }
  return self;
}

- (void)start
{
  // If cancelled just return
  if ([self isCancelled])
  {
    [self willChangeValueForKey:@"isFinished"];
    finished = YES;
    [self didChangeValueForKey:@"isFinished"];
    return;
  }

  // Now execute in main method a separate thread
  [self willChangeValueForKey:@"isExecuting"];
  [NSThread detachNewThreadSelector:@selector(main) toTarget:self withObject:nil];
  executing = YES;
  [self didChangeValueForKey:@"isExecuting"];
}

- (void)main
{
  @autoreleasepool
  {
    @try
    {
      if (![self isCancelled])
      {
        NSLog(@"Hello, World!");
        // Pause to simulate processing being performed by task
        [NSThread sleepForTimeInterval:3.0];
        NSLog(@"Goodbye, World!");
```

```
      [self willChangeValueForKey:@"isFinished"];
      [self willChangeValueForKey:@"isExecuting"];
      executing = NO;
      finished = YES;
      [self didChangeValueForKey:@"isExecuting"];
      [self didChangeValueForKey:@"isFinished"];
    }
  }
  @catch (NSException *ex) {}
  }
}

- (BOOL)isConcurrent
{
  return YES;
}

- (BOOL)isExecuting
{
  return executing;
}

- (BOOL)isFinished
{
  return finished;
}

@end
```

Compared to the nonconcurrent GreetingOperation implementation in Listing 17-17, there are a number of changes. First, observe the declaration of two private variables.

```
{
  BOOL finished;
  BOOL executing;
}
```

These variables are used to set and return the appropriate values for the isFinished and isExecuting methods. Recall that these methods (along with the isConcurrent method) must be overridden for concurrent operations. Now let's look at the implementation of the start method. This was not implemented for the nonconcurrent version of the GreetingOperation class. First, it checks to see whether or not the operation has been cancelled; if it has, it simply sets the finished variable appropriately for KVO notifications and returns.

```
if ([self isCancelled])
{
  [self willChangeValueForKey:@"isFinished"];
  finished = YES;
  [self didChangeValueForKey:@"isFinished"];
  return;
}
```

If not cancelled, the code sets up a new thread and uses it to invoke the `main` method that implements the associated task, while also performing the appropriate KVO notifications.

```
[self willChangeValueForKey:@"isExecuting"];
[NSThread detachNewThreadSelector:@selector(main) toTarget:self withObject:nil];
executing = YES;
[self didChangeValueForKey:@"isExecuting"];
```

Now let's examine the class's `main` method. This method has identical functionality to that of the `main` method in Listing 17-14, with the addition of KVO notifications to indicate the current operation state. Also note the statement that pauses the thread for three seconds to simulate task processing.

```
[NSThread sleepForTimeInterval:3.0];
```

Finally, the remaining methods implement the required `isExecuting`, `isFinished`, and `isConcurrent` methods, returning the appropriate value in each case.

OK, now that you have finished implementing the custom operation class, let's move on to the `main()` function. In the Xcode project navigator, select the **main.m** file and update the `main()` function, as shown in Listing 17-20.

Listing 17-20. GreetingOperation main() Function

```
#import <Foundation/Foundation.h>
#import "GreetingOperation.h"

int main(int argc, const char * argv[])
{
  @autoreleasepool
  {
    GreetingOperation *greetingOp = [GreetingOperation new];
    [greetingOp start];
    while (![greetingOp isFinished])
      ;
  }
  return 0;
}
```

The `main()` function begins by creating a `GreetingOperation` object. It then executes the operation by invoking its `start` method. Finally, a conditional expression using the object's `isFinished` method is used to end execution of the program when the concurrent operation is finished.

When you compile and run the program, you should observe the messages in the output pane shown in Figure 17-6.

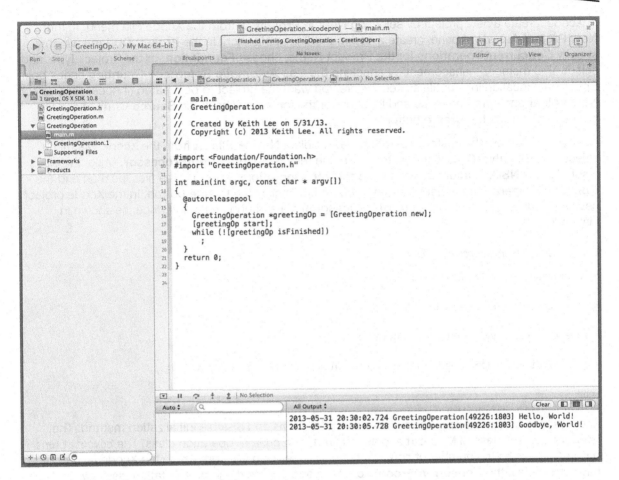

Figure 17-6. GreetingOperation program output

In the output pane, the task displays the initial greeting followed by a delay of approximately 3 seconds, and then the final message. The program exits when the thread finishes execution per the conditional expression. As you learned from this example, a considerable amount of additional functionality must be coded to correctly implement a custom concurrent operation class. Hence, you should only do this if you need to have an operation object execute asynchronously without adding it to a queue.

Using Operation Queues for Concurrency

You have implemented a concurrent program using threads and a concurrent operation, so now you will implement a program that uses operations and an operation queue for concurrency. This program contains the same functionality of the ConcurrentThreads program that you implemented earlier in this chapter. This will enable you to compare the use of the different APIs and mechanisms for concurrent programming.

In Xcode, create a new project by selecting **New ➤ Project ...** from the Xcode File menu. In the **New Project Assistant** pane, create a command-line application. In the **Project Options** window, specify **ConcurrentOperations** for the Product Name, choose **Foundation** for the Project Type, and select ARC memory management by checking the **Use Automatic Reference Counting** check box. Specify the location in your file system where you want the project to be created (if necessary, select **New Folder** and enter the name and location for the folder), uncheck the **Source Control** check box, and then click the **Create** button.

Next you will create the custom operation class. Select **New ➤ File ...** from the Xcode File menu, select the **Objective-C** class template, and name the class **ConcurrentProcessor**. Make the class a subclass of **NSOperation**, select the **ConcurrentOperations** folder for the files location and the **ConcurrentOperations** project as the target, and then click the **Create** button. In the Xcode project navigator pane, select the **ConcurrentProcessor.m** file and update the interface, as shown in Listing 17-21.

Listing 17-21. ConcurrentProcessor Interface

```
#import <Foundation/Foundation.h>

@interface ConcurrentProcessor : NSOperation

@property (readonly) NSUInteger computations;

- (id)initWithData:(NSInteger *)result computations:(NSUInteger)computations;

@end
```

The interface contains one property named `computations` and a single initialization method. The interface is a subclass of `NSOperation`, as required for a custom operation class. The `computations` property specifies the number of computations the operation will perform. In the Xcode project navigator, select the **ConcurrentProcessor.m** file and update the implementation, as shown in Listing 17-22.

Listing 17-22. ConcurrentProcessor Implementation

```
#import "ConcurrentProcessor.h"

@implementation ConcurrentProcessor
{
  NSInteger *computeResult;
}

- (id)initWithData:(NSInteger *)result computations:(NSUInteger)computations
{
  if ((self = [super init]))
  {
    _computations = computations;
    computeResult = result;
  }
  return self;
}
```

```
- (void)main
{
  @autoreleasepool
  {
    @try
    {
      if (![self isCancelled])
      {
        NSLog(@"Performing %ld computations", self.computations);
        [NSThread sleepForTimeInterval:1.0];
        for (int ii=0; ii<self.computations; ii++)
        {
          *computeResult = *computeResult + 1;
        }
      }
    }
    @catch (NSException *ex) {}
  }
}
@end
```

The implementation begins by declaring a private instance variable, computeResult, which contains the address of the memory location where the computation result is stored. The init: method sets the computations property and computeResult variable to the input parameters. The main method performs the compute task for the operation. It includes an autorelease pool and a try-catch block, as recommended for thread-based execution of operation objects. The main method also checks if the operation is cancelled in order to quickly terminate its execution if it is no longer needed. The computation logic simply increments the computation result for the number of computations specified. Notice here that, unlike with the concurrent operation shown in Listing 17-19 (the GreetingOperation program), thread execution state (i.e., isFinished and isExecuting) is not updated. This is performed automatically by the operation queue. Also note that, unlike the thread-based ConcurrentProcessor implementation (as shown in Listing 17-14), synchronization mechanisms are not required. This is due to the fact that interoperation dependencies can be declared. These prevent operations from concurrently accessing shared data and also synchronize the order that operations are executed.

Now let's move on to the main() function. In the Xcode project navigator, select the **main.m** file and update the main() function, as shown in Listing 17-23.

Listing 17-23. ConcurrentOperations main() Function

```
#import <Foundation/Foundation.h>
#import "ConcurrentProcessor.h"

int main(int argc, const char * argv[])
{
  @autoreleasepool
  {
    NSOperationQueue *queue = [[NSOperationQueue alloc] init];
    NSInteger result = 0;
```

```
    // Create operation objects
    ConcurrentProcessor *proc1 = [[ConcurrentProcessor alloc]initWithData:&result
                                                    computations:5];
    ConcurrentProcessor *proc2 = [[ConcurrentProcessor alloc]initWithData:&result
                                                    computations:10];
    ConcurrentProcessor *proc3 = [[ConcurrentProcessor alloc]initWithData:&result
                                                    computations:20];
    NSArray *operations = @[proc1, proc2, proc3];

    // Add inter-operation dependencies
    [proc2 addDependency:proc1];
    [proc3 addDependency:proc2];

    // Add operations to queue to start execution
    [queue addOperations:operations waitUntilFinished:NO];

    // Wait until all operations are finished, then display result
    [queue waitUntilAllOperationsAreFinished];
    NSLog(@"Computation result = %ld", result);
  }
  return 0;
}
```

The method begins by creating an operation queue and the variable, computeResult, which holds the result of the computation for the operations. Then three operation objects are created, each performing a different number of computations, and these are combined in an NSArray instance. Next, dependencies between the operations are defined. In this case, operation 1 (proc1) must complete before operation 2 (proc2), and operation 2 must complete before operation 3 (proc3). The operations are then added to the queue to begin asynchronous execution. The code waits until all of the operations have finished execution and then logs the computation result to the output pane.

When you compile and run the program, you should observe the messages in the output pane shown in Figure 17-7.

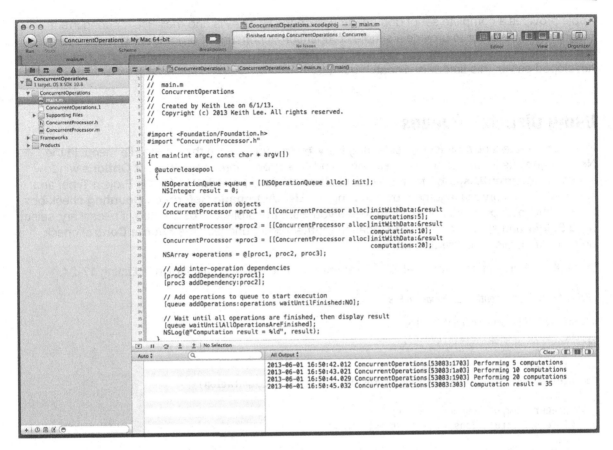

Figure 17-7. ConcurrentOperations program output

The results are identical to that obtained with the thread-based version of this program, with considerably less code complexity. This program demonstrates how operation objects and queues can greatly simplify concurrent programming. In effect, they enable you to execute tasks asynchronously and concurrently without having to perform low-level thread-based programming, and manage the resulting complexity. They enable you to manage dependencies among various operations, cancel or suspend them, and provide a higher-level, object-oriented abstraction for concurrent programming. In the next section, you will explore Grand Central Dispatch, a C-based mechanism for asynchronous/concurrent programming.

Grand Central Dispatch

Grand Central Dispatch (GCD) is a set of language features, C-based APIs, and system enhancements that support the use of dispatch queues for executing tasks. GCD dispatch queues can be used to execute code synchronously or asynchronously, and to perform tasks serially or concurrently. As with operation queues, dispatch queues are easier to use than threads and more efficient at executing asynchronous or concurrent tasks.

Apple provides a complete set of documentation on the GCD APIs and their use for concurrent programming. In order to provide a simple comparison of concurrent programming using operation queues and dispatch queues, you will now reimplement the ConcurrentOperations program that you developed earlier, this time with dispatch queues.

Using Dispatch Queues

In Xcode, create a new project by selecting **New ➤ Project ...** from the Xcode File menu. In the **New Project Assistant** pane, create a command-line application. In the **Project Options** window, specify **ConcurrentDispatch** for the Product Name, choose **Foundation** for the Project Type, and select ARC memory management by checking the **Use Automatic Reference Counting** check box. Specify the location in your file system where you want the project to be created (if necessary, select **New Folder** and enter the name and location for the folder), uncheck the **Source Control** check box, and then click the **Create** button.

In the Xcode project navigator, select the **main.m** file and update it as shown in Listing 17-24.

Listing 17-24. ConcurrentDispatch main.m File

```objc
#import <Foundation/Foundation.h>
typedef void (^ComputeTask)(void);

/* Retrieve a block used to download a URL */
ComputeTask getComputeTask(NSInteger *result, NSUInteger computation)
{
  NSInteger *computeResult = result;
  NSUInteger computations = computation;
  return ^{
    [NSThread sleepForTimeInterval:1.0];
    NSLog(@"Performing %ld computations", computations);
    for (int ii=0; ii<computations; ii++)
    {
      *computeResult = *computeResult + 1;
    }
  };
}

int main(int argc, const char * argv[])
{
  @autoreleasepool
  {
    NSInteger computeResult;

    // Create serial queue and group
    dispatch_queue_t serialQueue = dispatch_queue_create("MySerialQueue",
                                            DISPATCH_QUEUE_SERIAL);
    dispatch_group_t group = dispatch_group_create();
```

```
    // Add tasks to queue
    dispatch_group_async(group, serialQueue, getComputeTask(&computeResult, 5));
    dispatch_group_async(group, serialQueue, getComputeTask(&computeResult, 10));
    dispatch_group_async(group, serialQueue, getComputeTask(&computeResult, 20));

    // Block until all tasks from group are completed, then display results
    dispatch_group_wait(group, DISPATCH_TIME_FOREVER);
    NSLog(@"Computation result = %ld", computeResult);

  }
  return 0;
}
```

The listing includes, in addition to the main() function, a function named computeTask that is identical in functionality to that provided by the task in the ConcurrentOperations program, as shown in the main method in Listing 17-22.

The main() function uses GCD APIs to create and asynchronously dispatch three tasks for serial execution, thereby coordinating execution properly and preventing concurrent access to shared data. It creates a serial dispatch queue and a dispatch group.

```
dispatch_queue_t serialQueue = dispatch_queue_create("MySerialQueue",
                                          DISPATCH_QUEUE_SERIAL);
dispatch_group_t group = dispatch_group_create();
```

The code then dispatches the three tasks to the queue.

```
dispatch_group_async(group, serialQueue, getComputeTask(&computeResult, 5));
dispatch_group_async(group, serialQueue, getComputeTask(&computeResult, 10));
dispatch_group_async(group, serialQueue, getComputeTask(&computeResult, 20));
```

Notice that the task to be executed is specified by a block literal retrieved by the computeTask() function, each time providing a different argument for the number of computations. Again, this is identical to what was done for the ConcurrentOperations program. The GCD dispatch_group_async() function causes these tasks to be performed asynchronously and, as the queue is a serial queue, in serial order. Next, the GCD dispatch_group_wait() function is used to block the main thread until the tasks complete.

```
dispatch_group_wait(group, DISPATCH_TIME_FOREVER);
```

Now save, compile, and run the BlockConcurrentTasks program and observe the messages in the output pane (as shown in Figure 17-8).

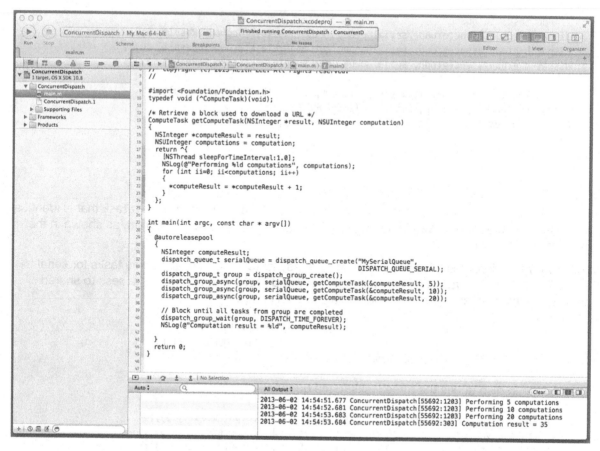

```
//
#import <Foundation/Foundation.h>
typedef void (^ComputeTask)(void);

/* Retrieve a block used to download a URL */
ComputeTask getComputeTask(NSInteger *result, NSUInteger computation)
{
    NSInteger *computeResult = result;
    NSUInteger computations = computation;
    return ^{
        [NSThread sleepForTimeInterval:1.0];
        NSLog(@"Performing %ld computations", computations);
        for (int ii=0; ii<computations; ii++)
        {
            *computeResult = *computeResult + 1;
        }
    };
}

int main(int argc, const char * argv[])
{
    @autoreleasepool
    {
        NSInteger computeResult;
        dispatch_queue_t serialQueue = dispatch_queue_create("MySerialQueue",
                                                DISPATCH_QUEUE_SERIAL);
        dispatch_group_t group = dispatch_group_create();
        dispatch_group_async(group, serialQueue, getComputeTask(&computeResult, 5));
        dispatch_group_async(group, serialQueue, getComputeTask(&computeResult, 10));
        dispatch_group_async(group, serialQueue, getComputeTask(&computeResult, 20));

        // Block until all tasks from group are completed
        dispatch_group_wait(group, DISPATCH_TIME_FOREVER);
        NSLog(@"Computation result = %ld", computeResult);

    }
    return 0;
}
```

```
2013-06-02 14:54:51.677 ConcurrentDispatch[55692:1203] Performing 5 computations
2013-06-02 14:54:52.681 ConcurrentDispatch[55692:1203] Performing 10 computations
2013-06-02 14:54:53.683 ConcurrentDispatch[55692:1203] Performing 20 computations
2013-06-02 14:54:53.684 ConcurrentDispatch[55692:303] Computation result = 35
```

Figure 17-8. Testing the ConcurrentDispatch project

The messages in the output pane show that the concurrent tasks were performed successfully. Compared to the ConcurrentOperations program, the version using GCD dispatch queues. Although it employs C-based APIs, it required much less code.

Choosing the Right API for Concurrent Programming

This chapter has covered a variety of approaches for concurrent programming, so you have several options to choose from. To recap, the following are the available options:

- *Asynchronous APIs*. The Foundation Framework (along with the Cocoa and Cocoa Touch frameworks) includes a variety of APIs that perform asynchronous processing; examples include the NSURLConnection, NSFileHandle, and NSPort classes.

- *Threads*. APIs that use threads to implement concurrent programming. This includes the Foundation Framework message passing APIs, the NSThread class, and the synchronization mechanisms.

- *Operation queues.* NSOperation and NSOperationQueue are Objective-C APIs that can be used to implement concurrent programming using queues.

- *Dispatch queues.* Grand Central Dispatch is a C-based API and set of services that can be used to implement concurrent programming using dispatch queues.

In general, you should use the asynchronous APIs to implement asynchronous/concurrent processing if possible. These APIs use various technologies (threads, queues, etc.) to provide concurrency that scales with the capabilities of the system and enable your program design to align with the program style and capabilities of the Objective-C platform.

Although the Objective-C platform provides a number of language features and APIs to support thread-based concurrent programming, threads are not the recommendation approach for concurrent programming. Operation queues and dispatch queues are the preferred mechanism for asynchronous, concurrent processing. These should be used to concurrently perform tasks that are not supported by the asynchronous APIs, such as executing a long computation, background data processing, and so forth.

Operation and dispatch queues provide an asynchronous, queue-based approach that eliminate the need for low-level thread management and maximize system utilization and efficiency compared to thread-based programming. Operation queues, being object-based, have more overhead and utilize more resources than GCD dispatch queues. However, the higher-level, object-oriented API is consistent with the Objective-C platform and may be easier to use. In addition, operation queues provide support for complex interoperation dependencies, constraint-based execution, and management of operation objects.

GCD, as it provides a lower-level (C-based) API, is lightweight and provides better performance than operation queues. As shown by the example ConcurrentDispatch program, the GCD block-based approach can result in fewer lines of code that may minimize overall program complexity.

Finally, as operation and dispatch queues do not address real-time constraints, threads are still an appropriate mechanism for concurrent programming of real-time systems.

Roundup

In this chapter, you learned about concurrent programming and the various mechanisms and APIs available to support asynchronous/concurrent processing. As the chapter has shown, there are numerous options to choose from. In addition, concurrent programming is challenging and it is very important to understand the tradeoffs involved with each option under consideration. The following are key takeaways from this chapter:

- Concurrent processing implies the simultaneous execution of multiple tasks. It is a function of design, whereas parallel computing is a function of hardware. The motivations for concurrent processing are numerous, some of which include increased application throughput, increased system utilization, improved application responsiveness, and better mapping to the problem domain.

- Concurrent processing refers to multiple logical control flows that may execute in parallel. Asynchronous processing, on the other hand, is effectively a mechanism for the asynchronous (i.e., nonblocking) invocation of methods/functions.

In other words, the caller invokes the method and can continue processing while the method is being executed. Asynchronous processing can be implemented using a variety of devices, including concurrent programming APIs and services.

- The most common mechanisms used to implement concurrent programming in Objective-C are message passing, threads, synchronization mechanisms, operation queues, and dispatch queues.

- The Foundation Framework NSObject class includes a collection of methods that use the message-passing paradigm to invoke a method on an object with a thread.

- The NSThread class provides APIs that can be used to *explicitly* create and manage threads. The Objective-C language and Foundation Framework also include mechanisms for synchronizing shared data/resource access between concurrent threads.

- Operation objects and operation queues provide an object-oriented mechanism for performing asynchronous/concurrent programming. They eliminate the need for low-level thread management, and simplify synchronization and coordination of execution for multiple interdependent tasks.

- Grand Central Dispatch (GCD) is a set of language features, C-based APIs, and system enhancements that support the use of dispatch queues for executing tasks. GCD dispatch queues can be used to execute code synchronously or asynchronously, and to perform tasks serially or concurrently. Dispatch queues are easier to use than threads and more efficient at executing asynchronous or concurrent tasks.

Congratulations! You have just completed this detailed examination of concurrent programming on the Objective-C platform. This chapter was by far the longest to date and the material is a lot to absorb, so don't feel as if you have to master this all at once. Take your time to review its contents, and tinker with the examples to let it all sink in. When you're ready, turn the page to begin the final chapter on key-value programming.

Chapter 18

Key-Value Programming

Here you are, at the start of the final chapter of this book. Congratulations on the great job you've done throughout this journey! The advanced topic for this chapter is *key-value programming*, a set of language mechanisms and APIs that can enable you to both simplify program design and also implement more extensible and reusable code. The Objective-C key-value programming features are collectively referred to as *key-value coding* (KVC) and *key-value observing* (KVO). Key-value coding enables your code to access and manipulate an object's properties indirectly, by name (i.e., key), rather than through accessor methods or backing instance variables. Key-value observing enables objects to be notified of changes to the properties of other objects. In this chapter, you will learn the fundamentals of these technologies, key implementation details, and how to use them in your programs.

Key-Value Coding

As stated earlier, key-value coding is a mechanism for accessing an object's properties. In Chapter 2 of this book, you learned that properties encapsulate an object's internal state. This state is not accessed directly, but rather using properties' accessor methods (also known as *getter* and *setter* methods). The compiler can generate these methods automatically (according to the property declaration). This reduces the amount of code to write and also facilitates program consistency and maintainability. In the following code fragment, a class named Hello declares a property named greeting of type NSString.

```
@interface Hello : NSObject
@property NSString *greeting;
...
@end
```

This property can be accessed using either standard property accessors or dot notation syntax (recall that the compiler transforms property dot notation expressions into their corresponding accessor method invocations). Given a Hello instance named helloObject, the value for the greeting property can be retrieved using either of the following expressions:

```
[helloObject greeting]
helloObject.greeting
```

Conversely, the value for the greeting property can be set using either of the following expressions:

```
[helloObject setGreeting:newValue]
helloObject.greeting = newValue
```

Recall that a property's backing instance variable can also be accessed directly if the object associated with the property is not fully constructed (i.e., if the variable is accessed within a class init or dealloc method). The init method for the Hello class accesses the backing instance variable of the greeting property in Listing 18-1.

Listing 18-1. Accessing a Property's Backing Instance Variable

```
@implementation Hello
- (id)init
{
  if ((self = [super init]))
  {
    _greeting = @"Hello";
...
}
```

Note that these mechanisms for accessing a property are compile-time expressions, and hence tightly couple the calling code to the receiver object. With that background, you can now examine key-value coding. In a nutshell, it provides a key-value pair mechanism for accessing a property, where the key is the property's name and the value is the property value. Now this mechanism should already be familiar to you, as it is identical to that used to access entries in a dictionary (e.g., an NSDictionary instance). For example, given a Hello instance named helloObject, the following expression uses key-value coding APIs to retrieve the value of the greeting property.

```
[helloObject valueForKey:@"greeting"]
```

Observe that the key provided is the name of the property, in this case greeting. Key-value coding APIs can also be used to set the value for the greeting property.

```
[helloObject setValue:@"Hello" forKey:@"greeting"]
```

OK, so this is all fine and good, but you may still be wondering, "What's the advantage of using KVC to access properties versus the standard property accessor methods?" Well to begin with, key-value coding allows you to access a property using a string that can be varied at runtime, and thus provides a more dynamic, flexible approach for accessing and manipulating an object's state. The following are several of the key benefits to key-value coding:

- Configuration-based property access. KVC enables your code to access properties using a parameter-driven, common API.

- Loose coupling. Use of KVC for property access reduces coupling between software components, thereby improving software maintainability.

- Simplifies code. KVC can reduce the amount of code that you have to write, particularly in scenarios where you need to access a specific property based on a variable. Instead of using conditional expressions to determine the correct property accessor method to invoke, you can employ one KVC expression using the variable as its parameter.

Let's say that you need to dynamically update the state of a model based on an input from the user. Listing 18-2 provides an implementation of this logic using standard property accessors.

Listing 18-2. Updating Model State Using Standard Property Accessors

```
- (void)updateModel:(NSString *)value forState:(NSString *)state
{
  if ([state isEqualToString:@"species"])
  {
    [self setSpecies:value];
  }
  else if ([state isEqualToString:@"genus"])
  {
    [self setGenus:value];
  }
  ...
}
```

As shown in Listing 18-2, this method uses conditional expressions and standard property accessors to update the value of the correct property. Although functional, this implementation doesn't scale well and is difficult to maintain because the code must be updated whenever the property names and/or number of properties changes. Contrast that with Listing 18-3, which implements the same logic using key-value coding.

Listing 18-3. Updating Model State Using Key-Value Coding

```
- (void)updateModel:(NSString *)value forState:(NSString *)state
{
  [self setValue:value forKey:state];
}
```

Comparing the two listings, it should be pretty obvious to you that the KVC-based implementation is a vast simplification over the earlier approach. As shown in Listing 18-3, KVC can greatly reduce the amount of code that you have to write to implement this type of logic. Compared to Listing 18-2, it is also easier to both maintain and evolve because changing the properties of the model does not require any updates to the method (shown in Listing 18-3) that uses KVC.

Keys and Key Paths

Key-value coding uses keys and key paths for property access. A *key* is a string that identifies a specific property. A *key path* specifies a sequence of object properties to traverse. The KVC APIs support accessing both individual and multiple properties of an object. The properties can be object types, basic types, or C structs; basic types and structs are automatically wrapped to/from corresponding object types.

Just as dot notation syntax enables you to traverse nested properties in an object graph, KVC provides this capability through key paths. As an example, imagine a Person class that declares a property named name of type Name, and the Name class declares a property named firstName of type NSString (see Figure 18-1).

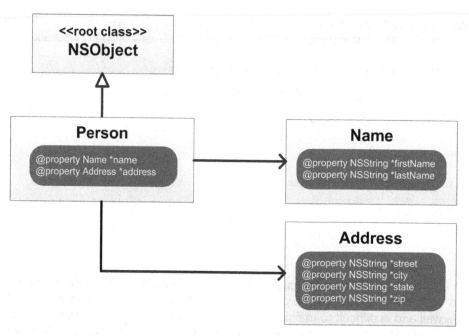

Figure 18-1. Person object graph

The object-oriented principle of composition is used here to create an object graph comprised of a Person object that has a Name instance and an Address instance. Given this object graph, for a Person instance named person, dot notation syntax could be used to retrieve the value of the firstName property, and then set the value of the firstName property as follows:

```
person.name.firstName = @"Bob";
```

The key-value coding mechanism includes an API that provides the same functionality (i.e., the setValue:forKeyPath: method). Its arguments include a key path that also uses dot notation.

```
[person setValue:@"Bob" forKeyPath:@"name.firstName"];
```

The valueForKeyPath: API would be used to retrieve a property value specified by a key path, for example

```
NSString *name = [person valueForKeyPath:@"name.firstName"];
```

As indicated earlier, key-value coding includes APIs for accessing multiple properties of an object. In the object graph depicted in Figure 18-1, a Person class declares a Name property and an Address property. Key-value coding can be used to retrieve the keys and corresponding values for an input collection of keys. Listing 18-4 uses the KVC dictionaryWithValuesForKeys: method to retrieve the keys and values for the name and address properties of a Person instance named person.

Listing 18-4. Using KVC to Retrieve Multiple Property Values

```
NSArray *personKeys = @[@"name", @"address"];
NSDictionary *personValues = [person dictionaryWithValuesForKeys:personKeys];
```

Conversely, Listing 18-5 uses the KVC setValuesForKeysWithDictionary: method to set values for the name and address properties of a Person instance named person.

Listing 18-5. Using KVC to Set Multiple Property Values

```
Name *tom = [Name new];
Address *home = [Address new];
NSDictionary *personProperties = @{@"name":tom, @"address":home};
[person setValuesForKeysWithDictionary:personProperties];
```

These are just some of the features that key-value coding provides. In the following paragraphs, you will examine this technology in more detail and learn some of its more advanced features.

KVC Design and Implementation

The design of key-value coding is based on the following two fundamental constructs:

- A mechanism that can be used to access the properties of an object indirectly by name (or key), rather than through direct invocation of accessor methods.

- A mechanism for mapping keys to the appropriate property accessor methods and/or property backing variables.

The NSKeyValueCoding informal protocol defines the mechanism for accessing objects indirectly by name/key. This protocol declares the key-value coding API, consisting of class and instance methods along with constant values. The methods enable you to get and set property values, perform property validation, and change the default behavior of the key-value coding methods for getting property values. Earlier in this chapter, you used several of these APIs (e.g., valueForKey:, selectValue:forKey:, etc.). NSObject provides the default implementation of the NSKeyValueCoding protocol, and thus any class that descends from NSObject has built-in support for key-value coding.

Key-Value Coding APIs

The NSKeyValueCoding informal protocol defines the standard key-value coding APIs. These methods enable you to get/set property values, perform key-value coding based property validation, and configure key-value coding operation. Depending upon the select method, its input parameters are a key, key path, value, and (for the validation APIs) an error object pointer. In the previous sections, you used several of the methods to get and set property values; now I'll provide an overview of a few other methods specified by this protocol.

The NSKeyValueCoding accessInstanceVariablesDirectly class method enables your class to control whether the key-value coding mechanism should access a property's backing variable directly, if no accessor method (for the property) is found. The method returns a Boolean value.

YES indicates that the key-value coding methods should access the corresponding instance variable directly, and NO indicates that they should not. The default (NSObject) implementation returns YES; your class should override this method to control this behavior.

Because key-value coding uses a key value (determined at runtime) to access a property, it also provides APIs to handle scenarios where the input key does not correspond to an object's properties. The NSKeyValueCoding valueForUndefinedKey: and setValue:forUndefinedKey: methods control how key-value coding responds to undefined key scenarios. Specifically, one of these methods is invoked when the valueForKey: or setValue:forKey: methods find no property corresponding to the input key. The default implementation of the undefined key methods raises an NSUndefinedKeyException, but subclasses can override these methods to return a custom value for undefined keys. Listing 18-6 overrides the valueForUndefinedKey: method of the Hello class implementation shown earlier (see Listing 18-1) to return the value of the property named greeting if the input key is "hi".

Listing 18-6. Hello Class Implementation of the valueForUndefinedKey: Method

```
@implementation Hello
...
- (id)valueForUndefinedKey:(NSString *)key
{
  if ((nil != key) && ([@"hi" isEqualToString:key]))
  {
    return self.greeting;
  }
  [NSException raise:NSUndefinedKeyException
              format:@"Key %@ not defined", key];
  return nil;
}
...
@end
```

The protocol defines two methods for validating a property value: validateValue:forKey:error: and validateValue:forKeyPath:error:. You'll examine these methods later in this chapter.

For collections, the NSKeyValueCoding protocol includes methods that can return a mutable instance of a collection (array or set) for a given key. The following code fragment uses the mutableArrayValueForKey: method to return a mutable array from an object named order for the key "items".

```
NSMutableArray *items = [order mutableArrayValueForKey:@"items"];
```

Note that these APIs return mutable collection instances, even if the property is a read-only collection.

Key-Value Search Patterns

So, when a KVC API is invoked, how does it get/set property values, given that its input parameters are a key/key path (along with a value for set methods)? KVC accomplishes this through use of a set of search patterns that rely on property accessor method naming conventions.

These search patterns attempt to get/set property values using their corresponding accessor methods, only resorting to directly accessing the backing instance variable if no matching accessor method is found. The NSObject default implementation of KVC includes several search patterns to support the various KVC getter/setter methods. The search pattern for the setValue:forKey: method is as follows:

1. KVC searches the target (i.e., receiver) class for an accessor method whose name matches the pattern set<Key>:, where <Key> is the name of the property. Hence, if your object invokes the setValue:forKey: method, providing a value of "name" for the key, KVC would search the class for an accessor method named setName:.

2. If no accessor is found, and the receiver's class method accessInstanceVariablesDirectly returns YES, then the receiver class is searched for an instance variable whose name matches the pattern _<key>, _is<Key>, <key>, or is<Key>. In this case, KVC would search for an instance variable named _name, _isName, name, or isName.

3. If a matching accessor method or instance variable is found, it is used to set the value. If necessary, the value is wrapped.

4. If no appropriate accessor or instance variable is found, the receiver's setValue:forUndefinedKey: method is invoked.

The search patterns support various categories of properties (attributes, object types, collections). As mentioned previously, your classes can also override the valueForUndefinedKey: and setValue:forUndefinedKey: methods to handle cases where a property can't be found for a given key.

Note   Key-value coding can be used to access three different categories of properties: simple attributes, to-one relationships, or to-many relationships. An *attribute* is a property that is a primitive (i.e., basic type), Boolean, string (NSString), or value object (NSDate, NSNumber, NSDecimalNumber, NSValue). A property that conforms to a *to-one relationship* is an object type and (potentially) has properties of its own. This includes framework classes (e.g., Foundation Framework) and your own custom classes. A property that conforms to a *to-many relationship* consists of a collection of similar type objects. These are most commonly collection types (NSArray, NSSet, etc.).

Property Accessor Naming Conventions

As you learned in the last section, the default NSObject key-value coding implementation relies on key-value compliant properties. Specifically, such properties must comply with the standard Cocoa naming conventions for property accessor methods. These can be summarized as follows:

- A getter method should use the <key> accessor form, where the method and property name are identical. For a property named firstName, the getter method should also be named firstName. This is true for all data types except for Boolean properties, for which the getter method should be prepended with the word is (e.g., isFirstName in the previous example).

- The setter method for a property should use the set<key> form, where the method name is the same as the property, prepended with the word set. For a property named firstName, the setter method should be named setFirstName:.

These conventions should be used for attribute and to-one relationship properties. As an example, given a property named person of type Type, the getter and setter accessor methods for the property should be named as follows:

```
- (Type)person;
- (void)setPerson:(Type)newValue;
```

In the preceding example, if the type of the property person is Boolean, the getter method could instead be named as follows:

```
- (BOOL)isPerson;
```

As another example, a property of type NSString * named address would have accessors with the following names:

```
- (NSString *)address
- (void)setAddress:(NSString *)
```

Note that if your properties are defined by autosynthesis (as explained in Chapter 2), the compiler automatically generates accessor methods that follow this convention.

Key-value coding depends on these naming conventions; hence, your code must follow these in order for key-value coding to work properly.

To-Many Property Accessor Naming Conventions

In addition to the <key> and set<key> accessor forms, to-many relationship properties (i.e., collections) should implement an additional set of accessor methods. These additional methods can improve the performance of KVC mutable collection APIs, enable you to model to-many relationships with classes beyond NSArray or NSSet (i.e., your own custom classes), and enable your code to use the KVC accessor methods to make modifications to collections.

To-many relationship properties have several accessor patterns, depending upon the type of collection. A class with properties that maintain an ordered, to-many relationship (these are typically of type NSArray or NSMutableArray) should implement the methods listed in Table 18-1.

Table 18-1. Methods to Implement for Ordered, To-Many Relationship Properties

Method	Ordered, To-Many Relationship	Mutable Ordered, To-Many Relationship
countOf<Key>	Required	Required
objectIn<Key>AtIndex: (or <key>AtIndexes:)	Required	Required
get<Key>:range:	Optional	Optional
insertObject:in<Key>AtIndex: (or insert<Key>:atIndexes:)		Required
removeObjectFrom<Key>AtIndex: (or remove<Key>AtIndexes:)		Required
replaceObjectIn<Key>AtIndex:withObject: (or replaceKeyAtIndexes:with<Key>:)		Optional

Implementing the optional methods of Table 18-1 can improve performance when accessing collection elements. Recall that Figure 18-1 depicts the object graph for a Person class. Imagine a to-many property named people (of type NSArray *). Listing 18-7 provides implementations of the countOf<Key> and objectIn<Key>AtIndex: methods for this property.

Listing 18-7. Example Implementations of Accessors for an Ordered, To-Many Property

```
- (NSUInteger)countOfPeople
{
  return [self.people count];
}

- (Person *)objectInPeopleAtIndex:(NSUInteger)index
{
  return [self.people objectAtIndex:index];
}
```

A class with properties that maintain an unordered, to-many relationship (typically of type NSSet or NSMutableSet) should implement the methods listed in Table 18-2.

Table 18-2. Methods to Implement for Unordered, To-many Relationship Properties

Method	Ordered, To-Many Relationship	Mutable Ordered, To-Many Relationship
countOf<Key>	Required	Required
enumeratorOf<Key>	Required	Required
memberOf<Key>:	Optional	Optional
add<Key>Object: (or add<Key>:)		Required
remove<Key>Object: (or remove<Key>:)		Required

Imagine that the to-many property named people is of type NSSet * (i.e., an unordered, to-many relationship property). Listing 18-8 provides implementations of the enumeratorOf<Key> and memberOf<Key> methods for this property.

Listing 18-8. Example Implementations of Accessors for an Unordered, To-Many Property

```
- (NSEnumerator *)enumeratorOfPeople
{
  return [self.people objectEnumerator];
}

- (Person *)memberOfPeople:(Person *)obj
{
  return [self.people member:obj];
}
```

Key-Value Validation

Key-value coding also provides infrastructure for validating property values. The KVC validation mechanism comprises a set of APIs and a standard convention for custom property validation methods. The KVC validation methods can be called directly, or indirectly by invoking the KVC validateValue:forKey:error: method.

Key-value validation specifies a convention for naming a property's validation method. The selector for a validation method is

validate<Key>:error:

<Key> is the name of the property. For example, given a property named person, its validation method is validatePerson:error:. Listing 18-9 provides an example implementation of the validation method for the city property of the Address class shown in Figure 18-1.

Listing 18-9. Example Validation Method Implementation for the City Property

```
- (BOOL)validateCity:(id *)value error:(NSError * __autoreleasing *)error
{
  if (*value == nil)
  {
    if (error != NULL)
    {
      *error = [NSError errorWithDomain:@"Invalid Property Value (nil)"
                                   code:1
                               userInfo:nil];
    }
    return NO;
  }
  return YES;
}
```

As shown in the preceding method implementation, the method returns a Boolean value of YES or NO. It returns NO if the object value is not valid and a valid value cannot be created and returned. In this case, an NSError object is also returned (via double-indirection) that indicates the reason that validation failed. A validation method returns YES under the following scenarios:

- If the input object value is valid, YES is returned.

- If the input object value is not valid, but a new object value that is valid is created and returned, then YES is returned after setting the input value to the new, valid value.

The KVC method that performs property validation (by invoking the corresponding validate<Key>:error: method) is declared as follows:

```
- (BOOL)validate<Key>:(id *)value error:(NSError **)error;
```

Note that key-value coding does not automatically invoke a property validation method. Your code must manually perform property validation, typically by calling its validation method directly or using the KVC validation API. Listing 18-10 illustrates an example usage of key-value validation on an Address instance named address to validate a value before setting it on the Address property named city.

Listing 18-10. Using Key-Value Validation

```
NSError *error;
NSString *value = @"San Jose";
BOOL result = [address validateValue:&value forKey:@"city" error:&error];
if (result)
{
  [address setValue:value forKey:@"city"];
}
```

Key-Value Coding Collection Operators

Key-value coding includes a set of operators that allow actions to be performed on the items of a collection using key path dot notation. The format of the specialized key path for the KVC collection operators is

```
collectionKeyPath.@operator.propertyKeyPath
```

This specialized key path is used as a parameter of the valueForKeyPath: method to perform collection operations. Note that components of this key path are separated by a period. The collectionKeyPath, if provided, is the key path of the array or set (relative to the receiver) on which the operation is performed. The operator (preceded by an ampersand) is the operation performed on the collection. Finally, the propertyKeyPath is the key path for the property of the collection that the operator uses. There are several types of collection operators: simple collection operators that operate on the properties of a collection, object operators that provide results when the operator is applied on a single collection instance, and collection operators that operate on nested collections and return an array or set depending on the operator.

The best way to illustrate how the collection operators work is by example, so that's what you'll do here. Listing 18-11 declares the interface to an OrderItem class that includes several properties.

Listing 18-11. OrderItem Class Interface

```
@interface OrderItem : NSObject

@property NSString *description;
@property NSUInteger *quantity;
@property float *price;

@end
```

Given a collection of OrderItem instances stored in an NSArray object named orderItems, the following expression uses the KVC valueForKeyPath: expression with the @sum collection operator to sum the prices of the items.

```
NSNumber *totalPrice = [orderItems valueForKeyPath:@"@sum.price"];
```

The number of objects in the orderItems collection can be determined using the @count collection operator, as follows:

```
NSNumber *totalItems = [orderItems valueForKeyPath:@"@count"];
```

The number of distinct order items, each with a different description, can be obtained by using the @distinctUnionOfObjects operator, as follows:

```
NSArray *itemTypes = [orderItems
                valueForKeyPath:@"@distinctUnionOfObjects.description"];
```

Now let's look at an example that uses a collection operator on a collection property. Listing 18-12 declares the interface to an Order class with a single property.

Listing 18-12. Order Class Interface

```
@interface Order : NSObject

@property NSArray *items;

@end
```

Given an Order instance named order, the @count operator can be used to determine the number of objects in the key path collection. In this case, the key path consists of the key path to the collection (items), followed by the @count operator.

```
NSNumber *totalItems = [order valueForKeyPath:@"items.@count"];
```

The preceding examples demonstrate usage of a subset of the available KVC collection operators. The Apple Key-Value Programming Guide provides a complete reference of the collection operators.

Key-Value Observing

Key-value observing (KVO) is a mechanism that enables objects to be notified of changes to the properties of other objects. It is essentially an implementation of the observer software design pattern, and is implemented in numerous software libraries and frameworks. In fact, it is a key component of the model-view-controller (MVC) design pattern, a central component of the Cocoa and Cocoa Touch frameworks. Key-value observing provides numerous benefits, including the decoupling of observer objects from the object being observed (i.e., the subject), framework-level support, and a full-featured set of APIs. The following example uses key-value observing to register an Administrator object as an observer of the name property of a Person instance named person.

```
Administrator *admin = [Administrator new];
[person addObserver:admin
        forKeyPath:@"name"
           options:NSKeyValueObservingOptionNew
           context:NULL];
```

Invoking the addObserver:forKeyPath:options:context: method creates a connection between the subject and the observer object. When the value of the observed property changes, the subject invokes the observer's observeValueForKeyPath:ofObject:change:context: method. In this method, an observer class implements logic to handle the property change. A subject automatically invokes this method when the value of an observed property is changed in a KVO-compliant manner, or the key on which it depends is changed. Observers must implement this method for key-value observing to work properly. Listing 18-13 provides an example implementation of this method for the Administrator class.

Listing 18-13. Example Implementation of observeValueForKeyPath:ofObject:change:context: Method

```
@implementation Administrator

...
- (void)observeValueForKeyPath:(NSString *)keyPath ofObject:(id)object
        change:(NSDictionary *)change context:(void *)context
{
  if ([@"name" isEqual:keyPath])
  {
    // Insert logic to handle update of person's name
    ....
  }
  // Invoke the superclass's implementation if it implements this!
  [super observeValueForKeyPath:keyPath
                       ofObject:object
                         change:change
                        context:context];
}
...

@end
```

The NSKeyValueObserving informal protocol defines the API for key-value observing. Its methods enable change notification, registering observers, notifying observers of changes, and customizing observing. NSObject provides the default implementation of the NSKeyValueObserving protocol, and thus any class that descends from NSObject has built-in support for key-value observing. In addition, you can further refine notifications by disabling automatic observer notifications and implementing manual notifications using the methods in this protocol.

Key-Value Observing or Notifications

In Chapter 12, you learned about the Foundation Framework notification classes (NSNotification, NSNotificationCenter, NSNotificationQueue). These APIs provide a mechanism for passing information between objects, similar to key-value observing. Because this is somewhat similar to the function of key-value observing, you may be wondering, "How do these two mechanisms compare, and which do you use?" Well, there are a variety of differences between key-value observing and the notification APIs that will influence which you choose for the scenario in question, so I'll compare the two here.

An NSNotification instance encapsulates generic information, so it supports a wide class of system events (including property changes), whereas key-value observing is strictly for notification of changes to properties of objects. As such, the KVO API is potentially simpler to use (vs. the notifications API) for property changes alone.

The notification classes employ a broadcast model of interaction, whereby information (encapsulated in an NSNotification object) is distributed via a centralized notification center (NSNotificationCenter instance). It allows a message to be sent to more than one object, and doesn't even require receivers to be registered to support notifications. The notification classes support both synchronous and asynchronous (using an NSNotificationQueue instance) posting of notifications. Key-value observing, on the other hand, utilizes a point-to-point interaction model, whereby the subject directly sends a notification to registered observers when a property changes, and blocks until the corresponding method finishes execution. Both mechanisms provide loose coupling; however, the notification APIs also provide nonblocking (i.e., asynchronous) interactions, and thus have the potential to provide greater application responsiveness.

Because the notification mechanism completely decouples the sender and receiver of notification events, there is no mechanism for direct, two-way communication between the two; both must register for notifications in order to provide bidirectional communication. Key-value observing, on the other hand, enables the observer to send a message to the subject, because the subject is provided as a parameter to the observer's observeValueForKeyPath:ofObject:change:context: method.

A notification is distinguished by its name, and hence the name must be unique to ensure that posted notifications are received by the correct observer(s). Apple specifies a set of naming conventions in the Coding Guidelines for Cocoa document to minimize the possibility of notification name collisions. Because property names are specific to a class (i.e., have class namespace) and subjects are directly bound to observers, naming collisions are not a concern.

Key-Value Observing APIs

The NSKeyValueObserving protocol APIs provide methods to both add and remove observers for an input key path. Invoking the addObserver:forKeyPath:options:context: method creates a connection between the subject and the observer object. Because this creates a strong reference to the observer, an object should be removed as an observer prior to the subject being deallocated.

The removeObserver:forKeyPath: method performs this function. It stops an object from receiving change notifications for a property with the specified key path. The addObserver:forKeyPath:context: performs the same function relative to a receiver and a context. When the same observer is registered for the same key-path multiple times, but with different contexts, the context pointer can be used to determine which observer to remove. Listing 18-14 demonstrates the use of these APIs to add and remove an Administrator object as an observer of the name property of a Person instance named person.

Listing 18-14. KVO Adding and Removing an Observer

```
Administrator *admin = [Administrator new];
[person addObserver:admin
        forKeyPath:@"name"
           options:NSKeyValueObservingOptionNew
           context:NULL];
[person removeObsserver:admin forKeyPath:@"name"];
```

Key-value observing provides APIs (declared in the NSKeyValueObserving protocol) to support both automatic and manual key-value change notification. They enable an observer to perform logic both before and after a property value is changed. The APIs support attributes, to-one, and to-many relationship properties.

- APIs for attributes and to-one relationship properties:

    - willChangeValueForKey:

    - didChangeValueForKey:

- APIs for to-many, ordered relationship properties:

    - willChange:valuesAtIndexes:forKey:

    - didChange:valuesAtIndexes:forKey:

- APIs for to-many, unordered relationship properties:

    - willChangeValueForKey:withSetMutation:usingObjects:

    - didChangeValueForKey:withSetMutation:usingObjects:

The default NSObject implementation automatically invokes the correct change notification methods on an observer when a corresponding property value is changed. Automatic/manual change notification is configured with the NSKeyValueObserving automaticallyNotifiesObserversForKey: method. The default NSObject implementation returns YES for this method, hence it performs automatic change notification. To perform manual change notification, your class must override the NSKeyValueObserving automaticallyNotifiesObserversForKey: method. For properties, you want to perform manual change notification; the method should return NO. In this case, your code must invoke the NSKeyValueObserving protocol method willChange: before changing the property value, and the didChange: method after changing the value. Listing 18-15 provides an example implementation of manual change notification for the name property of the Person class, as shown in Figure 18-1.

Listing 18-15. Example Implementation of KVO Manual Change Notification

```
- (void)changeName:(Name *)newName
{
  [self willChangeValueForKey:@"name"];
  self.name = newName;
  [self didChangeValueForKey:@"name"];
}
```

So why would you want to perform manual change notification? Reasons include more fine-grained control over the sending of change notifications, eliminating unnecessary notifications (e.g., cases when the new property value is the same as its old value), and grouping notifications.

The NSKeyValueObserving protocol also provides several methods for customizing observing. The keyPathsForValuesAffectingValueForKey: method retrieves the key paths for all properties whose values affect the value of the input key. This method is used to register dependent keys, when the value of one property depends upon that of one or more properties in another object. For to-one relationship properties, this method should be overridden to enable your code to return the appropriate set of dependent keys for the property. As an example, the Address class, as shown in Figure 18-1, declares street, city, state, and zip properties. A zip property depends on the other three properties; thus, an application observing the zip property should be notified if any of the other address properties changes. This can be accomplished by having the Address class override the method to return a collection of key paths consisting of the keys street, city and state, as shown in Listing 18-16.

Listing 18-16. Registering Dependent Keys for To-One Relationship Properties

```
+ (NSSet *)keyPathsForValuesAffectingValueForKey:(NSString *)key
{
  NSSet *keyPaths = [super keyPathsForValuesAffectingValueForKey:key];
  if ([key isEqualToString:@"zip"])
  {
    NSArray *affectingKeys = @[@"street", @"city", @"state"];
    keyPaths = [keyPaths setByAddingObjectsFromArray:affectingKeys];
  }

  return keyPaths;
}
```

It is also possible to register dependent keys for to-one relationship properties by implementing a class method that follows the naming convention keyPathsForValuesAffecting<Key>, where <Key> is the name of the attribute that is dependent on the values. Comparable methods and techniques are provided to register dependent keys for to-many relationship properties.

The observationInfo and setObservationInfo: methods enable you to get/set observation information about all the observers that are registered with the subject.

KVO Design and Implementation

Key-value observing is implemented through the power of the Objective-C runtime. When you register an observer on an object, the KVO infrastructure dynamically creates a new subclass of the object's original class. It then adjusts the isa pointer of the object to point to the subclass; thus messages to the original class will actually be sent to the subclass. You may recall from Chapter 8 that the isa pointer points to the object's class and this class maintains a dispatch table with pointers to the methods the class implements. The new subclass implements the KVO infrastructure. It intercepts messages to the object and inspects them for those matching certain patterns (such as the getters, setters, and collection access), posting notifications to observers, and so forth. This technique of dynamically swapping out the class that the isa pointer points to is called isa-swizzling.

Using Key-Value Programming

Now you will implement an example program that uses key-value programming to perform a variety of tasks. The program demonstrates the use of key-value coding and key-value observing in a system whose class diagram is depicted in Figure 18-2.

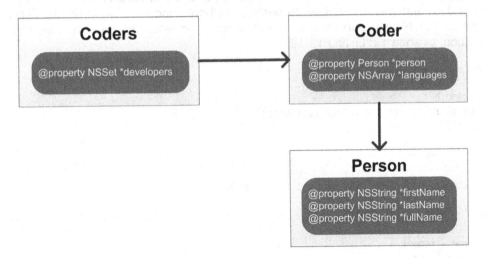

Figure 18-2. Coders class diagram

In Xcode, create a new project by selecting **New ➤ Project ...** from the Xcode File menu. In the **New Project Assistant** pane, create a command-line application. In the **Project Options** window, specify **Coders** for the Product Name, choose **Foundation** for the Project Type, and select ARC memory management by checking the **Use Automatic Reference Counting** check box. Specify the location in your file system where you want the project to be created (if necessary, select **New Folder** and enter the name and location for the folder), uncheck the **Source Control** check box, and then click the **Create** button.

You're going to create several classes here that declare various properties. Select **New ➤ File ...**
from the Xcode File menu, select the Objective-C class template, and name the class **Person**. Select
the **Coders** folder for the files location and the **Coders** project as the target, and then click the
Create button. Next, in the Xcode project navigator pane, select the **Person.h** file and update the
class interface, as shown in Listing 18-17.

Listing 18-17. Person Class Interface

```
#import <Foundation/Foundation.h>

@interface Person : NSObject

@property (readonly) NSString *fullName;
@property NSString *firstName;
@property NSString *lastName;

- (id)initWithFirstName:(NSString *)fname lastName:(NSString *)lname;

@end
```

The interface declares three properties and a single initialization method. A Person has a first name,
last name, and full name. The fullName property is read-only, and is derived from the firstName and
lastName properties. Next, use the Xcode project navigator to select the **Person.m** file and code the
implementation, as shown in Listing 18-18.

Listing 18-18. Person Class Implementation

```
#import "Person.h"
#define CodersErrorDomain    @"CodersErrorDomain"
#define kInvalidValueError   1

@implementation Person

- (id)initWithFirstName:(NSString *)fname lastName:(NSString *)lname
{
  if ((self = [super init]))
  {
    _firstName = fname;
    _lastName = lname;
  }

  return self;
}

- (NSString *)fullName
{
  return [NSString stringWithFormat:@"%@ %@", self.firstName, self.lastName];
}
```

```objc
- (BOOL)validateLastName:(id *)value error:(NSError * __autoreleasing *)error
{
    // Check for nil value
    if (*value == nil)
    {
        if (error != NULL)
        {
            NSDictionary *reason = @{NSLocalizedDescriptionKey:
                                        @"Last name cannot be nil"};
            *error = [NSError errorWithDomain:CodersErrorDomain
                                         code:kInvalidValueError
                                     userInfo:reason];
        }
        return NO;
    }
    // Check for empty value
    NSUInteger length = [[(NSString *)*value stringByTrimmingCharactersInSet:
                            [NSCharacterSet whitespaceAndNewlineCharacterSet]] length];
    if (length == 0)
    {
        if (error != NULL)
        {
            NSDictionary *reason = @{NSLocalizedDescriptionKey:
                                        @"Last name cannot be empty"};
            *error = [NSError errorWithDomain:CodersErrorDomain
                                         code:kInvalidValueError
                                     userInfo:reason];
        }
        return NO;
    }
    return YES;
}

+ (NSSet *)keyPathsForValuesAffectingValueForKey:(NSString *)key
{
    NSSet *keyPaths = [super keyPathsForValuesAffectingValueForKey:key];
    if ([key isEqualToString:@"fullName"])
    {
        NSArray *affectingKeys = @[@"firstName", @"lastName"];
        keyPaths = [keyPaths setByAddingObjectsFromArray:affectingKeys];
    }

    return keyPaths;
}

@end
```

The initWithFirstName:lastName: method is used to initialize a Person instance with the input first and last names. The accessor method fullName returns the derived value of a Person object's full name as the concatenation of the firstName and lastName property values. The validateLastName:error: method is used to perform KVC property validation on the lastName property. It returns NO and an NSError object if the input last name is nil or an empty string; otherwise, it returns YES. The keyPathsForValuesAffectingValueForKey: method registers dependent keys. The method utilizes the fullName property, which depends on the firstName and lastName properties, to obtain the keys that are added to the returned key path.

Next, you will implement the Coder class. Select **New ➤ File ...** from the Xcode File menu, select the **Objective-C** class template, and name the class **Coder**. Select the **Coders** folder for the files location and the **Coders** project as the target, and then click the **Create** button. In the Xcode project navigator pane, select the **Coder.h** file and update the class interface, as shown in Listing 18-19.

Listing 18-19. Coder Class Interface

```
#import <Foundation/Foundation.h>

@class Person;
@interface Coder : NSObject

@property Person *person;
@property NSMutableArray *languages;

@end
```

The class declares two properties: a Person property named person, and an NSMutableArray property named languages. The languages property is an array that contains the names of programming languages that a Coder uses. Notice that a @class directive is used to forward declare the Person class, thereby removing the need to import its header file in this interface. Now use the Xcode project navigator to select the **Coder.m** file and code the implementation, as shown in Listing 18-20.

Listing 18-20. Coder Class Implementation

```
#import "Coder.h"

@implementation Coder

- (NSUInteger)countOfLanguages
{
  return [self.languages count];
}

- (NSString *)objectInLanguagesAtIndex:(NSUInteger)index
{
  return [self.languages objectAtIndex:index];
}

- (void)insertObject:(NSString *)object inLanguagesAtIndex:(NSUInteger)index
{
  [self.languages insertObject:object atIndex:index];
}
```

```
- (void)removeObjectFromLanguagesAtIndex:(NSUInteger)index
{
  [self.languages removeObjectAtIndex:index];
}

- (void)observeValueForKeyPath:(NSString *)keyPath
                      ofObject:(id)object
                        change:(NSDictionary *)change
                       context:(void *)context
{
  NSString *newValue = change[NSKeyValueChangeNewKey];
  NSLog(@"Value changed for %@ object, key path: %@, new value: %@",
        [object className], keyPath, newValue);
}

@end
```

The Coder implementation includes the KVO-recommended methods for the ordered, to-many relationship of the languages property. The observeValueForKeyPath:ofObject:change:context: method is executed when a Coder property with the input key path is changed. In this case, the method just prints out the new value for the object and key path in question.

Finally, you will implement the Coders class. As depicted in Figure 18-2, the Coders class holds a collection (an NSSet) of Coder instances. Select **New ➤ File ...** from the Xcode File menu, select the Objective-C class template, and name the class Coders. Select the **Coders** folder for the files location and the **Coders** project as the target, and then click the **Create** button. Next, in the Xcode project navigator pane, select the **Coders.h** file and update the class interface, as shown in Listing 18-21.

Listing 18-21. Coders Class Interface

```
#import <Foundation/Foundation.h>

@class Coder;
@interface Coders : NSObject

@property NSSet *developers;

@end
```

The Coders interface declares a single property, an NSSet named developers that contains the collection of Coder objects. Now use the Xcode project navigator to select the **Coders.m** file and code the implementation, as shown in Listing 18-22.

Listing 18-22. Coders Class Implementation

```
#import "Coders.h"

@implementation Coders

- (NSUInteger)countOfDevelopers
{
  return [self.developers count];
}
```

```
- (NSEnumerator *)enumeratorOfDevelopers
{
  return [self.developers objectEnumerator];
}

- (Coder *)memberOfDevelopers:(Coder *)member object:(Coder *)anObject
{
  return [self.developers member:anObject];
}

@end
```

The Coders implementation includes the KVO-recommended methods for the unordered, to-many relationship of the developers property.

Now that you have finished implementing the classes, let's move on to the main() function. In the Xcode project navigator, select the **main.m** file and update the main() function, as shown in Listing 18-23.

Listing 18-23. Coders main() function

```
#import <Foundation/Foundation.h>
#import "Person.h"
#import "Coder.h"
#import "Coders.h"

int main(int argc, const char * argv[])
{
  @autoreleasepool
  {
    Person *curly = [[Person alloc] initWithFirstName:@"Curly" lastName:@"Howard"];
    NSLog(@"Person first name: %@", [curly valueForKey:@"firstName"]);
    NSLog(@"Person full name: %@", [curly valueForKey:@"fullName"]);
    NSArray *langs1 = @[@"Objective-C", @"C"];
    Coder *coder1 = [Coder new];
    coder1.person = curly;
    coder1.languages = [langs1 mutableCopy];
    NSLog(@"\nCoder name: %@\n\t  languages: %@",
          [coder1 valueForKeyPath:@"person.fullName"],
          [coder1 valueForKey:@"languages"]);

    Coder *coder2 = [Coder new];
    coder2.person = [[Person alloc] initWithFirstName:@"Larry" lastName:@"Fine"];
    coder2.languages = [@[@"Objective-C", @"C++"] mutableCopy];
    NSLog(@"\nCoder name: %@\n\t  languages: %@",
          [coder2 valueForKeyPath:@"person.fullName"],
          [coder2 valueForKey:@"languages"]);

    [curly addObserver:coder1
            forKeyPath:@"fullName"
               options:NSKeyValueObservingOptionNew
               context:NULL];
```

```
  curly.lastName = @"Fine";
  [curly removeObserver:coder1 forKeyPath:@"fullName"];

  Coders *bestCoders = [Coders new];
  bestCoders.developers = [[NSSet alloc] initWithArray:@[coder1, coder2]];
  [bestCoders valueForKey:@"developers"];
  NSLog(@"Number of coders = %@", [bestCoders.developers
                              valueForKeyPath:@"@count"]);
  NSError *error;
  NSString *emptyName = @"";
  BOOL valid = [curly validateValue:&emptyName forKey:@"lastName" error:&error];
  if (!valid)
  {
     NSLog(@"Error: %@", ([error userInfo])[NSLocalizedDescriptionKey]);
  }
 }
 return 0;
}
```

The function first creates a Person instance and then uses key-value coding to retrieve values for its properties. Next, a Coder instance is created, and its person and languages property are set. The key-value coding APIs are then used to retrieve the corresponding property values. Another Coder instance is then created and its property values are set accordingly. Key-value observing is then demonstrated, with a Coder instance registered to receive notifications when the fullName property of a Person instance is changed. A Coders instance (remember, the Coders class holds a collection of Coder instances) is then created and its developers property is assigned to the collection of Coder instances created previously. A collection operator is then used to return the total number of coders in the collection. Finally, key-value coding validation is demonstrated on the lastName property of a Person instance.

When you compile and run the program, you should observe the messages in the output pane shown in Figure 18-3.

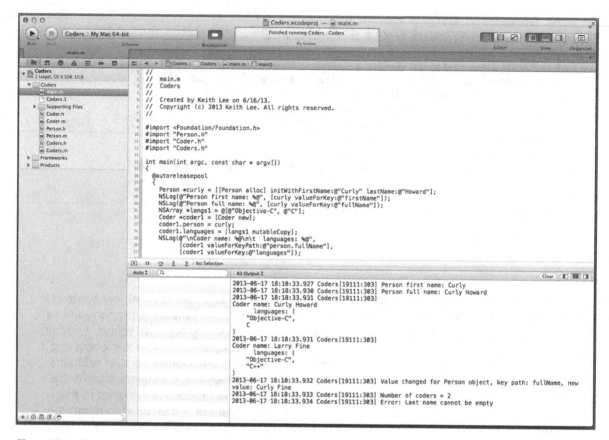

Figure 18-3. Coders program output

Excellent! This completes your in-depth examination of the key-value programming APIs and infrastructure. Knowledge of key-value coding and key-value observing will be extremely useful to you when programming with Objective-C and using Apple's various software frameworks and services.

Roundup

In this chapter, you learned about key-value programming, a powerful set of mechanisms and APIs in the Objective-C language. Key-value programming is an important component of general Objective-C programming, along with the Cocoa and Cocoa Touch frameworks, hence it is important to understand its details and how it can be effectively used in your programs. This chapter provided an in-depth examination of key-value programming infrastructure, specifically key-value coding and key-value observing. Its key takeaways include the following:

- Key-value coding enables your code to access and manipulate an object's properties indirectly, by name (i.e., key), rather than through accessor methods or backing instance variables.

- Key-value coding allows you to access a property using a string that can be varied at runtime, and thus provides a more dynamic, flexible approach for accessing and manipulating an object's state. Its key benefits include loose coupling, configuration-based property access, and code simplification.

- Key-value coding uses keys and key paths for property access. A key is a string that identifies a specific property. A key path specifies a sequence of object properties (within an object graph) that are traversed to identify a specific property. The KVC APIs support accessing both individual and multiple properties of an object. The properties can be primitives, C structs, object types (including collections). Primitives and structs are automatically wrapped to/from corresponding object types.

- The NSKeyValueCoding informal protocol defines the mechanism for accessing objects indirectly by name/key. This protocol declares the key-value coding API, consisting of class and instance methods along with constant values. The methods enable you to get and set property values, perform property validation, and change the default behavior of the key-value coding methods for getting property values.

- Key-value coding utilizes a mechanism for mapping keys to the appropriate property accessor methods and/or property backing variables. This mechanism utilizes a set of standard search patterns that rely on property accessor method naming conventions.

- Key-value coding also includes infrastructure for validating property values. The KVC validation mechanism comprises a set of APIs and a standard convention for custom property validation methods. The KVC validation methods can be called directly or indirectly.

- The key-value coding collection operators allow actions to be performed on the items of a collection using key path dot notation.

- Key-value observing enables other objects to be notified of changes to the properties of other objects. It is essentially an implementation of the observer software design pattern, and is implemented in numerous software libraries and frameworks. In fact, it is a key component of the model-view-controller (MVC) design pattern, a central component of the Cocoa and Cocoa Touch frameworks. Key-value observing is built on key-value coding.

- Key-value observing provides numerous benefits, including decoupling of observer objects from the object being observed (i.e., the subject), framework-level support, and a full-featured set of APIs. It provides event notification, similar to the Foundation Framework notification APIs, but a different set of features. Hence, you should compare the two before deciding which to use in your programs.

■ Key-value observing provides APIs that support both automatic and manual key-value property change notification. They enable an observer to perform logic both before and after a property value is changed. The APIs support attributes, to-one, and to-many relationship properties. Automatic property change notification is implemented by the default NSObject KVO implementation. Manual change notification provides more fine-grained control over the sending of change notifications, eliminates unnecessary notifications (e.g., for cases when the new property value is the same as its old value), and enables you to group notifications.

Congratulations, you should now be well on your way to mastering the Objective-C language! Perhaps there's some material that you want to review again, or maybe you would just like to give your brain a well-deserved rest. Go right ahead, but please take advantage of the numerous code listings and programs to thoroughly explore the topics covered. The more you do this, the more skilled you will become at Objective-C programming.

This is the final chapter of this book—but guess what, you're not done yet. The next stop is the appendices, where you'll explore a variety of additional topics that will further enhance your Objective-C skills.

Language Elements

Appendix A provides a concise summary of the basic elements of the Objective-C language. Its scope is the Objective-C language extensions to ANSI C. The fundamental elements of the C programming language are not covered here; they can be found in numerous other references.

Variables

The lexical rules for variable names in Objective-C are identical to those for ANSI C—a variable is defined with a letter or underscore, followed by any combination of letters, underscores, and the digits 0–9. Uppercase and lowercase letters are distinct.

Objective-C Reserved Words

In a programming language, a *reserved word* is a symbol that has a special meaning in the language, and hence should not be used as a variable name. Objective-C adds a number of reserved words to those already defined for ANSI C; these are listed in Table A-1.

Table A-1. Objective-C Reserved Words Not Used for Variable Names

_Bool	_cmd	_Complex	_Imaginary	atomic
bycopy	byref	BOOL	Class	id
IMP	inline	inout	instancetype	nil
NO	nonatomic	NULL	oneway	out
Protocol	restrict	retain	SEL	self
super	YES			

Variable Scope

The visibility and accessibility of a variable is dependent on its scope. A variable may exist within a statement block, a function, a method, an object instance (or related objects), throughout a file, or across multiple files. ANSI C defines four kinds of scope:

- *block*: A variable declared within a statement block has *block scope*. Variables declared within a block are only visible and accessible within this block.

- *file*: A variable that has *file scope* is visible and accessible only to code within the file where the variable is declared.

- *function*: A variable declared within a function/method has *function scope*. These variables are only visible and accessible within the associated function/method.

- *function prototype*: A variable declared within the list of parameters in a function/method prototype has *function prototype scope*. These variables are visible and accessible within the associated function/method.

Objective-C adds a set of access modifier directives that enable you to provide fine-grained access control to instance variables.

Access Modifiers

Objective-C defines several compiler directives to control the scope of instance variables; that is, the visibility of variables throughout a program.

- `@private`: The instance variable is only accessible within the class that declares it and other instances of this class type.

- `@protected`: The instance variable is accessible within the class that declares it and the instance methods of any of its subclasses. This is the default scope if a protection level is not specified for an instance variable.

- `@public`: The instance variable is accessible from everywhere.

- `@package`: The instance variable is accessible from any other class instance or function, but outside of the package, it is treated as private. This scope can be useful for libraries or framework classes.

These directives are referred to as *access modifiers*, and are used on instance variables declared within an instance variable declaration block. The class instance variable declaration of Listing A-1 declares a `counter` variable of type `int` that is accessible everywhere, a `temperature` variable of type `float` that is accessible within the declaring class and any subclasses, and a `description` variable of type `NSString*` that is accessible only within the declaring class.

Listing A-1. Instance Variable Declaration with Access Modifiers

```
{
  @public int counter;
  @protected float temperature;
  @private NSString *description;
}
```

Data Types

As Objective-C is a strict superset of the C programming language. It supports all of the standard ANSI C data types and type qualifiers. Objective-C also defines a number of language-specific data types (BOOL type, class instance types, id type, class definition types, block type). These are discussed in the following paragraphs.

BOOL Type

BOOL is an Objective-C type used to hold a Boolean value that can hold only two possible values: true or false. For the Objective-C BOOL type, these values are defined as YES and NO rather than true (1) or false (0). The amount of storage allocated for a BOOL is 1 byte. Objective-C also supports the C99 types _Bool and bool, although BOOL is the preferred Boolean type to use in Objective-C programs.

Class Instance Types

The class instance types represent objects, classes, and superclasses. The Objective-C runtime has several class instance types, of which the most commonly used is the id type.

id Type

The id type is the final supertype of all Objective-C object pointers and can be used to hold a reference to any Objective-C object, regardless of its type. The following statement declares a variable named myObject of type id.

```
id myObject;
```

The object instantiated for this variable can be of any type.

The runtime equivalent for the Objective-C id type is a C struct defined as a pointer to an objc_object (as shown in Listing A-2).

Listing A-2. id Type Definition

```
typedef struct objc_object
{
  Class isa;
} *id;
```

In other words, an id is just a pointer to a C struct with the identifier objc_object.

instancetype Keyword

The instancetype keyword is a contextual keyword that can be used as the result type of a method; it signals that the method returns a *related result type*. In Chapter 3, you learned that when a method returns a related result type, it returns an object that is an instance of the receiving class's type. A related result type can be inferred for the following types of methods:

- Class methods that begin with the words alloc or new.
- Instance methods that begin with the words autorelease, init, retain, or self.

The following statement creates an OrderItem object using the new keyword.

```
OrderItem *item = [OrderItem new];
```

Although the NSObject new method specifies id as the return type, the compiler infers the correct result type (in this case OrderItem *) based on the type of the receiving class instance named *item*.

The instancetype keyword can be used to explicitly indicate that a method returns a related result type. Listing A-3 provides an example of a class named OrderItem, whose interface declares a method that returns a related result type.

Listing A-3. Use of the instancetype Keyword to Return a Related Result Type

```
@interface OrderItem : NSObject
+ (instancetype)orderItemWithDescription:(NSString *)description price:(float)cost;
@end
```

Class Definition Types

The class definition types define Objective-C runtime data structures. They include the SEL, IMP, Class, and objc_object types.

SEL Type

The SEL type represents a method selector, a type that represents the name of a method in the Objective-C runtime. A variable of type SEL for a method selector named helloWorld can be created using the @selector compiler directive.

```
SEL myHelloMethod = @selector(helloWorld);
```

This selector can be used to invoke the helloWorld method on an object.

IMP Type

The IMP type represents a method pointer that points to the beginning address in memory for a function that implements a method. An IMP is defined as follows:

```
typdef id (*IMP)(id, SEL, ...);
```

As shown by the preceding type definition, the function pointed to by an IMP takes as its parameters an id, a method selector (SEL), variable arguments (represented by the variadic arguments ... symbol), and returns an id.

Class Type

The Class type represents an Objective-C class instance (i.e., an object) and is composed of various data elements. The Class data type is defined as follows:

```
typedef struct objc_class *Class;
```

As shown by the preceding type definition, the Class data type is a pointer to an opaque type with an identifier of objc_class. The members of the objc_class struct can only be accessed through functions defined specifically for it, specifically using the Objective-C runtime library functions.

objc_object Type

Objective-C objects have a corresponding runtime data type. When the compiler parses Objective-C code for objects, it generates code that creates a runtime object type, the objc_object type. This data type, declared in Listing A-4, is a C struct type with an identifier of objc_object.

Listing A-4. objc_object Data Type

```
struct objc_object
{
  Class isa;
  /* ...variable length data containing instance variable values... */
};
```

The objc_object type contains a variable named isa of type Class; in other words, a pointer to a variable of type objc_class.

Block Type

Blocks provide a way to create a group of statements (i.e., a block of code) and assign those statements to a variable, which can subsequently be invoked. They are similar to standard C functions, but in addition to executable code, they may also contain variable bindings to stack or heap memory. A block is an Objective-C object (of block type), and like all Objective-C objects, it is accessed via a pointer. As with Objective-C objects, the id type can be used to refer to a block object. The following statement declares a Block variable named incrementSum that has a single parameter of type int and returns nothing.

```
void (^incrementSum)(int);
```

The __block storage modifier can be used to create mutable block variables. It is applied to a variable outside of a Block literal but within the same lexical scope, and enables this variable to be modified within the Block. This storage modifier cannot be combined with the local storage modifiers auto, register, and static on the same variable. Listing A-5 illustrates the use of a __block variable.

Listing A-5. Correct Use of __block Storage

```
__block int totalSum = 0;
void (^incrementSum)(int) = ^(int amount){
  totalSum += amount;
  NSLog(@"Current total = %d", totalSum);
};
incrementSum(5);
```

When the code fragment displayed in Listing A-5 is executed, it outputs the following:

```
Current total = 5
```

Hence, the block variable totalSum is initialized with a value of 0 and then modified when the block literal is invoked.

Enumeration Types

Objective-C supports the standard C enumeration types and also provides support for specifying the type for an enumeration. An enumeration type consists of a set of named values (aka *enumerators*) that are defined using the enum keyword. A variable declared as an enumeration can be assigned any of the enumerator values. Listing A-6 defines an enumeration with a set of values: Red, Green, and Blue for the variable named color.

Listing A-6. Example enum Type Definition

```
enum
{
  Red,
  Green,
  Blue
} color;
```

The default type for enumerators is int. Objective-C provides support for explicitly specifying the type for an enumeration, also referred to as *enumerations with a fixed underlying type*. The types supported for an enumeration are any signed or unsigned integer type (char, short, int, and long). The type should be specified after the enum keyword, prefixed by a colon. Listing A-7 defines an enumeration with a set of values Red, Green, and Blue whose type is unsigned char for the variable named color.

Listing A-7. Example enum with a Fixed Underlying Type

```
enum : unsigned char
{
  Red,
  Green,
  Blue
} color;
```

Typically, a type definition is used to declare an enumeration type. Listing A-8 declares a type definition for an enumeration with a set of values Red, Green, and Blue (whose type is unsigned char), and then declares a variable named color of that type.

Listing A-8. Example typedef enum with a Fixed Underlying Type

```
typedef enum : unsigned char
{
  Red,
  Green,
  Blue
} ColorType;
ColorType color;
```

The preferred approach in Objective-C for defining enumeration types is to use the NS_ENUM macro. This provides a convenient mechanism to declare the underlying type for the enumeration values and define the name of the new type in a single statement. Listing A-9 illustrates use of the NS_ENUM macro to define the enumeration type previously defined in Listing A-8.

Listing A-9. Example enum Definition Using the NS_ENUM Macro

```
typedef NS_ENUM(unsigned char, ColorType)
{
  Red,
  Green,
  Blue
};
```

Listing A-9 shows that the first argument for the macro is the underlying type; whereas the second argument is the name of the new type. The values are stored inside the block, as usual.

Operators

Objective-C supports the operators defined for ANSI C, specifically

- Assignment operators

- Arithmetic operators

- Compound assignment operators

- Increment and decrement operators

- Logical comparison operators

- Logical Boolean operators

- Bitwise operators

- Compound bitwise operators

- Ternary operators

- Type cast operators
- sizeof operators
- Address (&) operators
- Indirection (*) operators
- Comma operators

The rules for arithmetic conversions, along with those for operator precedence and associativity, are as specified for ANSI C.

The caret (^) operator is used with block objects; specifically to declare objects of block type and to define block literals.

Statements

Objective-C supports the conditional, looping, and jump statements defined for ANSI C, specifically

- Conditional statements (`if`, `if else`, `if else if`, `switch`)
- Loop statements (`for`, `while`, `do while`)
- Jump statements (`return`, `goto`, `break`, `continue`)

Class Elements

An Objective-C class is comprised of several structural elements, which are logical organized into sections. This section provides an overview of these fundamental class elements.

Instance Variables

Instance variables, sometimes referred to as *ivars*, are variables declared for a class that exist and hold their value throughout the life of a class instance. The memory used for instance variables is allocated when an object is first created, and freed when the object is dellocated. Instance variables have an implicit scope and namespace corresponding to the object. Instance variables can be declared within the instance variable declaration block of a class interface, implementation, or extension. The ivar declaration block must be placed immediately below the corresponding interface, implementation, or class extension declaration. Listing A-10 depicts an example ivar declaration block for the `Hello` class.

Listing A-10. Hello Class Implementation Instance Variable Declaration Block

```
@implementation Hello
{
  // declare instance variables here.
  ...
}
...
@end
```

The recommended practice is to declare instance variables in the class implementation (rather than the public class interface). Instance variables are commonly declared in an extension for variables solely used within the corresponding class implementation file.

Instance Variables Ownership Qualifiers

An Objective-C ownership qualifier is a type qualifier that applies only to retainable object pointer types. An ownership qualifier is placed before an object pointer type in a variable declaration to specify the variable's ownership rules. Table A-2 lists the four ownership qualifiers.

Table A-2. Object Pointer Variable Ownership Qualifiers

Qualifier	Description
__autoreleasing	When the variable is assigned a new value, the new value is retained and autoreleased, and the previous value is sent a release message.
__weak	The variable uses simple assignment (i.e., the input value is not copied or retained). If the object is deallocated, the corresponding variable value is set to nil.
__unsafe_unretained	The variable uses simple assignment (i.e., the input value is not copied or retained).
__strong	When the variable is assigned a new value, the new value is retained and the previous value is sent a release message.

The default ownership qualifier (if none is provided) is __strong. The following statement declares a variable named hello (of type Hello *) with an ownership qualifier of __weak.

```
__weak Hello *hello;
```

Properties

In Objective-C a property provides a convenient mechanism, in the form of accessor methods (i.e., *getters* and *setters*), for accessing an object's shared state. A property differs from an instance variable in that it doesn't directly access an object's internal state. Objective-C declared properties enable the compiler to generate these methods automatically according to your provided specification.

A property is declared using the @property keyword, followed by an optional set of attributes (enclosed within parentheses), the property type, and its name.

```
@property (attributes) type propertyName;
```

Property declaration attributes are used to specify the storage semantics and other behaviors associated with a property. Table A-3 provides a list of the available property attributes.

Table A-3. *Property Attributes*

Attribute	Description	Comments
readwrite	Required.	Access qualifier. The default setting.
readonly	Required.	Access qualifier. Cannot select both readwrite and readonly.
assign	The setter method uses simple assignment (i.e., the input value is not copied or retained).	Ownership qualifier. Used under Manual Retain-Release (MRR) memory management. The default setting under MRR.
weak	The setter method uses simple assignment (i.e., the input value is not copied or retained). If the property instance is deallocated, its value is set to nil.	Ownership qualifier. Used under ARC memory management.
unsafe_unretained	The setter method uses simple assignment (i.e., the input value is not copied or retained).	Ownership qualifier. Used under ARC memory management.
copy	In the setter method, a copy method should be called for assignment and the old value should be sent a release message.	Ownership qualifier.
retain	In the setter method, the previous value will be sent a release message and the property uses retain on assignment.	Ownership qualifier. Similar to the strong attribute (used under Manual Retain-Release memory management).
strong	In the setter method, the previous value will be sent a release message and the property uses retain on assignment.	Ownership qualifier. Used under ARC memory management. The default setting under ARC.
getter=getterName	Names the getter method the specified getterName.	
setter=setterName	Names the setter method the specified setterName.	
nonatomic	Specifies that the accessor methods for this property are not atomic (the default). The nonatomic property setting has better performance, but does not guarantee that a whole value is always returned from a property getter or setter when being accessed by multiple threads.	

A property definition is performed in the implementation section of a class. In most cases, a property is backed by an instance variable, hence the property definition includes defining getter and setter methods for the property, declaring an instance variable, and using that variable in the getter/setter methods. Objective-C provides three methods for defining a property: explicit definition, synthesis via keyword, or autosynthesis.

Methods

Objective-C supports both instance methods and class methods. Instance methods are invoked on class instances (objects); as such, instance methods have direct access to an object's instance variables. Class methods are invoked on classes. Methods can be declared in a class interface, a protocol, and/or a category. Methods thus declared are defined in a corresponding class/category implementation.

A method declaration specifies the method type, a return type, its name, its parameter(s), and the corresponding parameter types. The *method type* identifier specifies whether the method is a class or instance method. A class method is declared with a plus (+) sign and indicates that the method has class scope, meaning that it operates at the class level and does not have access to the instance variables of the class (unless they are passed as parameters to the method). An instance method is declared with a minus (–) sign and indicates that the method has object scope. It operates at the instance level and has direct access to the instance variables of the object and its parent objects (subject to the access controls on the instance variables).

The method name includes parameters as part of its name, using colons. For each parameter, its type is specified in parentheses, followed by the method prototype parameter. The parameter name and type are separated by a colon; for example, in the following method declaration:

```
- (void)incrementSum:(int)value;
```

The method name is incrementSum: and it has a single parameter of type int named value. Multiple parameters require multiple name-parameter pairs; for example, the method declaration

```
- (int)addAddend1:(int)a1 addend2:(int)a2;
```

The method name is addAddend1:addend2: and it has two parameters of type int named a1 and a2.

The *return type* indicates the type of the returned variable from the method, if any. The return type is specified within parentheses, following the method type. If the method does not return anything, its return type is declared as void.

The following statement provides an example class method declaration for a method named hydrogenWithProtons:neutrons: that has two parameters of type unsigned int named nProtons and nNeutrons.

```
+ (id) hydrogenWithProtons:(unsigned)nProtons neutrons:(unsigned)nNeutrons;
```

Interface

A class interface specifies state and behavior of a class; encapsulated in its instance variables, properties and methods. A class interface declaration begins with the @interface directive and the name of the class; it ends with the @end directive. The formal syntax for declaring a class interface is shown in Listing A-11.

Listing A-11. Class Interface Syntax

```
@interface ClassName : SuperclassName
{
  // instance variable declarations
}

// Property and method declarations
@end
```

A superclass establishes a common interface and implementation, which specialized subclasses can inherit, modify, and supplement. Most classes inherit from the NSObject class, the root (i.e., base) class of most Foundation Framework class hierarchies, which provides a basic interface to the Objective-C runtime.

Forward Declarations

The @class directive is used to declare a class (in a class interface) prior to obtaining its complete specification. This tells the compiler that a class exists (and thus enables it to perform static type checking) without having to import its corresponding header file. Forward declarations can be useful in resolving circular dependencies between files.

Implementation

A class implementation defines a class's behavior by implementing defining its properties and implementing its methods. A class implementation declaration begins with the @implementation directive and the name of the class; it ends with the @end directive. The formal syntax for declaring a class implementation is shown in Listing A-12.

Listing A-12. Class Implementation Syntax

```
@implementation ClassName
{
  // instance variable declarations
}

// Property and method definitions
@end
```

The methods defined in a class implementation must directly map to its corresponding interface; for example, Listing A-13 depicts a Greeting class interface and its corresponding implementation.

Listing A-13. Greeting Class Interface and Implementation

```
#import <Foundation/Foundation.h>
@interface Greeting : NSObject

@property(readwrite) NSString *salutation;
- (void)hello:(NSString *)user;

@end
```

```
#import "Greeting.h"
@implementation Greeting
- (void)hello:(NSString *)user
{
  NSLog(@"%@, %@", self.salutation, user);
}
@end
```

Protocol

A protocol declares methods and properties that can be implemented by any class. A protocol declaration begins with the @protocol directive followed by the name of the protocol. It ends with the @end directive. Protocols can have both *required* and *optional* methods; optional methods do not require that an implementation of the protocol implement these methods. The directives @required and @optional (followed by the method name(s)) are used to mark a method appropriately. If neither keyword is specified, the default behavior is @required. The syntax of a protocol declaration is shown in Listing A-14.

Listing A-14. Protocol Declaration Syntax

```
@protocol ProtocolName
// Property declarations
@required
// Method declarations
@optional
// Method declarations
@end
```

One protocol can incorporate other protocols by specifying the name of each declared protocol within braces; this is referred to as *adopting* a protocol. Commas are used to separate multiple protocols (as shown in Listing A-15).

Listing A-15. Incorporating Other Protocols

```
@protocol ProtocolName<ProtocolName(s)>
// Method declarations
@end
```

An interface can *adopt* other protocols using similar syntax (shown in Listing A-16).

Listing A-16. Interface Adopting a Protocol

```
@interface ClassName : Parent <ProtocolName(s)>
// Method declarations
@end
```

Typically, a class interface and its corresponding implementation are physically organized in separate files; the interface in a header file suffixed with .h, and an implementation file suffixed with .m.

Category

A category enables the addition of new functionality to an existing class without subclassing it. The methods in a category become part of the class type (within the scope of the program) and are inherited by all its subclasses.

A category interface declaration begins with the @interface keyword, followed by the name of the existing class, and the category name in parentheses, followed by the protocols it adopts (if any). It ends with the @end keyword. Between these statements the method declarations are provided. The syntax of a category declaration is shown in Listing A-17.

Listing A-17. Category Declaration Syntax

```
@interface ClassName (CategoryName)
// Method declarations
@end
```

A category implementation is comparable to a class implementation, defining methods declared in a category interface. Its syntax is

```
@implementation ClassName (CategoryName)
// Method declarations
@end
```

Class Extension

A class *extension* can be considered as an anonymous (i.e., unnamed) category. The methods declared in an extension *must* be implemented in the main @implementation block for the corresponding class. As opposed to a category, an extension can declare instance variables and properties. The syntax of a class extension is shown in Listing A-18.

Listing A-18. Extension Declaration Syntax

```
@interface ClassName ()
{
  // Instance variable declarations
}

// Property declarations
// Method declarations
@end
```

A class extension is commonly placed in the same file as the class implementation file, and is used to group and declare additional required, private methods (e.g., not part of the publicly declared API) for use solely within a class.

Xcode Xposed!

Xcode is a comprehensive toolset for the development, management, and maintenance of software products that run on the Apple OS X and iOS platforms. It includes an IDE, compiler, debugger, and numerous other tools. Xcode also bundles the OS X and iOS Software Development Kits (SDKs) that comprise the Cocoa and Cocoa Touch frameworks. You have been using Xcode to develop and run the example applications presented throughout this book, so by now, you're already familiar with several of its basic features. In this appendix, you are going to "look under the hood" to explore some of Xcode's key features in depth. Specifically, you will examine the key concepts that form the foundation of Xcode and, by doing this, become more familiar with some of its key tools.

Basic Concepts

From a user perspective, Xcode is organized around several basic concepts: projects, workspaces, targets, schemes, and actions. In the next few paragraphs, you will learn more about these concepts and how they are used within Xcode.

Targets

A *target* is a fundamental concept in Xcode. It consists of a collection of instructions for building a software product. A target is comprised of rules and settings for how to build a product, and defines a set of *build phases*, the sequence of steps used to perform the actual software build.

Each target takes a collection of inputs (source files, resources, build instructions, etc.) and produces a product as its output. The product can be an application, software library, and so forth. An Xcode project can have multiple targets, each of which can have its own set of instructions for building a software product.

A target can have dependencies on other targets (e.g., *dependent targets*). Xcode automatically builds dependent targets when the selected target is built. Xcode provides capabilities for managing targets (create, update, delete, managing dependencies between them) and managing the files of a target (add, delete, setting role of header files).

Build Phases

Build phases define the stages by which your product is built. Three of these phases—Compile Sources, Link Binary With Libraries, and Copy Bundle Resources—are required, and others can be added as necessary. As build phases define how the target will be built, changing the build phases changes the build process.

Build Settings

Build settings define what to do at various stages of the build process, and hence provide a means of customizing this process. There are actually multiple lists of build setting values, each of which is called a *build configuration.* A build configuration is a named collection of build settings that are used to build a target's product in a particular way. They provide a mechanism for building different versions of the same target. You can also create build configuration files. These enable you to easily share a set of build setting definitions across targets, projects, and among developers.

Build Configurations

A project build configuration is used to build a software product. It contains build-setting definitions. These can be embedded in an Xcode project file or stored in a separate configuration settings file. When you create a project, Xcode provides two default embedded build configurations: *Debug* and *Release*, which differ primarily in the inclusion of debug information and in the degree to which the build is optimized. The *Debug* configuration is typically used throughout the development process, whereas the *Release* configuration is used for late-stage testing, when you want to check performance on a device. Several of the build settings for the Debug configuration are shown in Listing B-1.

Listing B-1. Debug Build Configuration Settings

```
ONLY_ACTIVE_ARCH=YES
CONFIGURATION_BUILD_DIR=build/Debug
COPY_PHASE_STRIP=NO
GCC_OPTIMIZATION_LEVEL=0
GCC_PREPROCESSOR_DEFINITIONS=DEBUG=1
```

A configuration settings file is a plain text file that specifies a list of build-setting definitions, one per line. If you are creating a new build configuration from an existing one, it must be based only on a configuration file that is in your project, not an external file.

Build Rules

Build rules provide instructions for processing files on a per-target basis. Xcode provides a set of default build rules, and you can add your own custom build rules to perform custom processing for specific file types.

Build rules specify how particular types of files are processed and which tool is used to process files during build phases. Each build rule consists of a condition and an action. The condition, which usually specifies a file type, determines whether a source file is processed with the associated action.

Xcode provides default build rules that process a variety of file types, including C-based files (such as Objective-C files) and assembly files. You can add custom build rules to process other types of files to each target. These are added in the Build Rules pane of the editor window, as shown in Figure B-1. Build rules are processed in the order they appear in the Rules pane.

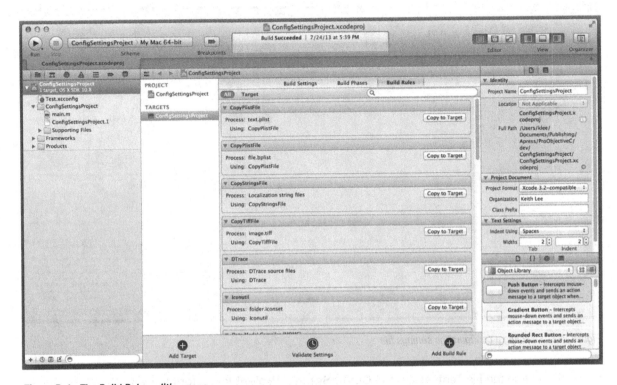

Figure B-1. The Build Rules editing pane

Creating a Configuration Settings File

In this example, you will use Xcode to create a plain-text build configuration settings file for a project.

1. In Xcode, create a new project by selecting **New ▶ Project …** from the Xcode File menu.

2. In the **New Project Assistant** pane, create a command-line application.

3. In the **Project Options** window specify **ConfigSettingsProject** for the Product Name, choose **Foundation** for the Project Type, and select ARC memory management by selecting the **Use Automatic Reference Counting** check box.

4. Specify the location in your file system where you want the project to be created (if necessary select **New Folder** and enter the name and location for the folder), uncheck the **Source Control** check box, and then click the **Create** button.

5. Now you will create the configuration settings file. Select **New ➤ File ...** from the Xcode File menu and select the **Configuration Settings File** template from the **Other** option under OS X (as shown in Figure B-2).

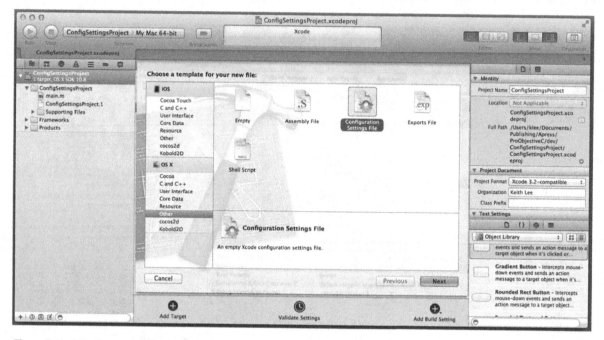

Figure B-2. Selecting a configuration settings file

6. Name the file **Test**, select the **ConfigSettingsProject** folder for the files location and the **ConfigSettingsProject** project as the target, and then click the **Create** button.

7. This creates an empty configuration settings file named Test.xconfig. Now update this file to support code coverage during testing. This is accomplished by setting the configuration flags to **Enable test coverage** and **Instrument program flow**.

```
GCC_GENERATE_TEST_COVERAGE_FILES=YES
GCC_INSTRUMENT_PROGRAM_FLOW_ARCS=YES
```

8. In Xcode, select and update the **Test.xconfig** file, as shown in Figure B-3.

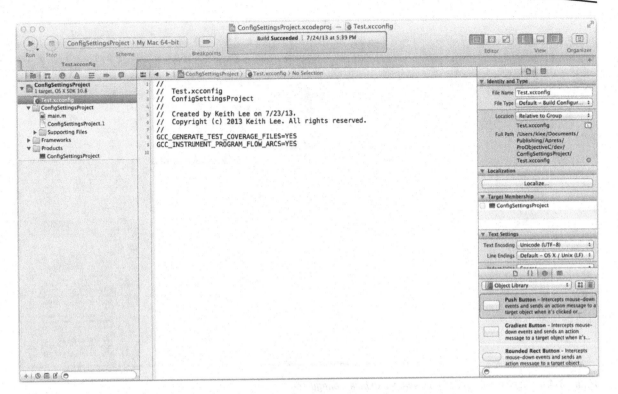

Figure B-3. Edit the configuration settings file to support code coverage

Now you need to add the settings from the file to the current build configuration for the project.

1. In the Xcode project navigator, select the **ConfigSettingsProject**, and then the **ConfigSettingsProject** in the Project Editor, and finally the **Info** tab in the Editor window. Note that the **Debug** configuration (under **Configurations** in the Editor window) has no configurations set.

2. Click the arrow next to Debug to display the ConfigSettingsProject, and then under the configuration file drop-down list select **Test** (as shown in Figure B-4) to update the Debug configuration settings with the values in the Test.xconfig file.

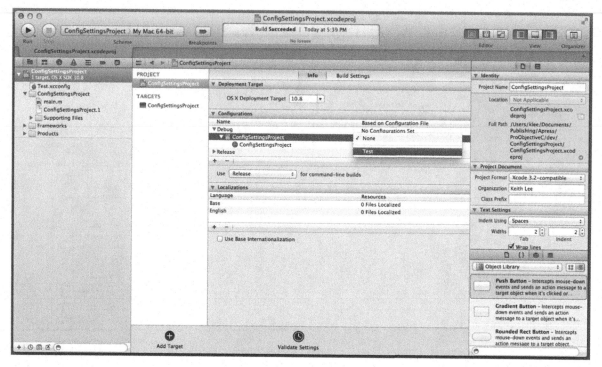

Figure B-4. *Assigning configuration file settings to build configuration*

The settings for the debug configuration have now been updated. You can check this by viewing the updated build settings for test coverage (see Figure B-5).

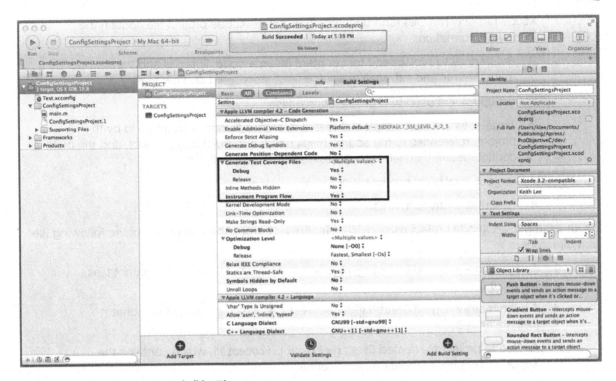

Figure B-5. Updated test coverage build settings

The Xcode Build Setting Reference provides a comprehensive reference for the various build settings available for Xcode.

Projects

An Xcode project is comprised of the artifacts for one or more software products, along with the mechanisms used to build these products and perform actions on them. As such, it contains not only all of the elements used to build a software product(s), but also maintains the relationships between these elements. Each Xcode project consists of the following items:

- *Project content*. The project content includes source files, resources, property list settings files, a precompiled header file, localization files, etc.).

- *Test content*. The test content consists of automated test source files and any required test resources.

- *Xcode project file*. The Xcode project file is actually a subdirectory. It contains various files and directories related to the project that it is a part of. The project file artifacts provide the infrastructure required to build a product and perform the selected actions on it. An Xcode project file is named according to the convention ProjectName.xcodeproj, where ProjectName is the name of the

Xcode project. The files (and directories) within an Xcode project file contain the following information:

- References to project and test content (source code, libraries and frameworks (both internal and external), resource files, storyboard and nib files).

- Group folders used to organize source files.

- Targets, where each target includes a reference to one product build by the project, references to the source file(s) needed to build that product, and the build configurations that can be used to build that product).

- Project-level build configurations.

- Executable environments.

As an example, an Xcode project named GreetingProject would be comprised of the following files and directories:

- A subdirectory named GreetingProject, in which all of the project content files are stored.

- A subdirectory named GreetingProjectTests, in which all of the test content files are stored.

- An Xcode project file named GreetingProject.xcodeproj, which contains the Xcode project file information listed earlier.

An Xcode project can be standalone or included in a workspace. You will learn about workspaces later in this appendix.

Executable Environment

An executable environment defines the configuration used to run a software product from Xcode. The configuration specifies the executable to launch when running/debugging the product, command-line arguments to be passed to the executable (if any), along with any environment variables to be set when running the program. The executable environment settings are edited via a project *scheme*. You will learn about schemes a little later in this appendix.

Workspaces

Workspaces are the Xcode mechanism for supporting and organizing multiple projects. A workspace groups projects and other related documents, thereby facilitating multi-product development. You can share code between projects without having to manually copy and paste project dependencies (e.g., libraries, along with their corresponding public header files), yet still manage each project individually. An Xcode workspace can discover implicit dependencies between projects, and thus resolve these dependencies automatically during build. In addition, workspaces also enable you to more easily create and use external (i.e., third-party) software libraries.

Each workspace is, in fact, an Xcode document composed of metadata that can contain any number of Xcode projects, plus any other files you want to include. In addition to organizing all the files in each Xcode project, a workspace provides implicit and explicit relationships among the included projects and their targets. The workspace document contains pointers to the included projects and other files, but no other data. A project can belong to more than one workspace.

You can include a project in a workspace by simply dragging the project file into the workspace (or by using an Xcode command to add files to a workspace) and it becomes available for use by all other projects in the workspace. However, projects in a workspace are still managed separately, and builds of software products within a workspace will automatically resolve dependencies between projects (and recompile these projects as necessary if their contents have been updated).

By default, all the Xcode projects in a workspace are built in the same directory, referred to as the *workspace build directory*. Each workspace has its own build directory. Because all of the files in all of the projects in a workspace are in the same build directory, all of these files are visible to each project. Therefore, if two or more projects use the same libraries, you don't need to copy them into each project folder separately.

Xcode examines the files in the build directory to discover implicit dependencies. For example, if one project included in a workspace builds a library that is linked against another project in the same workspace, Xcode automatically builds the library before building the other project, even if the build configuration does not make this dependency explicit. You can override such implicit dependencies with explicit build settings, if necessary. For explicit dependencies, you must create project references.

Each project in a workspace continues to have its own independent identity. To work on a project without affecting—or being affected by—the other projects in the workspace, you can open the project without opening the workspace, or you can add the project to another workspace. Because a project can belong to more than one workspace, you can work on your projects in any number of combinations without having to reconfigure any of the projects or workspaces.

You can use the workspace's default build directory or you can specify one. If a project specifies a build directory, the build directory of whatever workspace the project is in at the time you build the project overrides that directory.

Adding an Existing Project to a Workspace

In Xcode, perform the following steps to add an existing project to a workspace:

1. In the project navigator, Control-click in the empty space below the projects in the list. In the pop-up menu that follows, select **Add Files to "<WorkspaceName>"...**, where *WorkspaceName* is the name of the workspace.

2. Navigate to the folder containing the corresponding Xcode project file (it ends with .xcodeproj).

3. Select the project file and click **Add**.

The project is now part of the workspace, and thus its contents can be shared with other projects in the workspace.

Using Static Libraries in a Workspace

Now you will learn how to incorporate static libraries into a workspace. Briefly, the steps you will perform are as follows:

1. Create workspace.

2. Create static library.

3. Create app.

> **Note**   The following example program was developed using Xcode version 4.6.3. Xcode version 4.5 or greater is required for the configuration steps documented in this example (particularly those used to share static libraries) to work properly.

Creating a Workspace

First. you will create a workspace that you will use for the library and app.

1. In Xcode, create a new workspace by selecting **New ➤ Workspace ...** from the Xcode File menu.

2. Save the workspace as **HelloSpace** in a new folder named Hello. As shown in Figure B-6, a new workspace named HelloSpace.xcworkspace is displayed in the Xcode window.

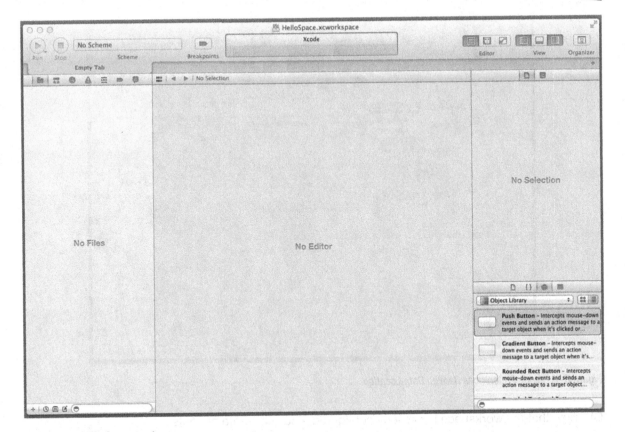

Figure B-6. HelloSpace workspace

As you learned earlier, a workspace builds its projects in a *Derived Data* directory. The location for this directory must be identical at the project level and as specified in the Xcode preferences pane.

3. In Xcode, open the preferences pane by selecting **Preferences ...** from the Xcode menu. In the preferences pane, select the **Location** tab, and then select **Default** from the **Derived Data:** drop-down list (as shown in Figure B-7).

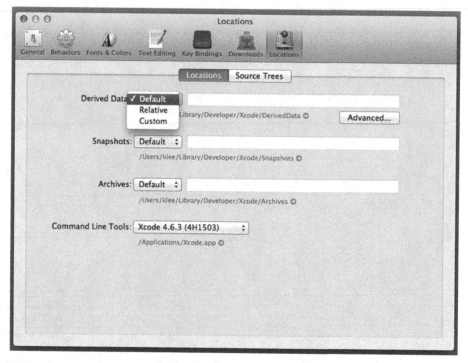

Figure B-7. Xcode Preferences Derived Data Location

OK, now that the workspace is properly configured, you will create projects.

Creating a Static Library

Now you will create a static library.

1. In Xcode, create a new project by selecting **New ➤ Project …** from the
    Xcode File menu.

2. In the **New Project Assistant** pane, create a Cocoa library by first selecting
    Framework & Library (under the Mac OS X section), and then selecting the
    Cocoa Library icon in the upper-right pane (as shown in Figure B-8).

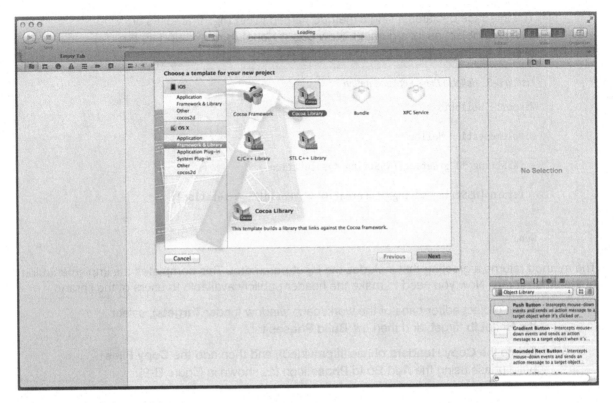

Figure B-8. Creating a Cocoa Library

3. The Project Options window is then displayed. Specify the Product Name as **HelloLib**, the Type drop-down list as **Static** (to create a static library), and select the check box to specify that the project will use **Automatic Reference Counting** for memory management. Do not select the check box for Include Unit Tests, and accept the defaults for the rest of the options.

4. Now click **Next** to bring up the **Project Options** window. In this window, specify **Hello** for location of the project, select **HelloSpace** in the **Add to:** drop-down list (to add this library to the HelloSpace workspace), and then click the **Create** button.

5. In the Xcode project navigator, observe that an empty HelloLib class is created. Select **HelloLib.h** and update the class interface as shown in Listing B-2.

Listing B-2. HelloLib Class Interface

```
#import <Foundation/Foundation.h>

@interface HelloLib : NSObject

- (NSString *) greeting:(NSString *)salutation;

@end
```

6. The interface declares a single method named `greeting:` that takes an NSString object as its argument. Now select **HelloLib.m** and update the class implementation as shown in Listing B-3.

Listing B-3. HelloLib Class Implementation

```
#import "HelloLib.h"

@implementation HelloLib

- (NSString *) greeting:(NSString *)salutation
{
  return [NSString stringWithFormat:@"%@, World!", salutation];
}

@end
```

The method returns a greeting that includes the input parameter. This completes the implementation of the static library. Now you need to make the header publicly available to users of the library.

1. In the project editor pane of the workspace window (under **Targets**), select the **HelloLib** target, and then the **Build Phases** tab.

2. Delete the **Copy Headers** phase (if provided), and then add the **Copy Files** build phase using the **Add Build Phase** icon (as shown in Figure B-9).

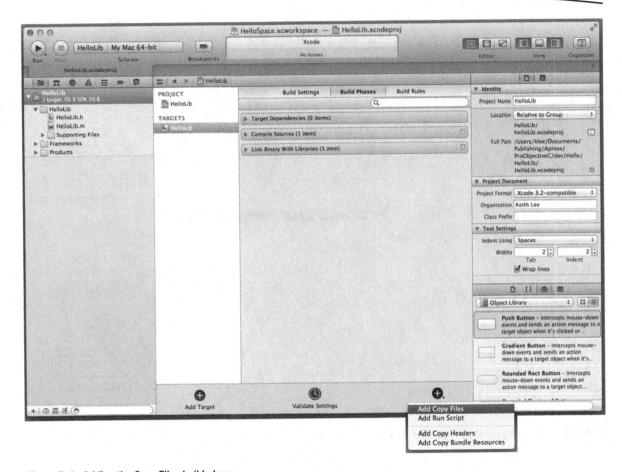

Figure B-9. Adding the Copy Files build phase

3. Now disclose for the **Copy Files** phase by clicking the neighboring triangle. You will see a location for adding files at the bottom of the window (it's labeled **Add files here**). From the project navigator, drag a copy of the **HelloLib.h** header into this area and release it. This will make this header file available to clients.

4. In the Copy Files area, set the **Subpath** to **include/${PRODUCT_NAME}**, and select **Products Directory** in the Destination drop-down list. The workspace window should now look as shown in Figure B-10.

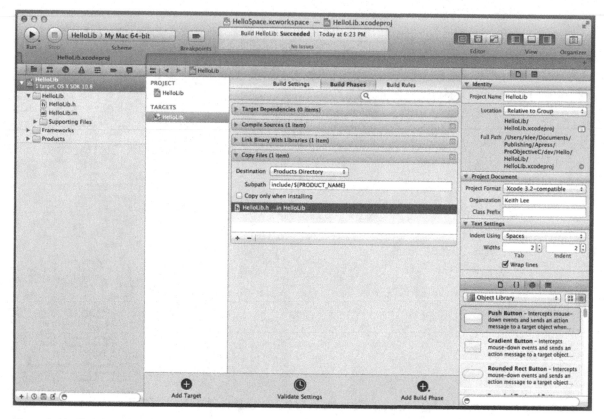

Figure B-10. *Updating the Copy Files build phase*

> **Note** The subpath setting will copy files into a folder named after the library (i.e., HelloLib), inside a folder named include, inside the workspace built products directory. This setting enables you to organize header files for different libraries by library name. The include folder inside a build products directory is in the default header search path for applications.

5. Finally, you should share the library, thereby making it available to any project using the workspace. In Xcode, select **Scheme ➤ Manage Schemes ...** from the Xcode Product menu. The Manage Schemes dialog will be displayed. Then locate the **HelloLib** scheme in this dialog and click the **Shared** check box.

6. Now select the **Build Settings** tab. Use the Search tool to find the **Skip Install** setting and set that to **Yes**; this prevents Xcode from creating a multiapplication bundle when projects that use this library are archived. This setting must be made for both the HelloLib project and HelloLib target.

With those steps completed, your static library is properly configured. Now let's create the app.

Creating the App

Now you will create the application that uses the static library.

1. In Xcode, create a new project by selecting **New ➤ Project …** from the Xcode File menu.

2. In the **New Project Assistant** pane, create a command-line application by selecting the **Command Line Tool** icon (from the **Application** selection under OS X template groups).

3. In the **Project Options** window, specify **HelloApp** for the Product Name, choose **Foundation** for the Project Type, and select ARC memory management by checking the **Use Automatic Reference Counting** check box. Specify the location in your file system where you want the project to be created (if necessary, select **New Folder** and enter the name and location for the folder) and uncheck the **Source Control** check box.

4. Finally, select **HelloSpace** in the **Add to:** and **Group:** drop-down lists (to add this library to the HelloSpace workspace), and then click the **Create** button.

The first thing you'll do is link the app against the static library.

1. Select the **HelloApp** project in the project navigator, and then select the **HelloApp** target in the project editor.

2. Select the **Build Phases** tab, disclose the **Link Binaries With Libraries** phase, and click the plus (+) button.

3. In the window, choose **libHelloLib.a** and click **Add** to add the library.

Next you'll update build configuration settings to link the library:

1. Select the **Build Settings** tab.

2. Find the **Other Linker Flags** build setting (using the search tool) and add the flag -ObjC to this setting's value, if not present (as shown in Figure B-11).

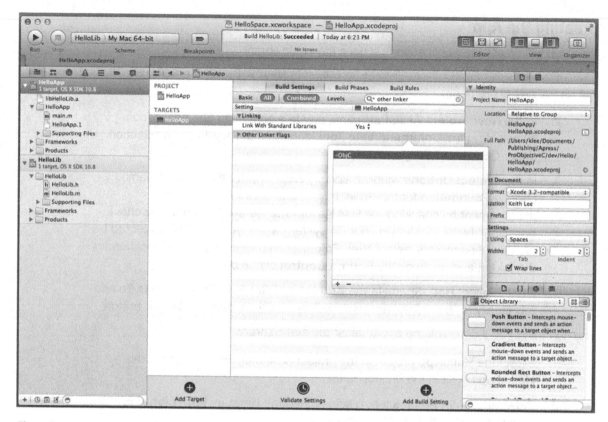

Figure B-11. *Updating the Copy Files build phase*

The -ObjC flag will tell the linker to link all Objective-C classes and categories from static libraries into your application, even if the linker can't tell that they are used (e.g., categories and/or classes added dynamically).

Now you need to import the header file for the static library.

The build products for all the projects in a workspace are located in the workspace build directory. Earlier, you copied the HelloLib.h header file into the Products Directory include directory. This directory is automatically included in the search path for all projects in the workspace. Because you specified a subdirectory named after the PRODUCT_NAME build setting (e.g., include/${PRODUCT_NAME}) in the subpath, the import statement should include that directory, for example:

```
#import "HelloLib/HelloLib.h"
```

OK, now you will add the code to the app to demonstrate use of the static library. In the project navigator, select the **main.m** file for the HelloApp and make the updates shown in Listing B-4.

Listing B-4. HelloApp main() Function

```
#import <Foundation/Foundation.h>
#import "HelloLib/HelloLib.h"

int main(int argc, const char * argv[])
{
  @autoreleasepool
  {
    HelloLib *hello = [HelloLib new];
    NSLog(@"%@", [hello greeting:@"Hello"]);
  }
  return 0;
}
```

The header file for the HelloLib static library is imported with the statement.

```
#import "HelloLib/HelloLib.h"
```

The main() function creates a HelloLib instance and invokes its greeting: method. When you compile and run the program, you should observe the messages in the output pane shown in Figure B-12.

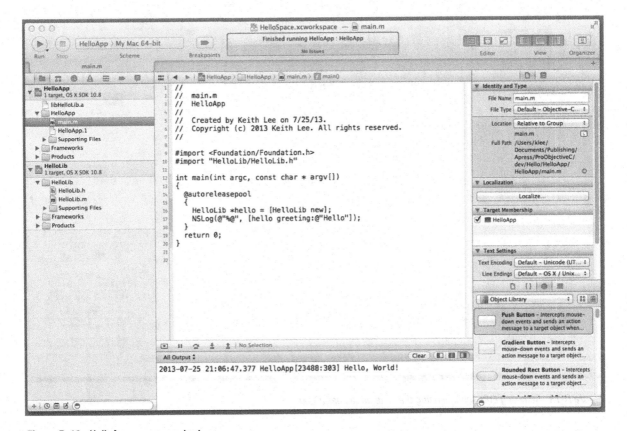

Figure B-12. HelloApp program output

Cool. This demonstrates how to incorporate static libraries into your projects using Xcode workspaces. The same techniques apply for other reusable software libraries (dynamic libraries, frameworks, bundles, etc.).

Schemes

An Xcode scheme groups one or more targets with a build configuration and an environment execution configuration, with respect to the purpose (i.e., action) for which you are building the product.

You can have as many schemes as you want, but only one can be active at a time. You can specify whether a scheme should be stored in a project—in which case it's available in every workspace that includes that project, or in the workspace—in which case it's available only in that workspace. When you select an active scheme, you also select a run destination (that is, the architecture of the hardware for which the products are built).

To edit a scheme, select **Edit Scheme...** from the Scheme toolbar menu in the Xcode workspace window, as shown in Figure B-13.

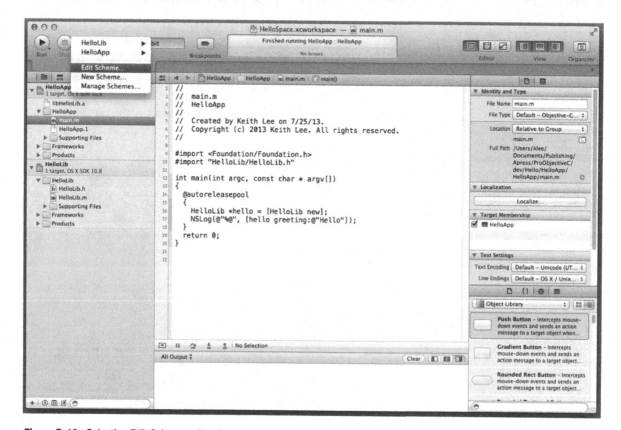

Figure B-13. Selecting Edit Scheme using the scheme toolbar menu

The Scheme pop-up dialog allows you to specify many settings that affect product build and the actions performed on a product. As shown in Figure B-14, the left column lists actions that correspond to commands in the Product menu: Run, Test, Profile, Analyze, and Archive. The Build option allows you to select the targets to build for each of these actions.

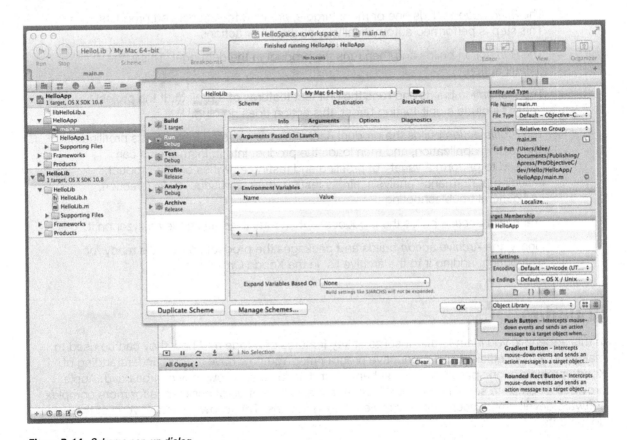

Figure B-14. Scheme pop-up dialog

As shown in Figure B-14, the tabs at the top of the scheme dialog vary according to the action performed on the product. They enable you to configure the build and the execution environment appropriately.

Actions

In Xcode, an action builds a target (thereby creating a product) and processes the product accordingly. Xcode defines the Build, Run, Test, Profile, Analyze, and Archive actions.

- The *Build action* builds one or more targets, creating the associated products. This step is performed automatically by all the other actions.

- The *Run action* builds and then runs the product in the debugger. This is the default action.

- The *Test action* builds and runs the unit test features of a project. If the project doesn't include a unit-testing target, this action does nothing.

- The *Profile action* builds the product, launches the selected Instruments profiling and testing application, and then loads the product into it. Instruments can be used to perform a variety of profiling and testing activities on the product, including performance analysis, stress testing, memory usage, leak detection, and general troubleshooting.

- The *Analyze action* builds the product and then runs the static code analyzer on it.

- Finally, the *Archive action* builds and packages the product so that it is ready for distribution, adding it to the archive list in the Xcode Organizer.

Roundup

In this appendix, you learned about some of key features of Xcode and how they can be used to make you a more efficient and productive programmer. You now have a good understanding of Xcode projects, workspaces, targets, schemes, and actions, and how they can be used. Apple provides a complete set of reference documents that will be of great assistance for more complex software development scenarios and project configurations. The following lists several of these documents.

- Xcode User Guide

- Xcode Release Notes

- Xcode Build Setting Reference

- Instruments User Guide

- Instruments User Reference

- App Distribution Guide

Using LLDB

Software development can be a complex and (at times) error-prone process. As you have learned over the course of reading this book, the Objective-C platform provides a myriad of features to make you a more efficient, productive programmer. However, the bottom line is that the programs you write will have bugs; so the question is how do you mitigate them? Specifically, how do you detect bugs, validate program correctness, and analyze program control flow? Or perhaps of even greater importance, what is the process you use for debugging code? For example, do you analyze program state by inserting debugging statements in your source code? The Xcode debugger is the key tool for detecting runtime and logical errors in your software. In addition, it provides a variety of features that can also make you better at debugging.

In this appendix, you will learn about debugging your programs in Xcode using the LLVM Debugger (LLDB). We'll begin by briefly reviewing the LLVM compiler infrastructure, several of whose components are leveraged by LLDB. Next, you will explore the design of LLDB and review its key components. You will then learn how Xcode supports debugging with LLDB, and finally debug a few example programs with LLDB, thereby becoming familiar with some of its key features. By the end of this appendix, you should be convinced of the power and capability of LLDB, and will use it whenever you program with Xcode using Objective-C.

LLVM Overview

LLVM (originally an acronym for *Low Level Virtual Machine*) was conceived as a compiler framework for programs written in arbitrary languages. Currently, the LLVM project consists of a collection of modular, reusable components (libraries, toolsets, runtimes) used for program analysis and compilation (as shown in Figure C-1).

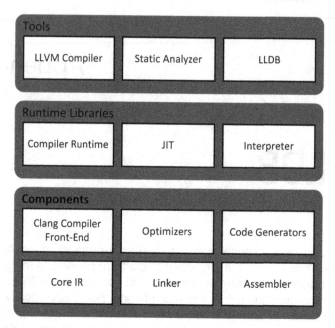

Figure C-1. LLVM project components

These components can be used as infrastructure to implement a variety of capabilities, such as compilers, optimizers, and debuggers. The following are brief definitions for several of the components under the LLVM project:

- *Clang compiler*: Clang is a modern compiler for the C, Objective-C, and C++ programming languages. It is responsible for parsing, validating, and diagnosing errors in the input code, and then translating the parsed code into LLVM intermediate representation (IR). Like the LLVM project, Clang is itself divided into modular, reusable libraries that expose public APIs.

- *Optimizers*: The LLVM optimizers perform code optimization, traversing some portion of code to either collect information or perform transformations. Their features include compile-time optimization, link-time optimization, and optimization across language boundaries.

- *Code generator*: The LLVM target-independent code generator is a framework that provides a suite of reusable components for translating the LLVM internal representation to the machine code for a specified target—either in assembly form (suitable for a static compiler) or in binary machine code form (usable for a JIT compiler).

- *Disassembler*: The disassembler takes an LLVM bitcode file and converts it into human-readable LLVM assembly language.

- *JIT*: The LLVM Just-in-Time (JIT) compiler performs runtime translation of LLVM IR code into machine code. It also performs runtime optimization based on dynamic information.

As depicted in Figure C-1, a few of the tools that have been built using the LLVM project components include the LLVM compiler (the standard compiler for Xcode), the static analyzer (also used by Xcode), and the LLDB debugger. Xcode's integration with LLVM components and tools provides many benefits in addition to Objective-C source code compilation. These benefits include real-time notification of warnings and errors as you type your code, suggested corrections for coding mistakes, improved code completion, source code static analysis, and comprehensive support for program debugging with LLDB, the default debugger for Xcode.

LLDB

LLDB is a modern, high-performance debugger for the C, C++, and Objective-C programming languages. It is built as a set of reusable components that leverage existing components and libraries of the LLVM Project (Clang compiler, JIT, disassembler, etc.). LLDB provides up-to-date C, C++, and Objective-C language support, support for expressions that can declare local variables and types, just-in-time compilation of expressions for improved performance, and a public API that enables LLDB to be used for other purposes (disassembly, object and symbol file introspection, etc.) in addition to debugging. The entire LLDB API is also available as Python functions through a script-bridging interface. This means the LLDB API's can be used directly from Python or, alternatively, Python can be used within the LLDB command-line tool. LLDB can be run standalone via its command-line tool or directly within Xcode.

Design

LLDB was developed using object-oriented design practices, including data encapsulation (no global variables) and a plug-in based architecture that facilitates modularity and extensibility. The next few paragraphs provide an overview of the libraries that comprise LLDB and examine in more detail a few of its significant design elements.

Libraries

LLDB is designed as a collection of libraries that are logically grouped, as follows:

- *API*: The LLDB public interface, currently written in C++. This API enables LLDB to be reused by other programs. It is also used by the LLDB command-line tool.

- *Breakpoint*: A collection of classes that implement debugging breakpoints. LLDB supports line breakpoints, symbolic breakpoints, and exception breakpoints. Exception breakpoints are hit anytime an exception is thrown or caught. Symbolic breakpoints cause program execution to pause when a symbol name (e.g., a method invocation or function call) is encountered.

- *Commands*: A collection of classes that implement the functionality for the textual commands of the LLDB command-line tool.

- *Core*: Classes that implement basic functionality required by LLDB.

- *Data formatters*: A collection of classes that implement the data formatters for LLDB. These are used to define custom display options for debugging variables.

- *Expressions*: These classes are used to perform expression parsing. They can evaluate DWARF expressions up to programming language (e.g., Objective-C) expressions using the Clang compiler front end. DWARF is a general-purpose debugging file format used to support source-level debugging. DWARF expressions describe how to compute a value or how to name a location during the debugging of a program. The expression classes enable a variety of features, including multiline expressions, local variable support, flow control, and persistent expression global variables.

- Host: A set of classes that provide an abstraction from the host on which LLDB is running (system functions, etc.).

- *Interpreter*: A collection of classes responsible for being the base classes needed for each command object. It is responsible for tracking and running command-line commands.

- *Symbol*: Classes that provide everything needed in order to parse object files and debug symbols. All the needed classes for compilation units (code and debug info for a source file), functions, lexical blocks within functions, inlined functions, types, declaration locations, and variables are in this section.

- *Target*: A set of classes that encapsulate data for a debug target (target, process, thread, stack frames, etc.).

- *Utility*: LLDB utility classes (string data extractors, etc.).

Expression Parsing

One of the most important features of a debugger is its ability to display the values of objects from the target program, also referred to as *expression evaluation*. Hence, a debugger's expression evaluation capabilities are a key element of its design and implementation. Most debuggers implement a custom expression parser, and thus also create custom type representations used by the parser. As a consequence, changes to these type representations (e.g., as a result of programming language changes) requires changes to the parser. In addition, the expression parser aims for compiler-level accuracy. This level of accuracy is extremely difficult (if not impossible) to achieve, and also makes it difficult for the debugger to remain current with changes to the language and/or compiler. These factors, among others, make it difficult to write and maintain a debugger.

LLDB mitigates these issues by utilizing the LLVM Clang compiler front end; specifically, it converts debugging information into Clang data types. This enables LLDB to use Clang to parse command expressions and thus directly support the latest C, C++, Objective C, and Objective C++ language features and runtimes. Debugger error reporting is improved because it is identical to that provided by the compiler. LLDB also leverages the compiler for other functionalities, including making function calls within expressions and disassembling instructions.

Plug-in Architecture

LLDB is designed with a plug-in-based architecture for portability and extensibility. This enables it to easily utilize different implementations for supported functionality and to incorporate new plug-ins with no impact on the existing codebase. The plug-in architecture is currently used for object file parsers (currently supports Mach-O and ELF files), object container parsers (Mach-O and BSD archives), debug symbol file parsers (DWARF and Mach-O symbol tables), symbol vendors, disassembly (LLVM and ARM/Thumb), and general debugger plug-ins for host and target-specific functions.

Multithreaded Debugging

Many programs have multiple threads, and debugging multithreaded applications can be difficult under even the best circumstances. LLDB is designed to support multithreaded debugging. It displays diagnostic information for each thread and provides a set of commands for operating on one or more threads within an application.

LLDB Commands

LLDB includes a comprehensive set of debugging commands that can be used with both Xcode and the command-line tool. The following are several of the commonly used LLDB debugger commands:

- `apropos`: Finds a list of debugger commands related to a particular word or subject.

- `breakpoint`: A set of commands that perform operations on breakpoints (set, clear, enable, disable, etc.). A breakpoint pauses execution of a target program, thereby enabling you to examine its current state. LLDB supports line breakpoints (set on a line of source code), symbolic breakpoints (set on a symbol [e.g., function/method name] in a program), and exception breakpoints (set when an exception is thrown or caught).

- `disassemble`: Disassemble bytes in a function, an address, and so forth.

- `expression`: Evaluates a C/C++/Objective-C expression in the current target using both user-defined variables and variables currently in scope.

- `frame`: A set of commands for operating on the current thread's stack frame (info, select, variable).

- `help`: Shows a list of all debugger commands.

- `log`: A set of commands for operating on logs.

- `memory`: A set of commands that performs operations on memory (e.g., read from, write to).

- `process`: A set of commands for operating on a process (launch, kill, attach, detach, connect, etc.).

- `register`: A set of commands used to access thread registers (read, write, etc.).

- **thread**: A set of commands used to operate on one or more threads (single step, step over, continue, etc.). This enables you to control execution of a target program being debugged.

- **watchpoint**: A set of commands for operating on watchpoints (set, clear, enable, disable, etc.). A watchpoint is a form of conditional breakpoints set on a variable. It causes the target to stop execution whenever the value of the watched variable is changed.

LLDB implements a structured command syntax that facilitates its use and provides a mechanism to construct aliases for commonly used commands. The command-line tool also supports command completion for source file names, symbol names, and so forth with the Tab key. The general syntax for LLDB CLI commands is as follows:

```
<noun> <verb> [-options [option-value]] [argument [argument...]]
```

Each command has a subcommand (i.e., the verb) along with its applicable options and arguments. Listing C-1 depicts an example of an LLDB debugging session of the application named FirstProject (recall that you developed this application in Chapter 1) using the command-line tool.

Listing C-1. Example LLDB Debug Session Using the Command-Line Tool:

```
% xcrun lldb
(lldb) target create FirstProject
(lldb) breakpoint set --name main
(lldb) process launch
(lldb) thread step-over
(lldb) breakpoint set --line 42
(lldb) thread continue
(lldb) expression (void)NSLog(@"Date = %@", dateTime)
(lldb) quit
```

As shown in Listing C-1, xcrun is an Xcode command that loads a binary contained within an Xcode bundle. This enables you to run LLDB from the command line. Next, the *target create* command loads the FirstProject application as a target for the debugger. The *breakpoint set* command sets a breakpoint at the main method. The expression (void)NSLog(@"Date = %@", dateTime) command evaluates an Objective-C expression that displays the current value for the dateTime object. The *quit* command ends the debugging session.

Xcode LLDB Integration

LLDB is the default debugger in Xcode, which augments the standard functionality of LLDB with a variety of features that can make you more efficient at debugging your code. Figure C-2 depicts an example debugging session in Xcode. In the following paragraphs, you will examine these features in more detail.

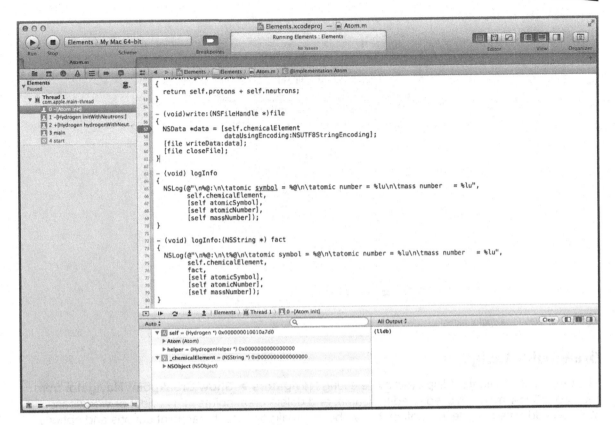

Figure C-2. Xcode debugging with LLDB

Debug Navigator

The debug navigator (displayed by selecting **Navigators ➤ Show Debug Navigator** from the Xcode **View** menu) displays the call stacks of your application when paused at a breakpoint. The navigator groups the stack frames by threads or queues (depending upon the view selected). It also enables you to view the memory of variables. The debug navigator opens automatically whenever you pause a running application or it hits a breakpoint. Figure C-3 depicts the debug navigator pane.

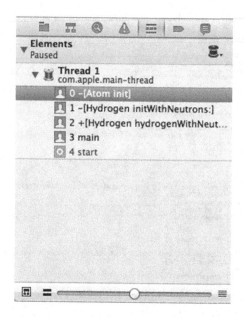

Figure C-3. Debug navigator pane

Breakpoint Navigator

The breakpoint navigator (displayed by selecting **Navigators ➤ Show Breakpoint Navigator** from the Xcode **View** menu) is used to edit, disable, and delete breakpoints in a project or workspace. You can add/delete a (line, exception, or symbolic) breakpoint, set breakpoint actions and options, specify the scope of a breakpoint, and share a breakpoint. Figure C-4 depicts the breakpoint navigator pane.

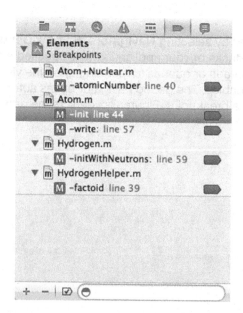

Figure C-4. Breakpoint navigator pane

Breakpoint Actions

A breakpoint action defines an operation performed when a target program reaches a breakpoint. Xcode provides the following breakpoint actions.

- *Debugger command*: This action evaluates a debugger command. As you recall from earlier in this appendix, the debugger is able to execute C/C++/Objective-C expressions, making this a very powerful tool.

- *Log message command*: This command logs a message to the output console or speaks a message.

- *Shell command*: This command executes a shell command (/usr/bin/ls, etc.).

- *Sound command*: This command plays a sound.

- *AppleScript command*: This command evaluates AppleScript code.

Breakpoint actions are configured when you edit a breakpoint. This can be done in the breakpoint navigator by Control-clicking the breakpoint, and then choosing **Edit Breakpoint...** from the shortcut menu (as shown in Figure C-5).

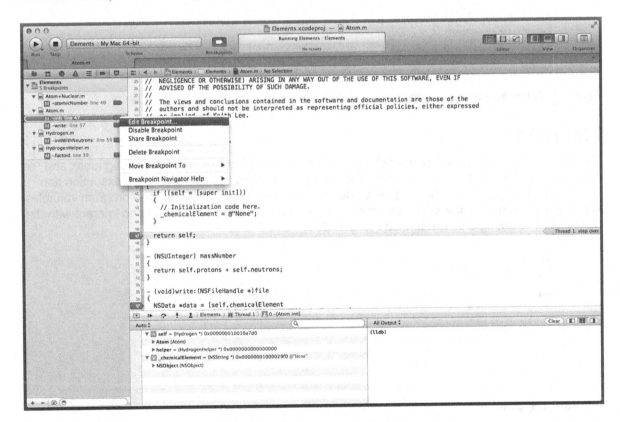

Figure C-5. Editing a breakpoint from the breakpoint navigator pane

The breakpoint action pop-up window enables you to select the type of command to be performed when the target program reaches a breakpoint. You can configure an option that defines additional breakpoint behaviors and you can set other properties specific to the type of breakpoint selected. Figure C-6 displays a breakpoint action configured to perform a debugger command that prints the value of the _chemicalElement instance variable, and then automatically continues program execution after the command is executed.

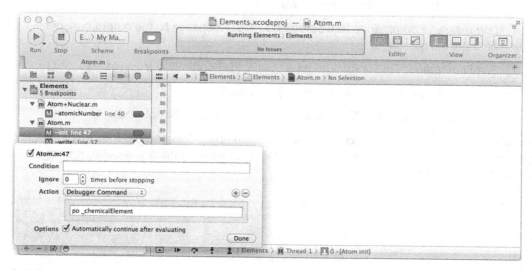

Figure C-6. *Configuring a breakpoint action*

Debug Area

The debug area is comprised of the debug bar (toolbar located at the top of the debug area), and the content pane (the remainder of the area). The debug bar is used to control program execution and to navigate through source code. The left side of the content pane is used to view program variables and registers. The right side of the content pane is used to view console output and interact with the debugger. The debug area is depicted in Figure C-7.

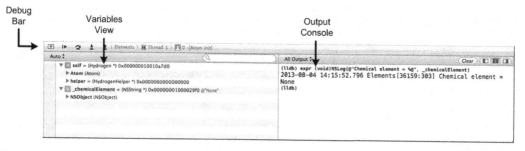

Figure C-7. *Debug area*

The debug bar is used to control target program execution and to navigate through its source code. There are five buttons on the left of the debug bar; from left to right, these buttons are used to

- Show/hide the debug area.

- Pause/resume program execution.

- Step over (i.e., execute) an instruction. If the instruction is a method/function call, it causes the whole method/function to be executed.

- Step into (i.e., execute) an instruction. If the instruction is a method/function call, it causes the debugger to jump to the first line of the method/function.

- Step out of the method/function. This causes the debugger to complete execution of the current method/function and jump to the next calling method/ function or back to the method/function that called it.

The remainder of the debug area displays a pop-up menu that enables you to choose a thread in the program to debug.

The content pane is used to display variables and also provide a command-line interface for entering debugging commands. As depicted in Figure C-7, the left side of the content pane displays the *variables view* (for displaying values the variables in the current context), while the right side displays the output console (for the LLDB command-line interface in which debugger commands are executed).

Disassembly View

Xcode provides a disassembly view that enables you to view the set of assembly-language instructions seen by the debugger while your program is running. You can configure Xcode to display disassembly only, or both the source code and corresponding disassembly. To choose the disassembly view, select **Debug Workflow ➤ Show Disassembly When Debugging** from the Xcode Product menu. Figure C-8 displays both the source and disassembly view in the Xcode split editor pane.

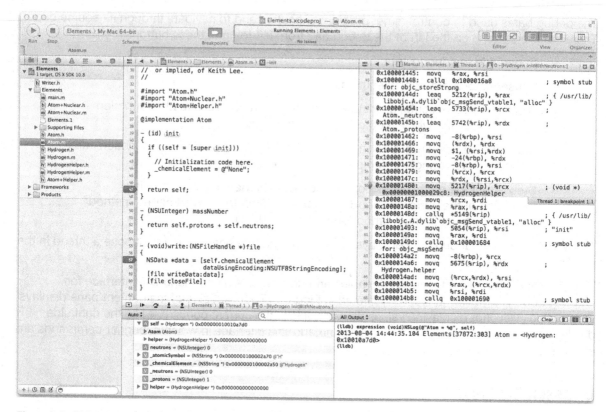

Figure C-8. Disassembly view

Using LLDB in Xcode

Now that you have received an overview of LLDB and debugging with Xcode, you will debug a program using Xcode. In Xcode, create a new project by selecting **New ➤ Project...** from the Xcode File menu. In the **New Project Assistant** pane, create a command-line application by selecting the **Command Line Tool** icon (from the **Application** selection under OS X template groups). In the **Project Options** window, specify **BrokenCalculator** for the Product Name, choose **Foundation** for the Project Type, and select ARC memory management by selecting the **Use Automatic Reference Counting** check box. Specify the location in your file system where you want the project to be created (if necessary, select **New Folder** and enter the name and location for the folder) and uncheck the **Source Control** check box.

Now create the calculator class. Select **New ➤ File...** from the Xcode File menu, select the **Objective-C** class template, and name the class **Calculator**. Select the **BrokenCalculator** folder for the files location and the **BrokenCalculator** project as the target, and then click the **Create** button. Next, in the project navigator pane, select the **Calculator.h** file and update the class interface as shown in Listing C-2.

Listing C-2. Calculator Class Interface

```
#import <Foundation/Foundation.h>

@interface Calculator : NSObject

- (NSNumber *) sumAddend1:(NSNumber *)adder1 addend2:(NSNumber *)adder2;

@end
```

The class declares a single instance method for returning the sum of two numbers. Next, use the Xcode project navigator to select the **Calculator.m** file and code the implementation as shown in Listing C-3.

Listing C-3. Calculator Class Implementation

```
#import "Calculator.h"

@implementation Calculator

- (NSNumber *) sumAddend1:(NSNumber *)adder1 addend2:(NSNumber *)adder2
{
    return [NSNumber numberWithInteger:([adder1 integerValue] +
                                        [adder2 integerValue])];
}
@end
```

The method returns the sum of the integer values of the two input parameters. OK, that's pretty straightforward, now let's move on to the main() function. In the project navigator, select the **main.m** file and update the main() function as shown in Listing C-4.

Listing C-4. BrokenCalculator main() Function

```
#import <Foundation/Foundation.h>
#import "Calculator.h"

int main(int argc, const char * argv[])
{
  @autoreleasepool
  {
    // Create instance and numbers to add
    Calculator *calculator = [[Calculator alloc] init];
    NSNumber *addend1 = [NSNumber numberWithInteger:10];
    NSNumber *addend2 = [NSNumber numberWithInteger:15];
    NSNumber *addend3 = [NSNumber numberWithInteger:-25];

    // Add numbers and validate correct sum returned
    NSNumber *sum1 = [calculator sumAddend1:addend1 addend2:addend2];
    NSCAssert(([sum1 intValue] == 25), @"Invalid sum computed");
```

```
    NSNumber *sum2 = [calculator sumAddend1:addend1 addend2:addend3];
    NSCAssert(([sum2 intValue] == 15),  @"Invalid sum computed");
  }
  return 0;
}
```

The method creates a `Calculator` instance and `NSNumber` instances, and then adds two numbers and validates that the correct sum is returned. When you compile and run the program, you should observe the messages in the output pane, as shown in Figure C-9.

Figure C-9. BrokenCalculator program output

Figure C-9 shows that an exception was thrown—specifically an assertion failed, indicating that the sum returned was not the expected value. Now you will use the debugger to determine the cause of the problem. In the breakpoint navigator, add an exception breakpoint by clicking the plus (+) symbol at the bottom left of the navigator pane and selecting **Add Exception Breakpoint...** from the pop-up menu (as shown in Figure C-10).

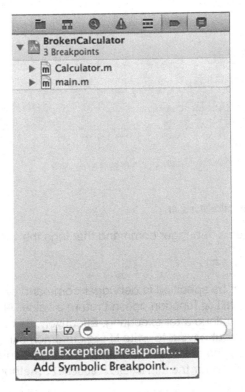

Figure C-10. Adding an exception breakpoint

In the exception breakpoint dialog, there are several settings. For **Exception**, select **All** (set on all exceptions), and for **Break**, select **On Throw** (set breakpoint when exception is thrown). When you compile and run the program, you should observe that the program pauses in the main function at the following line:

```
NSCAssert((([sum2 intValue] == 15),  @"Invalid sum computed");
```

You can see that this assertion fails, causing the exception to be thrown. Now you will set some line breakpoints to troubleshoot the program. You set a line breakpoint in Xcode by clicking the gutter next to the corresponding line in your source code. In the project navigator, select the **Calculator.m** file and set a breakpoint at the line with the following statement:

```
return [NSNumber numberWithInteger:([adder1 integerValue] +
                                    [adder2 integerValue])];
```

Next, in the `main()` function, set a breakpoint at the line with the following statement:

```
NSCAssert((([sum1 intValue] == 25),  @"Invalid sum computed");
```

Now edit this breakpoint to add a breakpoint action, as shown in Figure C-11.

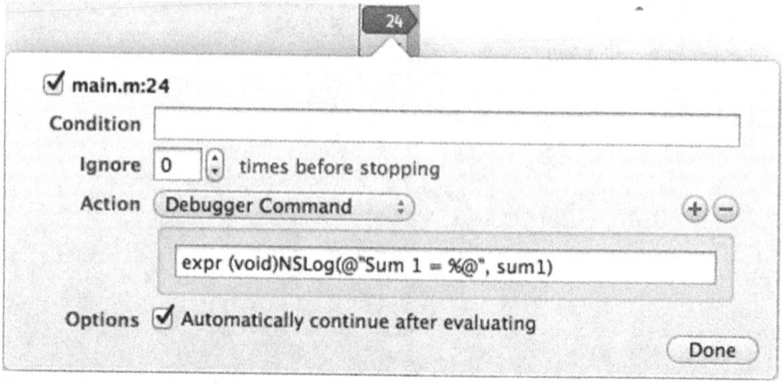

Figure C-11. *Edit breakpoint action for calculator sum*

This breakpoint action executes a debugger command that logs the value stored in variable `sum1`.

```
expr (void)NSLog(@"Sum 1 = %@", sum1)
```

Notice that the return type must be specified in debugger command expressions. In this case, the type is `void`, signifying that the `NSLog` function doesn't return a value. Also note that the breakpoint option is set to automatically continue after executing. Effectively, this enables you to display the value of a program variable without having to write `NSLog` statements in your code, and hence avoid cluttering your code with debugging statements! When you compile and run the program, it pauses execution at the line breakpoint set for the `sumAddend1:addend2:` method, as shown in Figure C-12.

Figure C-12. *Pausing execution at line breakpoint in sumAddend1:addend2: method*

In the debug area content pane, you can see that the values for variables adder1 and adder2 are as expected. Now you would like to validate the return value from this method. This can be done with the step-out command (located in the debug bar). This command executes the remaining lines of a method/function in which the current execution point lies, and then displays the next statement following the method/function call. Select this button two times. After that is done, the return value is displayed in the content pane display area (**Return Value**), as shown in Figure C-13.

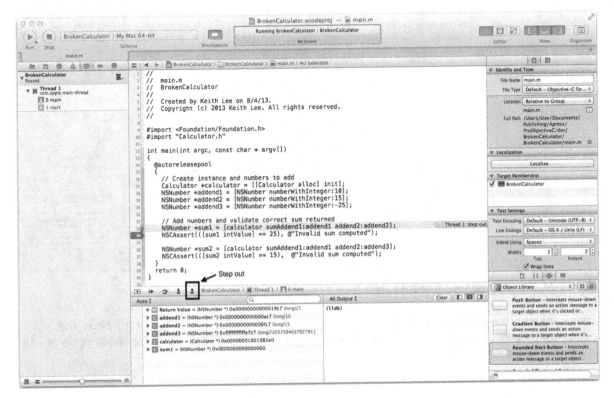

Figure C-13. *Displaying the return value of a method using the debugger*

The return value of 25 (shown in Figure C-13) is correct. Next, select **continue** in the debug bar (you may have to click the button two or three times). The output console logs Sum 1 = 25, per the breakpoint action debugger command that you configured earlier. Now observe that the debugger has paused again at the line breakpoint set for the sumAddend1:addend2: method. This time, use the debugger po command in the debug area content pane to display the values for the two parameters:

```
po adder1
po adder2
```

The output of these commands is shown in Figure C-14.

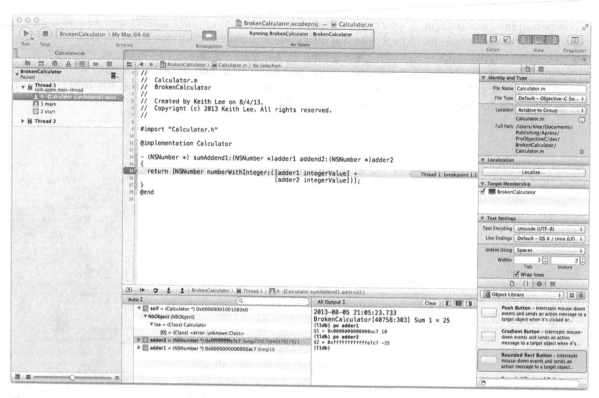

Figure C-14. Displaying the value of variables using Xcode debugger commands

These values (10, –25) are as expected, so select **continue** to advance the program. Next, the debugger pauses at the NSCAssert. Using the po command, the variable sum2 displays a value of –15 (as shown in Figure C-15).

Figure C-15. Displaying a value using the po command

This is the expected value, so why is the assertion failing? Looking at the assertion statement, you can see that the conditional expression is expecting a value of 15, when it should be –15!

```
NSCAssert((([sum2 intValue] == 15),  @"Invalid sum computed");
```

When you correct the assertion (by changing the value to –15) and run the program again, you will see that it runs successfully. Now even though this was a very contrived example, it illustrates a few of the capabilities of debugging in Xcode using LLDB. Apple provides a variety of documentation on Xcode debugging using LLDB, and the LLDB web site is an essential reference for more information.

Roundup

In this appendix, you learned about debugging using LLDB, the default debugger for Xcode. Debugging is a mandatory part of software development, so it's vital to master this skill to become a more efficient, productive programmer. By now I hope that you are convinced of the power and capability of LLDB, and that you will take the time to become skilled at using it on all of your Objective-C software development projects.

You have now reached the end of this book. I hope that it has been (and will continue to be) of use as you develop more OS X and iOS applications. Please feel free to contact me at ProObjectiveC@icloud.com with any questions or comments about this book or about Objective-C in general. Thank you for taking part in this wonderful journey, now signing out!!

Index

D

Z